D0142754

Social Media

Recent Titles in the

CONTEMPORARY WORLD ISSUES

Series

The Global Water Crisis: A Reference Handbook
David E. Newton

Youth Substance Abuse: A Reference Handbook
David E. Newton

Global Pandemic Threats: A Reference Handbook
Michael C. LeMay

Same-Sex Marriage: A Reference Handbook, second edition
David E. Newton

DNA Technology: A Reference Handbook, second edition
David E. Newton

Modern Sport Ethics: A Reference Handbook, second edition
Angela Lumpkin

Marijuana: A Reference Handbook, second edition
David E. Newton

Gun Control in the United States: A Reference Handbook, second edition
Gregg Lee Carter

The Right to Die: A Reference Handbook
Howard Ball

Student Debt: A Reference Handbook
William Elliott III and Melinda K. Lewis

Food Safety: A Reference Handbook, third edition
Nina E. Redman and Michele Morrone

Human Trafficking: A Reference Handbook
Alexis A. Aronowitz

Books in the **Contemporary World Issues** series address vital issues in today's society such as genetic engineering, pollution, and biodiversity. Written by professional writers, scholars, and nonacademic experts, these books are authoritative, clearly written, up-to-date, and objective. They provide a good starting point for research by high school and college students, scholars, and general readers as well as by legislators, businesspeople, activists, and others.

Each book, carefully organized and easy to use, contains an overview of the subject, a detailed chronology, biographical sketches, facts and data and/or documents and other primary source material, a forum of authoritative perspective essays, annotated lists of print and nonprint resources, and an index.

Readers of books in the Contemporary World Issues series will find the information they need in order to have a better understanding of the social, political, environmental, and economic issues facing the world today.

CONTEMPORARY WORLD ISSUES

Social Media

A REFERENCE HANDBOOK

Kelli S. Burns

An Imprint of ABC-CLIO, LLC
Santa Barbara, California • Denver, Colorado

Library of Congress Cataloging-in-Publication Data

Social Media: A Reference Handbook
Library of Congress Cataloging in Publication Control Number: 2016052707

ISBN: 978-1-4408-4355-6
EISBN: 978-1-4408-4356-3

21 20 19 18 17   1 2 3 4 5

This book is also available as an eBook.

ABC-CLIO
An Imprint of ABC-CLIO, LLC

ABC-CLIO, LLC
130 Cremona Drive, P.O. Box 1911
Santa Barbara, California 93116-1911
www.abc-clio.com

This book is printed on acid-free paper ∞

Manufactured in the United States of America

Preface, xvii

1 **Background and History, 3**

Introduction, 3

A Definition of Social Media, 6

Social Media Foundations: 1970s–1990s, 7

Early Social Media Communities: 1990s, 11

Emerging Social Media: Early 2000s, 14

Mainstream Social Media: Late 2000s, 25

Modern Social Media: 2010s, 33

Future Directions for Social Media, 39

References, 44

2 **Problems, Controversies, and Solutions, 59**

Introduction, 59

Social Media Addiction, 59

Influence of Curated Content, 67

Online Hoaxes, Rumors, and Scams, 71

Cyberbullying, Sexting, and Child Predators, 79

Negative Moods, Feelings of Loneliness, and Envy, 86

Pressure to Project the Ideal Self, 94

Social Media in the Workplace, 99

Relationships and Communication Skills, 105

Online Shaming and Attacks, 111

Social Media Privacy Concerns, 116

Conclusion, 121

References, 122

3 Perspectives, 139

Introduction, 139

The Female Body on Social Media *by Petya Eckler and Yusuf Kalyango Jr.*, 139

Exploring Victimization in the Digital Age: Perspectives on Social Media and Sexual Assault *by Rowena Briones Winkler*, 145

Posting, Sharing, and Tweeting a Brand's Politics: Social Media and the Recent Evolution of Online Corporate Activism *by Nathan Gilkerson*, 149

Consumers as Data Profiles: What Companies See in the Social You *by Joseph T. Yun and Brittany R. L. Duff*, 155

The Role of Social Media in Crisis Communication: Opportunities and Challenges for Crisis Communication Strategies in the Social Media Era *by Jae-Hwa Shin*, 161

Lessons from the Social Media Revolution?: A Look Back at Social Media's Role in Political Campaigns and Elections *by Terri L. Towner*, 167

Saving Face: Applying the Spiral of Silence Theory to Social Media: Self-Censorship in the Midst of Controversial Issues *by Juliana Maria (da Silva) Trammel*, 172

Live Tweeting: Fans and Celebrities *by Michelle Groover*, 177

4 **PROFILES, 183**

Introduction, 183

Movements, 184

ALS Ice Bucket Challenge (2014), 184

Arab Spring (2010–2011), 186

Occupy Wall Street (2011), 189

People, 191

Anderson, Tom (1970–), 191

Armstrong, Heather B. (1975–), 194

boyd, danah (1977–), 196

Dorsey, Jack (1976–), 198

Fake, Caterina (1969–), 200

Hoffman, Reid (1967–), 201

Hughes, Chris (1983–), 204

Karp, David (1986–), 207

Kjellberg, Felix (1983–), 208

Monty, Scott (1970–), 210

Parker, Sean (1979–), 212

Pincus, Mark (1966–), 214

Rose, Kevin (1977–), 217

Sandberg, Sheryl (1969–), 220

Silbermann, Ben (1982–), 223
Smith, Marc (1965–), 225
Solis, Brian (1970–), 227
Spiegel, Evan (1990–), 228
Stanton, Brandon (1984–), 230
Thiel, Peter (1967–), 233
Williams, Evan (1972–), 236
Zuckerberg, Mark (1984–), 238

References, 240

5 DATA AND DOCUMENTS, 255

Introduction, 255

Internet, Social Media, and Mobile Usage, 256

Table 5.1: United States Digital and Mobile Usage (January 2016), 256

Table 5.2: Worldwide Digital and Mobile Usage (January 2016), 257

Table 5.3: Social Media Adoption by Worldwide Region (January 2016), 257

Figure 5.1: Social Media Users among Adult Internet Users and All Adults in the United States as a Percentage of the Population (2005–2015), 258

Table 5.4: Social Media Users in the United States by Demographics (2015), 259

Smartphone Ownership and Social Media Usage on Devices, 260

Figure 5.2: Ownership of Devices among U.S. Adults (2015), 261

Table 5.5: Device Ownership over Time (U.S. Adults Aged 18–29), 261

Table 5.6: Top 12 Countries for Smartphone Penetration and Demographic Differences (2015), 262

Table 5.7: Worldwide Penetration of Smartphone, Computer, and Smartphone-Only Users (2014), 263

Figure 5.3: Worldwide Mobile Web Access by Online Adults (2011–2015), 264

Figure 5.4: Time Spent Online per Day on Mobile Phones, by Age among Global Users (2015), 265

Figure 5.5: Time Spent Online per Day on Mobile Phones, by Region (2015), 265

Figure 5.6: Average Time Spent on Digital Media per Day among U.S. Adult Users (2008–2015 YTD), 266

Figure 5.7: Share of Time Spent on Social Media across Platforms (2013–2015), 266

Social Media Addiction, 267

Figure 5.8: Worldwide Daily Average Time Spent on Social Media (2012–2016), 267

Figure 5.9: Proportion of Teens (13–18 Years Old) and Tweens (8–12 Years Old) Using Screen Media (February–March 2015), 268

Table 5.8: Teen Desire to Unplug and Other Frustrations (2012), 269

Table 5.9: Teen and Parent Addiction to Mobile Devices (May 2016), 270

Table 5.10: Mobile Apps Smartphone Users Check First in the Morning (November 2015), 272

Usage of Various Social Media Platforms, 272

Figure 5.10: Top 20 Social Media Platforms and Messaging Apps with the Most Monthly Active Users (January 2016), 273

Figure 5.11: Top Active Social Media Platforms in the United States (January 2016), 274

Figure 5.12: Membership, Visitation, and Active Usage of Top Social Media Platforms (2015), 275

Figure 5.13: Frequency of Usage by U.S. Social Media Platform Users (March–April 2015), 275

Figure 5.14: Social Media Platform Usage Penetration over Time (Ages 13–32), 276

Figure 5.15: Comparison of Daily Posting or Commenting: Teens versus Young Adults (2015), 277

Specific Platform Data, 277

Facebook, 277

Table 5.11: Worldwide Facebook Users (in Millions) (May 2016), 278

Table 5.12: Global Facebook Product Usage (2015), 278

Table 5.13: U.S. Facebook User Penetration (among Internet Users) (March–April 2015), 279

Figure 5.16: Top Facebook Actions Completed by Global Facebook Users within the Past Month (2015), 280

Figure 5.17: Top 12 Brands with the Most Facebook Fans (September 2016), 280

Twitter, 281

Table 5.14: U.S. Twitter User Penetration (among Internet Users) (March–April 2015), 281

Table 5.15: Twitter Users with the Most Followers (September 2016), 282

Table 5.16: Top 10 Most Popular Retweeted Tweets (March 2016), 283

Video, 284

Table 5.17: U.S. Digital Video and Television Viewing (2012–2017), 284

Figure 5.18: Frequency of Television or Movie Viewing on Smartphones by U.S. Consumers (2015), 285

Table 5.18: Top 10 Most Viewed YouTube Channels of All Time (September 2016), 286

Figure 5.19: Top 10 Most Viewed YouTube Videos of All Time (September 2016), 286

Pinterest, 287

Table 5.19: Pinterest Users in the United States by Gender, 2013–2019, 287

Table 5.20: U.S. Pinterest User Penetration (among Internet Users) (March–April 2015), 288

Instagram, 288

Table 5.21: U.S. Instagram User Penetration (among Internet Users) (March–April 2015), 289

Figure 5.20: Worldwide Instagram Net Mobile Ad Revenues (2015–2017), 289

Figure 5.21: Top 10 Instagram Profiles in Terms of Most Followed (October 2016), 290

LinkedIn, 290

Table 5.22: U.S. LinkedIn User Penetration (among Internet Users) (March–April 2015), 291

Table 5.23: LinkedIn Advertising Revenues, United States vs. non–United States (2014–2017), 291

Snapchat, 292

Table 5.24: U.S. Snapchat Penetration by Age (2013–2016), 292

Figure 5.22: U.S. Millennial Snapchat Users and Penetration (2014–2020), 293

Figure 5.23: Top 10 Snapchat Actions by Snapchat Users in the Past Month (2015), 293

Social Media for Marketing, 294

Figure 5.24: Social Media Platforms Used by Worldwide Marketers (May 2016), 294

Figure 5.25: Planned Increase in Social Media Usage by Worldwide Marketers (May 2016), 295

Figure 5.26: Worldwide Social Media Marketers' Perception of Social Platforms with Best ROI (March 2016), 295

Table 5.25: Social Network Ad Spending Worldwide and in North America (2013–2017), 296

Figure 5.27: Allocation of 2016 Digital Ad Spending by U.S. Ad Buyers, 297

Impact of Social Media on Online Shopping, 297

Figure 5.28: Adoption of Buy Buttons among U.S. Digital Retailers (August 2015), 298

Figure 5.29: Global Social Commerce Prospects (2015), 299

Figure 5.30: Social Media Activities That Influence Worldwide Shopping Behavior (September 2015), 300

Documents, 300

Children's Online Privacy Protection Act (1998), 300

Barack Obama, "It Gets Better" (2010), 302

Social Media in Disasters (2011), 304
Nebraska Workplace Privacy Act (2016), 308
Facebook Suppressing Conservative Views (2016), 311

References, 312

6 RESOURCES, 317

Introduction, 317

Books, 318

E-Books, 335

Blogs by Social Media Thought Leaders, 336

Corporate Social Media Blogs, 341

Online News Sites and Magazines, 343

TED Talks, Movies, and Videos, 348

Podcasts, 351

Research Organizations, 354

Nonprofit Organizations, 357

Legal, Government, and Social Service Resources, 359

Social Media Statistics, 362

7 CHRONOLOGY, 365

Glossary, 379
Index, 385
About the Author, 399

Social media have infiltrated nearly every aspect of modern society, enhancing opportunities to maintain and build interpersonal relationships, connect businesses to customers, collect donations for causes, build online professional networks for job searching, and even fuel political revolutions. Users can access news from media organizations through social media or act as citizen journalists to create and distribute their own news. Support for social issues can be expressed through hashtags on Twitter, images on Facebook, or videos on YouTube. People also use social media to publish and access travel, restaurant, and product reviews; play interactive games; engage in political conversations; and connect with fellow fans of their favorite television shows. Social media have opened windows to users' personal lives and made users obsess about the way they present themselves online. Consumers are increasingly buying products directly from social media sites, and marketers are diverting higher percentages of digital budgets to advertising on social media sites. Social media have produced new job opportunities, including social media marketers and online community managers, and some celebrities have risen to fame through social media. Furthermore, almost all industries have been impacted by the availability of social media, and new industries have emerged because of social media.

Behind the scenes, social media platforms and data companies are collecting the information users are sharing. The data are useful to marketers who target social media users with product advertising, political campaigns that want to encourage certain users to vote for their candidates, or hiring managers who are making decisions about job candidates. As a result, many users are becoming more concerned about how their data are being used.

Social media are a global phenomenon, with the Asia-Pacific region driving much of the growth. Worldwide, social media users grew 10 percent between 2015 and 2016 to 2.3 billion. During that time, social media users in the Asia-Pacific region increased 14 percent. Social media platforms are also increasingly being accessed from mobile devices. Between 2015 and 2016, active mobile social users grew 17 percent to almost 2 billion users (Kemp 2016).

As an inescapable part of our culture, social media have even had a profound impact on the English language. In 2014, the collegiate edition of the *Merriam-Webster* dictionary added the following Internet and social media–related words: *selfie, hashtag, catfish, crowdfunding, digital divide, gamification, paywall, tweep, social networking, hot spot,* and *unfriend* (Steinmetz 2014). In 2015, the unabridged version added *clickbait, emoji, meme, NSFW* (not safe/suitable for work), and *photobomb* (Izahim 2015). Social media and tech words added in 2016 to the unabridged version included *FoMO*, an acronym for the "fear of missing out," which impacts some social media users, and *nomophobia*, which is the fear of being without a cell phone (Steinmetz 2016).

This book has seven chapters that provide readers with an overview of the social media industry and references for social media resources. Chapter 1 starts with a definition of social media and then outlines the history of the industry by focusing on the launch and growth of a variety of important platforms and technologies. The chapter concludes with a discussion of future trends in social media.

Chapter 2 describes the unique problems and controversies of social media and suggests solutions. Social media have been targeted for a variety of societal ills, including an unhealthy addiction to social media and feelings of depression, loneliness, and envy as people are exposed to the seemingly more fabulous lives of others. This envy may also drive people to feel pressure to project idealized versions of their own lives. People also worry about privacy issues and the potential for online shaming when people jump on the bandwagon to attack someone through social media. Parents are particularly concerned about cyberbullying, sexting, and online predators. Users can also be targeted by online scammers or tricked by hoaxes or fake news stories. Whether social media have a positive or negative impact on relationships and communication skills is also addressed. The curation process used by social media platforms may also affect users who are exposed to a narrow worldview. Finally, practical issues related to social media in the workplace are discussed.

Chapter 3 provides a variety of perspectives from social media scholars and professionals on topics ranging from societal issues, such as the impact of social media on body image and on victims of sexual assault, to corporate concerns, such as corporate online activism, social media data mining, and using social media for crisis communication. The chapter also covers political campaigns, the suppression of a minority opinion, and engaging on Twitter with actors of a popular television program.

Chapter 4 first discusses three key movements that successfully engaged social media users. Then, the chapter profiles the founders of the most popular and important social media platforms as well as social media thought leaders, scholars, professionals, bloggers, and celebrities.

Chapter 5 reviews key data related to social media including Internet, social, and mobile users and usage, the increasing use of smartphones to access social media sites, and the amount of time spent on social media as well as feelings of addiction. This chapter also describes statistics that compare social media platform usage, presents data about users and usage of the most popular platforms, addresses the use of social media by marketers, and explores social commerce. Finally, key documents including legislation, testimonies, and speeches related to social media are provided.

Chapter 6 presents an annotated bibliography of print and nonprint resources for further research on social media including books, blogs, podcasts, videos, and leading research organizations.

Chapter 7 provides a chronology that tracks the development of social media from the technologies that made it possible to launch social media platforms through the founding, growth, sale, and even closure of some platforms. Also included are entries about social media usage and social media campaigns that attracted significant media attention.

The book concludes with a glossary of terms related to social media.

References

Izahim, Elahe. 2015. "Behold, the New Words Added to Merriam-Webster: Clickbait, WTF and Photobomb." *The Washington Post.* May 26. http://www.washingtonpost.com/news/morning-mix/wp/2015/05/26/behold-the-new-words-added-to-merriam-webster-clickbait-wtf-and-photobomb/.

Kemp, Simon. 2016. "Digital in 2016." *We Are Social.* January 27. http://wearesocial.com/uk/special-reports/digital-in-2016.

Steinmetz, Katy. 2014. "# Selfie, Steampunk, Catfish: See This Year's New Dictionary Words." *Time.* May 19. http://time.com/103503/merriam-webster-dictionary-selfie-catfish/.

Steinmetz, Katy. 2016. "Merriam-Webster Adds 'FOMO,' 'Mx.' and About 2,000 Other Words." *Time.* April 20. http://time.com/4299634/merriam-webster-fomo-mx-dox-update/.

Social Media

Introduction

In a relatively short period of time in human existence, social media changed the world. Users connect and communicate with others, share their lives, and spend their time in new ways. Corporations, governments, and many other organizations have had to pivot to adapt to the new opportunities. While changing the world, the world also changed social media. Users often defined how social media platforms would be used, which created opportunities for new entrants, caused some to alter their strategies, and forced others to close.

The growth of social media has been both swift and vast. At the beginning of 2016, when the worldwide population was almost 7.4 billion and more than 3.4 billion people actively used the Internet, over 2.3 billion people were active social media users (Kemp 2016). Putting the scale of Facebook alone into perspective, Facebook users total more than the population of any country, including China and India (Qualman 2015). The region of the world with the highest penetration of social media users is North America, where approximately 59 percent of the population has a social media account. In terms of individual countries, penetration in the United States also is 59 percent;

A blogger updates her blog from her home in Brooklyn, New York. In addition to changing the way people connect and communicate with others for professional purposes, social media have created many new jobs. (AP Photo/Bebeto Matthews) only South Korea, the UAE, Hong Kong, Singapore, and Argentina have higher penetration rates (Kemp 2016).

In terms of mobile, the world had almost 3.8 billion mobile users (including smartphones and non-Internet-enabled feature phones) and almost 2 billion active mobile social media users in 2016 (Kemp 2016). The ubiquity of mobile phones, which more people own than a toothbrush, may be driving the social web more than any other trend or development (Qualman 2015). As digital analyst Erik Qualman proclaimed, social and mobile media are not emerging, but merging.

Today, the social media industry rakes in billions of dollars. One source of revenue is advertising on social media sites, which is predicted to reach almost $36 billion in 2017 (eMarketer 2015a). The highest spending on advertising is in North America, followed by Asia-Pacific and Western Europe. Facebook receives the highest percentage of spending among all social media sites, representing almost 65 percent in 2014 (eMarketer 2015a). In addition to using social media to drive consumers to websites or stores to make purchases, some marketers are experimenting with online sales directly on social networks, called social commerce. For example, sites like Pinterest are starting to add "buy" buttons so that sales can be made directly from the social media site. The Social Media 500 report by Internet Retailer found that, of the 500 leading online retailers, social commerce totaled $3.3 billion in 2014, an increase from $2.6 billion in 2013 (C. Smith 2015).

Social media are phenomenal not only for their rapid growth and economic value, but also for the impact on the human experience. From a social standpoint, no other technological advancement has likely had such a significant impact on connection and communication as social media. A 2014 survey found the average adult Facebook user had more than 300 friends in his or her network with 15 percent of respondents having more than 500 friends, allowing them to engage with many more people than most could handle offline (A. Smith 2014). Social media bridge geographical distances, providing a means to continue relationships with friends who live elsewhere or make new connections.

Social media users have also learned how to share their lives with others in new ways, as private moments are now experienced publicly. All the milestones of life, including engagements, weddings, honeymoons, births, and even deaths, are shared within the network. As noted by *Guardian* reporter Jacob Silverman, "Sharing itself becomes personhood, with activities taking on meaning not for their basic content but for the way they are turned into content, disseminated through the digital network, and responded to" (Silverman 2015). Users are not just posting photos; many are also video blogging, aka vlogging. YouTube has been a popular repository for these vlogs, but newer social media entrants like Snapchat and Instagram allow users to send short videos to friends. Those who want to provide real-time access to their lives can use Periscope and Facebook Live.

Social media have changed not only interpersonal communication, but also communication by organizations. Most businesses, from Fortune 500 companies to small businesses, use social media to connect with customers, prospective customers, investors, suppliers, and others. Social media users are also active content creators of online reviews on sites like Yelp, travel site TripAdvisor, and restaurant site Urbanspoon, which can help or hurt a business. Television shows, movies, celebrities, bands, and studios all use social media to connect to fans. News organizations also use social media to share stories, changing the way people consume news. Instead of visiting the website of a news organization, many people receive their news as they scroll through news feeds on Facebook or Twitter. Certain stories will be more attractive on social media sites and appear higher on feeds, creating a new form of gatekeeper. Citizen journalists who can easily upload content to social media sites have also expanded the range of reporting. Political campaigns, social cause campaigns, and even revolutions have been impacted by social media.

Finally, social media have changed the job market. Based on research by Deloitte, Facebook alone is estimated to have spurred the creation of 4.5 million jobs around the world and added $227 billion to the worldwide economy (Goldman 2015). Facebook itself has 8,000 employees. A new job, called social media manager, did not exist before Facebook, and in 2014, approximately 189,000 people managed social media profiles for clients or their employers. Employees are creating profiles on LinkedIn to build professional networks and find jobs. Some social media users are creating their own empires through blogs, YouTube videos, or Instagram profiles, while others are launching the next social media platform.

This chapter starts with a definition of social media and then outlines the rise of social media by focusing first on the technological developments that made social media possible and then detailing the launch and growth of a variety of important platforms. Predictions for the future of social media are discussed at the end of the chapter.

A Definition of Social Media

Social media are Internet-based platforms that allow users to create profiles for sharing user-generated or curated digital content in the form of text, photos, graphics, or videos within a networked community of users who can respond to the content. The terms *social media* and *social networks* are often used interchangeably, but social media are the sites that allow users to share content and connect with other users, and social networks refer to the communities of users who are found on social media sites. In the early years, social media sites were often referred to as social network sites because many platforms emphasized the networking feature. For example, Friendster called itself "an online community that connects people through networks of friends for dating or meeting new friends" and MySpace's mission was that it "lets you share photos, journals and interests with your growing network of mutual friends."

In an influential paper on social networks, danah boyd and Nicole Ellison defined *social network sites* as "web-based services that allow individuals to (1) construct a public or semi-public profile within a bounded system, (2) articulate a list of other users with whom they share a connection, and (3) view and traverse their list of connections and those made by others within the system" (boyd and Ellison 2007). Reminiscent of a journal or diary, Don Schultz described social networks as "participatory and self-expressive Web sites . . . where members/participants expose, discuss, reveal, and expound on their personal lives, activities, hopes, dreams, and even fantasies for others to see and marvel upon" (Schultz 2007, 10).

Today, the term *social media* is more popular, bypassing the usage of *social network* in Google searches around 2009 (Veerasamy n.d.). The replacement of the word *network* or *networking* with the word *media* reflects the fact that many of these platforms now function as media, where content is shared and consumed much like a news site. Twitter once defined itself as "A global community of friends and strangers answering one simple question: What are you doing?" Now the site prompts users to share "what's happening?" and its mission is "to give everyone the power to create and share ideas and information instantly, without barriers." This change reflects a shift from serving as a social network for the purpose of forming and maintaining connections to a vibrant information source created by that network. Every social media platform offers a unique experience for the user and provides a range of uses and benefits.

Social Media Foundations: 1970s–1990s

Similar to any invention in modern history, many previous developments have led to the emergence of what is now known as social media. For all the successes of social media companies, most notably Facebook, many other companies failed to find the right formula. This sentiment is expressed by Gartner analyst Brian Blau who said in a 2013 interview, "The road is littered with dead companies that made the wrong move at the wrong time, the MySpaces of the world" (Bercovici 2013). Some entrepreneurs have been forgotten for their important contributions to later more commercially viable platforms. For example, Marcel Molina, whose short-form blogging platform called a tumblelog may have helped inspire David Karp's more popular Tumblr, which Karp sold to Yahoo for $1.1 billion, had this to say in 2013 about social media pioneers: "The people who plant the seed are often forgotten through history even though one could arguably associate substantial or equal credit to them. I'm not saying that's what I want. I just think it's interesting how the last one wins" (Alfonso 2013).

Before the platforms referred to today as *social media* developed, message and bulletin boards, LISTSERVs, online chat rooms, and instant messaging tools allowed users to connect with others through networked computers and later online. Bulletin board systems (BBSs) emerged shortly after the first generation of the home computer. The first use of a home computer to manage a BBS dates back to 1978. Ward Christensen and Randy Suess, who were members of the Chicago Area Computer Hobbyist Exchange, conceived the Computer Bulletin Board System during the Great Blizzard of 1978 in Chicago (Gilbertson 2010). Their BBS allowed the club to share messages through a computer network, rather than on a physical message board. Users would dial into a host computer, which would establish a connection via modem. Another development called Network News Transfer Protocol (NNTP) in 1979 by Duke University graduate students Tom Truscott and Jim Ellis allowed for the launch of Usenet Newsgroups. Instead of using personal computers, like BBSs, Usenet Newsgroups were hosted on a mainframe computer that could manage many users at the same time. Truscott and Ellis also developed the concept of organizing messages into categories (Apple II History n.d.).

In 1993, Internet service providers such as America Online (AOL) and CompuServe provided Usenet access to members (Apple II History n.d.). Users of Usenet groups could post or reply to messages posted on the boards, which allowed for threaded conversations. Providing networked conversation on a variety of topics, Usenet groups were the forerunners for the many discussion sites on the Web today. CompuServe offered thousands of forums on topics ranging from current events, entertainment, politics, and sports, which were visited by hundreds of thousands of users. Later versions allowed users to create profiles, but users were not able to create a list of friends or followers, which, according to boyd and Ellison (2007), made them fall short of being a true social network. Throughout the 1990s, interest in using BBSs and Usenet groups began to subside, mainly due to the rise of the Internet and the availability and wealth of information provided there. AOL discontinued its Usenet newsgroups in the early 2000s, replacing them with Web-based chat rooms and message or discussion boards.

LISTSERVs allow users to build online social networks through e-mail. Developed in 1986 by engineering student Eric Thomas, the LISTSERV software automates the management of e-mail lists, which had previously been set up manually (Manjoo 2010). LISTSERV users can join a group based on a topic of interest and then easily send and receive messages to and from the entire group. A moderator assists in managing the process. Although LISTSERV is a registered trademark of Thomas's company, people often use the term to refer to a generic e-mail discussion list. In the early years, hundreds and then thousands of groups were launched, mostly at universities for discussing research or technology (Manjoo 2010). LISTSERVs are still popular today to connect members of an industry or organization or for internal communication within a company on a specific topic of interest to employees. Although Twitter, Facebook, and other social media sites are increasingly serving as a substitute for LISTSERVs, a LISTSERV still offers value as a targeted communications tool.

In 1980, CompuServe developed CB Simulator, the first dedicated online chat service available to the general public, although the technology dates back to 1973 when Doug Brown and David R. Wolley introduced Talkomatic at the University of Illinois. Chat rooms allowed for real-time conversation in a space that users could join or leave with a simple click. AOL, then known as AppleLink, also developed a chat product. AppleLink's People Connection service provided virtual rooms for people to connect on such topics as genealogy and games (Wagstaff 2012). Chat room usage at AOL reached its peak in the late 1990s after the company introduced monthly (instead of hourly) pricing in 1996, allowing people to hang out in chat rooms as long as they wished (Wagstaff 2012). By 1999, AOL's subscriber base was 17 million users. AOL chat rooms were available until 2010, when the company decided to focus on other products (Wagstaff 2012).

Instant messaging services offered the ability to connect directly with specific users instead of a collection of random users, moving them one step closer to being a social network. For example, AOL Instant Messenger (AIM) employed instant messaging technology to allow users to chat with friends on their buddy lists, create profiles, and post away messages that could be read by others. Despite dominating the market in the late 1990s to early 2000s, AIM had dropped to a market share of 0.7 percent by 2011 (Abbruzzese 2014).

Another variation of a chat room existed in Internet Relay Chat (IRC), a real-time online conversation tool that allowed users to join channels on such topics as "macusers" or "teenchat." To see certain channels and interact with certain people, IRC requires users to connect to the same IRC network comprising one or more IRC servers. In August 1988, Jarrkko "WiZ" Oikarinen launched the first IRC client and server at the University of Oulu in Finland (Stenberg 2011). IRC emerged when Oikarinen added chat to his BBS software at tolsun.oulu.fi. The software was freed from the university so that it could be run on an offsite server. After installing a server, Oikarinen had the first IRC network. After friends at other universities also set up IRC servers, IRC quickly spread to the entire Finnish national network, then the Scandinavian branch of the Internet. By November 1988, IRC was used throughout the Internet.

IRC usage has decreased since 2004. At that time, the top four IRC networks had more than 100,000 daily users, with one called Quakenet receiving daily visits by 200,000 users (Stenberg 2011). By 2011, Quakenet had lost about half of those daily users but was the only network with more than 100,000 users (Stenberg 2011).

Early Social Media Communities: 1990s

In contrast to the previously discussed communication tools that facilitated an exchange of messages, GeoCities and blogs emerged in the 1990s to provide a personal space for users to share their own content. Wikis also arrived on the scene as a way for users to collaborate on content creation, and Six Degrees introduced early adopters to the concept of social networking.

GeoCities, launched in 1994, was a precursor to the first social networking platforms. The tool allowed users, aka "homesteaders," to create their own websites that were grouped into "neighborhoods," or themed content areas (1st Web Designer n.d.). A user with a technology-related site would be placed in "SiliconValley," while one with an entertainment focus would be located in "Hollywood." Yahoo bought the company for more than $3 billion in stock during the dotcom bubble and shut it down in 2009 (Ostrow 2009). GeoCities Japan still remains available to users in that country.

Blogs emerged primarily to share personal reflections, essays, articles, and other content. Although blogs do allow for two-way communication through the comments section, they are primarily a vehicle for one-way communication. Although previously available in other forms such as compilations of Web links, blogs exploded in popularity in the late 1990s. First called Web logs, blogs are characterized by reverse chronological entries of text, video, audio, or photos. Blogging was facilitated by a new technology that was launched in 1999, namely RSS, called either "Really Simple Syndication" or "Rich Site Summary." Credited to Dave Winer, RSS breaks data into discrete items that can be syndicated on the Web, and an RSS feed makes it possible to pull news stories, blog entries, and other content into a news aggregator. When a blog is in RSS format, a program such as a news aggregator can check the blog's feed for changes and update the news aggregator appropriately.

LiveJournal, launched in 1999 by programmer Brad Fitzpatrick to stay in touch with friends, allowed users to have a profile page, a friends list, and the ability to follow the blogs of friends, making it more similar to modern social media platforms. The friends list also provided the most recent journal entries by those friends. One differentiating point of LiveJournal was that the platform served as a primary site for fan discussion (Romano 2012). Since the founder's exit in 2005, LiveJournal angered its users by continuing to make business and site design changes without consulting or informing users, then failing to respond quickly and apologize in the wake of user outrage, and then reversing the decision (Romano 2012). The biggest corporate mistake, which occurred in 2007 after the company had been purchased by Six Apart, involved the deletion of 500 user journals with problematic keywords, such as those referring to rape and child molestation. At the same time, journals for rape survivor groups and character role-playing groups were also deleted. This corporate maneuver, known as Strikethrough because of the strike-throughs placed on the journal names, made national news (Romano 2012). Angry users who used the site to participate in fan communities left for fan-run sites like Dreamwidth and ArchiveOfOurOwn .org. LiveJournal was later sold to SUP Media, a Russian media company. The U.S. general manager of LiveJournal, Anjelika Petrochecko, discussed in an interview with the Daily Dot how the platform evolved in relevance: "Back when LiveJournal was first created], the Internet was really small. Think about how many websites you actually could use. You had to make do with LiveJournal and Yahoo, pretty much. Now, userbases are growing, more people have access to more websites, and there are so many interesting technologies. It's the natural evolution of the Internet. It's very different from what it was even three years ago, let alone 10 years ago" (Romano 2012).

Free blogging software was also released in 1999 by both Pitas and Blogger. The software provided users with a simple interface for designing and updating a blog, making it possible for a wider and less technical segment of the population to launch a blog. Blogging software Pitas was founded by Toronto programmer Andrew Smales, which during the last three months of its existence had been actively used by about 50,000 users (Phillips-Sandy 2013). Before launching Pitas, Smales had a Web page called "Every Link I Went to Today" and noted at the time that "there was a pretty distinct line between online diaries and weblogs that were mostly links with a little bit of commentary" (Phillips-Sandy 2013). When a fellow tech entrepreneur complimented Smales with the words "nice weblog," he had a name for what he was doing (Phillips-Sandy 2013). Smales's other project at the time was building an online community of diarists called Diaryland. Diaryland had about 2.2 million registered users in 1999, according to Smales, with about 20–30 percent of them active (Phillips-Sandy 2013). The site was an early version of a social network, allowing users to post content and also follow one another.

Blogger, founded by Evan Williams, Paul Bausch, and Meg Hourihan of Pyra Labs, differentiated itself from Pitas by providing an option to host the blog on the user's own server or the server of his or her choice, rather than the Blogger server. After users created more than 1 million blogs (200,000 of which were active) using the platform, Blogger was purchased by Google in 2003 (McIntosh 2003). In 2015, Blogger ranked fifth behind leader WordPress among content management systems (W3Techs n.d.). Blogging still remains a popular activity on the Web, but has evolved since the early days. New tools have been introduced, namely Tumblr, LinkedIn, and Medium, that provide additional opportunities for blogging.

Although the first wiki had been introduced by Ward Cunningham in 1995, it was not until 2001 when Jimmy Wales, Larry Sanger, and others launched online encyclopedia Wikipedia that most people become aware of the usefulness of a wiki. The name originates from the Hawaiian word "wiki wiki," meaning "very fast." Wikis are considered social media because users collaborate on creating and editing content. As of 2016, Wikipedia had more than 5 million English articles and experienced approximately 10 edits a second around the world (Wikipedia n.d.).

In 1997, MacroView CEO Andrew Weinreich launched Six Degrees, a site sometimes referred to as the first true social network. The name of the site was derived from the concept of "six degrees of separation," which suggests that everyone in the world can be connected to any other person through six connections or fewer. Six Degrees combined features from other sites, including the user profiles of dating sites like Match.com and the lists of friends and chat capabilities of messaging tools like AIM. A later feature allowed users to browse the connections of their friends. This early iteration of social networking ceased operations in 2001, just one year after being sold for $125 million, and its quick death can be blamed on the limited number of online users at the time and the fact that that the site served little purpose other than to collect friends, send messages, and see how friends were connected to other users (1st Web Designer n.d.). Users were also frustrated by incessant membership drives and the spam-like nature of the invitations (1st Web Designer n.d.). Around the same time as Six Degrees, sites such as AsianAvenue, BlackPlanet, and MiGente also emerged to connect niche audiences.

Emerging Social Media: Early 2000s

The developments previously discussed laid the foundation for the emergence of social media platforms in the early 2000s. By the middle of the decade, the popularity of social media started to explode with the introduction of some of today's most popular platforms. For some people, social media has pervaded their lives so intensely that it is difficult to remember how communication occurred before social media.

Ryze, launched in 2001 by Adrian Scott, sought to help business professionals connect online. Scott's inspiration came from networking mixers he organized at his San Francisco loft (Mieszkowski 2002). He developed the site to allow those attendees to connect between events. Members could create profiles; search the site for other professionals based on location, industry, and personal hobbies; and create tribes based on commonalities. The site quickly inspired another social networking site, Friendster, which was founded by Ryze member Jonathan Abrams and Peter Chin.

Friendster was launched in 2002 with a more user-friendly interface than predecessor Six Degrees. The site included profile photos, message boards, and links to "friendsters." Friendster attempted to find a niche in the online dating marketplace as an alternative to Match.com. Instead of meeting strangers, Friendster could help a user meet a friend of a friend, potentially leading to a more successful romantic relationship. Within its first three months, the site attracted 3 million members, representing 1 in every 126 Web users at the time (1st Web Designer n.d.). The platform's demise came after rapid growth created technical problems and an upset to the site's culture. Users also fretted about whether to allow acquaintances to become friendsters.

LinkedIn, the leading professional social networking site with 350 million users in more than 200 countries, was founded by Reid Hoffman and other former members of PayPal and SocialNet in 2002, and then was launched officially in 2003. The site provides a space for users to create a professional profile in a format similar to a resume, build their professional networks, share references with their contacts, and search for jobs. The site has evolved and now provides a space to share news stories and blog posts in a news feed.

For many social media users, MySpace was their first social networking experience. Launched on a limited basis in 2003 (and officially in 2004) by musician Tom Anderson and marketer Chris DeWolfe, MySpace was designed as a Friendster-like platform for musicians and bands to share music and connect with fans. The growth of the site was aided by Anderson's connections to and support from Hollywood and musician friends. DeWolfe promoted MySpace through e-mail spam to users of Friendster and online dating sites (Lapinski 2006). The year proved to be the right time for people to embrace social networking, and popularity of the site skyrocketed throughout 2004, breaking 1 million unique visitors per month in June 2004 (Jackson and Madrigal 2011). In July 2005, when the site was receiving 17 million unique monthly visitors, the founders sold the company to Rupert Murdoch's News Corp for $580 million (Rushe 2011). Just a year later with 46 million unique monthly visitors, MySpace became the most visited site on the Web representing 4.46 percent of all Internet traffic (Cashmore 2006). The quick rise eventually led to a dramatic fall, as Facebook surpassed MySpace in terms of unique worldwide visitors in April 2008 and unique U.S. visitors in May 2009 (Raphael 2009). News Corp took a financial hit in selling MySpace in June 2011 to Specific Media Group and Justin Timberlake for a reported $35 million (Rushe 2011). The site, rebranded as Myspace with a lowercase *s*, now focuses on the music industry.

A virtual experience in an online world was launched by Linden Lab and its founder Philip Rosedale in 2003 through the game Second Life. While in the game, players, represented by avatars, engage with other users, participate in activities, and create and trade property. Second Life may have been the first social media site to demonstrate the potential of users to spend money on virtual goods, such as a new hairstyle for an avatar. After 10 years in existence, more than 36 million people had created accounts and spent a total of $3.2 billion within Second Life (Linden Lab 2013). At the time, the company was still acquiring an average of 400,000 new users each month and users offered 2.1 million virtual goods for sale (Linden Lab 2013). Since then, Linden Lab geared up for a new version, expected to be released in 2016. The new version will support the Oculus Rift, a virtual reality headset, allowing users to not only watch their avatars on the screen, but also virtually see out of the eyes of their avatars (Linden Lab 2015).

A seminal year in the history of social media was 2004 when Mark Zuckerberg and several of his Harvard University classmates launched Facebook. At the time of the 10-year anniversary of Facebook, Zuckerberg reflected on the occasion by saying, "I remember getting pizza with my friends one night in college shortly after opening Facebook. I told them I was excited to help connect our school community, but one day someone needed to connect the whole world" (Zuckerberg 2014). At the time, this goal may have seemed far-fetched, but Facebook has indeed been successful at connecting billions of people worldwide. Facebook's early strategy was to restrict access to the social network to create an air of exclusivity. First, it was only open to Harvard students, attracting more than half of the student population to sign up in its first month (1st Web Designer n.d.). It later rolled out access to students at other universities, high school students, and finally, the general public after two years. Another decision was to accommodate other languages on Facebook. In 2007, Facebook started with Spanish and now offers approximately 80 languages. As of August 2016, Facebook had 1.71 billion monthly active users with 84.5 percent of those users outside the United States and Canada (Facebook n.d.). Facebook is by far the most dominant social media platform in the world.

In May 2012, Facebook had the largest Internet initial public offering in history at the time and raised $16 billion with a peak market capitalization of more than $104 billion (Spears and Frier 2012). After an initial tumble of its stock price, the price surged during the three-year period of 2013–2016 along with the rest of the stock market. By 2015, Facebook was worth more than Walmart, with a market valuation of $245 billion (La Monica 2015).

One of the early considerations of the Facebook founders and other key employees was a revenue model that would allow for continued access to the free service. An advertising model was adopted to allow marketers to purchase sidebar advertising or promote posts within users' News Feeds. Since then, advertising formats have continued to evolve. Revenue for 2015 was almost $18 billion, with much of that coming from advertising, representing a 44 percent increase of revenue from the previous year. Approximately 80 percent of all Facebook's advertising revenue is generated by mobile advertising (Lien 2016).

Despite its strength in terms of users and revenue, the growth of Facebook has not been without challenges and obstacles. The company was criticized following the introduction of the Facebook mobile app in 2010, mainly with complaints that it was buggy and slow (Casti 2013). The key problem was that the app was designed to work on any operating system, including iOS or Android, instead of being designed for a specific platform. Critics questioned whether the company would be able to dominate in mobile, but the company successfully redesigned the app. As of the end of the second quarter of 2016, Facebook had 1.57 billion monthly active mobile users, representing approximately 92 percent of all active monthly users (Facebook 2016).

The company has also made it possible for non-smartphone users to access Facebook through an app for feature phones called "Facebook for Every Phone." The app mimics a smartphone app and runs faster than the mobile website. The app is used by more than 100 million users in developing countries, such as India, Indonesia, and the Philippines (Makavy 2013). Facebook also introduced Facebook Messenger in late 2012, moving its messaging system out of the boundaries of Facebook and into a separate app. By 2014, all Facebook mobile users were required to download the app if they wanted to continue messaging through Facebook. The benefit of Messenger is that any user can access the app, not just Facebook users. The app also provides a means to connect with Facebook friends and other contacts either by phone, video calling, or text message.

Facebook is the only social media platform to date to have a Hollywood movie released about it. The 2010 movie *The Social Network* told the story of the founding and growth of Facebook and was based on the 2009 book *The Accidental Billionaires: The Founding of Facebook, a Tale of Sex, Money, Genius, and Betrayal* by Ben Mezrich. The central conflict in the book and subsequent movie was whether Zuckerberg had stolen the concept of Facebook from Harvard classmates, the Winklevoss twins, an allegation that was denounced in other sources, namely *The Facebook Effect* by David Kirkpatrick. In 2011, Facebook settled with the Winklevoss twins a second time in a dispute over who had conceived the idea of the social media site. The deal was worth more than $160 million at the time and included $20 million in cash and partial ownership of Facebook (Ionescu 2011).

Despite the popularity of Facebook, recent studies have suggested that Facebook is not as important as other social media platforms for younger users who prefer platforms where they can share content and communicate away from the eyes of their parents, teachers, and other adults (BI Intelligence 2015). Perhaps the younger demographic will move onto Facebook as they age and have less of a need to have private conversations among peers. Whatever the future holds for Facebook, its rise has been phenomenal and the benefits have been abundant. Zuckerberg said so himself in his 10-year anniversary post: "It's been amazing to see how all of you have used our tools to build a real community. You've shared the happy moments and the painful ones. You've started new families, and kept spread-out families connected. You've created new services and built small businesses. You've helped each other in so many ways" (Zuckerberg 2014).

Flickr, an early image-sharing social media platform, was launched in 2004 by husband-and-wife team Stewart

Butterfield and Caterina Fake. The site's tagline, "almost certainly the best online photo management and sharing application in the world," underscored its dominance in the early years. Flickr was built on the concept of not just photo sharing, but also social networking. Photo sharing could be controlled with much more granularity than sites like Facebook originally offered. For example, photos could be uploaded for private viewing, shared with a few select people, or posted for public consumption.

Just a year after launching, Yahoo acquired Flickr for a reported $22 million to $25 million. Instead of nurturing the community, Yahoo focused on monetizing the site through searches that accessed Flickr images (Honan 2012). To Yahoo, the site was a database, not a social network, at a time when social networks were on the rise. Under Yahoo's management, Flickr users were frustrated with a new system of signing in to Flickr with a Yahoo account. The company also pursued prescreening of user content before it was posted online.

Another problem with Flickr was that it was slow to introduce a mobile app. More than a year after the Apple iTunes store opened, Flickr finally launched its app, but reception was extremely critical of the inability of the app to upload several photos at one time and the reduction of image quality through the process of uploading (Honan 2012). At the same time, other photo apps emerged, which allowed users to apply creative filters to their images. Approximately one year after Flickr launched an app in the iTunes store, its biggest threat to future success, Instagram, appeared on the scene (Honan 2012).

Flickr has somewhat fallen out of favor with mainstream users for image sharing, as people generally choose Facebook as a place to share personal photos and Instagram as a place to share and view a range of photography. Flickr's usefulness as a storage platform for photography has also been replaced by services from Dropbox, Microsoft, Google, and Apple (Honan 2012). As of 2015, the site still reportedly had 92 million users, but traffic was much lower, suggesting that many of those users represent neglected accounts (Honan 2012). As of mid-2016, Quantcast estimated Flickr's traffic to be approximately 4.5 million users a month, a number that has been dropping over time (Quantcast n.d.). New developments, however, are continuing and the site now provides higher-resolution display for pro members and an improved photo editor tool. The site also offers users one terabyte of free storage with no size limits.

Social news sites emerged as early as 1997 with the technology-focused site Slashdot, but it was the launch of Digg in 2004 and Reddit in 2005 that social news sites started to attract mainstream attention. These sites allow users to share stories that can then be voted on by other readers. The more favorable the votes are, the higher the story will appear in the feed, while negative votes will move the story down. Digg, founded by Kevin Rose, Jay Adelson, Owen Byrne, and Ron Gorodetzky, provides users with a means to vote to either "digg" or "bury" a user-submitted story. Further contributing to making this site a social network, users can create profile pages with a catalog of their diggs that can be followed by friends. In 2012, Digg was acquired by Betaworks, a technology investment and development company, for just $500,000, a disappointing figure considering the estimated value of the site had once been around $160 million and investors had provided $45 million of funding through the years (Metz 2012). Data from comScore revealed that although Digg's traffic had been more than 29 million unique monthly visitors in January 2010, by May 2012, it had dropped to 7.3 million (Metz 2012).

Social news site Reddit, launched by University of Virginia graduates Steve Huffman and Alexis Ohanian, has fared much better than Digg. In 2006, Condé Nast acquired the site for an undisclosed price and started to attract a more mainstream audience. As of April 2016, Reddit had 244 million monthly unique visitors (Conger and Dickey 2016).

When the *New Oxford American Dictionary* named *podcast* as the word of the year in 2005, it signaled that podcasts had reached the mainstream. A podcast is an online audio program that can be downloaded or streamed. Although a podcast is not exactly social media any more than a song or television show is social media, it can be made social by providing a space for listeners to engage with the hosts. For example, questions for the hosts or answers to questions asked by the hosts could be tweeted or posted on Facebook. Furthermore, podcasts provide a way for many regular people to create shareable content because production requires little in terms of skill or tools.

The podcast "tipping point" is often considered to be June 28, 2005, when Apple's iTunes allowed for the podcast format and created a frenzy of activity with 1 million podcast subscriptions within just two days and listenership for some podcasts increasing at 10 times previous levels (Apple 2005). Although only a minority of the U.S. population listened to podcasts in 2016, listenership has been steadily growing. By 2016, 21 percent of Americans over age 12 had listened to a podcast in the past month and 36 percent had listened to a podcast at least once (Edison Research 2016). Additionally the rise of mobile phones has helped spur podcast listening, with 64 percent of those who have ever listened to a podcast indicating that they had done so "most often" on a mobile device. However, podcasts only represented a small sliver of total audio listening, at about 2 percent of the time compared with 54 percent of the time spent listening to AM/FM radio (Edison Research 2016).

The fastest growing website for the first half of 2006 was video-sharing site YouTube (O'Malley 2006). Founded by PayPal employees Chad Hurley, Steve Chen, and Jawed Karim in 2005, the site allows users to post videos and build a community of users who like and comment on videos, as well as subscribe to the user's feed. Less than a year after its official launch in November 2005, YouTube was purchased by Google for $1.65 billion in stock (Sorkin and Peters 2006). As of 2016, the site was the second largest search engine and the third most visited site (behind Google and Facebook). Approximately 300 hours of video are uploaded every minute, and YouTube's videos receive an average of more than 1 billion views a day (K. Smith 2016b). More than half of the views on YouTube come from mobile devices, and among millennials, YouTube is where they spend about two-thirds of their premium online viewing time (K. Smith 2016b).

A Daily Kos post from 2011 attempted to answer the question of how long it would take to watch all videos uploaded to YouTube to date. Estimates of the number of videos that have been uploaded ranged from Dr. Michael Wesch's suggestion of 80 million in March 2008, which was determined by using a wildcard search (typing "*" into the search bar), to programmer Artem Russakovskii's suggestion of 141–144 million videos in August 2008. The post's author performed a wildcard search in 2011, which yielded approximately 275 million video results. Wesch also studied video length and proclaimed that an average YouTube video at the time was 2.77 minutes. Calculations using 275 million videos at an average length of 2.77 minutes show that it would take 1,450 years for a single person to watch all YouTube content that had been uploaded at that time (SuperBowlXX 2011).

YouTube's business model relies heavily on paid advertising, and various forms are available to advertisers. Skippable or non-skippable ads run prior to the start of a video, overlay ads are semitransparent at the bottom of the video and can be closed, sponsored cards relevant to the video are placed directly to the right of the video, and display ads appear above the other suggested videos. Worldwide gross ad revenues for 2015 were expected to hit $9.5 billion, and after subtracting costs for traffic and content acquisition, net advertising revenues were expected to reach $4.28 billion (eMarketer 2015b). Although YouTube dominates as the worldwide leader in video views, the company is facing competition from Facebook, Twitter, Amazon, and Vimeo.

To encourage major users to stay with YouTube, the company launched the YouTube Partners Program in 2007 to share advertising revenue. According to YouTube, channel owners making more than six figures increased 50 percent between 2015 and 2016 (YouTube 2016). As of September 2016, the top YouTubers in terms of subscribers included established pop stars and musical groups such as Rihanna, Justin Bieber, One Direction, and Taylor Swift as well as YouTube sensations such as PewDiePie, HolaSoyGerman, and Smosh (Social Blade 2016). The annual earnings of leader PewDiePie, with almost 50 million subscribers and more than 13.1 billion video views as of mid-2016, were estimated to be $12 million for 2015 (Mandle 2015). As a result of user interest in creating videos with quality production, YouTube Spaces is now available in six cities around the world to provide video creators with studios to produce their video content and learn new skills.

Social networking site Bebo is an example of a social media site that crashed, burned, and then reinvented itself. The site was founded by husband-and-wife team Michael and Xochi Birch in San Francisco in 2005 and became popular among users in the United Kingdom, particularly Ireland. Its major competitor at the time was MySpace, but Bebo was considered more user-friendly. Similar to other social media sites, users could share blog posts, photos, music, videos, and surveys. AOL purchased the site in 2008 for $850 million, a deal considered by a BBC reporter to be "one of the worst deals ever made in the dotcom era" (BBC News 2010). After managing the site for two years, AOL announced that Bebo would be sold or closed for its inability to compete with Facebook and Twitter and its declining membership. After the site was sold to Criterion Capital Partners, the new owner declared bankruptcy, and the Birches bought Bebo back for $1 million (Grant 2013). Late in 2014, Bebo was reincarnated as a mobile messaging app. Users select avatars for their profiles, not personal photos. Hashtags are not just for following similar conversations, but they also control actions or unlock special activities within the app. For example, the hashtag #allthesingleladies places the avatar in a

Beyoncé video with backup dancers, #draw launches a drawing canvas, and #tictactoe opens the game (Solon 2014).

Mainstream Social Media: Late 2000s

By 2006, Facebook had opened its platform to all users over age 13 with a valid e-mail address, and many users were willing to explore not only Facebook, but also the other social media platforms that emerged during the late 2000s. Notable entrants during this time included Twitter, Tumblr, Foursquare, and WhatsApp. Also, social gaming grew in popularity, and the launch of the iPhone meant that mobile users had a chance to engage with social media through apps and the Web on a user-friendly mobile platform.

Twitter first received mainstream attention at the SXSW conference in 2007 and was the conference's breakout social media platform (Kessler 2011). Twitter is differentiated from other social media sites in that it is, by default, an open space for conversation. Most users keep their profiles set to public, instead of making them private. Also unlike other social media sites, Twitter users do not have to mutually accept a follower request to see tweets from another user. Users can follow anyone with a public account and see that user's tweets in their timelines, but can also block followers, which may occur if a follower harasses or bothers a user. Hashtags are used extensively on Twitter, which allow users to search and follow a thread of conversation. For example, users watching a television show might use the show's hashtag to follow and participate in conversations with other viewers. Hashtags are also used to build support for issues or causes, such as #BlackLivesMatter for violence and injustice against African Americans, #bringbackourgirls for the Nigerian schoolgirls who were abducted by Boko Haram, #alsicebucketchallenge for the ALS Ice Bucket Challenge, or #whyistayed and #whyileft for domestic abuse.

The story behind the founding of Twitter has been hotly debated in popular media and often neglects the involvement of

Noah Glass, original founder of Odeo, a podcasting platform start-up and the company that later launched Twitter. Odeo investor Evan Williams (who later became CEO), former Google employee Biz Stone, and NYU undergraduate student Jack Dorsey are usually credited for the founding of Twitter. In a 2011 *Business Insider* article, Nicholas Carlson provides a version of the founding that highlights Glass's contribution (Carlson 2011).

After Glass founded Odeo, Williams became more involved than investors generally are with start-ups (Carlson 2011). Odeo even moved its operations to Williams's former apartment when he moved into a house. Williams eventually became the CEO, and along the way, Stone and Dorsey were also hired. Although an early invention of Glass's was turning a phone message into an MP3 that could be hosted online, Odeo's first product was an online platform for podcasting. Within months, however, Apple announced that iTunes would be able to host podcasts and that the service would be preloaded on iPods. Odeo then grew disenchanted with podcasts.

Dorsey had the idea of sharing "status," or what the user was doing right then. In early 2006, Glass, Dorsey, and contract developer Florian Weber presented an idea to the company whereby users would send a text that would be shared with all their connections (Carlson 2011). Glass was in charge of the development team. This service was called twttr, a name imagined by Glass. After they purchased the domain name from its owner, twttr became Twitter. The first message on the site was posted by Dorsey, who tweeted on March 21, 2006: "just setting up my twttr."

To clarify who deserves credit, Carlson explained: "Everyone agrees that original inkling for Twitter sprang from Jack Dorsey's mind. Dorsey even has drawings of something that looks like Twitter that he made years before he joined Odeo. And Jack was obviously central to the Twitter team. But all of the early employees and Odeo investors we talked to also agree that no one at Odeo was more passionate about

Twitter in the early days than Odeo's co-founder, Noah Glass" (Carlson 2011). One illustration of how Glass is often overlooked in the platform's start-up story is an interview of Stone by radio host Howard Stein where he said, "So Jack and I built the prototype. We took two weeks and built the working early model of Twitter and showed the rest of the team. We said, 'What do you guys think?' People were pretty underwhelmed" (Carlson 2011).

Twitter had a rough start, gaining only 5,000 registered users within its first two months (Carlson 2011). Williams saw its value, but felt investors were not justified in investing in Odeo now that its direction had changed. He purchased back all the stock in mid-2006, therefore becoming not only the CEO but also the owner. Although this sum was not reported, it is speculated to have been approximately $5 million (Carlson 2011). Five years later, the company was valued at $5 billion. Questions remain as to whether Williams tricked investors by downplaying the potential of Twitter (Carlson 2011). In 2006, Williams started a new company called Obvious Corporation, which promptly purchased Odeo. Williams then made the decision to fire Glass. Twitter was later spun out of Obvious as its own company and went public in late 2013. At the time of its IPO, shares of Twitter were priced at $26 per share, but the price has been on the relative decline ever since. As of 2016, Twitter had about 310 million monthly average users and over 1.3 billion registered users, with slightly less than half of those accounts having ever sent a tweet (K. Smith 2016a).

Although most of the social media platforms discussed so far involve connecting with friends for conversation and content sharing, social gaming, where networks of people can participate collaboratively or competitively in a game setting, is another important development within the realm of social media. One of the early leaders in social gaming was the company Zynga, founded in 2007 by Mark Pincus who had also previously launched early social networking site Tribe.net. Zynga's games were first available to MySpace users and later moved onto Facebook. As Facebook exploded in popularity, so too did Zynga's games, with some Facebook users even joining the social networking site to be able to access the games. Zynga's first game for Facebook, launched in September 2007, was a social poker game called Texas Hold 'Em Poker, providing friends a way to organize a poker game and participate remotely. Another popular Zynga product, Mafia Wars, launched in 2008, has been called "the smallest, marginal step up from a text-based game," involving just pictures, progress bars that moved from empty to full, and numbers that increased (Thier 2012). Zynga's most popular game, FarmVille, which launched in 2009 after being in development for just five weeks, had more than 1 million new daily active users a week on average (Keating 2015). FarmVille was followed by Café World the same year. After being introduced in late 2011, Zynga's Mafia Wars 2, despite significant updates, started losing users from day one. As of 2012, it had 100,000 fewer daily active users than its predecessor (Thier 2012). By 2013, three of the five most popular games on Facebook were Zynga games FarmVille 2, Zynga Poker, and ChefVille.

The business model of Zynga allowed for free participation in games, but offered virtual goods that could be purchased to enhance the gaming experience. Pincus said in a recorded talk to app developers, "I did every horrible thing in the book just to get revenues" (Popken 2009). Some of his tactics included announcements cluttering the Facebook News Feed, providing paid in-game boosts to regenerate energy quicker, and using lead-generating offers that involved answering questions that might trick users into opting in to receiving spam, installing malware or adware, or subscribing to a credit card charge. In the same talk, Pincus also said, "I mean we gave our users poker chips if they downloaded this zwinky toolbar which was like, I don't know, I downloaded it once and couldn't get rid of it" (Popken 2009). Users were also incentivized to recruit friends to the game and allow promotional messages to be presented to friends on Facebook.

During the final quarter of 2011, Zynga earned 80 percent of its revenue from Facebook users, while 43 percent of Facebook's revenues were coming from Zynga (Tam 2012). By the end of the following year, Zynga and Facebook had negotiated a new deal to reduce the reliance of each company on the other. The companies agreed that Zynga would no longer be required to display Facebook ads on its site, use Facebook credits to make in-game purchases, or solely develop for the Facebook platform. In return, Zynga no longer had the ability to cross-promote through Facebook by placing Zynga.com ads in Zynga games played on Facebook, publishing game updates that link to the Zynga site, or sending e-mails to Facebook users (Tam 2012).

Zynga's initial success failed to translate into long-term stability for the company. When the company first filed for an IPO in 2011, the valuation was $20 billion, a number that quickly dropped to $9 billion, and finally, by the time of its IPO, had dropped further to $7 billion with shares priced at $10 (Thier 2012). From May 2014 to August 2016, share prices hovered around $3. Even though Zynga is not as much of an industry player as it once was, the mobile gaming industry has been on the rise and was expected to hit $30 billion in sales in 2015, which surpasses $25 billion in 2014 (Keating 2015). Mobile gamers are also increasing and represented 35 percent of all gamers in 2015 (Keating 2015).

The blogs of the early day of social media were reinvented with the introduction of tumblelogs, with the most popular being Tumblr, which was developed and released by David Karp in 2007. A tumblelog is a short-form blog service that allows each post to be just one paragraph and the content of posts includes not just text, but also photos, GIFs, and pulled quotes. Although Karp often receives credit for inventing this new format, his design was likely inspired by earlier developers, including a German high school student named Chris Neukirchen who created a tumblelog called anarchaia in 2005 and Marcel Molina and Sam Stephenson who launched Projectionist, which they referred to as a "tumble log" (Alfonso 2013). What Karp was able to do was take these existing concepts and provide regular users with tools to create their own tumblelogs.

Tumblr users not only had their own blogs that they could manage, but also a dashboard that provided a feed of updated content on other Tumblrs they followed and comments on their own posts. Originally founded as an advertising-free platform, the business model changed in 2012 to embrace paid advertising, called sponsor products (Lardinois 2012). One of Tumblr's first major advertisers was Adidas, for whom the company created a soccer Tumblr and promoted it on the home page. In 2013, Tumblr was purchased by Yahoo for $1.1 billion, making Karp about $250 million richer. By the end of 2015, Tumblr had about 550 million monthly users and 280 million blogs (Heine 2015).

In 2016, Tumblr added paid advertising to users' blogs, but allowed users to opt out (Olivarez-Giles 2016). The ads provide an additional way to monetize the free service and also offer a way for users to make money from their blogs through a partner program. The inability of Tumblr to have a viable monetization strategy for so many years resulted in the company having a hard time convincing marketers to spend money on Tumblr (Walters 2016). Around the same time as the advertising announcement, Tumblr's parent company, Yahoo, sold to Verizon, placing Tumblr under the umbrella of the telecommunications giant.

Although not a social media platform, the emergence of the iPhone and other smartphones can be tied to an increased use of social media. Smartphones can be traced back to and the launch of the IBM Simon in 1992 (McCarty 2011). That phone offered a touchscreen that could be operated by a stylus and the ability to send and receive faxes and e-mails, but failed to gain popularity among mainstream consumers. Several years later, Nokia and Ericsson also introduced smartphones, a term coined by Ericsson. By the early 2000s, Palm, Research in Motion (the maker of BlackBerry), and Windows all had entrants into the smartphone market, but nothing changed dramatically in the marketplace until Apple CEO Steve Jobs announced at the Macworld convention in January 2007 that the iPhone would be on the market later that year (Chen 2008). Instead of a phone for business people, the iPhone would be geared toward the average consumer.

An initial limitation of the iPhone was that third-party applications could not be added, but within six months, Apple opened up the platform to developers. The first third-party app developed for the iPhone was OneTrip, a digital shopping list (Moynihan 2007). Around the same time, the Android operating system was also in development, and this system was able to run on a number of devices, including first HTC and later Samsung, LG, and Motorola (McCarty 2011). Third-party apps for all these phones are located on either Apple's App Store or Google's Android Market, now called Google Play. As of June 2016, the number of apps available in the Apple App Store was estimated to be 2 million apps, which was second to Google Play with 2.2 million apps, with both app sources dwarfing Amazon Appstore, Windows Store, and BlackBerry World (Statista 2016b). Apple apps have experienced 140 billion downloads between July 2008 and September 2016 (Statista 2016a). In May 2016, the most popular apps in the world included WhatsApp with 42 million downloads that month, followed by Messenger, Facebook, Snapchat, Instagram, and YouTube (Richter 2016).

By 2015, 64 percent of American adults owned a smartphone, a steep increase from 2011 when the percentage was 35 percent (A. Smith 2015). Among all mobile phone users in the United States, 79 percent own a smartphone (comScore 2016). Ten percent of American adults have a smartphone, but not high-speed Internet at home, making them particularly reliant on this device (A. Smith 2015). Smartphones keep social media sites at the fingertips of users at all times. Furthermore, the functions of the phone, namely the photo and video camera, allow users to capture content for easy sharing to social media sites. By the end of 2015, almost 80 percent of social media users' time on social media was spent accessing the sites from predominately smartphones (67 percent of time) but also tablets (12 percent of time), which had increased from 67 percent of time for both types of devices at the end of 2013 (comScore 2016).

The increasing penetration of smartphone usage has led to the development of social media apps to be used solely on a smartphone. Foursquare, created in 2009 by Dennis Crowley and Naveen Selvadurai, was launched as a location-based social networking site that incorporates the phone's location services to allow users to "check in" to their location. Crowley had previously developed Dodgeball, which was a mobile service that texted location to a user's friends.

Foursquare included social networking features by providing a way to connect users with friends also at the same location. Additionally, the app had a game component that gave users an opportunity to unlock a variety of badges based on their check-ins and also become the "mayor" of a location by having the most visits during a time period. The app appealed to businesses that could present users with deals or discounts based on their check-ins. For example, Chili's provided a free order of chips and salsa to patrons who had checked in the restaurant on Foursquare.

Foursquare grew dramatically in the early years, surpassing 45 million users and 5 billion check-ins by December 2013; however, since then, the platform has not fared as well (C. Smith 2014). Foursquare's initial purpose shifted in 2014, and the app that is Foursquare now provides suggestions about the "best places to eat, drink, shop, or visit in any city in the world" with "access to over 75 million short reviews from local experts," according to its home page. The company also launched the app Swarm for checking in and finding nearby friends, which had both been features of the original Foursquare. The check-in data in the early years was particularly important at that time because phones were not sophisticated enough to pinpoint a user's location with much precision or know what venues were in the area, a data point that was relevant to users of the data. As the technology and data developed, the check-in became less important to the company. The company also learned that sharing a check-in was not nearly as interesting as sharing a selfie or other content that could be done on other social media platforms (Popper and Hamburger 2014).

A major player in the messaging arena is WhatsApp, which was purchased by Facebook in 2014 for $19 billion five years after its founding in 2009 by Jan Koum and Brian Acton. Facebook already had a successful messaging app in Facebook Messenger, but even after the acquisition of WhatsApp, users continued to grow for both services. WhatsApp grew steadily from August 2013 to September 2015, adding approximately 1 million users every four months to hit 900 million users with Messenger trailing slightly with 700 million (Baidya 2015). Acton explained at Facebook's 2015 F8 conference that each platform will grow through independent development and that Facebook has no plans to merge the two platforms in the near future (McGarry 2015).

Modern Social Media: 2010s

As social media increased in usage and moved to mobile, many social networks fell into one of two categories: those that focus on photos and those that focus on messaging (Pierce 2015). Even Facebook, despite its dominance in these two areas, purchased platforms that emphasize photos, such as Instagram, and platforms for messaging, such as WhatsApp. Journalist David Pierce stated, "[Facebook] understood before anyone that our online social interactions can't be captured in a single feed. Instagram, Messenger, and Facebook all have different purposes, different uses; trying to cram them all into a single bucket doesn't make any sense. It took Google a while, but it too seems to be finally recognizing that" (Pierce 2015). This section covers visual platforms Pinterest, Instagram, and Vine, messaging apps Kik and Snapchat (which also emphasizes visual content), and live-streaming apps Facebook Live, Meerkat, and Periscope.

Pinterest, the virtual pinboard or bulletin board site, is full of visual content ranging from home design and fashion to party ideas and recipes. The site, launched in 2010 by Ben Silbermann, Paul Sciarra, and Evan Sharp, provides users with a platform reminiscent of a bulletin board or scrapbook for uploading or "pinning" either their own content to the site, content shared by others on the site, or content shared elsewhere that offers a Pinterest button. The pins are organized onto boards that can be named by the user. The Pinterest feed on the home page allows users to see the content shared or liked by others. Despite offering social networking functions, Silbermann views Pinterest as a "catalogue of ideas" that is more like a search engine (Barbaschow 2015).

Pinterest users surpassed 100 million in September 2015 and they were pinning approximately 1.5 billion pins a month (Barbaschow 2015). As of March 2015, Pinterest was valued at $11 billion, a number that had tripled during the previous 18 months (de la Merced 2015). At 85 percent, the majority of users are women (eMarketer 2014) and an estimated 42 percent of women in the United States use Pinterest (Duggan et al. 2015). One of the main sources of revenue for the site is "promoted pins" purchased by advertisers to attract interest in products and drive sales through links to websites for online purchases. In June 2015, Pinterest launched Buyable Pins indicated by blue price tags that allow users to make purchases directly from the site (Barbaschow 2015). Advertisers also create their own profiles for branding purposes. The visual beauty available on Pinterest has impacted society in many ways, inspiring people to be more creative when planning everything from weddings to baby gender reveal parties to children's birthday parties. Pinterest also offers countless recipes and photos of food pinned by restaurants, food manufacturers, grocery stores, food bloggers and home chefs. Fashion, crafting, organizing, and decorating ideas also flourish on the site. The site is also filled with inspirational quotes as well as "life hacks," which are methods of making a task easier.

The site is particularly useful for marketers interested in reaching the predominantly female audience of consumers. Grocery store Whole Food's Pinterest page, for example, offers approximately 60 boards on such topics as "Beautiful Summer Berries," "Sweet Tooth," and "How Does your Garden Grow?" Marketers also identify Pinterest influencers, who are users with large followings, for sponsored content or design collaborations. For example, in 2014 Target selected several Pinterest party-planning influencers and partnered with them to create product lines that would be sold in stores and featured on the influencers' Pinterest boards (Target 2014).

Also launched in 2010 was Instagram, the brainchild of Kevin Systrom and Mike Krieger. Instagram began as a photo-sharing site that offered a range of artsy digital filters for enhancing photos. Since then, it has also added video-sharing capabilities and a "stories" feature where users can string together photos and videos into a slideshow that disappears. Similar to Twitter, Instagram also incorporates hashtags to allow users to tag and then search for content sharing the same tag. Advertisers also encourage the use of certain hashtags for users to share a photo to enter a contest or participate in another type of promotion. As of June 2015, Instagram had 300 million active users who post 75 million photos per day (Newtek 2015). Purchased by Facebook in April 2012 for $1 billion, the company has not yet developed a monetization model. It is, however, exploring ways to connect advertisers with consumers (Newtek 2015).

The popularity of Instagram has led to "the Instagram effect" described by *Adweek* as "that filtered, shadowed, sharpened, brightened, tilted, faded, structured, saturated way of seeing life through a lens" (Swant 2015). The site's impact has even extended to brands, which are replacing their overly staged photography with visuals that look more organic not only for Instagram, but also for other online and offline advertising placements. Researchers at Canva studied more than 1 million Instagram images and found that those filtered with Clarendon, Skyline, Normal (not using a filter), and Valencia tend to get the most likes (Williams 2016). Analytics provide information about how viewers are responding to these styles, and Instagram is a good source for ideas to make branded photos blend in with other popular styles.

Google launched social networking site Google+ in 2011 to compete with Facebook and Twitter, but despite its attempts to differentiate itself with concepts such as "Circles," which limit conversation to a specific group of friends, and "Hangouts," which allow a group of people to video chat, Google+ could not gain a significant advantage over the leaders (Fiegerman 2015). Users with a large network on Facebook had little motivation to recreate that network on another site, and Facebook eventually incorporated a similar tool to Google Circles to manage the receivers of any post. Furthermore, as noted in *Mashable*, Google+ launched "without a clear plan to differentiate the service from Facebook . . . bet on a charismatic leader with a flawed vision, ignored troubling indications about the social network's traction (or lack thereof) with users and continued throwing features at the wall long after many had written Google+ off for dead" (Fiegerman 2015).

The original Google+ integrated with other Google products, namely Search, Gmail, and Drive, helping its adoption and allowing users to seamlessly move between products. Google+ represented Google's fourth attempt to successfully launch a social network following products Google Buzz, Google Friend Connect, and Orkut. Orkut survived for a while because of high usage among Brazilian and Indian users, but the site was eventually closed in 2014. In early 2015, Google+ spun off "Photos" and "Streams" as separate products (Fiegerman 2015). Photos allows users access to photo storage, editing and sharing tools, organization and search capabilities, and a clean layout. Streams is the rebranded news feed of Google+ that offers opportunities for users to share and read content provided by their connections. Google Hangouts had already been a stand-alone product, offering messaging, video calls, and voice calls from any device. Although Google has not released usage statistics for Hangouts, it has serious competition from other messaging apps including WhatsApp with 700 million active users and WeChat with 500 million users as of January 2015 (tech2 News Staff 2015). Hangouts is failing by not being as mobile-friendly as other chat apps in a mobile world (tech2 News Staff 2015).

The video-sharing site Vine, created by Dom Hofmann, Rus Yusupov, and Colin Kroll, allowed users to create six-second video clips through an iOS or Android app. Twitter quickly purchased Vine in 2012 and officially launched the platform in 2013. Vine grew from 77,000 visitors in January 2013 to 3.6 million by May 2013, according to Compete.com (Tate 2013). Although not the first app of its kind, Vine was the one that was able to differentiate itself from the competition. Advertisers employed the platform to create stop-motion animation videos. Other users included journalists who captured a small slice of the news story they were covering, celebrities who used it to connect with fans, and record labels for promoting new albums or artists. As of 2016, Vine suspended uploads to the platform, but will continue to make current content available for several months. Twitter is expected to close the app in 2017 (Perez 2016).

Other social media platforms launched in the early to mid-2010s included mobile messaging apps, such as Kik and Snapchat, which are popular with teens and young adults. These apps give teens a way to communicate with each other while avoiding the watchful eyes of their parents. Launched in 2010, Kik is similar to short message service (SMS) text messaging, but instead uses data or Wi-Fi to transmit messages, which makes it attractive to users with text limits. Additionally, users only need to know the Kik username of someone they wish to message, not their phone number like with SMS messaging.

Snapchat was founded by Stanford students Evan Spiegel, Bobby Murphy, and Reggie Brown in 2011. With more than 150 million people using the service by mid-2016, Snapchat surpassed Twitter usage that year (Frier 2016). Snapchat's messages disappear after being viewed for several seconds, which makes it a particularly compelling app for private sharing of photos and videos. Snapchat engages users with effects such as filters for changing the photo's tones as well geofilters that indicate location; graphics that add elements to a selfie, such as a flower crown; and animated effects, such as a rainbow being vomited from a subject's mouth.

Live-streaming video platforms were a social media development that attracted significant attention in 2015. The two major players in this arena are Periscope and Facebook Live, which allow users to live broadcast (with about a two-second lag) from their phones and interact with followers who can post messages. One of the early entrants into the live-streaming market was the now-defunct Meerkat, founded by Ben Rubin, which gained traction at the SXSW conference in 2015. Celebrities and television personalities such as Julia Louis-Dreyfus, Jimmy Fallon, and Al Roker followed with "Meerkats" shortly after (Newton 2015). Some of the appeal of the app may have resulted from the announcement that Twitter was cutting off access to Meerkat as a result of its acquisition of similar tool Periscope, a move that incited people to show interest in the smaller company (Newton 2015). Shortly before SXSW 2015, Twitter quietly purchased Periscope for an amount reported to be slightly under $100 million, its largest acquisition (Koh and Rusli 2015). Periscope, founded by Kayvon Beykpour and Joe Bernstein, had 10 million downloads by August 2015 (Wagner 2015). The applications for live streaming are varied and include concerts, sporting events, other live productions, backstage moments from television shows, breaking news stories, and political campaigning.

Facebook also launched its own live-streaming service called Live in 2015, but the feature was first only available on

Facebook Mentions, an app that allows celebrities and other high-profile verified users to engage with fans (Mangalindan 2015). Facebook users can view the live stream in their News Feed when a celebrity they follow launches the app. In 2016, the company made Live available to all users with an iPhone. This strategic move by Facebook helped prevent Periscope and other competitors from enjoying a significant amount of the live-steaming market, encouraged people to spend an increasing amount of time on Facebook engaging with videos, and served people's desire to create and watch live streaming (Barnett 2016).

Future Directions for Social Media

"We're still in the first minutes of the first day of the Internet revolution," remarked Intuit cofounder Scott Cook back in 2000 (Levingston and International Herald Tribune 2000). Less than two decades after its emergence, the social media industry still seems to be in its early days as well. The developments that users might see in the future include growth of existing platforms, new platforms, and new features in current platforms. Other trends include the popularity of niche social networks, online sharing and crowdfunding platforms, virtual and augmented reality apps, and messaging apps. Social media monetization strategies will continue to evolve, and popular culture products will continue to incorporate social media in new and creative ways.

Niche social networks are increasingly popular because they allow users to connect with a smaller group of people who share a common interest instead of a mass audience. Because a viable competitor to Facebook may never emerge, the only way to create a competitive advantage may be to focus on an untapped niche market. The social networking platform, Nextdoor, for example, allows neighbors to connect and share community news, post items for sale, or find lost pets. Path, another social networking site, connects users with no more than 150 contacts, which is considered the optimal number of people in a network. Other trends include Social-Local-Mobile apps, aka SoLoMo apps, like Highlight or Ban.jo that allow users to connect socially with others and events in the local area through their mobile phones. SoLoMo apps benefit from the high rates of social media use on mobile phones and the needs of some people to meet up with friends who are in their vicinity or learn about events in the area.

Social media have been a critical component in the flourishing of an online sharing economy (Reynolds 2015). The emergence of social media sites, such as Facebook and Twitter, had an impact on users by fostering the sharing of information and recommendations. Some of these recommendations, particularly those on Twitter, are shared with strangers, which is an important component of a sharing economy. Also, because users often share under their real identities, this transparency, as opposed to anonymity, creates trust. The social network also provides users with a way to know whether reviewers are within their social graph as friends of friends (Holmes 2014). A report by Vision Critical found that 40 percent of Americans have participated in this collaborative economy by either buying or selling pre-owned goods or services (Holmes 2014).

One of the popular sharing sites is Airbnb, a site for sharing homes or rooms with strangers for a price. Airbnb and similar sites allow users to first view photos of the accommodations and then the two parties involved can learn about one another through verified profiles and reviews. Uber and Lyft have also grown in popularity to provide transportation services. Other sharing sites have emerged that provide pet sitting services, such as DogVacay, conference rooms through sites like Liquid Space and ShareDesk, car rentals from Turo and Getaround, and bike sharing through Liquid.

Social media users are also connecting on crowdfunding sites like GoFundMe to launch and support fund-raising campaigns that raise money for health emergencies or other personal needs. Another popular site is Kickstarter, which is dedicated to fund-raising for creative products, not personal campaigns. Small donation site Kiva crowdfunds to provide loans, not donations, to people around the world to support their small business ventures.

Products for virtual and augmented reality are also expected to change the social media landscape. Virtual reality engages users in a simulated environment while augmented reality blends virtual reality with real life, such as overlaying useful information about the user's surroundings. When Facebook purchased Oculus VR in 2014 for $2 billion, it gained access to the company's virtual reality headset, the Oculus Rift. Lower-priced competitors Google Cardboard and Samsung Gear VR, among others, have also entered the marketplace. Other players are creating virtual and augmented reality apps. For example, the *New York Times* in 2015 shipped Google Cardboard headsets to its subscribers and encouraged them to download its virtual reality app. The app was downloaded more than 600,000 times, making it more successful that any app in its history (Griffith 2016). Even more popular was Pokémon Go, released in 2016, an augmented reality game that quickly captured mass attention and participation. While engaging with the game, users seek virtual characters by looking at their actual surroundings through a smartphone. As of the end of July 2016, Pokémon Go downloads were estimated to be 7.5 million in the United States alone (Etherington 2016).

Conversations have also been moving to messaging platforms, such as Snapchat, Messenger, WhatsApp, WeChat, and Kik, in such large numbers that messaging apps now have a user base that is on par with the four largest social media platforms combined (Revis 2016). In the future, messaging platforms will continue to look for ways to engage users with new features to enhance messages, such as emojis, gif apps, and stickers; expand the range of items for purchase; and offer improved tools for group chats. On apps like China's popular WeChat, where users can order a taxi, book a hotel, buy movie tickets, check into airline flights, access bank statements, and make appointments, the purpose of the app becomes to help manage a user's life, rather than just send messages (Natanson 2016). These interactions with banks, airlines, and movie theaters utilize third-party apps that act like websites on the chat user interface. Also on the horizon is the use of "bots" to engage with users of messaging platforms, with conversations triggered by keywords typed into messaging systems. For example, users who are chatting about going out to eat might receive a recommendation from a bot, and then after a reservation is made through the app, another bot might start recommending menu items.

Many social media platforms have a monetization strategy that depends heavily on advertising, but many are also incorporating social commerce that allows users to make purchases directly from the social media sites. The key to social commerce is a "buy" button directly on the Facebook post, Twitter tweet, or Pinterest pin. The buy buttons reduce the steps it takes to purchase the product, thus simplifying the sales funnel process. Facebook introduced its buy button in 2015, and users can purchase a product without leaving the site as all the information is input into a pop-up window. Also in 2015, Pinterest launched Buyable Pins, and Twitter started offering buy buttons on ads. Among the first marketers using the feature on Twitter were ticket merchants for sporting events and concerts (Del Rey 2015). Advertising formats will also continue to evolve. Facebook and YouTube have both added 360-degree video ads for more engaging experiences.

Social media platforms will also continue to engage popular culture consumers in new and creative ways. For example, movie trailers or television shows have premiered on social media sites. In 2011, Twitter was used by both Paramount for the release of the trailer for its movie *Super 8* and the Sundance Channel for the second season premiere of *Girls Who Like Boys Who Like Boys*. Two weeks before the AMC show *Halt and Catch Fire* premiered on television in 2014, it was released on Tumblr. As a show about computers, it was the perfect fit for a social media launch. Additionally, social media conversation can also create buzz for a show or a film. The 2013 Syfy made-for-television movie *Sharknado* about a tornado of sharks that hits a Los Angeles community illustrates the power of social media to create considerable interest in a media product. The network released promos on YouTube and started tweeting and retweeting in the hours before the movie's premiere in addition to promoting the film through traditional methods. During the airing, fans were tweeting at an estimated rate of 5,000 tweets per minute quickly making *Sharknado* a trending topic on the site (Twitter 2013).

Social media continue to offer viewers a richer experience to engage with television content. When viewers use their smartphones or tablets during a television show to access additional content related to the show or interact with other viewers, they are having what is called a "second-screen experience." Some of the techniques for engaging viewers in a second screen while watching a television show include providing hashtags on the screen, voting via a social media site or app, sharing reality show participants' social media sites, or providing apps to engage specifically with other viewers. For the television miniseries *World without End*, for example, users of the series' app were provided with extra content that was made available in real time, such as character-related content when a character appeared. The app also functioned to allow conversations with other fans. *The Walking Dead* and other AMC shows also use a similar product called Story Sync.

With all the developments during the past two decades, it may be difficult to imagine that a new social media platform or class of platform could emerge that will connect more users, significantly impact the culture, or greatly shift the way that lives are managed. That being said, entrepreneurs, inspired by today's social media founders and success of the most popular platforms, are working on projects that will likely once again change the world. New social media platforms continue to be launched every day to compete with the major players by offering more appealing features for a similar tool, targeting an untapped audience, or introducing a completely new concept.

References

Abbruzzese, Jason. 2014. "The Rise and Fall of AIM, the Breakthrough AOL Never Wanted." *Mashable.* April 15. http://avalaunchmedia.com/history-of-social-media/Main.html.

Alfonso, Fernando, III. 2013. "The Real Origins of Tumblr." *The Daily Dot.* May 23. http://www.dailydot.com/business/origin-tumblr-anarchaia-projectionist-david-karp/.

Apple. 2005. "iTunes Podcast Subscriptions Top One Million in First Two Days." *Apple.* June 30. https://www.apple.com/pr/library/2005/06/30iTunes-Podcast-Subscriptions-Top-One-Million-in-First-Two-Days.html.

Apple II History. n.d. http://apple2history.org/history/ah22/.

Baidya, Amartya. 2015. "The Growth of WhatsApp to 900 Million Active Users and Effect on Mobile Messaging Industry." *DazeInfo.* September 7. http://dazeinfo.com/2015/09/07/whatsapp-facebook-messenger-wechat-hike-monthly-active-users/.

Barbaschow, Asha. 2015. "Pinterest Surpasses 100 Million Monthly Users." *ZDNet.* September 18. http://www.zdnet.com/article/pinterest-surpasses-100-million-monthly-users/.

Barnett, Brian. 2016. "Facebook Livestreaming Opens Up to Everyone with an iPhone." *Wired.* January 28. http://www.wired.com/2016/01/facebook-livestreaming-opens-up-to-everyone-with-an-iphone/.

BBC News. 2010. "Bebo Sold by AOL after Just Two Years." *BBC News.* June 17. http://www.bbc.com/news/10341413.

Bercovici, Jeff. 2013. "Tumblr: David Karp's $800 Million Art Project." *Forbes.* January 3. http://www.forbes.com/

sites/jeffbercovici/2013/01/02/tumblr-david-karps-800-million-art-project/.

BI Intelligence. 2015. "Facebook is Losing its Grip on Teens as Visual Social Networks Gain Popularity." *Business Insider*. June 17. http://www.businessinsider.com/facebook-is-losing-its-grip-on-the-teen-demographic-as-visual-social-networks-gain-popularity-2015-6.

boyd, danah m., and Nicole B. Ellison. 2007. "Social Network Sites: Definition, History, and Scholarship." *Journal of Computer-Mediated Communication* 13 (1).

Carlson, Nicholas. 2011. "The Real History of Twitter." *Business Insider*. April 13. http://www.businessinsider.com/how-twitter-was-founded-2011-4.

Cashmore, Pete. 2006. "MySpace, America's Number One." *Mashable*. July 11. http://mashable.com/2006/07/11/myspace-americas-number-one.

Casti, Taylor. 2013. "The Evolution of Facebok Mobile." *Mashable*. August 1. http://mashable.com/2013/08/01/facebook-mobile-evolution.

Chen, Brian X. 2008. "June 29, 2007: iPhone, You Phone, We All Wanna iPhone." *Wired*. June 28. https://www.wired.com/2009/06/dayintech_0629/.

comScore. 2016. "Cross-Platform Future in Focus 2016." https://www.comscore.com/Insights/Presentations-and-Whitepapers/2016/2016-US-Cross-Platform-Future-in-Focus.

Conger, Kate, and Megan Rose Dickey. 2016. "Reddit Is Still in Turmoil." *TechCrunch*. July 21. https://techcrunch.com/2016/07/21/reddit-is-still-in-turmoil/.

de la Merced, Michael J. 2015. "Pinterest Valuation at $11 Billion after New Round of Fund-Raising." *New York Times*. March 16. http://www.nytimes.com/2015/03/17/business/dealbook/pinterest-valuation-at-11-billion-after-new-round-of-fund-raising.html.

Del Rey, Jason. 2015. "Twitter Beging Selling Sports Tickets, Starting with the NBA Playoffs." *Recode*. April 20. http://www.recode.net/2015/4/20/11561672/twitter-begins-selling-sports-tickets-starting-with-the-nba-playoffs.

Duggan, Maeve, Nicole B. Ellison, Cliff Lampe, Amanda Lenhart, and Mary Madden. 2015. "Social Media Update 2014." *Pew Internet & American Life Project.* January 9. http://www.pewinternet.org/2015/01/09/social-media-update-2014/.

Edison Research. 2016. "The Podcast Consumer 2016." *Edison Research.* May 26. http://www.edisonresearch.com/wp-content/uploads/2016/05/The-Podcast-Consumer-2016.pdf.

eMarketer. 2014. "Females Press the Pin Button." *eMarketer.* June 2. http://www.emarketer.com/Article.aspx?R=1010878.

eMarketer. 2015a. "Social Network Ad Spending to Hit $23.68 Billion Worldwide by 2015." *eMarketer.* April 15. http://www.emarketer.com/Article/Social-Network-Ad-Spending-Hit-2368-Billion-Worldwide-2015/1012357.

eMarketer. 2015b. "What Do Marketers Think of YouTube Data and Analytics?" *eMarketer.* August 25. http://www.emarketer.com/Article/What-Do-Marketers-Think-of-YouTube-Data-Analytics/1012903.

Etherington, Darrell. 2016. "Pokémon Go Has an Estimated 7.5M U.S. Downloads, $1.6M in Daily Revenue." *TechCrunch.* July 11. https://techcrunch.com/2016/07/11/pokemon-go-daily-revenue-downloads/.

Facebook. n.d. *Facebook.* Accessed August 9, 2016. http://newsroom.fb.com/company-info/.

Facebook. 2016. "Facebook Reports Second Quarter 2016 Results." *Facebook Investor Relations.* July 27. https://investor.fb.com/investor-news/press-release-details/2016/Facebook-Reports-Second-Quarter-2016-Results/default.aspx.

Fiegerman, Seth. 2015. "Inside the Failure of Google+, a Very Expensive Attempt to Unseat Facebook." *Mashable.* August 2. http://mashable.com/2015/08/02/google-plus-history/#dJv6UdGlVPqm.

1st Web Designer. n.d. "A History You Will Love: How Online Social Networking Began." *1st Web Designer.* http://www.1stwebdesigner.com/history-social-networking/.

Frier, Sarah. 2016. "Snapchat Passes Twitter in Daily Usage." *Bloomberg News.* June 2. http://www.bloomberg.com/news/articles/2016-06-02/snapchat-passes-twitter-in-daily-usage.

Gilbertson, Scott. 2010. "Feb. 16, 1978: Bulletin Board Goes Electronic." *Wired.* February 16. http://www.wired.com/2010/02/0216cbbs-first-bbs-bulletin-board/.

Goldman, David. 2015. "Facebook Claims It Created 4.5 Million Jobs." *CNN.* January 20. http://money.cnn.com/2015/01/20/technology/social/facebook-jobs/.

Grant, Rebecca. 2013. "Bebo Bargain: After Selling to AOL for $850M in 2008, Founders Buy It Back for . . . $1M." *Venture Beat.* July 1. http://venturebeat.com/2013/07/01/bebo-bargain-after-selling-to-aol-for-850m-in-2008-founders-buy-it-back-for-1m/.

Griffith, Erin. 2016. "Can Virtual Reality Save Journalism?" *Fortune.* May 2. http://fortune.com/2016/05/02/virtual-reality-nyt-newfronts/.

Heine, Christopher. 2015. "Here Are the Top 25 Tumblr Posts Sponsored by Brands in 2015." *Adweek.* December 16. http://www.adweek.com/news-gallery/technology/here-are-top-25-tumblr-posts-sponsored-brands-2015-168653.

Holmes, Ryan. 2014. "Social Media Jumpstarted the Sharing Economy." *The Wall Street Journal.* April 16. http://blogs.wsj.com/accelerators/2014/04/16/ryan-holmes-social-media-jumpstarted-the-share-economy/.

Honan, Matt. 2012. "How Yahoo Killed Flickr and Lost the Internet." *Gizmodo.* May 15. http://gizmodo.com/5910223/how-yahoo-killed-flickr-and-lost-the-internet.

Ionescu, Daniel. 2011. "Winklevoss Twins v. Facebook: Case Closed." *PCWorld*, April 12. http://www.pcworld.com/article/224933/Winklevoss_Twins_v_Facebook_Case_Closed.html.

Jackson, Nicholas, and Alexis C. Madrigal. 2011. "The Rise and Fall of MySpace." *The Atlantic.* January 12. http://www.theatlantic.com/technology/archive/2011/01/the-rise-and-fall-of-myspace/69444/.

Keating, Lauren. 2015. "Gaming-on-the-Go: Where Has Zynga Been Now That Mobile Gaming Has Exploded?" *Tech Times.* September 3. http://www.techtimes.com/articles/81491/20150903/gaming-go-where-zynga-gone-now-mobile-exploded.htm.

Kemp, Simon. 2016. "Digital in 2016." *We Are Social.* January 27. http://wearesocial.com/uk/special-reports/digital-in-2016.

Kessler, Sarah. 2011. "Six Successful SXSW Startup Launch Stories." *Mashable.* March 5. http://mashable.com/2011/03/05/sxsw-launches.

Koh, Yoree, and Evelyn M. Rusli. 2015. "Twitter Acquires Live-Video Streaming Startup Periscope." *The Wall Street Journal*, March 9. http://www.wsj.com/articles/twitter-acquires-live-video-streaming-startup-periscope-1425938498.

La Monica, Paul R. 2015. "Facebook Now Worth More than Walmart." *CNN.* June 23. http://money.cnn.com/2015/06/23/investing/facebook-walmart-market-value/.

Lapinski, Trent. 2006. "MySpace: The Business of Spam 2.0 (Exhaustive Edition)." *Gawker.* September 11.

http://gawker.com/199924/myspace-the-business-of-spam-20-exhaustive-edition.

Lardinois, Frederic. 2012. "Tumblr Finally Wants to Make Some Money, Launches Its First Ads." *TechCrunch.* May 2. https://techcrunch.com/2012/05/02/tumblr-finally-wants-to-make-some-money-launches-its-first-ads/.

Levingston, Steven, and International Herald Tribune. 2000. "Internet Entrepreneurs Are Upbeat Despite Market's Rough Ride." *New York Times.* May 24. http://www.nytimes.com/2000/05/24/business/worldbusiness/internet-entrepreneurs-are-upbeat-despite-markets.html.

Lien, Tracey. 2016. "Facebook Ends 2015 with Strong Revenue Growth and Profits." *The Los Angeles Times.* January 27. http://www.latimes.com/business/technology/la-fi-tn-facebook-earnings-20160127-story.html.

Linden Lab. 2013. "SL10B Infographic: Ten Years of Second Life." *Second Life.* June 20. https://community.secondlife.com/t5/Featured-News/SL10B-Infographic-Ten-Years-of-Second-Life/ba-p/2053857.

Linden Lab. 2015. "Linden Lab Invites First Virtual Experience Creators to Project Sansar Testing." *Linden Lab.* August 18. http://www.lindenlab.com/releases/linden-lab-invites-first-virtual-experience-creators-to-project-sansar-testing.

Makavy, Ran. 2013. "Feature Phone Milestone: Facebook for Every Phone Reaches 100 Million." Facebook. July 22. http://newsroom.fb.com/news/2013/07/feature-phone-milestone-facebook-for-every-phone-reaches-100-million/.

Mandle, Chris. 2015. "Forbes Names PewDiePie as Highest-Earning YouTuber with Annual Income Reaching $12m." *The Independent.* October 15. http://www.independent.co.uk/news/people/forbes-names-pewdiepie-as-highest-earning-youtuber-with-annual-income-reaching-12m-a6695536.html.

Mangalindan, J.P. 2015. "Facebook Launches Live Streaming, but Only for Famous People." *Mashable.* August 5. http://mashable.com/2015/08/05/facebook-live-streaming-celebrities.

Manjoo, Farhad. 2010. "The Joy of LISTSERVs." *Slate.* August 5. http://www.slate.com/articles/technology/technology/2010/08/the_joy_of_listservs.html.

McCarty, Brad. 2011. "The History of the Smartphone." *The Next Web.* December 6. http://thenextweb.com/mobile/2011/12/06/the-history-of-the-smartphone/.

McGarry, Caitlin. 2015. "How Facebook Messenger, Instagram, and WhatsApp Coexist under Facebook." *Macworld.* March 26. http://www.macworld.com/article/2902226/how-facebook-messenger-instagram-and-whatsapp-coexist-under-facebook.html.

McIntosh, Neil. 2003. "Google Buys Blogger Web Service." *The Guardian.* February 18. https://www.theguardian.com/business/2003/feb/18/digitalmedia.citynews.

Metz, Rachel. 2012. "Why Did Reddit Succeed Where Digg Failed?" *MIT Technology Review.* July 18. https://www.technologyreview.com/s/428520/why-did-reddit-succeed-where-digg-failed/.

Mieszkowski, Katharine. 2002. "The Ryze Surprise." *Salon.* October 2. http://www.salon.com/2002/10/02/ryze/.

Moynihan, Tim. 2007. "First Third-Party iPhone App: A Shopping List." *CNET.* June 28. https://www.cnet.com/news/first-third-party-iphone-app-a-shopping-list/.

Natanson, Elad. 2016. "Messaging Platforms, Bots and the Future of Mobile." *Forbes.* April 8. Social Media Trends 2016.

Newtek. 2015. "The Monetization of Instagram." *Forbes,* June 19. http://www.forbes.com/sites/thesba/2015/06/19/the-monetization-of-instagram/.

Newton, Casey. 2015. "How Meerkat Conquered All at SXSW." *The Verge.* March 17. http://www.theverge.com/2015/3/17/8234769/how-meerkat-conquered-all-at-sxsw.

Olivarez-Giles, Nathan. 2016. "Tumblr Brings Ads to Its Blogs, but You Can Opt Out." *The Wall Street Journal.* July 28. http://www.wsj.com/articles/tumblr-brings-ads-to-its-blogs-but-you-can-opt-out-1469732367.

O'Malley, Gavin. 2006. "YouTube Is the Fastest Growing Website." *Advertising Age.* July 21. http://adage.com/article/digital/youtube-fastest-growing-website/110632/.

Ostrow, Adam. 2009. "GeoCities to Shutdown; What Was GeoCities, You Ask?" *Mashable.* April 23. http://mashable.com/2009/04/23/geocities-shutdown/#bMHZd1X60EqJ.

Perez, Sarah. 2016. "Twitter Is Shutting Down Vine." *TechCrunch.* October 27. https://techcrunch.com/2016/10/27/twitter-is-shutting-down-vine/.

Phillips-Sandy, Mary. 2013. "A Conversation with Andrew Smales, Founder of Diaryland." *Medium.* June 25. https://medium.com/@maryps/a-conversation-with-andrew-smales-founder-of-diaryland-15e3d1ffc7dc.

Pierce, David. 2015. "Google+ as We Knew It Is Dead, But Google Is Still a Social Network." *Wired.* March 2. http://www.wired.com/2015/03/google-knew-dead-google-still-social-network/.

Popken, Ben. 2009. "Mafia Wars CEO Brags about Scamming Users from Day One." *Consumerist.* November 9. https://consumerist.com/2009/11/09/mafia-wars-ceo-brags-about-scamming-users-from-day-one/.

Popper, Ben, and Ellis Hamburger. 2014. "Meet Swarm: Foursquare's Ambitious Plan to Split Its App in Two." *The Verge.* May 1. http://www.theverge.com/2014/5/1/5666062/foursquare-swarm-new-app.

Qualman, Erik. 2015. *Social Media Revolution 2015 #Socialnomics.* YouTube, January 26. https://www.youtube.com/watch?v=jottDMuLesU.

Quantcast. n.d. "Flickr.com." *Quantcast.* Accessed August 18, 2016. https://www.quantcast.com/flickr.com.

Raphael, J.R. 2009. "Facebook Overtakes MySpace in U.S." *PCWorld.* June 16. http://www.pcworld.com/article/166794/Facebook_Overtakes_MySpace_in_US.html.

Revis, Layla. 2016. "Social Media Trends 2016." *Huffington Post.* January 5. http://www.huffingtonpost.com/layla-revis/social-media-trends-2016_b_8914190.html.

Reynolds, Cormac. 2015. "Why Social Media Is Necessary for the Sharing Economy." *Social Media Week.* May 18. http://socialmediaweek.org/blog/2015/05/social-media-necessary-sharing-economy/.

Richter, Felix. 2016. "The Most Popular Apps in the World." *Statista.* June 17. https://www.statista.com/chart/5055/top-10-apps-in-the-world/.

Romano, Aja. 2012. "The Demise of a Social Media Platform: Tracking LiveJournal's Decline." *The Daily Dot.* September 6. http://www.dailydot.com/culture/livejournal-decline-timeline/.

Rushe, Dominic. 2011. "Myspace Sold for $35m in Spectacular Fall from $12bn Heyday." *The Guardian.* June 30. https://www.theguardian.com/technology/2011/jun/30/myspace-sold-35-million-news.

Schultz, Don E. 2007. "Social Call: Can Our Brands Thrive or Even Survive in the Social Networked World?" *Marketing Management* 10–11.

Silverman, Jacob. 2015. "'Pics or It Didn't Happen'—The Mantra of the Instagram Era." *The Guardian.* February 26. https://www.theguardian.com/news/2015/feb/26/pics-or-it-didnt-happen-mantra-instagram-era-facebook-twitter.

Smith, Aaron. 2014. "Six New Facts about Facebook." *Pew Research Center.* February 3. http://www.pewresearch.org/fact-tank/2014/02/03/6-new-facts-about-facebook/.

Smith, Aaron. 2015. "U.S. Smartphone Use in 2015." *Pew Internet & American Life Project.* April 1. http://www.pewinternet.org/2015/04/01/us-smartphone-use-in-2015/.

Smith, Cooper. 2014. "Foursquare's New Big Data Initiative Is Going to Help It Thrive, Even as the Check-In Withers." *Business Insider.* January 14. http://www.businessinsider.com/foursquare-surpasses-45-million-registered-users-and-begins-collecting-data-in-new-ways-2-2014-1.

Smith, Cooper. 2015. "It's Time for Retailers to Start Paying Close Attention to Social Media." *Business Insider.* June 30. http://www.businessinsider.com/social-commerce-2015-report-2015-6.

Smith, Kit. 2016a. "44 Twitter Statistics for 2016." *Brand Watch.* May 17. https://www.brandwatch.com/2016/05/44-twitter-stats-2016/.

Smith, Kit. 2016b. "36 Fascinating YouTube Statistics for 2016." *Brand Watch.* June 8. https://www.brandwatch.com/2016/06/36-youtube-stats-2016/.

Social Blade. 2016. "Top 100 YouTubers by Subscribed." *Social Blade.* September 24. http://socialblade.com/youtube/top/100/mostsubscribed.

Solon, Olivia. 2014. "Bebo Is Back as a Bonkers Messaging App—Here's Everything You Need to Know." *Mirror.* December 18. http://www.mirror.co.uk/news/technology-science/technology/bebo-back-bonkers-messaging-app-4832300.

Sorkin, Andrew Ross, and Jeremy W. Peters. 2006. "Google to Acquire YouTube for $1.65 Billion." *New York Times.* October 9. http://www.nytimes.com/2006/10/09/business/09cnd-deal.html.

Spears, Lee, and Sarah Frier. 2012. "Facebook Stalls in Public Debut after Record $16B in IPO." *Bloomberg.* May 18. http://www.bloomberg.com/news/articles/2012-05-17/facebook-raises-16-billion-in-biggest-technology-ipo-on-record.

Statista. 2016a. "Cumulative Number of Apps Downloaded from the Apple App Store from July 2008 to September 2016 (in Billions)." *Statista.* September. https://www.statista.com/statistics/263794/number-of-downloads-from-the-apple-app-store/.

Statista. 2016b. "Number of Apps Available in Leading App Stores as of June 2016." *Statista.* June. https://www.statista.com/statistics/276623/number-of-apps-available-in-leading-app-stores/.

Stenberg, Daniel. 2011. "History of IRC (Internet Relay Chat)." March 29. http://daniel.haxx.se/irchistory.html.

SuperBowlXX. 2011. "Fun with Mathematics: The Finite and Infinite Universe of YouTube." *Daily Kos.* May 19. http://www.dailykos.com/story/2011/05/19/976539/-Fun-with-Mathematics-The-Finite-and-Infinite-Universe-of-YouTube#.

Swant, Marty. 2015. "How Instagram Is Changing the Way Brands Look at Photography, Online and Beyond: Embracing the 'Perfectly Imperfect.'" *Adweek*, August 24. http://www.adweek.com/news/advertising-branding/how-instagram-changing-way-brands-look-photography-online-and-beyond-166385.

Tam, Donna. 2012. "Under New Deal, Zynga Less Tied to Facebook." *CNET.* November 29. http://www.cnet.com/news/under-new-deal-zynga-less-tied-to-facebook/.

Target. 2014. "Pinterest-Worthy Party Planning Tips from Top Pinners." *A Bullseye View*. July 25. https://corporate.target.com/article/2014/07/pinterest-party-planning-tips-joy-cho-jan-halvarso.

Tate, Ryan. 2013. "Twitter Can't Control Rapid Growth of Its Vine." *Wired.* June 20. http://www.wired.com/2013/06/twitter-vine-growth/.

tech2 News Staff. 2015. "Here's Why Google Hangouts Isn't as Popular as WhatsApp, WeChat or Others." *tech2.* January 24. http://tech.firstpost.com/news-analysis/heres-why-google-hangouts-isnt-as-popular-as-whatsapp-wechat-or-others-251452.html.

Thier, Dave. 2012. "Why Zynga Is Doomed." *Forbes.* January 9. http://www.forbes.com/sites/davidthier/2012/01/09/why-zynga-is-doomed/#470184a814a9.

Twitter. 2013. "When a #Sharknado attacks! How the Phenomenon Happened on Twitter." *Twitter.* July 12. https://blog.twitter.com/2013/when-a-sharknado-attacks-how-the-phenomenon-happened-on-twitter.

Veerasamy, Visakan. n.d. "Social Networking Sites and Social Media: What's the Difference?" *ReferralCandy.* http://www.referralcandy.com/blog/difference-between-social-networks-and-social-media/.

W3Techs. n.d. "Usage of Content Management Systems for Websites." *W3Techs.* http://w3techs.com/technologies/overview/content_management/all.

Wagner, Kurt. 2015. "Periscope Has Ten Million Users (Kinda)." *Recode.* August 12. http://recode.net/2015/08/12/periscope-has-10-million-users-kinda/.

Wagstaff, Keith. 2012. "AOL's Longest-Running Employee on the History of AOL Chat Rooms." *Time.* July 6. http://techland.time.com/2012/07/06/aols-longest-running-employee-on-the-history-of-aol-chat-rooms/.

Walters, Eric. 2016. "What Verizon's Acquisition of Yahoo Means for Tumblr and Flickr." *Paste Magazine.* July 27. https://www.pastemagazine.com/articles/2016/07/what-verizons-acquisition-of-yahoo-means-for-tumbl.html.

Wikipedia. n.d. "Wikipedia: Statistics." *Wikipedia.* Accessed August 9, 2016. https://en.wikipedia.org/wiki/Wikipedia:Statistics.

Williams, Casey. 2016. "How to Use Five Instagram Filters to Get More Likes." *Huffington Post.* February 16. http://www.huffingtonpost.com/entry/how-to-get-instagram-likes_us_56c2055be4b0c3c5505205e5.

YouTube. 2016. "YouTube Statistics." *YouTube.* Accessed September 24, 2016. https://www.youtube.com/yt/press/statistics.html.

Zuckerberg, Mark. 2014. *Facebook.* February 4. https://www.facebook.com/zuck/posts/10101250930776491.

Introduction

New technologies are often both widely hailed for their positive contributions and fiercely criticized for their negative impact on society and individuals. Although social media platforms have more than 2 billion willing users, the impact on users has been the subject of much concern, derision, debate, and confusion. Some users will recognize the potential for social media to help them initiate and maintain relationships, achieve personal growth and development, and provide an outlet for creativity. Others will view social media as a potential threat to their relationships, jobs, ability to communicate, and possibly even safety. Furthermore, the news media often exaggerate the harmful effects in an effort to both educate consumers and attract readership and viewership, which stimulates more concern among users. This chapter will discuss some of the most prominent issues related to social media, highlight social media controversies, and propose valid solutions.

Social Media Addiction

Some users are so consumed by social media that they ignore or neglect offline responsibilities and relationships in an effort to connect with others online, share content about personal lives,

Teenagers have a daily connection with social media, primarily through their smartphones. This constant use of technology had led to new dangers such as cyberbullying, sexting, and media addiction. (iStockPhoto.com)

or read or watch engaging content. The time spent on social media may then detract from attending to job responsibilities, completing schoolwork, engaging with family members or friends face-to-face, or contributing to society in other meaningful ways. Most press coverage of the distractions from "real life" caused by social media is targeted at teens, parents, and employees, but any user is susceptible to social media addiction. A commentary on the plight of social media addicts is depicted in a 2013 video, which has received approximately 50 million views. "I Forgot My Phone" illustrates a day in the life of a young woman without her cell phone for the day, who experiences isolation from the many people she encounters who are interacting with their phones (charstarleneTV 2013).

Statistics show that social media consume a significant amount of daily attention. On a worldwide basis, Facebook estimates that the average user spends 50 minutes per day on Facebook and its products (Instagram, Messenger, and WhatsApp), while comScore estimates the number to be only 35 minutes for U.S. users (Stewart 2016). Other studies have found more disturbing trends. For example, GlobalWebIndex (2016) found that worldwide social media users spend almost two hours per day on social media. A study by Common Sense of teens found that teen girls who are social media users spend just under two and a half hours per day on social media, while teen boys who use social media spend slightly more than one and a half hours (Rideout 2015). The collective time spent on Facebook by all users each day amounts to 39,757 years (GO-Globe 2014).

What is it about social media sites that make them so addictive for users? Some users may be driven to social media sites like Facebook because they suffer from FoMO, or fear of missing out. In August 2013, the *Oxford English Dictionary* proposed the following definition of FoMO: "Anxiety that an exciting or interesting event may currently be happening elsewhere, often aroused by posts seen on a social media website" (Hogan 2015). Another study defined FoMO as "a pervasive apprehension that others might be having rewarding experiences from which one is absent . . . the desire to stay continually connected to what others are doing" (Przybylski et al. 2013). Przybylski et al. found that younger people were more likely to exhibit high levels of FoMO, with young men being more susceptible than women. Additionally, those with stronger FoMO had lower scores on basic psychological needs, such as autonomy and competence, and lower levels of life satisfaction and positive moods. Those with high FoMO scores also tended to use social media just before going to sleep and just after waking up as well as during meals and lectures.

In addition to FoMO, other reasons for the addictiveness of Facebook have been identified. The technology itself makes the site particularly addictive because only a minimal effort is needed to post, comment, or like to help maintain a relationship to others. The platform also allows users to share content and updates with a vast network simultaneously. Users also have access to a wealth of information including news stories, videos, and photos that are curated by a network of similar people as well as an opportunity to be a voyeur in the lives of others, commonly referred to as Facebook stalking. Others may be addicted to how Facebook strokes their egos. They have an opportunity to share an accomplishment, a photo from an exciting vacation, or even a selfie, and then wait for the positive feedback to follow. Facebook and other social media sites also help users fulfill their universal need for human connection and to remind people that they are not alone. The site can also offer entertainment in times of boredom. Facebook has traditionally featured a strong gaming element from games such as Candy Crush Saga and Clash of Clans, which draw tens of millions of daily users to the site to play the games (Conrad 2011). Furthermore, social media sites like Facebook also offer the promise of more exciting content as the user scrolls down the News Feed. If certain content is not interesting, users are enticed by the possibility of more interesting content if they continue scrolling, an activity that requires very little effort.

Neuroscience can be used to explain some of the addiction created by social media sites. Connecting with others online activates the neurotransmitter dopamine, which controls the reward and pleasure centers of the brain (Rock 2012). As Dr. David Rock, the director of the NeuroLeadership Institute, noted, "Social media can be so rewarding, that it overwhelms our ability to focus on other things. . . . The circuitry activated when you connect online is the seeking circuitry of dopamine. Yet when we connect with people online, we don't tend to get the oxytocin or serotonin calming reward that happens when we bond with someone in real time, when our circuits resonate with real-time shared emotions and experiences. . . . An overabundance of dopamine—while it feels great, just as sugar does—creates a mental hyperactivity that reduces the capacity for deeper focus" (Rock 2012).

Could social media be harder to quit than cigarettes or alcohol, as suggested by a study conducted by researchers in the Booth School of Business at the University of Chicago (Relph 2012)? While social media addiction is currently not classified as a psychological condition, researchers have been investigating this possibility. The American Psychiatric Association is considering adding "Internet-use disorder" to the list of official conditions in the *Diagnostic and Statistical Manual of Mental Disorders* (Jurgenson 2013). In 2012, University of Bergen researchers developed a scale to measure Facebook addiction (Andreassen et al. 2012). The researchers found Facebook dependency to occur more likely in younger users, women, people who are anxious or socially insecure, those who are less organized and ambitious, and extroverts. Answering "always" or "often" to at least four of the six following items may indicate Facebook addiction, according to the researchers: spending a lot of time thinking about Facebook or planning usage of Facebook, feeling urges to use Facebook more and more, using Facebook to forget about personal problems, trying to cut down on Facebook usage without success, experiencing feelings of restlessness if prohibited from using Facebook, and believing that Facebook usage has had a negative effect on work or school (Andreassen et al. 2012).

A 2013 Pew Internet & American Life study explored disengagement from Facebook and found that 61 percent of Facebook users had taken a break from the platform at least once for several weeks or longer (Rainie, Smith, and Dugan 2013). Of those who do not use Facebook, 20 percent of respondents had used the site at one time and only a small percentage (8 percent) of nonusers were interested in becoming a user in the future. The users who had taken an extended break mentioned they did so for a variety of reasons, including being too busy with other demands and not having time for Facebook (21 percent), lack of interest in the site (10 percent), lack of compelling content (10 percent), too much gossip or drama (9 percent), or concerns that they needed a break from the site because it was consuming too much time (8 percent).

Combating social media addiction often involves a digital detox, also called a disconnection or unplugging, where the user takes an extended or permanent break from a social media platform. High-profile people in the tech industry, such as Paul Miller of the website The Verge and *Fast Company* columnist Baratunde Thurston, have taken and then written about breaks from the Web (Jurgenson 2013). Thurston's detox revealed features of these social media sites that make them difficult to suspend usage (Thurston 2013). For example, unlike e-mail that offers an auto-reply vacation message, social media sites offer no such option. If a user wants to take a break and indicate that he or she is not checking social media, he or she has to be creative and possibly change the profile photo to a special message, as Thurston did by changing his profile photo to a message about his break.

An experiment by a team of Cornell University researchers encouraged people to take a break from Facebook and, during that time, change their profile photos to a graphic that read "99 Days of Freedom" and stay off the site for that length of time. Researchers followed up with participants after 33, 66, and

99 days. The key finding was that those participants who experienced addiction-associated feelings during the experiment, had focused on impression management while they used Facebook, experienced negative moods during the experiment, and replaced Facebook with other social media but used these sites to reflect upon and renegotiate their relationship with Facebook were more likely to eventually return to Facebook (Baumer et al. 2015).

Other programs have also emerged to help people disengage with social media. For example, public radio station WNYC's program *Note to Self* launched a project in 2015 called "Bored and Brilliant" to help participants break their addiction to checking their smartphones, including social media sites (WNYC 2015). The rationale for the importance of the project included the statistic that, 67 percent of the time, people check their smartphones without being prompted by any kind of notification. The project encouraged participants to download the app Moment (for iPhone) or BreakFree (for Android), both of which track phone usage. Challenges involved tasks such as keeping the phone in a bag (instead of a pocket) and deleting the apps considered the most distracting.

Digital detox camps such as Camp Grounded in Northern California give adults addicted to technology an opportunity to take a break from their screens. *Experience Life* magazine's Heidi Wachter attended the camp and wrote about the following suggestions that any digital addict can follow: create tech-free zones in the home, call or send handwritten notes to friends instead of texting, enjoy tech-free dinners with friends, and start or end the day with yoga, meditation, or another reflective activity (Wachter 2015).

Social media users interested in a digital detox should keep the following suggestions in mind (Hall 2014). First, users should recognize that feelings of withdrawal are temporary and detoxing from digital devices and social media is a process. Also, the time away should be replaced with a focus on offline relationships and living their lives more fully. Instead of feeling

FoMO, those taking a break from digital devices can embrace JoMO, which is the joy of missing out. Time spent looking at a screen can be replaced by real experiences that provide happiness as well as give detoxers an opportunity to reignite a passion for a particular hobby.

Studies have shown that unplugging is not easy for users. University of Maryland researchers found that when forced to unplug from technology for an entire day, nearly four in five students experienced significant mental and physical distress, panic, confusion, and extreme isolation (Relph 2012). Social media users who want to try detoxing for just one day can participate in the Annual Day of Unplugging, a project by the organization Reboot. The Annual Day of Unplugging, which runs from sundown to sundown starting on the first Friday in March each year, is supported with organized events around the world. Users who visit the website nationaldayofunplugging.com can sign the pledge, access resources, learn about events, and upload a photo of themselves holding a sign that shares what they plan to do when they unplug.

Extensive social media usage not only impacts daily life, but it can also cause physical ailments. The Ford 2014 Trend Report found that 94 percent of respondents from the United States and 75 percent worldwide agree that "Finding time to disconnect and be alone with myself is important to my health" (Ford 2013). In addition to the mental health benefit of disconnecting, users who control their social media addictions on smartphones can also prevent some of the physical ailments caused by smartphone use. For example, heavy smartphone users may experience headaches and neck aches. Florida chiropractor Dean Fishman coined the term "text neck" to describe the reversal in the curvature of the spine that happens after extended smartphone use (Dayton 2015). The weight of the head, when tilted forward, puts increased pressure on the cervical spine and supporting muscles. Suggestions to prevent and overcome the problem of text neck include holding the smartphone up to eye level, taking frequent breaks, and performing exercises that strengthen muscles behind the neck and between the shoulder blades (Dayton 2015). Focusing on a small screen to read text can also cause eyestrain, and users are encouraged to look into the distance occasionally to give their eyes a break (Chan 2011).

A study from Harvard Medical School also found that use of smartphones, laptops, and iPads at bedtime delays the release of sleep-inducing melatonin, which causes interference with sleep schedules (Gale 2014). A simple solution is to set a technology curfew and avoid using gadgets in bed. Those users who have a hard time not using devices in bed can use yellow-based lighting in the evening to block a screen's blue wavelength light, which has been shown to affect melatonin production (Harvard Medical School 2012). They can also use the software f.lux, which alters the intensity and spectrum of light produced by screens according to the time of day. In 2016, Apple released iOS 9.3, which included a feature called Night Shift that changes the colors on the screen to warmer tones, away from blue light, depending on the time of day.

The relationship between social media use and sleep disturbances has been explored in several studies. Researchers at the University of Pittsburgh School of Medicine surveyed 1,788 adults to collect information about social media usage and sleep patterns and found that the average amount of time spent per day on social media was 61 minutes and the average number of visits to social media sites per week was 30 (Levenson et al. 2016). Approximately 30 percent of respondents also reported sleep issues. When respondents were divided into light and heavy users, those who checked social media more during the week were more likely than those who checked less to have sleep disturbances, and similarly, those who spent more time on social media per day were more likely than those who spent less to have sleep problems. In studies like this, it is important to note that although these two variables appear to move together, one does not necessarily cause the other. If a causal relationship exists, social media may cause sleep loss by displacing sleep, by creating so much arousal making it difficult to sleep, or by being used on devices that emit light that impacts circadian rhythms. In contrast, sleep loss may increase social media usage as users pick up their devices when they cannot sleep.

Influence of Curated Content

Social media platforms with news feeds like Facebook and Twitter would overwhelm users if they presented all posted content in real time. The average Facebook user might have 1,500 posts that could appear on the News Feed when he or she opens the site, and through an algorithm that ranks content and selects the content the user is most likely to engage with, Facebook selects approximately 300 posts for viewing (Boland 2014). Users with many Facebook connections could interact with 15,000 potential posts during each session, making content curation in the News Feed even more important. Facebook defends this practice as providing a more positive and engaging experience for Facebook users who will be more likely to see content that engages them (Boland 2014).

Content publishers and other organizations that use Facebook and other sites to promote their businesses, causes, products, or services are particularly concerned with how to make their posts appear organically in the feeds of their followers without having to promote them through paid ads. For example, if a local restaurant posts content on Facebook, the restaurant would like those posts to appear in the News Feeds of followers. Organic reach refers to the average percentage of content posted by a page owner that its followers would see in their News Feeds. Over time, organic reach of Facebook posts has been diminishing dramatically. In February 2012, the average page follower would see 16 percent of posts made by a page owner. By March 2014, that percentage per follower had decreased to 6.51 percent (EdgeRank Checker 2014).

Facebook attributed the decrease in organic reach to increased content sharing (Boland 2014). As more content was being posted and user engagement with the site remained unchanged, then it followed that users would be exposed to a smaller percentage of all content. Users are also liking more pages, by an average increase of 50 percent in 2013, which further intensifies the competition among all these pages for placement on the News Feed (Constine 2014).

Facebook News Feed director of product management Will Cathcart described to *TechCrunch* reporter Josh Constine how the visibility of posts is determined by a score calculated by 100,000 factors (Constine 2014). The most important factors, according to Cathcart, included previous interest of the user in interacting with the content creator, the post's performance among other users, the performance of past content posted by the content creator, the type of post (status, photo, video, or link), and the recency of the post. Despite this technical description, the algorithm has been called "surprisingly inelegant, maddeningly mercurial, and stubbornly opaque" (Oremus 2016).

A study of Facebook conducted by EdgeRank Checker found that news outlets and others that create content that can be consumed on social media have more reach than companies who are posting marketing messages about their products. As Constine noted, "You can Like both *The New York Times* and Oreos, but you can actually read the *NYT* on News Feed whereas you can't eat a cookie there. So it makes sense that the *NYT* would reach a higher percentage of its fans—its posts are more interesting" (Constine 2014).

Others have challenged Facebook's explanations, criticizing the company for forcing marketers into paid advertising for their posts to appear in the feed. Facebook, however, has disputed that claim (Boland 2014). The challenge for marketers is to earn a spot on the News Feed by publishing posts that will get likes, comments, shares, and click-throughs. If users do not interact with posts, the reach for future posts will be impacted, setting off a spiral into potential oblivion.

In 2016, Facebook once again tweaked its algorithm based on the results of survey research. The company employs a feed quality panel of more than 1,000 users who rate their Facebook experiences and describe what improvements to content they would like to see. Additionally, the company surveys tens of thousands of people each day to understand how appealing they find stories in their feeds. According to the company, through this research, "we are able to better understand which stories people would be interested in seeing near the top of their News Feed even if they choose not to click, like or comment on them—and use this information to make ranking changes" (Zhang and Chen 2016). Research demonstrated that users had better experiences when they like the top stories in their feed. Stories that move to the top are those Facebook thinks people might take action on, such as liking, commenting, or sharing, and what people may want to see at the top of their feed. The company contends that most page owners will see few changes in their Facebook referral traffic, but that others may receive increases or declines (Zhang and Chen 2016).

The best way for page owners to get posts in front of consumers and other audiences is to pay for advertising. At one time, Facebook placed paid ads only in the sidebar. Now, promoted or sponsored posts appear in the News Feed alongside posts from friends, and any post created by a page owner can easily be converted into a paid advertisement. Other social media platforms have followed Facebook's lead and now offer the opportunity for promoted posts.

Although Facebook curates content in its News Feed, it has yet to segment content on another part of the site. In contrast, Twitter has made changes to its platform to curate content for users on a tab called Moments, which organizes tweets and other content by topic. However, like Facebook, Twitter's timeline is expected to undergo significant changes in the way content is presented. In 2015, visitors to the site started seeing "while you were away" tweets near the top of their timelines. In early 2016, a BuzzFeed report announced that Twitter was on the verge of introducing an algorithmic timeline, which sent users into panic mode (Kantrowitz 2016). Instead of a chronological feed, users would see content that Twitter believes they would be most interested in viewing. According to BuzzFeed News, "an algorithmic timeline represents a way for Twitter to elevate popular content, and could solve some of Twitter's signal-to-noise problems. It is also widely assumed to be anathema to the platform's typically vocal power users" (Kantrowitz 2016). Opponents of this change believe that the organic and unfiltered stream of news differentiates Twitter from other social media and news sites. With an algorithm, important tweets that have not achieved the appropriate metrics to be highlighted could instead be buried. The protest in Ferguson, Missouri, for example, built steam on Twitter through the unfiltered feed while news stories about the event did not crack the Facebook algorithm (Kantrowitz 2015).

Other social media platforms such as Snapchat and Instagram are also providing curated content for users. Presenting content organized around a theme helps users explore a topic in more depth and also increases the opportunities for the platform to offer brand sponsorships and advertising around an event. Snapchat, for example, started offering Live Stories in 2014 to follow live events such as concerts, sporting events, or political rallies. The advertising and sponsorship business model clicked, and the company increased live event coverage from one to two a week to several a day. The live events have proven their ability to attract millions of views, with the daily audience for Live Stories averaging 20 million people (Wagner 2015).

Although content curation offers organized content for users and opportunities for sponsored content or advertising for marketers, the content selected may have a profound impact on users. Users may find themselves in what has been called a "filter bubble" or an "echo chamber," where the content they see is consistent with their political, cultural, or ideological beliefs. Facebook, in particular, has been criticized for using its algorithm to highlight posts that are consistent with a user's viewpoint and suppressing posts from those who have dissenting viewpoints. Some of the awareness about the possibility of this practice has been generated by activist and author Eli Pariser, who gave a 2011 TED talk called "Beware Online 'Filter Bubbles,'" which has been viewed by several million people. His talk describes how Facebook removed his conservative friends from his feed because the algorithm must have picked up that he clicked more on the links posted by liberal friends. A research study that explored this issue, however, found that content in the News Feed is only marginally more consistent with users' own ideologies and that the nature of their friends and the content clicked on are more likely to predict the diversity of content in their feeds (Bakshy, Messing, and Adamic 2015).

In 2016, a former Facebook curator for the "Trending Topics" section revealed that Facebook was suppressing conservative stories (Nunez 2016). Even when trending organically, stories about Rand Paul, Mitt Romney, and other conservative issues were excluded from the list by workers. Conversely, when Facebook users were not reading stories deemed important by management from 10 specified news sites, other former curators described how they were instructed by management to place these stories in Trending Topics to gain some traction. After this exposé, Facebook fired the curating team and replaced them with engineers who would instead manage an algorithm to determine Trending Topics.

Online Hoaxes, Rumors, and Scams

Sharing content is a popular activity on social media sites, dramatically changing the ways users become aware of issues and form opinions. Sometimes the source of the content is a reputable news organization, blog, or other website, but the rush to post breaking news may result in the publication of false information. In some instances, however, the content intentionally includes unfounded rumors, pranks, hoaxes, scams, or fake news stories. Because sharing on social media is as easy as clicking a button, fabricated stories and rumors can spread rapidly.

Research has shown that Facebook users will select content to share provided that it is an accepted message and fits into what they already believe (Del Vicario et al. 2016). Because Facebook users tend to clump into homogeneous clusters, friends on social media are likely to process content through the same lens and share similar opinions, lessening the opportunity that any posted content would be challenged. Under these circumstances, it is possible for rumors and other unfounded content to proliferate.

A popular social media prank is to encourage people to post a message on their Facebook profiles under the false pretense that the post will result in a positive outcome or prevent a negative one. In 2015, Facebook users shared a post declaring copyright protection of all personal information on Facebook, including photos and videos (Dugle 2015). Facebook responded to this hoax by explaining that users already own the content they post to Facebook, making such a statement unnecessary. It is also unlikely that Facebook would ever cull through the profiles of its billions of users to see who had and had not made the copyright declaration.

Another prank in 2015 had people sharing messages on their Facebook profiles in hopes of receiving $4.5 million of the $4.5 billion worth of Facebook stock that Mark Zuckerberg was purportedly giving away "to people like YOU and ME!" as the post read (Emery 2015). The message explained that the prize money was a "way of saying thank you for making Facebook such a powerful vehicle for connection and philanthropy." In fact, Zuckerberg had announced that he was going to donate 99 percent of his fortune to the Chan Zuckerberg Initiative, a company created by Zuckerberg and his wife, but not to users. The Facebook post was merely a prank.

A common Facebook scam uses a post with a coupon for $100 off for stores like Target or Walmart. One purpose of the scam is to motivate people to like, share, or comment on the post so that it will spread further (Online Threat Alerts 2015). The click-throughs from the post also help to make a certain Web page popular so that the site can then be sold to the highest bidder, along with the names and other information of people who interacted with the post. Furthermore, those who click through might be asked to complete a survey, and the scammers get paid from third-party sites for these completed surveys.

Another scam involves creating a cloned account for a Facebook user. If a user friends an unknown person, it is possible for that Facebook "friend" to collect information about the user's friends, clone the account to pose as the user, and then send friend requests to those friends (Kristof 2013). Once the scammer has built up a strong following among the user's friends, the scammer sends a message, such as "OMG. I'm overseas and was just robbed! I don't even have enough to get home!" The scammer then requests financial contributions from the user's friends. In such situations, friends are likely to be suspicious and may even reach out with a text to check on the user, which is when the scam will be discovered. Another strategy of scammers is to send what looks like a link to interesting content to the user's friends but instead the link downloads malware onto their computers if they click on it.

These scam situations can be avoided if users apply diligence and common sense in their use of Facebook and other social media sites. Users are advised to not accept friend requests from people they do not know and to also review the profiles of people they think they know who make requests. The profile should be consistent with what the user knows about the friend. If not, it could be a cloned profile. If a user discovers a cloned profile, it can be reported to Facebook for removal. When money is requested by a friend for an emergency situation, those who are considering making a contribution should use other methods to ensure the request is legitimate. A friend in a desperate situation is likely to seek help from one person who can help, such as a parent or close friend, rather than sending a blast to all Facebook friends. Finally, although it is tempting to open links for "a funny video of you," such wording often indicates the link will download malware.

Online hoaxes have also occurred on YouTube, often in the form of entertainers portraying themselves in a false light. The seemingly homemade videos of singer Marié Digby posted on YouTube in early 2007 attracted quite a following, and she started to generate radio airplay and have her music featured on the MTV program *The Hills*. A press release in August 2007 described how "Breakthrough YouTube Phenomenon Marié Digby Signs with Hollywood Records." Although positioned by her record label as a breakout star who had been recently discovered and signed, Digby had actually been signed by Hollywood Records in late 2005, prior to posting YouTube videos. Before a *Wall Street Journal* reporter started investigating Digby's background in 2007, the artist even had "none" checked under record label on her MySpace page. In the end, both the artist and her label admitted to and defended their efforts, describing their strategy as building a following before the launch of her album (Smith and Lattman 2007).

Also in the early days of YouTube, a video series posted by lonelygirl15 involved a hoax that attracted a huge following. The videos appeared to showcase the real-life struggles of an average American teenager named Bree. After much speculation, Bree's identity was revealed to be New Zealand actress Jessica Rose, who was working in collaboration with filmmakers Ramesh Flinders and Miles Beckett (Heffernan and Zeller 2006). Additionally, Creative Artists Agency was behind the creation of the videos.

The World Economic Forum has listed digital misinformation as a main threat to society (Del Vicario et al. 2016). Google and Facebook have both taken steps to highlight false or untrustworthy content. Google's current algorithm bases search results on inbound links, so if a site has a lot of other sites linking to it, it is judged to be of higher quality and, therefore, deserves a higher rank in the search results. The problem with this method is that if many people link to a site of misinformation, it will continue to attract attention because it will appear higher in search results. Google's more recent program to rank Web pages on the accuracy of information is called "Knowledge-Based Trust" (Hodson 2015). Google has collected information and other known facts in a database called Knowledge Graph, which was first introduced in 2012. Using Knowledge-Based Trust, pages are ranked by comparing facts on the website with those stored in the Knowledge Graph. In early tests, the system was able to reliably predict the trustworthiness of the sources. The downside to this technology is that the trust scores of Web pages with facts not in the Knowledge Graph are more difficult to determine.

In 2015, Facebook tweaked its algorithm to limit the impact of stories that might be false (Oremus 2015). Although the stories were not removed, they were instead downplayed in the News Feed. Facebook added the option for users to flag a story as false when it appeared in their feeds. Facebook's algorithm also examined how many users who shared the story later deleted it, based on the assumption that they may have had regrets about posting a fake story. Furthermore, a flagged post was also marked with a warning that it could contain incorrect information.

Despite these efforts, the presidential campaign of 2016 was likely impacted by the onslaught of fake news websites that used Facebook and Twitter to spread fake stories. According to the Pew Research Center, almost half of the U.S. population and about two-thirds of Facebook users are getting news from the site (Gottfried and Shearer 2016). The fake news and political websites that flourished during this election were mostly only interested in traffic from social media sites for the purpose of driving up revenues through advertisements hosted on the websites. The more outrageous the news story, particularly if it reflected negatively on Democratic nominee Hillary Clinton, the more likely it was to receive clicks. Some of these sites have been traced to teens in Macedonia seeking to profit from the U.S. election. BuzzFeed identified more than 100 of these websites from this Greek region with names like WorldPoliticus.com, TrumpVision365.com, USConservativeToday.com, DonaldTrumpNews.co, and USADailyPolitics.com (Silverman and Alexander 2016).

One of the most popular stories included that Facebook, Twitter, and Google were burying news of an FBI investigation of Clinton, which was tweeted by Donald Trump. Other popular fake stories included one posted on a fake ABC News site that reported a man was paid $3,500 by the Clinton campaign to protest at a Trump rally (which was retweeted by Eric Trump, Ann Coulter, and Trump's former campaign manager Corey Lewandowski) and a tweet from a fake CNN account reporting a significant lead for Trump in Florida on election day just after polls opened. Other fake sites included the "Denver Guardian," which ran a story about how an FBI investigator into the Clinton e-mail scandal was found dead, and a "Christian Times Newspaper" story that reported 10,000+ sealed ballots with Clinton's name selected were being stored in ballot boxes in an Ohio warehouse. (*Christian Times* newspaper is a legitimate source, but is not affiliated with the website that appropriated its name.) A story from the Macedonian site ConservativeState.com proclaimed that Hillary Clinton said in 2013, "I Would Like to See People Like Donald Trump Run for Office; They're Honest and Can't Be Bought," which racked up almost 500,000 likes, shares, and comments. Other false claims from Macedonian sites included that the Pope endorsed Trump and that Mike Pence said Michelle Obama is the "most vulgar first lady we've ever had," which combined with two other fake posts reviewed by BuzzFeed received more than 1 million likes, shares, and comments (Silverman and Alexander 2016). In the wake of the election after recognizing the impact fake news can have on public opinion and facing a public outcry, Facebook introduced some experiments to more aggressively address and combat the issue of fake news (Isaac 2016).

In addition to fake tweets during the 2016 election, Twitter users were previously fooled by other false reports of news. In 2015, a story about an impending Twitter buyout for $31 billion was created by an unidentified scammer, who posted it on a fake *Bloomberg News* site after which it was circulated by journalists and others on Twitter and through other means (Farrell 2015). The rumor increased the stock price by 8 percent within eight minutes. When the story was confirmed by a *Bloomberg News* source to be false, the stock price sunk to lower than it was prior to the rumor. Even though the error was quickly corrected, the scammer and others still had enough time to benefit from the rumor. Hackers have even gained access to high-profile Twitter accounts and distributed false information. One of the more infamous examples involved the hacked Twitter account of the Associated Press and the resulting tweet: "Breaking: Two Explosions in the White House and Barack Obama Is Injured." Although only up for a few minutes, the tweet was retweeted 3,000 times and incited a 143-point plunge in the stock market (Kelly 2013).

The Boston Marathon bombing and Ebola cases in the United States are two examples of crises that spurred rumors throughout social media. A study by University of Washington researchers of the Boston Marathon rumors found that tweets with incorrect information spread faster and wider than tweets with correct information (Starbird et al. 2014). One tweet incorrectly stated that an eight-year-old girl running in the marathon had died in the bombing, and the research team found this rumor was tweeted more than 90,000 times and the correction only 2,000. Another popular Boston Marathon rumor was that the perpetrators may have been part of U.S. military special operations, possibly Navy SEALs. The source of this rumor was a photo widely circulated on social news site Reddit and bulletin board 4chan of two men standing together in similar clothes and backpacks with one wearing a hat with an emblem. The researchers found Twitter conversation about this tweet generated about 4,500 tweets with a significant number of the tweets referencing misinformation instead of corrections. The final rumor studied involved the misidentification of a missing Brown University student as one of the bombers. In photos released by the FBI, it was noted that the student resembled "Suspect #2," and the rumor went viral when Twitter users, including high school classmates of the student, tweeted about the resemblance. The almost 30,000 tweets misidentifying the bomber still exhibited many more with misinformation than corrections until the Tsarnaev brothers were named as suspects, which ended the spread of misinformation shortly thereafter.

In the case of the fatal disease Ebola, residents of Newark, Miami, and Washington, D.C., continued to tweet rumors suggesting Ebola had been unleashed in those cities even after the isolated potential cases in those cities tested negative (Luckerson 2014). Iowa residents believed that Ebola had afflicted someone in the state, and the state's Department of Public Health had to step in to dispel the rumor. Other tweets inaccurately suggested that Ebola is spread through air, water, and food, therefore creating more of a panic.

Sometimes citizen journalism is to blame for false information that is widely distributed on Twitter. People on the scene of a particularly hectic situation, such as a bombing, riot, or natural disaster, interpret the events through their first-hand perspective, but will not necessarily report the events accurately on social media sites, such as Twitter. Twitter is particularly viral in these crisis situations because it offers a public site that pulls all forms of content from a variety of viewpoints from officials and news organizations to eyewitnesses on a platform easily searchable using a hashtag or a keyword.

Visual content sites like Pinterest and Instagram are also targets of hoaxes and scams. On these sites, a common hoax involves photoshopped images. Users may believe that, in nature, one can find purple trees, blue watermelons, or rainbow-colored owls. Some Pinterest users manage boards to debunk Pinterest hoaxes, such as the board available at: pinterest.com/

trainrgrl/hoaxes. Scammers on these platforms may also set up bogus accounts to follow users with the hope of gaining followers so that the promoted images will be seen or the links will be clicked, which may earn scammers click-through fees. Surveys are also used in exchange for a free gift, but the scammers instead receive a "gift" of the user's personal information.

Most social media hoaxes and scams are relatively harmless, ranging from those that encourage people to post content on their social media profiles to entertainers who do not portray themselves authentically. Sites like Snopes provide background that can help users determine whether something shared on social media is a hoax or scam; therefore, it is recommended that concerned social media users check that site for any information. Users are also cautioned against clicking on quizzes, images, and other content that might help scammers gather personal information to sell or download viruses on victims' computers.

Cyberbullying, Sexting, and Child Predators

Cyberbullying, sexting, and child predators on social media sites are common concerns of parents, teenagers, educators, and law enforcement. Other issues related to teen use of social media include solicitations to engage in sexual talk or behavior and exposure to sexual content online. These negative aspects of social media will often be featured in the news because they make frightening stories that capture the attention of a general audience. Not every teen, however, who uses social media will be exposed to these abuses, but it is still important for vulnerable groups to be educated on how to avoid and handle these situations.

Online victimization has been categorized into three types, which include solicitation to engage in sexual talk or behavior, unwanted exposure to sexual materials, and Internet harassment, commonly referred to as cyberbullying (Finkelhor, Mitchell, and Wolak 2001). The Youth Internet Safety Surveys conducted in 2000, 2005, and 2010 with a sample of 1,500 teenagers aged 10 to 17 demonstrate changes in sexual solicitation, unwanted exposure to content, and online harassment during an important time when Internet users moved away from the chat rooms and websites of the early 2000s to the social media platforms that emerged and grew in popularity by the end of the decade (Jones, Mitchell, and Finkelhor 2012).

Throughout the time period studied in the Youth Internet Safety Surveys, unwanted sexual solicitation decreased from 19 percent in 2000 to 9 percent in 2010. The researchers suggested that the decline may be a result of teens moving from chat rooms with strangers to social networks where they are interacting with peers. The teens may also be more educated about online predators and are therefore more cautious about their online interactions. Although 34 percent experienced unwanted exposure to pornography in 2005, the percentage decreased to 23 percent by 2010. Some of the decline may be attributed to spam filters that remove this content from inboxes and increased sophistication of users who understand the possible consequences of clicking on unfamiliar links or opening unknown content. In contrast, experiences with online harassment either as a victim or as a perpetrator increased from 6 percent in 2000 to 11 percent in 2010. The researchers attributed this increase to more online interactions with peers and the lagging efforts of educational campaigns about cyberbullying at a time when more focus was placed on issues such as online sexual solicitation. They also added that bullying may not be increasing, but that the bullying that occurs offline has migrated online over time (Jones, Mitchell, and Finkelhor 2012).

Risk factors of online victimization have been classified into those that are technology-based, interpersonal, and intrapersonal (Call and Burrow-Sanchez 2010). First, using technology obviously increases the risk for online victimization, and common mistakes in using technology include misspelling a word in a Google search, downloading content from a file-sharing site, and disclosing personal information online, which could be used by a predator to target a potential victim. Often, teens who engage in risky behaviors are not aware of online dangers. A major interpersonal factor is forming online friendships with strangers, especially when the user is willing to share personal information or engage in sexual talk. Aggressive behavior in online communication, such as posting rude comments, also increases the likelihood of victimization. Parent–child relations are also important, as children who have been given more guidance by parents as well as children with less conflict in the home are less likely to be online victims. Offline physical and sexual abuse is another predictor of online victimization. Finally, certain intrapersonal factors may make a teen more likely to be victimized, such as the demographics of gender and race. The relationships formed online are also impacted by intrapersonal factors, such as mental illness, homosexuality, or difficulty with offline relationships (Call and Burrow-Sanchez 2010).

Defined as bullying that occurs on a digital platform, cyberbullying is found throughout the spectrum of social media sites. Although some people may reject the concept of cyberbullying with the argument that bullying occurred long before the introduction of online media, cyberbullying is particularly problematic for its victims. Hurtful comments and rumors are easily launched within the online environment, and depending on the social network, the sender may remain anonymous or hide behind a fake profile. Additionally, social media provide a means to both capture and distribute embarrassing content which can spread to a wide network very quickly. The content can also be difficult to completely remove from social media and the Internet as copies are easily made and posted. Finally, social media are available to users 24/7. The messages are difficult for bullied teens to ignore, given that they are often placed on the social media sites frequented by the victim and even the victim's own profile. Even if the target of the bully avoids social media, the messages may still be viewable to others.

The Youth Risk Behavior Surveillance survey for 2013 conducted by the Centers for Disease Control and Prevention examined cyberbullying rates as well as demographic factors. The study found that approximately 15 percent of high school student respondents reported they had experienced electronic bullying (Centers for Disease Control and Prevention 2014). More girls (21 percent) than boys (8.5 percent) reported being the victims of online bullies. The practice also decreased with grade, with ninth-graders (16.1 percent) experiencing more online bullying than twelfth-graders (13.5 percent).

Cyberbullying can lead to criminal charges. For example, in November 2013, police arrested a 15-year-old Florida girl who they said sent hundreds of threats over an eight-day period using the messaging app Kik such as, "You're a pathetic piece of s—," "Nobody likes you, "and "I hate you so much." Another message informed the recipient that she should commit suicide to avoid being murdered. The bully was charged with three counts of aggravated stalking and one count of tampering with a witness (Phippen 2013).

The most tragic cyberbullying cases are those that end with the victim committing suicide. One of the prominent early cases of social media cyberbullying occurred on MySpace when 13-year-old Megan Meier formed an online friendship with 16-year-old Josh Evans. In the beginning, Josh helped to build Megan's self-esteem, but then he quickly turned on Megan with messages that became increasingly more cruel, including statements such as "The world would be a better place without you." Other classmates also piled on to post hurtful messages. One day in October 2006, Megan walked away from her computer, went to her bedroom, hanged herself in her closet, and died the following day. Later, it was discovered that "Josh" was actually a fake profile created by neighbor Lori Drew, Drew's employee, and Drew's daughter, a former friend of Megan's. Although Drew had been indicted on one count of conspiracy and three counts of Computer Fraud and Abuse Act violations, she was later acquitted (Zetter 2009).

Recommendations for parents to deal with cyberbullying include talking to teens about what to do if they are the victim of a bully as well as how to avoid being one themselves, equipping them with tools to deal with bullying, encouraging them to sign a no-bullying pledge, asking them to stand up for victims, and explaining how to take action if the teen is a victim. In these conversations, teens need to realize that the consequences of what they say online can be very serious. Although rude or derogatory comments might be protected by the First Amendment, threatening statements may not be. Advice for teens is to avoid using social media as a tool to hurt others and to let parents know about any hurtful messages posted online about them. Several anti-bullying sites, such as StopBullying.gov and the Cyberbullying Research Center, provide guides to state laws, explain ways to report cyberbullying, and offer additional resources.

Another issue related to technology and social media is sexting, which is sending sexually explicit messages and photos, usually through texts. Sexting is related to cyberbullying in that the sexual content can be used to target or bully a student (called sextortion), especially if the content gets out of the hands of the original recipient and is shared with others on social media sites or elsewhere. When a naked photo of a teenager under the age of 18 is distributed, many states classify such content as child pornography, and those who create and/or distribute the content can then be charged as perpetrators of child pornography. A recent trend has been to reduce the penalties for minors who snap sexting selfies to misdemeanors or warnings. Florida, for example, is one state that before 2011 would have charged teens with a felony and required registration as a sex offender for such offenses, but new legislation eased the penalties for the first offense to community service and a small fine (CNN Wire Staff 2011).

Teens and other social media users may also be lured into a relationship with someone they meet online, which can lead to serious consequences. A 2014 study sponsored by Cox

Communications found that 18 percent of respondents have considered meeting someone in person that they first met online, while 58 percent of those teens have actually done so (The Futures Company 2014). Many of these relationships may be harmless, such as someone who is connected to a known person, such as the cousin of a friend. However, teens can easily be lured into meeting someone in real life who is posing as a fellow teen in order to cause harm. For example, a teen girl might think she has been building a relationship with a teen boy online, but that teen boy is actually a man.

YouTuber Coby Persin conducted an online experiment with three teenage girls (with parental permission) by first creating a fake Facebook profile, friending the girls, and then seeing what kind of judgment they would display when invited to meet him in person (Mahoney 2015). The scenarios included meeting Persin in a park, allowing him over to a girl's house, and getting into a car with him, all of which were done by the girls. The video featuring the three scenarios garnered more than 43 million views and was followed by one that used a girl's profile to lure boys, which was equally successful in its experiment and received more than 17 million views. Most of the parents who were interviewed beforehand believed that their child would not be willing to meet a complete stranger and were shocked at the outcome.

Monitoring behavior of teens on social media sites is a concern of many parents. In order to protect their children, parents should investigate a variety of approaches such as using software to monitor accounts or having user names and passwords to their children's social media accounts. A 2016 study by the Pew Research Center found that 60 percent of respondents with children aged 13–17 have reviewed their children's social media accounts for questionable or unsavory content (Sass 2016). Of the respondents, 56 percent have friended their children on various social media platforms and 35 percent know the passwords to their children's social media accounts. Only 16 percent use tracking tools. A Cox Communications study found similar results in that 51 percent of parents monitor their children's social media usage in some way (The Futures Company 2014).

Another preventative measure is to encourage parents to talk to their children about Internet safety, with an emphasis on not disclosing personal information and engaging in conversation with strangers. The Cox Communications study found that 9 of 10 teens have talked to their parents about Internet safety, with 86 percent of those teens having had the talk in the past year (The Futures Company 2014). The problem with this intervention, however, is that it avoids addressing some of the key risk factors that lead to victimization (Call and Burrow-Sanchez 2010). The following four components to an Internet safety education program are suggested: (1) informing teens about dangers and ways to engage in positive communication, (2) using peers as positive change agents, (3) including family members in the promotion of Internet safety, and (4) addressing the needs of the most vulnerable teens (Call and Burrow-Sanchez 2010).

Despite all the risks, many teens are savvy about social media, with some of these digital natives being more sophisticated than their parents. As a result, almost half of respondents admitted to hiding their online behavior from their parents, taking such actions as clearing their search history and cookies (46 percent), using a private browsing option (20 percent), or disabling the software their parents had installed on their phones, tablets, or computers (8 percent) (The Futures Company 2014). Parents who have access to their children's social media accounts, either through a password or a friend relationship, should not remain too complacent about their ability to monitor online activity. Some other teen tactics include moving to social media sites that are unfamiliar to or not used by their parents. For example, although a parent might have access to their child's Facebook account, the child may be having conversations and sharing content on sites like Snapchat or Instagram or even create a second, more private profile on a particular platform.

Negative Moods, Feelings of Loneliness, and Envy

If social media platforms always made users feel sad, they would not be nearly as popular as they are. Social media are similar to other forms of media such as television and newspapers in their ability to evoke both positive and negative reactions. Since the introduction of the uses and gratifications approach to studying media by Katz, Blumler, and Gurevitch (1973–1974) in the early 1970s, many other studies have explored how people use media and the benefits they receive from their usage. Bartsch and Viehoff (2010) summarized the results of some of the studies on emotional gratifications from media usage, which include intense sensations, management of mood, an escape from real-life relationships, the building of parasocial relationships with characters, the opportunity to have vicarious experiences, and downward social comparisons. Even though social media can be compared to traditional forms of media, social media are distinctive in that they allow for real-time two-way communication with people in a user's online social network, many of whom are typically also offline connections.

Some studies have suggested that social media usage impacts mood, feelings of loneliness, and envy when users compare their lives to that of others. Other studies describe positive emotions that result from building and maintaining relationships on social media platforms. Presented with a unique set of challenges, social media users are learning how to negotiate these platforms to avoid negative emotions and enhance positive ones. The direction of the emotional response may, in fact, be situational. For example, passive browsing on Facebook could result in feelings of envy for the lifestyles showcased in the photos of friends, while active engagement in conversations with friends could prove satisfying. Furthermore, the personality, mood, or offline experiences of the user may predict how social media usage will impact his or her emotional response.

A growing body of research has provided insight into the effects of Facebook on mood. A controversial 2012 experiment by Facebook, conducted unknowingly on almost 700,000 users, found that the nature of Facebook posts impact mood, a phenomenon called emotional contagion (Kramer, Guillory, and Hancock 2014). One group in the study was exposed to posts lacking words that are considered to evoke positive emotions, while another group saw posts lacking words thought to evoke negative emotions. In turn, the group shown posts with fewer positive words subsequently wrote posts with fewer positive words, while those shown posts minimizing negative words wrote posts with fewer negative words.

Other research has demonstrated that extensive use of Facebook, despite the nature of the posts seen, results in a belief that the participant's time was not used in meaningful way, contributing to a worse mood (Sagioglou and Greitemeyer 2014). In this study, researchers allowed participants to browse either Facebook or the Web for 20 minutes. Those in the Facebook group reported being in a worse mood, which was attributed to how they felt about the meaningfulness of the time spent online. The researchers concluded that users will continue to return to Facebook because of an "affective forecasting error," which is the mistaken assumption that they would actually feel more positive after spending time on Facebook.

Social media users can experience a feeling of validation when their friends acknowledge posts through comments and likes. A study of online interpersonal neglect by Greitemeyer, Mügge, and Bollermann (2014) found that having a large network of friends does not compensate for the psychological dissatisfaction felt when social media users receive few responses to their posts. The researchers explored this relationship by having participants view their birthday wishes from their last birthday and then respond to questions about mood. The study found that posts on a user's profile can impact his or her needs for belonging, self-esteem, control, and meaningful existence. The lack of birthday greetings on Facebook may even be more devastating to a user because it is displayed publicly and showcases the user's value to his or her network.

Despite serving as a robust social network, Facebook may also contribute to feelings of loneliness. Eric Klinenberg, author of *Going Solo: The Extraordinary Rise and Surprising Appeal of Living Alone*, wrote, "Reams of published research show that it's the quality, not the quantity of social interaction that best predicts loneliness" (Klinenberg 2013). Scholars and other critics are now questioning whether Facebook and other social media sites distance people from "real" offline relationships or allow for opportunities to bring people together in new ways. Most users can probably think of circumstances where Facebook and other social media sites have both hindered and helped personal relationships. Someone might spend so much time on Facebook that it becomes an entertainment substitute for other opportunities, such as going to dinner or a party with friends. At the same time, Facebook might help connect a user with an old friend when one is traveling to the other's hometown or help maintain bonds between friends who now live in distant cities so that the relationship does not decay over time. In the 1990s, the term *Internet paradox* was coined to describe how technology causes users to both connect and disengage with society (Kraut et al. 1998). In a world where people are more connected than ever, is it possible to experience such loneliness and detachment?

An Australian study found that Facebook users had lower levels of social loneliness, which describes a feeling of lacking friendship bonds, and higher level of family loneliness, where they did not feel connected to family (Ryan and Xenos 2011). Therefore, Facebook may connect people to friends outside the home to the detriment of the relationships they have with their family within the household. The researchers also looked at personality traits and found Facebook users to be more extroverted and narcissistic than nonusers, while nonusers were more conscientious and socially lonely. They also concluded that Facebook use depends on certain personality factors.

A study of adolescents found that feelings of loneliness are related to motives for using Facebook (Teppers et al. 2014). The researchers concluded that "In general, our findings showed that peer-related loneliness is an important personality characteristic that predicts adolescents' Facebook motives and, in turn, is positively predicted by the social skills compensation motive and negatively by the meeting people motive" (Teppers et al. 2014, 695). If teens are using Facebook to make connections and communicate with friends, usage of the site is predicted to lessen their feelings of loneliness over time. Users will receive an emotional gratification from this expanded network and feel less lonely. However, the researchers found feelings of loneliness may escalate if the teen has poor social skills and uses Facebook to compensate for other forms of interpersonal contact. The researchers hypothesized that teens with poor social skills feel lonelier as a result of Facebook use and suggested the following reasons: (1) teens are not able to transfer the comfort they feel communicating on Facebook to offline situations, (2) the time spent in superficial communication with online friends may displace time that would have been spent building deeper offline relationships, and (3) Facebook use impacts social comparisons leading to dissatisfaction.

Social media usage is linked to the acquisition of social capital, which is defined as the benefits attained from the social structure (Ellison, Steinfield, and Lampe 2007). Social capital is segmented into bridging social capital, or information acquired through a diverse network, and bonding social capital, or emotional support provided by friends. A study that compared directed communication on Facebook, which includes the posts, comments, and likes of friends, to consumption of the content posted by friends found that while directed communication correlates with heightened feelings of bonding social capital and lower loneliness, consumption is related to lower bridging and bonding social capital and increased loneliness (Burke, Marlow, and Lento 2010). The most counterintuitive result to the research team was that consumption was not related to increased feelings of bridging social capital. Additionally, overall activity on Facebook, particularly friend count, is positively related to both forms of social capital and negatively related to loneliness. The researchers interpreted the results in the following ways. First, socially connected people are attracted to sites that reaffirm those relationships. Next, Facebook allows for the building and maintenance of distant or new relationships. Finally, social media platforms offer a positive feedback loop whereby liking and commenting on the content of others will be returned to that user in the form of likes and comments on his or her content.

Some of the questions about social media sites and feelings of depression, loneliness, and other negative emotions are those of causation. Does Facebook cause these emotions or do people experiencing these emotions turn to Facebook for comfort? A study by Kross et al. (2013) of 82 Facebook users whose mood was tracked via surveys five times a day for two weeks found that the use of Facebook between surveys contributed to a worse mood and that overall satisfaction with life for those who were frequent Facebook users during the course of the study declined. Those participants who had made social contacts in the real world either by phone or in person between surveys reported more positive feelings. The researchers concluded that the decline in well-being that is linked to Facebook use is not because depressed people are more likely to gravitate to Facebook, but that Facebook itself has an impact on users.

Social media sites, especially Facebook, may also create feelings of envy when users view the seemingly endless photos and posts showcasing vacations, engagement rings, weddings, babies, parties, homes, athletic or academic achievements of children, cars, and job promotions. In addition to the amount of information that can be viewed about others, social media users may also be anxious that others will view their profiles less favorably in comparison. The environment increases the need for impression management, whereby a user highlights certain positive aspects of his or her life while downplaying others, creating a perception that is better than reality.

Researchers studying social media envy found that slightly more than 20 percent of recent scenarios where the participants were envious occurred on Facebook with the main areas of envy on Facebook being the vacations, happiness, and the online social interaction of others (Krasnova et al. 2013). Those users in their mid-thirties were more likely to envy family happiness, and women of all ages were more likely to envy physical beauty. The researchers also found that envy mediates the relationship between passive Facebook following and life satisfaction. Intense passive following (i.e., looking at profiles and not interacting with users) leads to social comparison and feelings of envy, which then have an impact on life satisfaction. Social media envy inevitably leads to pain, which the user will attempt to minimize through avoidance of particular friends or even unfriending those friends. Other responses may include more self-promotion on the part of the user, possibly through an exaggeration of accomplishments. The researchers referred to this behavior as the *self-promotion-envy spiral.* When users are exposed to the self-promotional content of others that makes them envious, they counter with their own self-promotional content, which may make other users envious. They found that men were more likely to discuss accomplishments as a form of self-promotion while women highlighted their looks and social lives.

Another study on Facebook envy surveyed users and found that browsing Facebook resulted in symptoms of depression when comparisons to the lives of others created feelings of envy (Tandoc, Ferucci, and Duffy 2014). When browsing did not lead to envy, users experienced lower levels of depression. In another examination of Facebook users, the researchers found that those who spent more time on the site as well as those who had Facebook friends they did not know personally were more likely to agree that others had better lives than themselves

(Chou and Edge 2012). Users who spent more time on Facebook were also more likely to have the perception that others were happier than themselves and less likely to agree that life is fair. On the positive side, those users who have more Facebook friends were less likely to agree that others were happier and more likely to agree that life is fair. To curb perceptions that others are happier or their lives are better, the researchers encouraged deeper interactions with friends in offline settings, which offer a more balanced view of the lives of friends instead of just the positive information they choose to post on Facebook.

Despite these findings, other studies have found positive emotional outcomes from social media use. For example, the majority of teens in the 2012 Common Sense Media study indicated that social media did not impact their emotional well-being, and of those who reported having been affected by social media, more teens reported positive outcomes rather than negative results (Rideout 2012). For example, social media usage was linked to greater confidence by 20 percent of respondents (4 percent said less), feeling more outgoing by 28 percent of respondents (5 percent said less), feeling more popular by 19 percent of respondents (4 percent said less), lower levels of depression by 10 percent of respondents (5 percent said more), and lower levels of shyness by 29 percent of respondents (3 percent said more). Additionally, 15 percent of users said they felt better about themselves because they use social media, while 4 percent said they felt worse.

Other circumstances highlight contexts when Facebook use may improve or at least have no negative impact on the mood of the user. In a study, Sagioglou and Greitemeyer (2014) found that making plans or connecting with friends on Facebook heightens mood. Lin and Utz (2015) found that positive emotions are more likely than negative to be experienced while using Facebook and are more likely to occur when a "strong tie" friend as opposed to a "weak tie" acquaintance makes a positive post. Verduyn et al. (2015) found that although passive Facebook usage, such as browsing, has led to decreases in affective well-being through feelings of envy, active Facebook usage had neither a positive nor a negative effect.

Verduyn et al. (2015) discussed why people continue to use Facebook passively (at a rate of 50 percent more than active users) if it negatively impacts their well-being. First, research has documented the addictive powers of Facebook and other social media sites, and similar to other addictive behaviors, people will continue to engage despite the negative consequences. Second, users enjoy interacting with others and exposure to interesting and entertaining content on social media sites, so it is possible that users consider the pros of usage to outweigh the cons. Finally, people may be unaware of the connection between their feelings and Facebook usage.

To combat problems related to social media use and mood, depression, loneliness, and envy, social media users should consider how to use the platforms in a way that increases positive emotions and suppresses negative ones. One suggestion is to block friends whose posts are troublesome, such as those who boast too much about accomplishments or post political content about a party, candidate, or issue not supported by the user. Users can also follow pages that post positive content, such as Upworthy, The Happiness Project, 1,000 Awesome Things, or the Huffington Post: Good News. Users should also maximize the features of the platforms for their personal gain. For example, users can maintain relationships on Facebook, but then use the site to organize real-life interactions. LinkedIn and Twitter are both beneficial for making professional contacts. Social media users might also be interested in participating in a happiness or gratitude project, where they share specific content on social media. Users can also share uplifting or positive content they find on the Web, such as an inspirational video or quote. In the end, it is important to remember that social media is a tool, and if it is not offering desirable content, useful features, or valuable relationships expected by the user, the user can always become a nonuser.

Pressure to Project the Ideal Self

The popular 2013 song "Selfie" by The Chainsmokers expressed the attitudes of many social media users who are focused on projecting a favorable image on social media sites. The lyrics include the following lines about a selfie: "I only got 10 likes in the last 5 minutes/Do you think I should take it down?" The subsequent lyrics answer the question by suggesting taking another selfie.

Social media sites allow users to create an idealized or curated version of their lives and then connect with others who can view this particular presentation of self. As described by Marche (2012), "Self-presentation on Facebook is continuous, intensely mediated, and possessed of a phony nonchalance that eliminates even the potential for spontaneity . . . Curating the exhibition of the self has become a 24/7 occupation." A 2014 trend report by Ford found that 74 percent of respondents in the United States believe that people portray themselves more favorably on social media than they do in real life (Ford 2013). Respondents from China were even more likely to agree with this statement (84 percent) while respondents in Japan (70 percent), Germany (58 percent), and Brazil (52 percent) were less likely. With complete control afforded by social media sites over profile content, users may choose to share the most attractive or interesting photos and other content. Similarly, users also often have the power to not share information about personal and professional failures, unattractive photos, or other content that would portray them in an unfavorable light.

Self-presentation has changed since the emergence of social media. Jurgenson (2013) discussed how the virtual world has replaced people's offline identity with "the simulated second life that uproots and disembodies the authentic self in favor of digital status-posturing, empty interaction, and addictive connection." Early social media sites and Web spaces allowed users anonymity, and users often took advantage of this option. For example, early MySpace users could create a display name of their choosing and opt to reveal their real name or not when interacting with other users or when others viewed their profiles. Nicknames were also popular among users of online bulletin boards and chat rooms as well as graphic avatars in place of a profile photo. When Facebook started growing in popularity, MySpace then began encouraging users to display their real names, as was the standard on Facebook from the beginning (Arrington 2008). Self-presentation became more of a concern with the emergence of social media sites like Facebook and Instagram that rely more on presentation through visual content, such as photos and videos. This type of content allows for opportunities to share much more about users' personal lives and manipulate this content as well. At the same time users are revealing more about their lives through photos on social media, they are making sure those photos represent them in the most favorable light, which may be artificial and inauthentic.

Photo apps are available that airbrush or otherwise alter photos to make the subject appear younger, thinner, or more attractive. Some of these apps include Perfect365, FaceTune, ModiFace, Pixtr, and Visage Lab. Some social media platforms have built-in features for photo manipulation. Not surprisingly, teens and young adults as well as women are the most active users of these apps. Seventy percent of FaceTune's users, for example, are women, and two-thirds of Perfect365's users are under age 24 (Bosker 2013).

Researchers who study social media presentation often draw upon impression management or self-presentation theories, which were influenced by sociologist Erving Goffman and his 1959 book *The Presentation of Self in Everyday Life* (Goffman 1959). Goffman viewed self-presentation as a performance and advocated impression management for its ability to foster friendship and avoid conflicts. Although his concepts originated long before the emergence of social media, Goffman's work remains applicable in modern times. Self-presentation has been the theoretical foundation of studies of personal websites by several academicians, including Nicola Döring (2002), Schau and Gilly (2003), and Anna-Malin Karlsson (1998). Others have looked at social networking sites, such as online dating sites (Ellison, Heino, and Gibbs 2006). Ellison et al.'s (2006) study explained reasons for deceptive profiles on online dating sites as resulting from a "foggy mirror" issue, where users cannot view themselves as others see them, or from a tendency to describe their "ideal selves," which could be a deliberate or unintentional process.

Self-affirmation is another theory that relates to social media presentation (Toma and Hancock 2013). This theory is based on the idea that people desire to view themselves as valuable, worthy, and good, and this drive will motivate their behavior. People will then avoid any information that will negatively impact their self-worth while embracing information that confirms it. Building self-worth requires self-affirmation, which demands an awareness of values, relationships, and individual characteristics. One of the processes in self-affirmation is the need to seek confirming information after an ego threat in order to repair self-worth, which will make people less defensive and more resistant to subsequent threats.

Toma and Hancock (2013) argued that self-affirmation applies to Facebook because the platform provides an opportunity to present key personal attributes within a network of personal relationships. Users will seek self-affirmation within this context and try to increase their perceptions of self-worth. As the researchers note, "this analysis suggests that Facebook profiles have the potential to confer upon users self-affirmational benefits because they encapsulate a flattering, socially connected, meaningful, and accurate self-portrait" (Toma and Hancock 2013, 323). In two studies of Facebook users, Toma and Hancock found that Facebook profiles are self-affirming and can satisfy the needs of users for building self-worth and self-integrity and that Facebook users are likely to browse their own Facebook profiles after a blow to their egos to attempt to repair their own feelings of self-worth. This study is particularly important in demonstrating how beneficial Facebook can be in helping people deal with life's setbacks and repair damage to their egos.

The reasons for participating in online self-presentation include a longing to make a favorable impression on others or project an identity that is consistent with one's ideals (Herring and Kapidzic 2015). Many of the studies in this area have focused on teens and young adults. Herring and Kapidzic (2015) explored differences in how teen girls and boys manage their online presentations. Girls are more likely to limit profile visibility through privacy settings while boys are more likely to share their profiles publicly. The researchers also compared textual presentations and found boys more likely to project assertiveness through their writing style and tone while girls demonstrated their desire to please boys and encourage social interaction. From the perspective of the visual presentation, girls posted more photos reflecting a desire to be attractive and sexually appealing, while boys did not demonstrate a clear pattern. Overall, the teens studied demonstrated the importance of displaying gendered identities on social media profiles, which is consistent with offline patterns of development of their social identity (Herring and Kapidzic 2015).

Focus groups with teens conducted by the Pew Internet & American Life Project found teens to be proactive in managing the content and appearance of their social media profiles (Madden et al. 2013). Participants viewed "likes" as an indicator of social status, and teens are strategic in their attempts to maximize "likes" and will remove content with few "likes." Deleting content is the most popular strategy (59 percent have done so), and some of their other tactics for managing their profiles include deleting comments from others (53 percent), removing a tag from photos posted by others (45 percent), and deleting their entire profile (31 percent).

Other studies have examined how young adult social media users present themselves in their posted photos. In a 2011 study of 288 Facebook users, Kapidzic found that young adults who chose profile photos where they had posed and dressed seductively were more likely to have internalized media messages about stereotypical looks (Kapidzic 2011). Not surprisingly, stronger results were found among females.

For some, the pressure to project and maintain a certain appearance can become an unhealthy obsession. Research studies have explored whether social media platforms change people in a way that they are more concerned about their self-presentation. A study of Australian social media users found that "Facebook users have higher levels of total narcissism, exhibitionism, and leadership than Facebook nonusers . . . In fact, it could be argued that Facebook specifically gratifies the narcissistic individual's need to engage in self-promoting and superficial behavior" (Ryan and Xenos 2011). Ryan and Xenos contend that social media platforms are more attractive to those who are already narcissistic and attention-seeking, and although the sites cultivate this behavior, they do not create it.

Managing a social media profile includes, for some people, excessively monitoring the likes and nature of the comments on posted photos. The more likes or positive comments, the more the user may feel worthy or validated. Ford's 2014 Trend Report noted that the public self that is shared on social media may require more validation than the offline, authentic self (Ford 2013). The report noted that 62 percent of adults agreed that they feel more positive about themselves when people respond to their social media posts. Seventy-two percent of adults over age 34 agreed that they post content on social media sites that they believe their followers will like, making them more self-conscious than the 40 percent of those aged 34 and younger who agreed with the statement. The report expanded on this idea:

> We are living in a world of hyper self-expression, complete with "selfies," chronic public-journaling and other forms of digital self-expression. As authors, we have the opportunity

> to craft our own identity and tell the stories that are unique to us. What looks like—and perhaps started as—vanity showmanship is now a deep desire for validation. A Facebook "like" or two makes us feel good. A dozen "likes" makes us feel great, creating a quiet but fierce need to revisit the pieces of our narrative, to tweak, color and edit them to our liking—and to the liking of others. But as we smooth out the rough edges of our public self, do we gloss over our real character? (Ford 2013, 20)

The ability to effectively manage a social media profile and maintain a positive self-presentation is a skill that benefits a range of people, from those seeking jobs or admission to college to those desiring a romantic relationship or a tight network of friends. Social media users, however, are cautioned to avoid obsessing over acquiring likes and comments from friends, altering photos to look as attractive as possible, and presenting one's life in a false light on social media sites. Users, particularly teens and young adults, who spend too much time creating their online personas may miss opportunities to develop their offline selves.

Social Media in the Workplace

Social media are an integral part of workplace life. Reasons for using social media for work purposes include the performance of job duties, particularly for employees in the marketing or communications fields; internal employee communication and team management; job hunting; monitoring employees; or recruiting and screening prospective employees. Social media can also create distractions for some employees on the job, which seriously impacts productivity (Vitak, Crouse, and LaRose 2009). This section focuses specifically on the use of social media for recruiting and screening prospective employees, the practice of employers requiring social media log-in information from current and prospective employees, the extent to which the National Labor Relations Act (NLRA) protects employees, and considerations when crafting a corporate social media policy. Finally, this section ends with a discussion of how prospective employees can use social media to enhance their job search.

The human resources function, in particular, is one area that has raised questions about the appropriate use of social media for recruiting and screening prospective hires. A 2016 study by the Society for Human Resource Management found that 43 percent of respondents use social media or a Google search to screen job applicants and 36 percent have rejected an applicant based on information discovered (Society for Human Resource Management 2016). Some of the reasons for rejection included illegal activity or factual inconsistencies with applications. The study also found 84 percent of respondents said they recruit using social media, an increase from 56 percent of those who used social media in 2011, and another 9 percent are planning to use it. For most recruiters, LinkedIn is the primary social media recruiting tool, used by 96 percent, but Facebook and Twitter are also popular platforms.

A study of 228 hiring professionals had similar results and found that almost 80 percent of respondents used LinkedIn to screen candidates, followed by Facebook (35.9 percent) and Twitter (14.8 percent) (Sameen and Cornelius 2015). Most of the hiring managers surveyed (67.2 percent) used social media to target passive candidates instead of active ones. The point in the hiring process where social media was most likely to be reviewed was after receiving the application (39.8 percent), and 43.8 percent said that final hiring decisions were not based on information in the social media profiles. For those who did use social media profiles to make final decisions (31.3 percent), some of the reasons included personality fit with organization, additional support for professional qualifications, and communication skills. Most (59.4 percent) would not reject candidates based on information found on social media profiles, but if they did, reasons included lying about qualifications, poor communication skills, sharing confidential information about the previous employer, and posting negative comments about the previous employer.

Another issue related to the usage of social media by recruiters is the possibility of discrimination based on information provided or observable on a social media profile, whether gender, age, race, religion, sexual orientation, or physical disability. The availability of candidate information on social media challenges the enforcement of federal employment discrimination laws. Suggestions to combat this problem include using social media as one of many tools for recruiting and involving a third party to review social media profiles as a background check (U.S. Equal Employment Opportunity Commission 2014).

A recent privacy invasion trend has been employers who demand the social media usernames and passwords from either prospective or current employees. Employers may defend this behavior by arguing they are monitoring whether employees are releasing proprietary information or setting them up for potential legal liabilities, but employees often see the practice as an invasion of privacy. According to the terms of agreement for many social media sites, users are expected to protect their passwords, therefore making it against the terms of agreement if recruiters or employers require prospective and current employees to turn over this information. By 2016, more than 25 states had passed laws that prohibit employers from collecting this information from both applicants and current employees and many other states are considering this legislation (National Conference of State Legislators 2016). At the same time, Congress is pursuing a federal law on this matter. For this reason, many recruiters and employers have access to only publicly available information.

For the most part, job applicants probably do not realize the extent to which they are being profiled. Some companies use scoring services to make data-driven decisions about promotions or hiring (Pasquale 2015). Anything from joining the wrong Facebook group or using inappropriate language can give an employee a black mark. Little regulation exists in this area, but states could pass legislation that would require employers to share the outside intelligence reports collected on current and prospective employees. As noted by Frank Pasquale in an op-ed piece for the *Los Angeles Times*, "Without such notification, we may be stigmatized by secret digital judgments" (2015). Employees and applicants should have an opportunity to know what data are being used to make decisions by employers as well as have a chance to correct any misinformation.

Many employees operate with the assumption that First Amendment protection of free speech applies to their social media posts. However, free speech protection is only provided to public sector employees posting on matters of public concern. Instead, workers have some protection from the NLRA. The NLRA allows employees to collectively discuss work-related issues for the purposes of collective bargaining or mutual protection without interference from the employer, and these conversations may occur on social media sites (Patterson 2014).

The act created the National Labor Relations Board (NLRB), a federal agency that receives tens of thousands of employee complaints annually, including an increasing number of social media–related cases (NLRB n.d.). In some of these complaints, employees are commenting on work-related issues or working conditions. In others, they are displaying behavior deemed inappropriate to the employer. It is important for both employees and employers to understand what kinds of posts are legally protected. Employers who fire employees over social media posts could face wrongful termination lawsuits if the content posted on social media sites represents protected speech or protest. Some of the rulings on recent cases have determined that a "like" may not be protected concerted activity; that the employee may not be protected if the post is a malicious attack on the employer's products, services, or reputation; and that an individual employee is not protected if posting alone without engaging in conversation with at least one other employee (Schmidt and O'Connor 2015).

Recent decisions by the NLRB also indicate that the agency is closely scrutinizing employer social media policies and looking for unlawful language. A 2012 study by the Society for Human Resource Management found that 40 percent of organizations have social media policies and the 33 percent of those with policies have used them to discipline an employee in the past year (Society for Human Resource Management 2012). Employers are advised to develop social media policies that provide guidelines for employees on what is acceptable and unacceptable on social media sites, but employers also need to understand the legal limits of what can be included. For example, in 2014, the NLRB reviewed a situation at Triple Play Sports Bar and Grill where two employees were fired for violating social media conduct policies by using profane language to criticize an owner on Facebook. One employee started the conversation with the following post: "Maybe someone should do the owners of Triple Play a favor and buy it from them. They can't even do the tax paperwork correctly!!! Now I OWE money . . . Wtf!!!" Then another employee added, "I owe too. [The boss is] such an a**hole" (Schmidt and O'Connor 2015). The NLRB ruled that because the language was used in discussions of problems by the employer in withholding the correct amount of state income tax from paychecks, it was protected as speech used to "seek and provide mutual support looking toward group action to encourage the employer to address problems in terms and conditions of employment, not to disparage its product or services or undermine its reputation" (Patterson 2014). The board also found the company's social media policy violated the NLRA because it "proscrib[ed] any discussions about their terms and conditions of employment [that the employer] deemed 'inappropriate'" (Patterson 2014).

In another decision issued in 2014, the NLRB determined that the firing of five employees from a nonprofit organization who discussed a coworker who was planning to complain to management about their performance was in violation of the NLRA. The board found the posts to be concerted activity, which is protected (NLRB n.d.). Another widely publicized employee firing as a result of a social media post created more bad news for troubled Chipotle, who was trying to bounce back after an *E. coli* outbreak and sexual discrimination lawsuit. Two weeks after tweeting "@ChipotleTweets, nothing is free, only cheap #labor. Crew members make only $8.50hr how much is that steak bowl really?" Chipotle employee James Kennedy was fired for the tweet and filed a wrongful termination lawsuit. The NLRB found Chipotle's social media policy, which prohibited posting "disparaging, false" statements on social media sites, to be in violation of labor laws (The Associated Press 2016).

Schmidt and O'Connor (2015) reviewed NLRB cases that resulted from social media terminations and provided recommendations to those crafting corporate social media policies. They suggested that employers provide employees with the freedom to share legitimate concerns about their workplace, but not embarrass the company or the customers. Policies should be as specific as possible in listing examples of prohibited behavior, but still allow employees to air grievances and not place limits on the use of profanity, sharing of gossip, or rude posts. It is also suggested that employers review other NLRB cases to learn from the mistakes of other organizations and stay abreast of case law in the area of social media.

A *National Law Review* article suggested that employers include in their social media policies the activities protected by NLRA and a statement that the policy will not interfere with those rights (Patterson 2014). Then, employers can include unprotected social media posts and activities that may result in disciplinary action, such as disclosure of proprietary company information, threats of violence, statements that are obscene or used to bully, rumors or other false statements about the company or employees, and posts that are racist, sexist, or discriminatory intended to create a hostile work environment.

A report issued by the NLRB in 2012 offered two major points for employers and employees to keep in mind as they relate to employer social media policies and employee postings on social media sites. First, "[e]mployer policies should not be so sweeping that they prohibit the kinds of activity protected by federal labor law, such as the discussion of wages or working conditions among employees." Second, "[a]n employee's comments on social media are generally not protected if they are mere gripes not made in relation to group activity among employees" (NLRB n.d.).

Although certain content on social media sites might disqualify applicants from jobs, social media can be used strategically by job seekers to improve their chances of being hired. Many prospects are located through LinkedIn, and therefore, job seekers should not only have a LinkedIn profile, but also add as many professional details as possible, build a strong network of connections, and join LinkedIn groups such as alumni organizations or industry associations. Job seekers may also consider building a personal website to showcase their work, which is particularly recommended in creative fields. Job seekers should also remove unfavorable social media content from their own social media profiles, including negative comments about current or prospective employers, or ask it to be removed from other profiles. Finally, even though employers are bound by anti-discrimination laws, applicants may also consider removing personal information from their social media profiles.

Relationships and Communication Skills

In today's digital society, people are both more connected and more disconnected than ever before. Social media provide users a link to a vast and potentially geographically dispersed network of friends and acquaintances with whom they can interact at any time. Through social media, friendships made throughout a lifetime can be maintained, and new friendships can be formed. Another benefit is that it is possible to manage many relationships through social media sites. Despite these advantages, social media interactions have been criticized for being superficial, lacking the necessary depth to form even closer bonds. Digital conversations may also be less fulfilling than other forms of communication. Consider, for example, the difference between receiving birthday wishes from many friends on Facebook versus a phone call from a friend. The Facebook greetings require little commitment in terms of time, while a phone call is more meaningful and personal. Social media interactions may also have a detrimental impact on the ability of people, especially youth, to communicate offline.

Because social media facilitate connections with other people and enhance the opportunity to meet new people, the technology may also threaten relationships with significant others. Anecdotal evidence has provided many examples of people who left a spouse to rekindle a relationship with a past love interest or start a relationship with a new social media connection. Even if a user is not engaging with social media to cheat on his or her partner or attempt to find a new partner, research has demonstrated that excessive use of the Internet can have detrimental effects on a relationship. A 2011 study found that when one partner spent significant amounts of time on the Internet, the relationship suffered from conflict (Kerkhof, Finkenauer, and Muusses 2011). Reasons suggested included that the non-Internet-using partner felt ignored or neglected and that the partner using the Internet was suspected of concealing or not sharing information about his or her life. A later study on Facebook usage and relationships also found that digital communication led to relationship conflict (Clayton, Nagurney, and Smith 2013). The researchers found a correlation between Facebook usage and conflict related to Facebook, and, in turn, a correlation between this conflict and negative relationship outcomes for the couple, such as cheating or the dissolution of the relationship (Clayton, Nagurney, and Smith 2013). For those in shorter relationships (36 months or less), Facebook use was more likely to lead to conflict, but this connection was not present for couples in relationships for more than three years.

Some of the research on the use of social media by youth to manage relationships has explored how social media usage leads to anxiety or isolation from family and friends (Turkle 2011), while other research has focused on how teens develop important relationships through social media (Ito et al. 2010). A study by Common Sense Media showed how social media can provide a tool for young people to communicate with friends, develop an identity, learn social skills, and extend friendships (Rideout 2012). When it comes to relationships with friends, this study of 13- to 17-year-olds found that more than half (52 percent) of teens said social media usage has enhanced relationships with friends versus just 4 percent who said usage has negatively affected those relationships. Some of the benefits included keeping in touch with friends they cannot see regularly (88 percent), getting to know students at school better (69 percent), and connecting with others who share a common interest (57 percent). The teens surveyed, however, preferred face-to-face communication as their favorite way to communicate with friends (49 percent) followed by texting (33 percent), with social media communication at just 7 percent. The two top reasons for preferring face-to-face communication included that it is more fun (38 percent) and easier to understand what people mean (29 percent).

Studies of self-reported communication preferences do not acknowledge how technology may rewire the user's brain pathways and impact the ability of users to develop strong interpersonal relationships. This process works through chemicals called neurotransmitters in the brain that function to transfer information between nerves. As a child develops, pathways are expanded based on stimulation and are used to help organize information as it is acquired. Digital use, however, changes the neural pathways and can impact some traits and abilities such as concentration, self-esteem, building personal relationships, and empathy (Johnson 2014).

Relationships can also be explored from the perspective of social capital, which are the resources that one acquires through relationships with people in a network (Coleman 1988). The concept of social capital is particularly relevant in a social media setting. Social capital could take the form of information or relationships that can be helpful to others in the network. For example, a user might be able to offer his connections knowledge about companies that are hiring or specialists who might be able to cure a disease. Social capital is often described as either bridging or bonding, with bridging resulting from "weak ties" or loose connections that can offer information but not emotional support and bonding resulting from people in close relationships, such as family members or dear friends (Ellison, Steinfield, and Lampe 2007). A study by Ellison, Steinfield, and Lampe (2007) of college students found certain kinds of Facebook use to be more useful in creating or maintaining bridging social capital. Students who did not use Facebook as intensely and had low satisfaction with college life and low self-esteem experienced much lower bridging capital than more intense users. The researchers suggested that Facebook use could help those unhappy students adjust to college life by offering information and opportunities. Facebook use was found to be less critical for maintaining or creating bonding social capital than bridging, but still important, particularly for maintaining preexisting close relationships.

Another study of youth and communication tools examined pairs of close female friends (Sherman, Michikyan, and Greenfield 2013). The research team found that the most bonding occurred when the pairs interacted in person, followed by video chat, audio chat, and then instant messaging. Additionally, the use of technology impacted bonding for the participants. For example, those who used video chat and audio chat frequently reported more bonding than those who did not. Furthermore, even though less bonding occurred during instant messaging than other communication methods, affiliation cues such as emoticons, typed laughter, and excessive capitalization improved bonding.

In addition to directly impacting relationships, social media have been criticized for sabotaging the development of solid communication skills needed to build and maintain relationships. Parents and other adults worry that children are not acquiring the skills to manage face-to-face conversations. Single people sometimes resort to texting and social media as an important tool for managing their dating relationships, even relying on digital media as a method for communicating the end of a relationship to avoid an uncomfortable face-to-face situation. Some people also find themselves distracted by social media in settings where they have the opportunity to engage with people face-to-face.

In an interview with WBUR, scholar Sherry Turkle stated that she believes digital communication is "dumbing down" communication skills and that some young people are even intimidated by the prospect of talking to people IRL (in real life). Turkle continued by adding that digital communication "is not so good for the sort of nuanced understanding and relationship-building you get when you are present with your friends—for sharing intimacies, for sharing difficult news, for saying you are sorry, for really getting to know someone. It gives us that sense of connection without the demands of intimacy and the responsibilities of intimacy" (Adler 2013). In the same interview, Microsoft researcher Nancy Baym advocated a contrasting opinion, saying that "the evidence consistently shows that the more you communicate with people using devices, the more likely you are to communicate with those people face to face" (Adler 2013).

For young people as well as others, screen time may impact the ability to recognize nonverbal cues, an important element of face-to-face communication that is absent in digital communication. A team of researchers performed a field experiment where a group of preteens spent five days at an overnight nature camp without any screens, including television, computers, and mobile devices. Compared to the control group who had access to screens, the preteens who did not engage with screens had better recognition of nonverbal emotional cues in facial expressions presented in photos and videotaped scenes. The researchers concluded that "the short-term effects of increased opportunities for social interaction, combined with time away from screen-based media and digital communication tools, improves a preteen's understanding of nonverbal emotional cues" (Uhls et al. 2014, 387).

A 2009 study on digital communication found that teens who spend more time communicating using online social sites, instant messages, and texts have more anxiety symptoms than when communicating face-to-face (Pierce 2009). This phenomenon is even more pronounced in girls. The question then arises as to whether people who are more socially anxious turn to technology for communication or whether it is the use of technology that drives them to be more anxious. In the end, the question is irrelevant because, either way, the teen is not having as much of an opportunity to build in-person social skills.

Social media may improve communication skills for those who lack the confidence to communicate in face-to-face situations. For those who are quiet or introverted, social media can level the playing field by giving them an opportunity for their voice to be heard or allowing them to show another side of themselves. The quiet person in a face-to-face situation might offer humorous comments, creative content, or thoughtful insights online. Some people or even certain situations may require more time to craft responses, and social media allow them opportunities to do so. Social media also provide an outlet for creative written and visual communication through the use of blogs, images, or videos.

Building and maintaining strong offline relationships and communication skills can be improved through practice and by not relying solely on social media as a crutch to avoid face-to-face communication. Social media users should recognize how social media communication can be used as a tool to foster personal relationships and as a bridge for offline communication, but not allow it to become a substitute for all face-to-face communications. For example, social media can be used to facilitate organization of an outing with friends, learn that a friend lives in a city where the user is planning to travel, or rekindle a relationship with a high school friend. Parents can help their children learn to build personal relationships by regulating the usage of their children's digital devices and setting up rules and boundaries. Furthermore, parents should also exhibit behaviors their children can model by creating boundaries for their own usage. For example, family dinners and other family events may be deemed device-free times. Children and teens should also be encouraged to talk in person to teachers, coaches, and other adults and not rely on digital communication.

Online Shaming and Attacks

With today's technology, people's public and even private behavior and statements as well as anything posted on social media can easily be captured, shared, downloaded, or forwarded to a network of followers, making it easy to launch and propagate online attacks. Unleashing an attack on someone for their morally reprehensible behavior is as easy as sending a tweet or sharing a photo. Depending on the site, attacks can even be made anonymously. In the wake of a controversial event, social media users tend to jump on the attack bandwagon and raise the profile of the event to something that may receive national and even international attention. In addition to public shaming, attackers sometimes call for the person to be destroyed, which often takes the form of a job firing. Another form of attack is committed by online trolls, who were active even before social media on websites and bulletin boards and often attack on a whim. With social media, however, people are now more exposed to trolls than ever before. Unlike the mobs who participate in public shaming, trolls often focus on a variety of targets and are not likely to pile on to a public situation.

relations professional Justine Sacco made several
iile traveling from New York to Cape Town, South
uring late 2013, commenting on a passenger's body
dental problems of Londoners, and finally, prior to
leg of her trip, the AIDS epidemic in Africa when she
oing to Africa. Hope I don't get AIDS. Just kidding.
e!" (Ronson 2015). Sacco's 170 followers did not have
ediate reaction to the tweet before she boarded her
our flight. During her flight while she was offline, her
eated a Twitterstorm of backlash and tens of thousands
ts. One said, "How did @JustineSacco get a PR job?!
el of racist ignorance belongs on Fox News. #AIDS can
iyone!" The situation was so critical that her employer,
lt compelled to engage in the conversation adding, "This
utrageous, offensive comment. Employee in question
ly unreachable on an intl flight." Another Twitter user
ded with, "We are about to watch this @JustineSacco
get fired. In REAL time. Before she even KNOWS she's
fired." Because Sacco was off the grid while the situation
ed, Twitter users created the hashtag #HasJustineLand-
accelerating the drama of the situation and making Sacco
p trending topic worldwide on Twitter. Because of the
Sacco did lose her job, moved to Africa to work in public
ons for a nongovernmental organization, and then moved
to New York for another public relations position at an
closed company (Ronson 2015).

other target of online vilification was Walter Palmer, the
iesota dentist who shot the beloved Cecil the Lion, a major
st attraction in Hwange National Park, while on a hunt-
rip in Zimbabwe. The killing was gruesome, with Palmer
ting Cecil with a bow and arrow, then allowing the lion
iffer for 40 hours before Palmer finally killed him (Bever
5). The fallout for Palmer was significant. The resulting
ne shaming and threats as well as offline protests caused
to shut down his dental practice. The garage of Palmer's
ition home in Florida was spray painted with the words

"Lion Killer." Additionally, Palmer's Yelp page was bombarded with negative reviews and boycott requests. Even celebrities, such as Ricky Gervais, Ian Somerhalder, Jerry O'Connell, Sharon Osbourne, and Shannon Doherty, jumped into the fray to criticize the dentist (Hilton 2015). The courts in Zimbabwe determined that Palmer had obtained legal authority to hunt, and he was not charged with any crime (BBC News 2015). The hunt guide he worked with, however, was arrested. After two months, Palmer was able to reopen his dental clinic.

Another online victim was Lindsey Stone, who in 2012 posted a photo on Facebook of herself "giving the finger" to and appearing to scream near a sign at Arlington National Cemetery that requested visitors offer "Silence and Respect." After the photo went viral, Stone received thousands of negative online comments and threats and was fired from her job (Regan 2015). In another example, the chief financial officer of a medical device manufacturer, Adam Mark Smith, posted a video of himself berating a Chick-fil-A employee about the company's antigay marriage stance. After the video went viral, he lost his $200,000-a-year job as well as his home. After finding a new job, Smith was promptly fired when the new boss realized that he was the man from the infamous video (Towner and Nye 2015). Alicia Ann Lynch also suffered the vitriol from social media users who objected to her Halloween costume of a Boston Marathon bombing victim just months after the attacks (Giacobbe 2014). The backlash included publicizing racy photos Lynch had previously uploaded to Tumblr, calling her parents and saying they would "slit her throat," contacting her boss, posting negative online reviews for the company they thought employed her father, threatening her best friend, and posting comments about how Lynch deserved to be raped and how they hoped her mom would get cancer (Giacobbe 2014). Although Lynch apologized, the threats continued and she was fired from her job.

Why does this phenomenon occur? Why are people so quick to pile on to these situations? Social media make it easy to share opinions, and these online condemnations might make insecure people feel better about themselves. Those who participate in online shaming may experience *schadenfreude*, which refers to the pleasure that comes from knowledge of the misfortune of others. Also, attacks do not need to be delivered face-to-face, so the sender can somewhat hide behind an online profile. By joining in the attack, people have an opportunity to be part of popular conversation and serve as moral police. Jon Ronson, who wrote the book *So You've Been Publicly Shamed*, described in the *New York Times* how public shaming grew along with the technology:

> Still, in those early days, the collective fury felt righteous, powerful and effective. It felt as if hierarchies were being dismantled, as if justice were being democratized. As time passed, though, I watched these shame campaigns multiply, to the point that they targeted not just powerful institutions and public figures but really anyone perceived to have done something offensive. I also began to marvel at the disconnect between the severity of the crime and the gleeful savagery of the punishment. It almost felt as if shamings were now happening for their own sake, as if they were following a script. (Ronson 2015)

Ronson views public shaming as a form of power, which gives a voice to voiceless people and provides a way to create drama. The sad consequence of the drama is that it often ruins a life or career.

For those who fear online shaming, one solution is to be more careful about what is shared in social media posts. Content can be misunderstood or taken out of context. Social media users also need to realize that people have different value systems and moral codes. An activity, such as hunting lions, may be acceptable to some people, but egregious to others. At the same time, social media users cannot completely control their online personas because others may capture offline behavior or comments and share that content on social media sites. Again, an awareness that anything said or done might be posted online may cause people to police their own offline behavior. Those who attack, criticize, or attempt to embarrass others through social media should consider whether the punishment called for fits the crime and also recognize that people, especially young people, will make mistakes they will later regret.

Trolls perform another type of online attack, often targeting people at random. Unlike online shaming, the target has usually not done anything egregious or controversial. Journalist Lindy West, herself a victim of a troll, defined trolling as "recreational abuse—usually anonymous—intended to waste the subject's time or get a rise out of them or frustrate or frighten them into silence" (West 2015). Sadly, trolls often prey on those who have lost family members, even children, and will write revolting comments on social media sites and online news stories. Those in the public eye, such as journalists and celebrities, are often targeted by numerous trolls.

In West's situation, a troll had set up a Twitter profile using the name PawWestDonezo, which was loosely based on West's deceased father's name, Paul West. The bio read: "Embarrassed father of an idiot. Other two kids are fine, though." His listed location was "Dirt hole in Seattle," and a photo of her father was used as the profile picture. West responded by writing about online trolls, which inspired the troll to e-mail West to apologize. His explanation for trolling West: "I think my anger towards you stems from your happiness with your own being. It offended me because it served to highlight my unhappiness with my own self" (West 2015).

Because trolls are trying to get a reaction from their targets, the best way to deal with them is to ignore their comments. Replying, even with a comment such as "please stop" or "go away, troll," will only feed the beast (Gordon 2014). Some users may get lured into the conversation with the troll, and in that case, it is best to try to deflate them with kindness

(Gordon 2014). Finally, recognizing that trolls are people who are probably bored or have low self-esteem may help a user discredit the attacks.

Social Media Privacy Concerns

The classic 1993 *New Yorker* cartoon that reads "Nobody on the Internet knows you are a dog" perfectly describes the sentiment in the beginning days of the Internet and early social media sites. Since then, consumer concerns about online privacy and security have increased as both technology and users have become more sophisticated (Pasierbinska-Wilson 2015).

When many users first went online in the early to mid-1990s, they were using dial-up services and paying by the hour for online access, two factors that limited opportunities for others to collect personal information. Furthermore, users at the time were often accessing the Internet through controlled portals such as AOL and the Microsoft Network. Additionally, the technology to steal personal information was not as available nor as advanced as it is today. Therefore, at the time, most consumers, businesses, and Internet service providers were not greatly concerned about privacy (Pasierbinska-Wilson 2015). That being said, movement toward privacy activism was taking place in organizations, such as the Electronic Privacy Information Center, which formed in 1994 to serve as a nonprofit research center to "protect privacy, freedom of expression, democratic values, and to promote the Public Voice in decisions concerning the future of the Internet" (Electronic Privacy Information Center n.d.). At the time, the American Civil Liberties Union also started to raise awareness of online privacy issues and the behavior of governments and corporations.

The privacy of children became an issue in the mid- to late 1990s as people began to worry about child pornography and marketers taking advantage of children under the age of consent (Pasierbinska-Wilson 2015). In 1998, Congress passed the

Children's Online Privacy Protection Act to require commercial websites to gain parental consent before collecting, using, and/or disclosing information from children under the age of 13 and to also outline the contents of a privacy policy, including the responsibility of a website operators to protect the privacy and safety of children on their sites.

The 2000s saw the rise in popularity of online social networks such as MySpace and Facebook, where users willingly shared personal information including their name, personal photos, birthdate, geographic location, and favorites (Pasierbinska-Wilson 2015). Legislation at the time, including the California Online Privacy Protection Act of 2003, focused on privacy policies. The act outlined that website operators who collect personal data must post a privacy policy in an obvious spot on the site that explains the nature of the data collected, how the data are shared with other parties, and how users can access their stored data, if the process exists. At the time, privacy concerns were somewhat addressed through awareness of policies.

By the 2010s, however, users wanted to not only know about how their data would be used, but also have more control over that data. High-profile stories related to online privacy and security covered by the news media highlighted the sophistication of individuals, governments, and corporations, heightening consumer concern (Pasierbinska-Wilson 2015). The National Security Agency surveillance reports, for example, revealed the once-secret bulk e-mail collection and wiretapping authorized by President George W. Bush and drew attention to all the online and offline data that are legally attainable. Similarly, Julian Assange's launch of WikiLeaks, a site that reveals secret information and news leaks, generated more concern from average citizens about online privacy.

In 2012, Havas Worldwide conducted a study of more than 7,000 adults in 19 countries on privacy concerns. The survey found that 55 percent of worldwide respondents aged 35–54 were worried that "technology is robbing us of our privacy," with the percentage higher than 60 percent among U.S. respondents

(Havas Worldwide 2012). Agreement was also high with that same age group (62 percent) for the statement "People share too much about their personal thoughts and experiences online; we need to go back to being more private." Despite concerns about privacy, a 2015 study by International Data Corporation and Kaspersky Lab of 18,000 consumers found several behaviors that leave social media users open to hackers and stalkers. In terms of friending, 12 percent responded they would add anyone to their network who made a friend request even if the person was a stranger, and 31 percent would add a "friend of a friend" (Kaspersky Lab 2015).

Online privacy and security is often a power struggle between website operators who find significant value in user data and users who want to protect their personal information. The business models of many websites and social media sites often involve providing collected data to advertisers and other third parties. Consumer scorn is often directed at advertisers and marketers who gather data that can be used to deliver relevant ads to users. Social networking sites such as Facebook and LinkedIn that provide a free platform to users generate revenue through advertising sales. Advertisers find value not only in getting ads in front of targeted prospective customers, but also in the data provided to them by the sites. In addition to for-profit businesses, the government and political parties are also interested in acquiring the data.

Users should be concerned with how social media companies are using and selling their personal information as well as how much information about them is known to third parties. Many Facebook users have noticed how a Google search results in subsequent targeted advertising on Facebook. For example, a consumer who is shopping on Zappos.com for a pair of boots may then notice Zappos ads for boots the next time they are on Facebook. A 2013 Pew Internet & American Life Project study found that most social media users are not interested in receiving targeted advertising based on surfing behavior or personal information (Davis 2016). Most social media sites provide users an option to turn off targeted ads in the settings or block ads from a specific source. For example, Facebook allows users to click directly on posts in the News Feed to decline or hide ads from a particular advertiser in the future. User information is collected not only through surfing the Web but also through apps that can be allowed access to phone content such as photos or contacts. In 2012, Twitter was exposed for copying contacts of iPhone Twitter app users to its own servers (Waugh and Cohen 2012).

A Pew Research Center study of 802 teens found that a higher percentage were sharing more information about themselves on social media in 2012 than they did in 2006 (Madden et al. 2013). Sharing a birth date (82 percent did so), school name (71 percent), city where they live (71 percent), or cell phone (20 percent) may also compromise the privacy or safety of the user. Additionally, sharing photos can be problematic for users. Photos taken on a cell phone have metadata attached to them, which can reveal the location of the user when the photo was taken. In 2012, a Burger King employee posted on the site 4chan a photo of lettuce on the floor of the restaurant with the caption: "This is the lettuce you eat at Burger King." Despite posting anonymously, the photo's metadata revealed the exact location of the restaurant, which eventually led to the firing of that employee and two others. Users should also be particularly concerned about broadcasting their locations through check-ins and posting photos from trips, which is a signal to others that their homes are unoccupied. To protect location data, users who take photos on phones and post to social media should turn off location services for social media sites and adjust the settings so that photos do not store metadata. Another strategy is for users not to post travel photos until they return home from a trip.

Another privacy concern is the extent of posted content that is available to "non-friends." These "non-friends" may access information through public social media profiles or might be accepted as friends by users they do not actually know. The best strategy for users to protect their information is to understand the privacy settings of social media sites. For most platforms, the default is a public account so the user must be savvy to know how to control access to their information. Users should also not accept friend requests from people not known to them personally, especially on sites like Facebook where a great deal of personal information is shared.

Social media sites also make it possible for privacy to be violated by another user posting personal information or photos about a friend, acquaintance, or even a stranger. In the Havas Worldwide study, almost half of the total sample (47 percent) and a majority of those aged 18–34 worry that inappropriate personal information about them will be shared online (Havas Worldwide 2012). On Facebook, users can require approval before being tagged in a photo, but that does not prevent users from uploading an embarrassing photo.

More concerning is the facial recognition technology used by Facebook to provide a suggested tag for uploaded photos. To do this, Facebook compares the faces in an uploaded photo to friends of the user, making a suggestion to tag specific users. The Privacy Commissioner of Canada had this to say about the future of facial recognition technology: "The availability of cheap facial recognition for the masses may have the effect of normalizing surveillance over time. We are not yet at the point where we can take pictures of people on the street with our smartphones, identify them, and gain access to information about them. However, this reality may not be too far off" (Roberts 2015). Although Facebook users are encouraged to opt out of auto-tagging, merely having photos on Facebook connected to a user's name provides data that can be used for other purposes.

Another privacy question of users is who owns the rights to the content posted on social media sites, including text, photos, and videos. Instagram users created such an uproar after Instagram announced that the site owned all content uploaded by users that the company had to retract the policy (McCullagh

2012). Facebook states that the company provides "a non-exclusive, transferable, sub-licensable, royalty-free, worldwide license to use any IP content that you post on or in connection with Facebook" (Facebook 2015). Therefore, while users own their content, Facebook can freely use it without compensation.

Conclusion

This chapter presented a range of issues related to social media use including addiction and the impact on relationships and communication skills. Other negative outcomes such as online shaming, scams and hoaxes, fake news, cyberbullying, and feelings of loneliness, depression, and envy were also covered. Finally, the chapter addressed the impact of content curation on social media feeds, the desire to project an ideal image, social media in the workplace, and privacy issues. Despite these problems, social media can have positive benefits if users approach social media with a meaningful, conscious, and informed mindset.

One of the questions often pondered about social media is how social media are changing users, but perhaps a better question is how social media users are changing the world. Recent examples of the large-scale impact of the power of social media include fund-raising campaigns, natural disaster response, and political revolutions (Roesler 2014). Without social media, more than $220 million worldwide would not have been raised for the ALS Association as a result of the viral Ice Bucket campaign (Holan 2014). Without social media, victims of the earthquake and tsunami in Japan 2011 would have fewer methods to seek information about loved ones and get updates about the situation, which was particularly dangerous because of damage to a nuclear reactor (Roesler 2014). Without social media, protesters in the political uprisings of the Arab Spring in 2011 would have fewer means to organize protesters, communicate with activist leaders, discuss government injustices, and demonstrate to the world the depravity of the situation

(Pontin 2011). Despite the many problems of social media platforms, they can offer unparalleled, large-scale, and meaningful benefits.

References

Adler, Iris. 2013. "How Our Digital Devices Are Affecting Our Personal Relationships." *WBUR*. January 17. http://www.wbur.org/2013/01/17/digital-lives-i.

Andreassen, Cecile S., Torbjorn Torsheim, Geir Scott Brunborg, and Stale Pallesen. 2012. "Development of a Facebook Addiction Scale." *Psychological Reports* 110 (2): 501–17.

Arrington, Michael. 2008. "MySpace Quietly Begins Encouraging Users to Use Their Real Names." *TechCrunch*. December 17. http://techcrunch.com/2008/12/17/myspace-quietly-begins-encouraging-users-to-use-their-real-names/.

The Associated Press. 2016. "Judge: Chipotle's Social Media Policy Violates U.S. Labor Laws." *ABC News*. March 16. http://abcnews.go.com/Technology/wireStory/judge-orders-chipotle-rehire-worker-fired-tweets-37688371.

Bakshy, Eytan, Solomon Messing, and Lada Adamic. 2015. "Exposure to Ideologically Diverse News and Opinion." *Science* 348 (6239): 1130–32.

Bartsch, Anne, and Reinhold Viehoff. 2010. "The Use of Media Entertainment and Emotional Gratification." *Procedia Social and Behavioral Sciences* 5: 2247–55.

Baumer, Eric P.S., Shion Guha, Emily Quan, David Mimno, and Geri K. Gay. 2015. "Missing Photos, Suffering Withdrawal, or Finding Freedom? How Experiences of Social Media Non-Use Influence the Likelihood of Reversion." *Social Media and Society* 1 (2): 1–14.

BBC News. 2015. "Cecil the Lion: No Charges for Walter Palmer, Says Zimbabwe." *BBC News*. October 12. http://www.bbc.com/news/world-africa-34508269.

Bever, Lindsey. 2015. "Walter Palmer, Dentist Who Hunted and Killed Cecil the Lion, Returns to Work." *The Washington Post.* September 8. https://www.washingtonpost.com/news/morning-mix/wp/2015/09/08/walter-palmer-dentist-who-hunted-and-killed-cecil-the-lion-returns-to-work/.

Boland, Brian. 2014. "Organic Reach on Facebook: Your Questions Answered." *Facebook.* June 5. https://www.facebook.com/business/news/Organic-Reach-on-Facebook.

Bosker, Bianca. 2013. "New Selfie-Help Apps Are Airbrushing Us All into Fake Instagram Perfection." *Huffington Post.* December 5. http://www.huffingtonpost.com/2013/12/05/selfie-instagram_n_4391220.html.

Burke, Moira, Cameron Marlow, and Thomas Lento. 2010. "Social Network Activity and Social Well-Being." CHI 2010 Proceedings of the SIGCHI Conference on Human Factors in Computing Systems. Atlanta: ACM. 1909–12.

Call, Meghan E., and Jason J. Burrow-Sanchez. 2010. "Identifying Risk Factors Enhancing Protective Factors to Prevent Adolescent Victimization on the Internet." In *Adolescent Online Social Communication and Behavior: Relationship Formation on the Internet*, edited by Robert Zheng, Jason Burrow-Sanchez, and Clifford Drew, 152–166. Hershey, PA: Information Science Reference.

Centers for Disease Control and Prevention. 2014. "Youth Risk Behavior Surveillance: United States 2013." *Morbidity and Mortality Weekly Report.* June 13. http://www.cdc.gov/mmwr/pdf/ss/ss6304.pdf.

Chan, Amanda. 2011. "Why Your Eyes Hurt after Staring at Your Smartphone." *Huffington Post.* September 24. http://www.huffingtonpost.com/2011/07/25/smartphone-eye-hurt_n_909025.html.

charstarleneTV. 2013. "I Forgot My Phone." *YouTube.* August 22. https://www.youtube.com/watch?v=OINa46HeWg8.

Chou, Hui-Tzu Grace, and Nicholas Edge. 2012. "'They Are Happier and Having Better Lives than I Am': The Impact of Using Facebook on Perceptions of Other's Lives." *Cyberpsychology, Behavior, and Social Networking* 15 (2): 117–21.

Clayton, Russell B., Alexander Nagurney, and Jessica R. Smith. 2013. "Cheating, Breakup, and Divorce: Is Facebook Use to Blame?" *Cyberpsychology, Behavior, and Social Networking* 16 (10): 717–20.

CNN Wire Staff. 2011. "Florida Eases Penalties for Teen Sexting." *CNN*. October 1. http://www.cnn.com/2011/10/01/us/florida-sexting/.

Coleman, James S. 1988. "Social Capital in the Creation of Human Capital." *American Journal of Sociology* 94 (Suppl): S95–S120.

Conrad, Brent. 2011. "Why Is Facebook Addictive? Twenty-One Reasons for Facebook Addiction." *Tech Addiction.* November. http://www.techaddiction.ca/why-is-facebook-addictive.html.

Constine, Josh. 2014. "Why Is Facebook Page Reach Decreasing? More Competition and Limited Attention." *TechCrunch.* April 3. http://techcrunch.com/2014/04/03/the-filtered-feed-problem/.

Davis, Wendy. 2016. "Pew: People Willing to Disclose Personal Data, but Wary about Its Use." *MediaPost: The Daily Online Examiner.* January 14. http://www.mediapost.com/publications/article/266619/pew-people-willing-to-disclose-personal-data-but.html.

Dayton, Lily. 2015. "Teens' Compulsive Texting Can Cause Neck Injury, Experts Warn." *Los Angeles Times.* April 3. http://www.latimes.com/health/la-he-text-neck-20150404-story.html.

Del Vicario, Michela, Alessandro Bessi, Fabiana Zollo, Fabio Petroni, Antonio Scala, Guido Caldarelli, H. Eugene

Stanley, and Walter Quattrociocchi. 2016. "The Spreading of Misinformation Online." *PNAS* 113 (3): 554–59. http://www.pnas.org/content/113/3/554.full.pdf.

Döring, Nicola. 2002. "Personal Home Pages on the Web: A Review of Research." *Journal of Computer-Mediated Communication* 7 (3).

Dugle, Dawn. 2015. "Hoax! Don't Copy and Paste That 'Copyright' Facebook Message." *USA Today*, January 5. http://www.usatoday.com/story/news/nation-now/2015/01/05/facebook-copyright-protection-scam/21288289/.

EdgeRank Checker. 2014. "Providing Stats & Metrics to the Eat24 Facebook Discussion." *EdgeRank Checker.* April 1. https://www.socialbakers.com/edgerankchecker/blog/2014/04/providing-stats-metrics-to-the-eat24-facebook-discussion/.

Electronic Privacy Information Center. n.d. "Press Kit." *Electronic Privacy Information Center.* https://epic.org/presskit/.

Ellison, Nicole B., Charles Steinfield, and Cliff Lampe. 2007. "The Benefits of Facebook 'Friends': Social Capital and College Students' Use of Online Social Network Sites." *Journal of Computer-Mediated Communication* 12 (4): 1143–68.

Ellison, Nicole, Rebecca Heino, and Jennifer Gibbs. 2006. "Managing Impressions Online: Self-Presentation Processes in the Online Dating Environment." *Journal of Computer-Mediated Communication* 11 (2): 415–41.

Emery, David. 2015. "Zuckerberg Gives Millions to Facebook Users?" *About.com.* December 27. http://urbanlegends.about.com/od/facebook/ss/Zuckerberg-Gives-Millions-to-Facebook-Users-Hoax.htm.

Facebook. 2015. "Statement of Rights and Responsibilities." *Facebook.* January 30. https://www.facebook.com/terms.

Farrell, Maureen. 2015. "Twitter Shares Hit by Takeover Hoax." *The Wall Street Journal.* July 14. http://www.wsj.com/articles/twitter-shares-hit-by-takeover-hoax-1436918683.

Finkelhor, David, Kimberly Mitchell, and Janis Wolak. 2001. "Highlights of the Youth Internet Safety Survey." *OJJDP Fact Sheet.* March. https://www.ncjrs.gov/pdffiles1/ojjdp/fs200104.pdf.

Ford. 2013. "Looking Forward with Ford: 2014 Trends." https://media.ford.com/content/dam/fordmedia/North%20America/US/2013/12/12/Ford_2014_TrendReport.pdf.

The Futures Company. 2014. "2014 Teen Internet Safety Survey." http://www.cox.com/wcm/en/aboutus/datasheet/takecharge/tween-internet-safety-survey.pdf.

Gale, Jason. 2014. "Bedroom-Invading Smartphones Jumble Body's Sleep Rhythms." *Bloomberg Business.* January 7. http://www.bloomberg.com/news/articles/2014-01-07/bedroom-invading-smartphones-jumble-body-s-sleep-rhythms.

Giacobbe, Alyssa. 2014. "Six Ways Social Media Can Ruin Your Life." *Boston Globe.* May 21. https://www.bostonglobe.com/magazine/2014/05/21/ways-social-media-can-ruin-your-life/St8vHIdqCLk7eRsvME3k5K/story.html.

GlobalWebIndex. 2016. "GWI Social Summary: Q3 2016." *GlobalWebIndex.* http://insight.globalwebindex.net/hubfs/GWI-Social-Q3-2016-Summary.pdf.

Goffman, Erving. 1959. *The Presentation of Self in Everyday Life.* New York: Doubleday.

GO-Globe. 2014. "Social Media Addiction: Statistics and Trends." *GO-Globe.* December 26. http://www.go-globe.com/blog/social-media-addiction/.

Gordon, Whitson. 2014. "How to Stop Caring about Trolls and Get On with Your Life." *Lifehacker.* May 16.

http://lifehacker.com/5854053/how-to-stop-caring-about-trolls-and-get-on-with-your-life.

Gottfried, Jeffrey, and Eliza Shearer. 2016. "News Use Across Social Media Platforms 2016." Pew Research Center. May 26. http://www.journalism.org/2016/05/26/news-use-across-social-media-platforms-2016/.

Greitemeyer, Tobias, Dirk O. Mügge, and Irina Bollermann. 2014. "Having Responsive Facebook Friends Affects the Satisfaction of Psychological Needs More than Having Many Facebook Friends." *Basic and Applied Social Psychology* 36 (3): 252–58.

Hall, Alena. 2014. "A Digital Detox Can Change Your Life. Here's What to Know before You Do It." *Huffington Post.* March 7. http://www.huffingtonpost.com/2014/03/07/what-to-expect-from-your-_0_n_4899237.html.

Harvard Medical School. 2012. "Blue Light Has a Dark Side." *Harvard Health Letter.* May 1. http://www.health.harvard.edu/staying-healthy/blue-light-has-a-dark-side.

Havas Worldwide. 2012. "This Digital Life." http://www.slideshare.net/HavasWorldwide/havas-worldwide-this-digital-life-39489236.

Heffernan, Virginia, and Tom Zeller Jr. 2006. "The Lonelygirl That Really Wasn't." *New York Times*, September 13. http://www.nytimes.com/2006/09/13/technology/13lonely.html.

Herring, Susan C., and Sanja Kapidzic. 2015. "Teens, Gender, and Self-Presentation in Social Media." In *International Encyclopedia of Social and Behavioral Sciences*, edited by J. D. Wright. Oxford: Elsevier. http://info.ils.indiana.edu/~herring/teens.gender.pdf.

Hilton, Perez. 2015. "Celebs React to the Heinous Murder of Cecil the Lion." *Perez Hilton.* July 28. http://perezhilton.com/2015-07-28-celebs-twitter-react-cecil-the-lion.

Hodson, Hal. 2015. "Google Wants to Rank Websites Based on Facts Not Links." *New Scientist.* February 28.

https://www.newscientist.com/article/mg22530102.600-google-wants-to-rank-websites-based-on-facts-not-links.

Hogan, Michael. 2015. "Facebook and the 'Fear of Missing Out' (FoMO)." *Psychology Today.* October 14. https://www.psychologytoday.com/blog/in-one-lifespan/201510/facebook-and-the-fear-missing-out-fomo.

Holan, Mark. 2014. "Ice Bucket Challenge Has Raised $220 Million." *Washington Business Journal.* December 12. http://www.bizjournals.com/washington/news/2014/12/12/ice-bucket-challenge-has-raised-220-million.html.

Isaac, Mike. 2016. "Facebook Mounts Effort to Limit Tide of Fake News." *New York Times.* December 15. http://www.nytimes.com/2016/12/15/technology/facebook-fake-news.html.

Ito, Misuko et al. 2010. *Hanging Out, Messing Around, and Geeking Out: Kids Living and Learning with New Media.* Cambridge, MA: MIT Press.

Johnson, Chandra. 2014. "Face Time vs. Screen Time: The Technological Impact on Communication." *Deseret News.* August 29. http://national.deseretnews.com/article/2235/face-time-vs-screen-time-the-technological-impact-on-communication.html.

Jones, Lisa M., Kimberly J. Mitchell, and David Finkelhor. 2012. "Trends in Youth Internet Victimization: Findings from Three Youth Internet Safety Surveys 2000–2010." *Journal of Adolescent Health* 50 (2): 179–86.

Jurgenson, Nathan. 2013. "The Disconnectionists." *The New Inquiry.* November 13. http://thenewinquiry.com/essays/the-disconnectionists/.

Kantrowitz, Alex. 2015. "An Algorithmic Feed May Be Twitter's Last Remaining Card to Play." *BuzzFeed News.* June 29. http://www.buzzfeed.com/alexkantrowitz/an-algorithmic-feed-may-be-twitters-last-remaining-card-to-p#.ojgx2pDRBw.

Kantrowitz, Alex. 2016. "Twitter to Introduce Algorithmic Timeline as soon as Next Week." *BuzzFeed News.* February 5. http://www.buzzfeed.com/alexkantrowitz/twitter-to-introduce-algorithmic-timeline-as-soon-as-next-we.

Kapidzic, Sanja. 2011. "The Influence of Personality and Internalization of Media Ideals on Facebook Image Selection." Indiana University Bloomington. Unpublished Master's thesis.

Karlsson, Anna-Malin. 1998. "Selves, Frames, and Functions of Two Swedish Teenagers' Personal Homepages." Sixth International Pragmatics Conference. Reims, France.

Kaspersky Lab. 2015. "Are You Cyber Savvy?" https://press.kaspersky.com/files/2015/09/Cyber_savvy_quiz_report.pdf.

Katz, Elihu, Jay G. Blumler, and Michael Gurevitch. 1973–1974. "Uses and Gratifications Research." *Public Opinion Quarterly* 37 (4): 509–23.

Kelly, Heather. 2013. "The Power of One Wrong Tweet." *CNN.* April 24. http://www.cnn.com/2013/04/23/tech/social-media/tweet-ripple-effect/.

Kerkhof, Peter, Catrin Finkenauer, and Linda D. Muusses. 2011. "Relational Consequences of Compulsive Internet Use: A Longitudinal Study among Newlyweds." *Human Communication Research* 37 (2): 147–73.

Klinenberg, Eric. 2013. *Going Solo: The Extraordinary Rise and Surprising Appeal of Living Alone.* New York City: Penguin Books.

Kramer, Adam D.I., Jamie E. Guillory, and Jeffrey T. Hancock. 2014. "Experimental Evidence of Massive-Scale Emotional Contagion through Social Networks." *PNAS* 111 (24): 8788–90.

Krasnova, Hanna, Helena Wenninger, Thomas Widjaja, and Peter Buxmann. 2013. "Envy on Facebook: A Hidden Threat to Users' Life Satisfaction?" Wirtschaftsinformatik

Proceedings 2013. http://www.wi2013.de/proceedings/WI2013%20-%20Track%2011%20-%20Krasnova.pdf.

Kraut, Robert, Michael Patterson, Vicki Lundmark, Sara Kiesler, Tridas Mukopadhyay, and William Scherlis. 1998. "Internet Paradox: A Social Technology That Reduces Social Involvement and Psychological Well-Being?" *American Psychology* 53 (9): 1017–31. http://www.ncbi.nlm.nih.gov/pubmed/9841579.

Kristof, Kathy. 2013. "Impostor Scam Cons Your Facebook Friends." *CBS News.* December 26. http://www.cbsnews.com/news/imposter-scam-cons-your-facebook-friends/.

Kross, Ethan, Philippe Verduyn, Emre Demiralp, David Seungiae Lee, Natalie Lin, Holly Shablack, John Jonides, and Oscar Ybarra. 2013. "Facebook Use Predicts Declines in Subjective Well-Being in Young Adults." *PLoS ONE* 8 (8). http://journals.plos.org/plosone/article?id=10.1371/journal.pone.0069841.

Levenson, Jessica C., Ariel Shensa, Jaime E. Sidani, Jason B. Colditz, and Brian A. Primack. 2016. "The Association between Social Media Use and Sleep Disturbance among Young Adults." *Preventive Medicine* 85 (April): 36–41.

Lin, Ruoyun, and Sonja Utz. 2015. "The Emotional Responses of Browsing Facebook: Happiness, Envy, and the Role of Tie Strength." *Computers in Human Behavior* 52: 29–38.

Luckerson, Victor. 2014. "Fear, Misinformation, and Social Media Complicate Ebola Fight." *Time.* October 8. http://time.com/3479254/ebola-social-media/.

Madden, Mary, Amanda Lenhart, Sandra Cortesi, Urs Gasser, Maeve Duggan, Aaron Smith, and Meredith Beaton. 2013. "Teens, Social Media, and Privacy." *Pew Research Center.* http://www.pewinternet.org/2015/04/09/teens-social-media-technology-2015/.

Mahoney, Sean. 2015. "Child Predator Social Experiment by Cody Person Reveals 'Dangers of Social Media.'" *Inquisitr.*

August 12. http://www.inquisitr.com/2331071/child-predator-social-experiment-by-coby-persin-reveals-dangers-of-social-media/.

Marche, Stephen. 2012. "Is Facebook Making Us Lonely?" *The Atlantic.* May. http://www.theatlantic.com/magazine/archive/2012/05/is-facebook-making-us-lonely/308930/.

McCullagh, Declan. 2012. "Instagram Says It Now Has the Right to Sell Your Photos." *CNET.* December 17. https://www.cnet.com/news/instagram-says-it-now-has-the-right-to-sell-your-photos/.

National Conference of State Legislators. 2016. "State Social Media Privacy Laws." *National Conference of State Legislators.* July 6. http://www.ncsl.org/research/telecommunications-and-information-technology/state-laws-prohibiting-access-to-social-media-usernames-and-passwords.aspx.

National Labor Relations Board. n.d. "The NLRB and Social Media." *National Labor Relations Board.* https://www.nlrb.gov/news-outreach/fact-sheets/nlrb-and-social-media.

Nunez, Michael. 2016. "Former Facebook Workers: We Routinely Suppressed Conservative News." *Gizmodo.* May 9. http://gizmodo.com/former-facebook-workers-we-routinely-suppressed-conser-1775461006.

Online Threat Alerts. 2015. "Facebook Scam: 'Get a $100 Target Coupon' or 'Target Is Giving Away $100 in Coupons'." *Online Threat Alerts.* February 18. https://www.onlinethreatalerts.com/article/2015/2/18/facebook-scam-get-a-100-target-coupon-or-target-is-giving-away-100-in-coupons/.

Oremus, Will. 2015. "Facebook Is Cracking Down on Viral Hoaxes. Really." *Slate.* January 20. http://www.slate.com/blogs/future_tense/2015/01/20/facebook_hoaxes_news_feed_changes_will_limit_false_news_stories.html.

Oremus, Will. 2016. "Who Controls Your Facebook News Feed?" *Slate.* January 3. http://www.slate.com/articles/

technology/cover_story/2016/01/how_facebook_s_news_feed_algorithm_works.html.

Pasierbinska-Wilson, Zuzanna. 2015. "The History of Data Privacy in Social Data and Its Milestones." *DataSift Blog.* February 26. http://blog.datasift.com/2015/02/26/the-history-of-data-privacy-in-social-data-and-its-milestones/.

Pasquale, Frank. 2015. "We're Being Stigmatized by 'Big Data' Scores We Don't Even Know About." *Los Angeles Times.* January 15. http://www.latimes.com/opinion/op-ed/la-oe-0116-pasquale-reputation-repair-digital-history-20150116-story.html.

Patterson, George M. 2014. "NLRB Continues Aggressive Crackdown on Social Media Policies." *National Law Review.* September 3. http://www.natlawreview.com/article/nlrb-continues-aggressive-crackdown-social-media-policies.

Phippen, Weston. 2013. "15-Year-Old St. Pete Girl Charged with Stalking in Cyberbullying Case." *Tampa Bay Times.* November 7. http://www.tampabay.com/news/public safety/crime/15-year-old-st-pete-girl-charged-with-stalking-in-cyber-bullying-case/2151342.

Pierce, Tamyra. 2009. "Social Anxiety and Technology: Face-to-Face Communication versus Technological Communication among Teens." *Computers in Human Behavior* 25 (6): 1367–72.

Pontin, Jason. 2011. "What Actually Happened: Did Social Media Matter in the Arab Spring? We Sent a Reporter to Ask the Revolutionaries." *Technology Review.* August 23. http://www.technologyreview.com/fromtheeditor/425124/what-actually-happened/.

Przybylski, Andrew K., Kou Murayama, Cody D. DeHaan, and Valerie Gladwell. 2013. "Motivational, Emotional, and

Behavioral Correlates of Fear of Missing Out." *Computers in Human Behavior* 29 (4): 1841–48.

Rainie, Lee, Aaron Smith, and Maeve Dugan. 2013. "Coming and Going on Facebook." *Pew Internet & American Life Project.* February 5. http://www.pewinternet.org/2013/02/05/coming-and-going-on-facebook/.

Regan, Helen. 2015. "Cecil the Lion, Walter Palmer and the Psychology of Online Shaming." *Time.* July 30. http://time.com/3978216/online-shaming-social-media-walter-palmer-cecil-lion/.

Relph, Mridu Khullar. 2012. "Why Is Facebook So Hard to Quit?" *Brain World Magazine.* September 9. http://brainworldmagazine.com/why-is-facebook-so-hard-to-quit/.

Rideout, Victoria. 2012. "Social Media, Social Life: How Teens View Their Digital Lives." *Common Sense Media.* https://www.commonsensemedia.org/file/socialmediasociallife-final-061812pdf-0.

Rideout, Victoria. 2015. "The Common Sense Census: Media Use by Tweens and Teens." *Common Sense.* https://www.commonsensemedia.org/sites/default/files/uploads/research/census_executivesummary.pdf.

Roberts, John Jeff. 2015. "Who Owns Your Face? Weak Laws Give Power to Facebook." *Fortune.* June 17. http://fortune.com/2015/06/17/facebook-moments-privacy-facial-recognition/.

Rock, David. 2012. "Your Brain on Facebook." *Harvard Business Review.* May 18. https://hbr.org/2012/05/your-brain-on-facebook/.

Roesler, Peter. 2014. "Six Ways Social Media Changed the World." *Inc.*, November 17. http://www.inc.com/peter-roesler/6-ways-social-media-changed-the-world.html.

Ronson, Jon. 2015. "How One Stupid Tweet Blew Up Justine Sacco's Life." *New York Times.* February 12. http://www.ny

times.com/2015/02/15/magazine/how-one-stupid-tweet-ruined-justine-saccos-life.html.

Ryan, Tracii, and Sophia Xenos. 2011. "Who Uses Facebook? An Investigation into the Relationship between the Big Five, Shyness, Narcissism, Loneliness, and Facebook Usage." *Computers in Human Behavior* 27 (5): 1658–64.

Sagioglou, Christina, and Tobias Greitemeyer. 2014. "Facebook's Emotional Consequences: Why Facebook Causes a Decrease in Mood and Why People Still Use It." *Computers in Human Behavior* 35: 359–63.

Sameen, Sara, and Samia Cornelius. 2015. "Social Networking Sites and Hiring: How Social Media Profiles Influence Hiring Decisions." *Journal of Business Studies Quarterly* 7 (1): 27–35.

Sass, Erik. 2016. "Six in Ten Parents Have Checked Kids' Social Media Profiles." *Social Media & Marketing Daily.* January 7. http://www.mediapost.com/publications/article/266160/six-in-ten-parents-have-checked-kids-social-media.html.

Schau, Hope Jensen, and Mary C. Gilly. 2003. "We Are What We Post? Self-Presentation on Personal Web Space." *Journal of Computer Research* 30 (3): 385–404.

Schmidt, Gordon B., and Kimberly W. O'Connor. 2015. "Fired for Facebook: Using NLRB Guidance to Craft Appropriate Social Media Policies." *Business Horizons* 58 (5): 571–79.

Sherman, Lauren E., Minas Michikyan, and Patricia M. Greenfield. 2013. "The Effects of Text, Audio, Video, and In-Person Communication on Bonding between Friends." *Cyberpsychology: Journal of Psychosocial Research on Cyberspace* 7 (2): article 3. http://www.cdmc.ucla.edu/PG_Media_biblio_files/Sherman%20et%20al.pdf.

Silverman, Craig, and Lawrence Alexander. 2016. "How Teens in the Balkans are Duping Trump Supporters with

Fake News." *BuzzFeed.* November 3. https://www.buzzfeed.com/craigsilverman/how-macedonia-became-a-global-hub-for-pro-trump-misinfo.

Smith, Ethan, and Peter Lattman. 2007. "Download This: YouTube Phenom Has a Big Secret." *The Wall Street Journal.* September 6.

Society for Human Resource Management. 2012. "An Examination of How Social Media Is Embedded in Business Strategy and Operations." https://www.shrm.org/hr-today/trends-and-forecasting/research-and-surveys/pages/2anexaminationofhowsocialmediaisembeddedinbusinessstrategyandoperationssurveyfindings.aspx.

Society for Human Resource Management. 2016. "Using Social Media for Talent Acquisition—Recruitment and Screening." https://www.shrm.org/hr-today/trends-and-forecasting/research-and-surveys/Documents/SHRM-Social-Media-Recruiting-Screening-2015.pdf.

Starbird, Kate, Jim Maddock, Mania Orand, Peg Achterman, and Robert M. Mason. 2014. "Rumors, False Flags, and Digital Vigilantes: Misinformation on Twitter after the 2013 Boston Marathon Bombing." *iConference 2014.* Berlin, Germany. http://faculty.washington.edu/kstarbi/Starbird_iConference2014-final.pdf.

Stewart, James B. 2016. "Facebook Has 50 Minutes of Your Time Each Day. It Wants More." *New York Times.* May 5. http://www.nytimes.com/2016/05/06/business/facebook-bends-the-rules-of-audience-engagement-to-its-advantage.html.

Tandoc, Edson, Patrick Ferucci, and Margaret Duffy. 2014. "Facebook Use, Envy, and Depression among College Students: Is Facebooking Depressing?" *Computers in Human Behavior* 43: 139–46.

Teppers, Eveline, Koen Luyckx, Theo A. Klimstra, and Luc Goossens. 2014. "Loneliness and Facebook Motives in

Adolescence: A Longitudinal Inquiry into Directionality of Effect." *Journal of Adolescence* 37 (5): 691–99.

Thurston, Baratunde. 2013. "#Unplug: Baratunde Thurston Left the Internet for 25 Days, and You Should, Too." *Fast Company.* June 17. http://www.fastcompany.com/3012521/unplug/baratunde-thurston-leaves-the-internet.

Toma, Catalina L., and Jeffrey T. Hancock. 2013. "Self-Affirmation Underlies Facebook Use." *Personality and Social Psychology Bulletin* 39 (3): 321–31.

Towner, Myriah, and James Nye. 2015. "Medical Exec Who Was Fired Three Years Ago Over Video of Him Berating Chick-fil-A Staff Is Still Unemployed and on Food Stamps." *Daily Mail.* March 26. http://www.dailymail.co.uk/news/article-3013044/Ex-CFO-father-four-food-stamps-looking-job-viral-video-protesting-Chick-fil-left-unemployed.html.

Turkle, Sherry. 2011. *Alone Together: Why We Expect More from Technology and Less from Each Other.* New York: Basic Books.

Uhls, Yalda T., Minas Michikyan, Jordan Morris, Debra Garcia, Gary W. Small, Eleni Zgourou, and Patricia M. Greenfield. 2014. "Five Days at Outdoor Education Camp without Screens Improves Preteen Skills with Nonverbal Emotion Cues." *Computers in Human Behavior* 39: 387–92.

U.S. Equal Employment Opportunity Commission. 2014. "Social Media Is Part of Today's Workplace but Its Use May Raise Employment Discrimination Concerns." *U.S. Equal Employment Opportunity Commission.* March 12. http://www.eeoc.gov/eeoc/newsroom/release/3-12-14.cfm.

Verduyn, Philippe, David Seungjae Lee, Jiyoung Park, Holly Shablack, Ariana Orvell, Joseph Bayer, Oscar Ybarra, John Jonides, and Ethan Kross. 2015. "Passive Facebook Usage Undermines Affective Well-Being: Experimental and Longitudinal Evidence." *Journal of Experimental Psychology* 144 (2): 480–88.

Vitak, Jessica, Julia Crouse, and Robert LaRose. 2009. "Personal Internet Use at Work: Understanding Cyberslacking." *Computers in Human Behavior* 27 (5): 1751–59.

Wachter, Heidi. 2015. "Digital Detox." *Experience Life*. January/February. https://experiencelife.com/article/digital-detox/.

Wagner, Kurt. 2015. "Snapchat Is Making Some Pretty Serious Money from Live Stories." *Recode*. July 17. http://recode.net/2015/06/17/snapchats-making-some-pretty-serious-money-from-live-stories/.

Waugh, Bob, and Tamara Cohen. 2012. "Now Twitter Admits 'Harvesting' Users' Phone Contacts without Telling the Owners as Apple Announces Crackdown." *Daily Mail*. February 16. http://www.dailymail.co.uk/sciencetech/article-2101934/Apple-moves-stop-Facebook-Twitter-accessing-iPhone-users-address-books-permission.html.

West, Lindy. 2015. "What Happened When I Confronted My Cruellest Troll." *The Guardian*. February 2. http://www.theguardian.com/society/2015/feb/02/what-happened-confronted-cruellest-troll-lindy-west.

WNYC. 2015. *The Case for Boredom*. January 12. http://www.wnyc.org/story/bored-brilliant-project-part-1/.

Zetter, Kim. 2009. "Judge Acquits Lori Drew in Cyberbullying Case, Overrules Jury." *Wired*. July 2. https://www.wired.com/2009/07/drew_court/.

Zhang, Cheng, and Si Chen. 2016. "News Feed FYI: Using Qualitative Feedback to Show Relevant Stories." *Facebook*. February 1. http://newsroom.fb.com/news/2016/02/news-feed-fyi-using-qualitative-feedback-to-show-relevant-stories/.

Introduction

The essays in this chapter authored by communication scholars and professionals provide a range of perspectives on social media. The issues covered explore societal topics including the impact of social media on young women's perceptions of their bodies and how social media both helps and hurts victims of sexual assault. Corporate concerns are also covered in essays about online corporate activism on issues such as lesbian, gay, bisexual, and transgender (LGBT) rights, the practice of social media data collection, and how social media both create crises for organizations and can be used for the purpose of organizational crisis communication. Finally, the essays also cover the role of social media in political campaigns, how social media suppress the minority opinion, and the practice of live tweeting during popular television shows. The authors provide insights that encourage readers to think about the issues and often propose solutions to the problems presented.

The Female Body on Social Media

Petya Eckler and Yusuf Kalyango Jr.

Today's teenagers and young adults have grown up with social media and often lead the way in using new digital platforms for

---

Actors Brett Davern and Beau Mirchoff attend the *Awkward* live tweet event at The Microsoft Lounge in Venice, California. Social media allow celebrities to engage with fans and build online followings. (Photo by Casey Rodgers/Invision for Microsoft/AP Photo)

communication. Indeed, of U.S. online users, 18- to 29-year-olds are on Facebook, Twitter, Instagram, and Pinterest in the largest proportion among all age groups, according to the Pew Research Center, and have adopted these platforms faster than others (Perrin 2015). Teenagers, on the other hand, are online daily, and some "almost constantly," primarily via mobile devices, says another Pew report (Lenhart 2015). This constant connectedness via social media has been both lauded and scorned by parents, academics, and experts, but despite the vast differences in opinion, one thing is certain: social media do affect the attitudes, behaviors, and relationships of many young people. One type of impact is on body image.

Body image encompasses the thoughts, feelings, and behaviors about one's physical shape, size, and appearance. It goes beyond how people feel about themselves and often affects how they behave toward their bodies. For example, poor body image is a stronger trigger of disordered eating than actual weight among college women (Cooley and Toray 2001) and is a risk factor for low self-esteem, depressive symptoms, eating disorders, and obesity (Grabe, Ward, and Hyde 2008). Body image can affect many aspects of a young person's life and therefore is important to be studied further, especially in relation to social media.

The link between social media and body image is still being explored but some trends are starting to occur. More time spent on Facebook has been linked to increased drive for thinness, internalization of the thin ideal, dissatisfaction with one's weight, and signs of disordered eating (Mabe, Forney, and Keel 2014; Tiggemann and Slater 2013). Some specific behaviors, such as photo-related activities, have been singled out for their negative consequences, although the relationship cannot point to definite cause and effect (Meier and Gray 2014).

Furthermore, users with particular physical or psychological attributes have different experiences. Our research has found that college women wanting to lose weight pay more attention to the physical appearance of others on Facebook and experience more negative body attitudes than women who do not want to lose weight (Eckler, Kalyango, and Paasch 2014). Women who tend to make more appearance comparisons, on the other hand, experience greater appearance discrepancies after spending time on Facebook (Fardouly and Vartanian 2015).

Thus, we know that spending more time on social media could be harmful to some. However, the reasons for this are yet unknown. A recent study the authors conducted on U.S. college women looked into the body-related content they posted on Facebook as a way to better understand the above relationship. Of the 882 participants, 111 (12.6 percent) said they had posted on their News Feeds about weight, body image, dieting, or weight loss in the past month. They made four such updates on average, ranging from 1 to 30, which shows a great difference in willingness to discuss such topics.

Women disclosed the contents of their last post and of a typical post, and their answers (total of 188) were analyzed qualitatively and several dominant themes emerged. For last and typical posts, exercise was the most dominant theme and covered primarily the practice of exercising ("how much I have exercised" or "working out at the gym"). Two other themes were equally present: weight loss and food/diet. The majority of comments about weight loss concerned outcomes or success, such as "how much weight I lost," "updates on weight loss," "could fit into a smaller size pants," or simply "losing weight." Other comments, although not as common, concerned the desire for weight loss, such as "needing to lose weight" and "thinking about losing weight." Common subthemes in the food/diet theme were healthy food alternatives ("trying a new healthy meal recipe") or starting a diet.

Body image was the final theme to emerge. Some women talked about negative perceptions of their bodies and how they wanted to look differently: "feeling huge," "I wish I was confident in my body," "how I wish I was taller," "I feel too skinny," "being too tall," and "I wish I was thinner or prettier."

Others used this platform to send empowering and positive messages, such as "I believe I look good," "my dress emphasized by curves," and "bigger being better." Overall, however, negative messages outweighed positive ones and the majority of the negative messages across all themes were concentrated in the body image theme. Messages about exercise, weight loss, and diet were primarily neutral in tone.

We concluded from our study that few women posted body-related updates on Facebook and most of them did so with a neutral tone and focused on exercise, weight loss, or dieting. But few women did post about body image and the majority of what they disclosed was negative. The small overall share of these negative body image posts may be reassuring to some, but we have reasons to believe that the predominance and influence of such communication over Facebook is larger than this initial study can attest. First, we have analyzed here only the responses of women who said they posted on their own timelines (12.6 percent of the overall sample). But another 27.4 percent had commented on friends' posts or photos on the same issues, which shows an additional communication stream about these topics. Furthermore, posts and comments on Facebook do not have to be about weight or shape to affect body image, as other research has shown that women who write status updates about their personal lives (unrelated to appearance or weight) and receive extremely negative comments are more likely to have concerns about their shape, weight, and eating (Hummel and Smith 2015).

What female Facebook users can take from all this is the knowledge that negative comments they write to others, even if unrelated to their appearance, may hurt their friends' body image. Also, the very amount of time they spend on Facebook may affect their own body image negatively and may push them into more comparisons with others. Social media offer access to more friends, more photos, and more updates, and comparisons are often the mechanism through which Facebook exerts its influence. Awareness of that may be helpful in reducing somewhat the urge to compare to others. Finally, it is important to realize that many users carefully manage their presentations online and often create ideal images of themselves, which is far from their real selves (Gonzales and Hancock 2011; Goodings and Tucker 2014). This could be one reason why so few female social media users post updates on body-related issues, when we know that these are highly relevant to many of them. Knowing this may push women into questioning the realism and veracity of the content they see on social media and thus guard them against false comparisons to others and extreme expectations from themselves.

References

Cooley, Eric, and Tamina Toray. 2001. "Body Image and Personality Predictors of Eating Disorder Symptoms during the College Years." *International Journal of Eating Disorders* 30 (1): 28–36.

Eckler, Petya, Yusuf Kalyango Jr., and Ellen Paasch. 2014. "Facebook and College Women's Bodies: Social Media's Influence on Body Image and Disordered Eating." Paper presented at the annual meeting of the International Communication Association, Seattle, Washington, May 22–26.

Fardouly, Jasmine, and Lenny R. Vartanian. 2015. "Negative Comparisons about One's Appearance Mediate the Relationship between Facebook Usage and Body Image Concerns." *Body Image* 12: 82–88.

Gonzales, Amy L., and Jeffrey T. Hancock. 2011. "Mirror, Mirror on My Facebook Wall: Effects of Exposure to Facebook on Self–Esteem." *Cyberpsychology, Behavior, and Social Networking* 14 (1–2): 9–83.

Goodings, Lewis, and Ian Tucker. 2014. "Social Media and the Co-Production of Bodies Online: Bergson, Serres, and Facebook's Timeline." *Media, Culture & Society* 36 (1): 37–51.

Grabe, Shelly, L. Monique Ward, and Janet Shibley Hyde. 2008. "The Role of the Media in Body Image Concerns among Women: A Meta-Analysis of Experimental and Correlational Studies." *Psychological Bulletin* 134 (3): 460–76.

Hummel, Alexandra C., and April R. Smith. 2015. "Ask and You Shall Receive: Desire and Receipt of Feedback via Facebook Predicts Disordered Eating Concerns." *International Journal of Eating Disorders* 48 (4): 436–42.

Lenhart, Amanda. 2015. "Teens, Social Media & Technology: Overview 2015." *Pew Research Center.* April 9. http://www.pewinternet.org/2015/04/09/teens-social-media-technology-2015/.

Mabe, Annalise G., K. Jean Forney, and Pamela K. Keel. 2014. "Do You 'Like' My Photo? Facebook Use Maintains Eating Disorder Risk." *International Journal of Eating Disorders* 47 (5): 516–23.

Meier, Evelyn P, and James Gray. 2014. "Facebook Photo Activity Associated with Body Image Disturbance in Adolescent Girls." *Cyberpsychology, Behavior, and Social Networking* 17 (4): 199–206.

Perrin, Andrew. 2015. "Social Media Usage: 2005–2015." *Pew Research Center*. October 8. http://www.pewinternet.org/2015/10/08/social-networking-usage-2005-2015/.

Tiggemann, Marika, and Amy Slater. 2013. "NetGirls: The Internet, Facebook, and Body Image Concern in Adolescent Girls." *International Journal of Eating Disorders* 46 (6): 630–33.

Petya Eckler, PhD, is a lecturer in journalism at University of Strathclyde in Glasgow. She studies social media and health communication with a recent focus on body image. Eckler's professional experience includes working as an assistant editor, managing editor, health writer, reporter, copy editor, and public relations coordinator in the United States and Bulgaria.

Yusuf Kalyango Jr., PhD, is professor and director of the Institute for International Journalism in the E. W. Scripps School of Journalism at Ohio University. He has published the books Global Journalism Practice & New Media Performance *(2015),* Why Discourse Matters *(2014), and* African Media and Democratization *(2011) and serves as editor of the* International Communication Research Journal.

Exploring Victimization in the Digital Age: Perspectives on Social Media and Sexual Assault

Rowena Briones Winkler

In recent years, the issue of sexual assault (SA) has come to the forefront due to the power of social media. Nonprofit organizations, politicians, activists, and survivors alike have harnessed these technologies to help spread the word and increase awareness of this issue that continues to pervade and challenge our society on a daily basis. With this said, it is imperative to explore how social media are used to communicate about a serious issue that is in need of more awareness, mobilization, and action. Therefore, this essay aims to describe social media communication surrounding SA from a variety of different perspectives. By exploring the social media conversation surrounding SA, an often taboo and stigmatized topic, this essay can provide much needed insight on how to handle prevention efforts and victim support, as well as how social media communication can be used to address social issues like SA in the future.

One way that social media has allowed activists to build online dialogue is through hashtags, which are defined as tags or identifiers that help to categorize conversations (Stache 2014). For SA in particular, this tactic has mostly been used via Twitter as depicted by several recent examples:

- The #yesallwomen hashtag shared stories of women who were ignored by law enforcement and school administrators when they sought help after being assaulted to discuss violence against women and the unfair sexual expectations directed at women. The woman who created the hashtag, however, was forced to shut down her personal Twitter account after being harassed violently on the site.

- Christine Fox asked "What were you wearing when you were assaulted?" on Twitter in response to the victim-blaming around suggestive clothing that typically occurs after an assault. Following the activity on Twitter, artist Adrienne Simpson created a series of images that more visually displayed the tweets and added the hashtag #RapeHasNoUniform, which was frequently shared.
- Hannah Giorgis created the #WhyIDidntReport hashtag to offer individuals an outlet to share stories as to why they remained silent after being assaulted. Within several days, Giorgis received over 15,000 tweets in response to the hashtag, along with over 600 anonymous stories that were shared on Tumblr (Giorgis 2014).
- Wagatwe Wanjuki created the hashtag #survivorprivilege in response to *Washington Post* columnist George Will's opinion piece that sparked major backlash for calling rape a "supposed campus epidemic" and tagging rape victims as a "coveted status" on college campuses (Will 2014, 1). Many survivors angry with the piece participated in the hashtag, arguing that there is nothing privileged about life after rape.

Not surprisingly, anti-rape social media efforts have particularly strong roots within the college campus community. With 94 percent of first-year college students using social media sites (Tunheim 2012), several campaigns were developed by student-led efforts to hold schools accountable for victim advocacy and support. Due to their ease with technology and social media in particular, rapid collaborations have taken place both within and between college campuses, allowing messages to spread quickly to create an anti-rape movement throughout the nation. Two examples are The IX Network, a private Facebook group created to provide solidarity for victims, and Know Your IX, a group that provides assistance for students who want to file federal complaints and put pressure on university leaders. Faculty members have also gotten involved, participating in online-based organizations such as Faculty against Rape.

With hashtag campaigns and online advocacy groups emerging in response to the rape epidemic, there are definitely benefits to increasing awareness of this issue via social media. However, there are complications and negative consequences to consider as well, otherwise known as the "horrific Catch-22 of rape in the Internet age" (Friedman 2013, 1). Even though there is more willingness to confront SA head-on via social media, a question remains: *Is this a healthy step in recovery for victims in particular, or does it only perpetuate online shaming and undermine the therapy process?* For many victims, the harassment and social stigma surrounding the aftermath of the experience are difficult to endure. Several cases explicate this: 17-year-old Rehtaeh Parsons, who took her own life after photos of her rape circulated at Cole Harbour High School in Nova Scotia; 15-year-old Audrie Pott, who killed herself only eight days after Facebook photos of her naked body were circulated throughout her social circle; and 16-year-old Daisy Coleman, who attempted suicide after accusations of being a slut were spread on Facebook following a party—one of the only times she went out after being raped by a football player two years prior to the incident.

These cases, among many others, illustrate how the bystander effect can play a role with social media and accounts of SA. According to Darley and Latané (1968), the bystander effect refers to the notion that the more individuals are present in a distressing situation, the less likely one single person will stop to help the person in need. Some argue that this very phenomenon is occurring when it comes to rape cases spread on social media; oftentimes, students who are forwarded photos are too scared to speak up in fear of judgment from peers, or that they too will be cyberbullied. Even more troubling, friends of the victim also fail to report a problem out of a misguided respect for the victim, believing that the victim would just want to forget about the assault and move on. Thus, the bystander effect, along with the catch-22 of social media and SA, paints a very complex picture for all parties involved. For the first time in years, what has been traditionally recognized as an intensely private issue is suddenly becoming increasingly more public. As Friedman (2013, 1) states:

> Now that cases regularly crop up in which photos and videos of sexual assaults are circulated on social media, it's becoming harder to argue that rape is anything but a public scourge. We are all bystanders . . . when we see photos and videos of a teen girl's body or of a high school boy bragging about taking advantage of her, this reality is thrown into stark relief. And when we see ordinary kids engaged in extraordinarily terrible behavior, we don't always look away. Often, we click "share."

All hope is not lost, however. With the increasing awareness of these issues also comes a stronger fight against rape culture, both online and offline.

References

Darley, John M., and B. Bibb Latané. 1968. "Bystander Intervention in Emergencies: Diffusion of Responsibility." *Journal of Personality and Social Psychology* 8 (4, Pt.1): 377–83.

Friedman, Ann. 2013. "When Rape Goes Viral." *Newsweek.* July 24. http://www.newsweek.com/2013/07/24/when-rape-goes-viral-237742.html.

Giorgis, Hannah. 2014. "My Body Is More Than a Crime Scene: #WhyIDidntReport and What I Learned from Talking about It." http://www.youngist.org/why-I-didnt-report.

Stache, Lara C. 2015. "Advocacy and Political Potential at the Convergence of Hashtag Activism and Commerce." *Feminist Media Studies* 15 (1): 162–64.

Tunheim. 2012 "How College Students Use Social Media." *Tunheim Blog.* March 9. http://blog.tunheim.com/2012/03/09/how-college-students-use-social-media/129.

Will, George F. 2014. "George Will: Colleges Become the Victims of Progressivism." *Washington Post.* June 6. https://www.washingtonpost.com/opinions/george-will-college-become-the-victims-of-progressivism/2014/06/06/e90e73b4-eb50-11e3-9f5c-9075d5508f0a_story.html.

Rowena Briones Winkler, PhD, is the managing director of the Oral Communication Program in the Department of Communication at the University of Maryland. Her research agenda explores how digital media impact public relations and health contexts, particularly in the areas of social justice, crisis communication, and risk communication.

Posting, Sharing, and Tweeting a Brand's Politics: Social Media and the Recent Evolution of Online Corporate Activism

Nathan Gilkerson

In the short decade since the dramatic rise of social media platforms such as Facebook and Twitter, companies have evolved from primarily using these tools for basic marketing and public relations purposes, such as communicating sales and promotions to customers, to an environment in which brands and corporate CEOs have become online participants in the national political dialogue of the day. Although once a practice most companies strived to avoid, more and more corporations have now begun to strategically engage in online political activism, often as a viable method for strengthening customer relationships, building corporate reputation, and improving internal and external relations. In fact, many consumers now expect brands to use social media to "weigh in" on and show visible support (or opposition) toward certain hot-button political issues, such as gay marriage. Some social media users today are quick to pressure companies to take a stand and join their cause, publicly calling out organizations that remain neutral. In particular, Twitter has become a popular venue for companies to express support for political causes.

Recent headlines have highlighted several high-profile examples of this trend, with mixed results for companies willing to use social media to wade into the political debate. Several corporate CEOs utilized social media to express concern and condemn legislation passed in Indiana in 2015 that made it legal for businesses in the state to deny services to gay, lesbian, and transgender individuals based on religious beliefs. In response to the law's passage, Marc Benioff, CEO of the cloud computing company Salesforce.com, announced on Twitter that his company was reducing its investments in Indiana and would be canceling events requiring employees to travel to the state, tweeting, "Today we are canceling all programs that require our customers/employees to travel to Indiana to face discrimination" (Barbaro and Eckholm 2015). Surrounding the 2014 protests and civil unrest in Ferguson, Missouri, Starbucks CEO Howard Schultz initiated a short-lived companywide campaign intended to promote candid conversations about race in the United States through the hashtag #RaceTogether (Sanders 2015). Although the Starbucks effort was widely criticized by business and social commentators as being tone-deaf and superficial, many also applauded the company's initiative to engage its customers on such a hot-button topic. Around the same time, Twitter itself took a political stance and made headlines in both social and traditional media by prominently painting the hashtag #BlackLivesMatter on an office wall of its San Francisco headquarters. Including a photo of the painting, one Twitter employee proudly tweeted to her followers, "Honored to work for a company like this. Truly" (Mandaro 2014).

While it has become more common for companies to use social media to comment on political and social issues, it seems some topics are viewed as safer to engage in than others. Although a few brands spoke out on race issues during the height of the Ferguson protests, or more recently, during the summer of 2015 debate over removal of the Confederate flag in Southern state capitals, a long list of companies quickly took to social media to show their support for the historic June 2015 decision by the U.S. Supreme Court regarding the legality of gay marriage. Using trending hashtags such as #MarriageEquality and #LoveWins, major corporate Twitter accounts including brands like Ben & Jerry's, Gap, Visa, and American Airlines posted images and messages to convey their support for the controversial court decision (Griswold 2015).

Beginning around 2012, a number of companies began publicly voicing either support or opposition in the political debate over gay marriage. Among the earlier most noteworthy examples, several Fortune 500 companies including Amazon, Starbucks, Microsoft, and Nike formally supported legislation legalizing same-sex marriage in Washington state. Alternately, the family-owned fast-food chain Chick-fil-A, which closes its locations on Sundays and is known for its CEO's strongly held Christian beliefs, gained national media attention and online notoriety by using the company's charitable organization to contribute millions of dollars to conservative groups opposing gay marriage (Webley 2012). Consumers across the political spectrum have taken to social media to express outrage and call for boycotts against companies that have conveyed political stances they oppose. As just one example, some Facebook users called for a boycott against Oreo when the brand posted a photo featuring a rainbow-colored cookie on its Facebook page in an effort to highlight and show support for LGBT Pride Month (Webley 2012).

Despite the risk of angering and alienating some consumers, recent industry and academic research has supported the notion that corporate involvement in politics can be a winning business strategy. Academic research in the field of public relations has formally conceptualized this activity as "corporate social advocacy" and positioned the approach between two other traditional areas of public relations practice: issues management and corporate social responsibility efforts (Dodd and Supa 2014). Strategic issues management within public relations can be thought of as the proactive monitoring of and responding to issues (and critics or opponents, etc.) that can affect the success or operations of an organization. Alternatively, corporate social responsibility activities are voluntary actions taken by a company that are not specifically concerned with maximizing profits, but instead are more focused on benefiting society, such as efforts to help employees, the environment, or the local community. Corporate social advocacy, Dodd and Supa argue, specifically "refers to an organization making a public statement or taking a public stance on social-political issues" (2014, 5) and can occur either in the form of a planned, intentional communication issued from a company—such as a formal announcement of corporate support for a cause or certain legislation on Twitter or Facebook—or through a less intended or planned action, such as a remark made by a CEO to a journalist during an interview or to a crowd at a public event.

Dodd and Supa (2014) explored the dynamics of consumer reactions to corporate social advocacy, using experimental research to test the shifts in "purchase intentions" among study participants exposed to information about organizational advocacy efforts. Gauging both the participants' political attitudes and their self-expressed intention to purchase products or services from the companies described in the experiment, the researchers found that subjects who were in agreement with a company's stated political stance were significantly more likely to express purchase intent toward that company and, alternately, that lesser subject agreement with a company's political position resulted in a reduction in stated purchase intent. Put another way, the researchers found evidence that consumers do care about the political positions taken by a company, and reward those companies they agree with by giving them their business, while avoiding doing business with organizations espousing politics they disagree with.

Research indicates that not only do many consumers consider a company's politics, but also many of today's consumers are in fact *expecting* political involvement from the corporate sphere. A 2014 study published by Global Strategy Group, a U.S. public affairs and research firm, also examined the dynamics of corporate involvement in politics and the potential impact on business and reputation. Surveying a U.S. adult population, the research found that 56 percent of respondents agreed that "Corporations should stand up for what they believe politically regardless of whether or not it is controversial," with an 89 percent majority expressing they felt companies have the power to positively influence social change (Global Strategy Group 2014). The study explored attitudes toward "corporate political engagement" related to companies conveying public stances on issues such as the minimum wage, gun control, same-sex marriage, and the environment. The research concluded that when done strategically, with consideration of shifting public attitudes and key audiences' opinions about controversial issues, taking a political stance is generally viewed as appropriate and can serve to enhance the company's reputation. The study noted that respondents were generally more supportive of companies' political involvement if the issue was viewed as connected to their core business, and that millennial respondents were the most likely to indicate strong support for corporate advocacy related to specific issues, such as LGBT-related causes (Global Strategy Group 2014). While the Global Strategy Group study did not specifically report on social media usage or respondents' willingness to take to sites like Facebook or Twitter to publicly praise or chastise a company based on its politics, data from the Pew Research Center (2013) have shown that millennials remain the highest-percentage age group in usage of social networking sites and that a strong majority

(66 percent) of all social media users today report having used the tools for civic or political activities (Rainie et al. 2012).

References

Barbaro, Michael, and Erik Eckholm. 2015. "Indiana Law Denounced as Invitation to Discriminate against Gays." *New York Times.* March 27. http://www.nytimes.com/2015/03/28/us/politics/indiana-law-denounced-as-invitation-to-discriminate-against-gays.html.

Dodd, Melissa D., and Dustin W. Supa. 2014. "Conceptualizing and Measuring 'Corporate Social Advocacy' Communication: Examining the Impact on Corporate Financial Performance." *Public Relations Journal* 8 (3). http://www.prsa.org/Intelligence/PRJournal/Vol8/No3/.

Global Strategy Group. 2015. "Business and Politics: Do They Mix? 2014 Annual Study." October 1. http://globalstrategygroup.com/wp-content/uploads/2014/10/2014-Business-and-Politics-Report.pdf.

Griswold, Alison. 2015. "Brands Are Draping Their Logos in Rainbows to Celebrate Marriage Equality." *Slate.* June 26. http://www.slate.com/blogs/moneybox/ 2015/06/26/ brands_celebrate_marriage_equality_with_rainbows_and_supportive_tweets.html.

Mandaro, Laura. 2014. "Twitter Paints #blacklivesmatter on Office Wall," *USA Today.* December 5. http://www.usatoday.com/story/tech/2014/12/05/twitter-blacklivesmatter-tech-diversity/19935443/.

Pew Research Center. 2013. "Social Networking Fact Sheet." December 27. http://www.pewinternet.org/fact-sheets/social-networking-fact-sheet.

Rainie, Lee, Aaron Smith, Kay Lehman Schlozman, Henry Brady, and Sidney Verba. 2012. "Social Media and Political Engagement." *Pew Research Center.*

October 19. http://www.pewinternet.org/2012/10/19/social-media-and-political-engagement/.

Sanders, Sam. 2015. "Starbucks Will Stop Putting the Words 'Race Together' on Cups." *NPR.org*. March 22. http://www.npr.org/sections/thetwo-way/2015/03/22/394710277/starbucks-will-stop-writing-race-together-on-coffee-cups.

Webley, Kayla. 2012. "From Chick-fil-A to Amazon, Why Companies Take a Stand on Social Issues," *Time*. July 31. http://business.time.com/2012/07/31/when-companies-go-political-from-chick-fil-a-to-amazon-why-companies-choose-to-take-a-stand-on-social-issues/.

Nathan Gilkerson (PhD, University of Minnesota, 2012) is assistant professor of strategic communication at Marquette University. His research interests include political communication and public relations, social media, and communication measurement and evaluation. Gilkerson worked professionally in politics, advertising, and public relations and has published research in a variety of academic journals.

Consumers as Data Profiles: What Companies See in the Social You

Joseph T. Yun and Brittany R. L. Duff

Each day 500 million tweets are posted to Twitter's social media feed (Twitter 2015). Facebook has 1.71 billion monthly active users (Facebook 2016). These astounding numbers of social media users produce an equally mind-boggling amount of data. It is generally assumed that social media companies might use data for their own business purposes, but there is a growing group of other players that are storing and analyzing social media data that many people are not aware of. Data mining of social media is a burgeoning subfield of data mining, and techniques are being created for further discovery in this realm (Barbier and Liu 2011). While users are aware that they are posting to public or semipublic venues, they may not be aware that their posts can be cataloged as a long-term record. With the ever-growing body of social data being stored and the computational techniques alongside it, we are presented with both an exciting future of data discovery and potential for concern when it comes to privacy.

The reality of widespread data aggregation went from an abstract idea to a very concrete reality with the revelation of highly classified documents showing mass data collection of U.S. citizens. On June 5, 2013, Edward Snowden, a former CIA employee and government contractor, leaked documents that showed that the National Security Agency (NSA) was collecting metadata on U.S. citizens, which was previously unknown. What the general public once thought was conspiracy theory hit home as they realized that it was their own personal data that were being stored and accessed in ways previously unimaginable.

With the computational power available in the era of big data, data are being stored, accessed, and mined with staggering ease. This holds true for social media data that individuals and groups publicly post every day. Whether it is public comments on news sites, posting of statuses to Facebook, broadcasting an image on Instagram, tweeting 140 characters (or less) on Twitter, or even expressing one's thoughts over Weibo (a Chinese social media platform), if the posting is public, it is being stored in data warehouses for analysis. Data warehouses are physical computer storage repositories where organizations centrally store data from various sources. In the case of social media, numerous companies now aggregate and store the data from as many public social media feeds as they can. Some examples of these data aggregator companies are Crimson Hexagon, Salesforce Radian6, Gnip, Sysomos, and BrandWatch. They connect to each social media feed's public application programming interfaces (a set of programming requirements that allow one application to talk to another application, or in this case, a way for a data aggregating company to get data from the social media company) or, in many cases, they have a business relationship with the social media company to obtain the full stream of data from its platform. These data aggregator companies store all of the publicly posted social media data they can acquire in their data warehouses and then also apply their own tools to allow for easy analysis and mining. As public social media data and social media platforms continue to grow daily, so does the aggregation of these data into data warehouses. For example, topsy.com indicates that its Twitter database includes all publicly posted tweets from 2006 until present day (Topsy 2015).

With the aggregation of "easy to access" public social media data comes a vast open landscape for research opportunities in both the business and the academic sectors. Researchers have already attempted to predict future societal trends (i.e., stock market movement) with social media data (Asur and Huberman 2010) and project personality types of individuals based on the content and connections of their social data (Golbeck, Robles, and Turner 2011). In the past, it was only possible to access, store, and analyze smaller amounts of social media data, but now with data aggregation and highly accessible computational tools, finely tuned consumer profiles are being utilized by numerous companies. Companies such as Google and Facebook are well known for their targeted advertising, which is driven by the data that are collected from each customer, but these companies still largely rely on data that are proprietary to their platforms and their organizations. Pieces of our personal data are strewn throughout the digital world, but it seems likely that consumer research will most likely be accelerated by the combination of data storage and the computational power that exists today. An example of the potential power of combining data aggregation and supercomputing is IBM Watson Bluemix, which has cognitive services that give detailed analyses of social data in the realms of personality, message resonance (matching a message with an individual's preferences and personality), and cognitive insights (insights into the mind of the individual) (IBM 2015).

Various open source and commercial tools exist for large-scale analysis of social media text as well. Commercial packages, such as Crimson Hexagon ForSight, allow individuals to analyze social text and categorize that text into categories such as positive, negative, or neutral sentiment (Crimson Hexagon 2015). Open source products, such as NodeXL, provide the ability to construct a bird's eye view perspective on the structure of social networks through the data from social media feeds (NodeXL 2015). The science of network analysis can shed light on questions such as which individuals and/or groups have positions of power and influence within a social network. Websites such as overviewproject.org allow for researchers to organically compute what sorts of topics or themes arise from bodies of social media conversation (Overview 2015). The algorithms that make up topic modeling are allowing companies and people to gain better insight into the topics encompassed in a large body of social text (Blei 2012). It is likely that these tools and algorithms, when paired with the vast stores of social media data, will increase the accessibility and, therefore, use of social media data to profile topics, trends, and people. Consumers will indeed become associated with highly detailed individual data profiles in the very near future, profiles that could utilize individual social media postings going back several years.

With the revelation of NSA collection of metadata on U.S. citizens, researchers began considering whether or not this mass data collection violates the Fourth Amendment (unreasonable search or seizure) (Atkins 2014). A similar question may be asked with regard to the mass collection of social data and provision of services and tools to mine these data. One major difference between these two would be that U.S. citizens were largely unaware of their personal metadata being captured and stored by these government programs, whereas individuals knowingly post to social media and understand the public nature of their posts. Would social media behaviors change if everyone knew the permanence of their posts, the widespread storage of years of their posts beyond the social media feeds that they post to, and the growing ability to easily mine and analyze their posts? Even if a user decides to delete a post from social media and/or delete his or her whole account, what happens to the posts that are already stored in data warehouses? The assumption may be that these companies would have an agreement with the social media companies to ensure that databases are synced between the two, especially with regard to data deletion, but this is not necessarily guaranteed.

Another major problem of privacy is anonymized social data. A common practice by companies when it comes to sharing social data is to anonymize the data by removing personal names or aliases from data sets. This assumes that it would take extensive effort to reidentify individuals in these social data sets, and therefore modeling would be built around larger themes as opposed to around any single individual. However, researchers at the University of Texas at Austin created an algorithm that allowed them to use one set of social data from Flickr to ascertain individual identities in anonymized social data from Twitter (Narayanan and Shmatikov 2009). By analyzing the structure of the social networks (connection patterns between people on social media and measures of those connections), they were able to correctly reidentify 30.8 percent of the anonymous users. Only about 12 percent were identified incorrectly and the rest were not able to be identified; but of the 12 percent that were incorrectly identified, almost half of were close enough to allow for human insight to help reidentify the individuals. As computational power increases and algorithms become more refined, the potential for true anonymity of data will become increasingly unlikely.

References

Asur, Sitaram, and Bernardo Huberman. 2010. "Predicting the Future with Social Media." WI-IAT '10 Proceedings of the 2010 IEEE/WIC/ACM International Conference on Web Intelligence and Intelligent Agent Technology, 1: 492–99.

Atkins, Elizabeth. 2014. "Spying on Americans: At What Point Does the NSA's Collection and Searching of Metadata Violate the Fourth Amendment." *Washington Journal of Law, Technology & Arts* 10 (1): 51–88. https://digital.law.washington.edu/dspace-law/bitstream/handle/1773.1/1390/10wjlta051.pdf

Barbier, Geoffrey, and Liu, Huan. 2011. "Data Mining in Social Media." In *Social Network Data Analytics*, edited by C. C. Aggarwal, 327–51. Berlin: Springer Science+Business Media.

Blei, David M. 2012. "Probabilistic Topic Models." *Communications of the ACM* 55 (4): 77–84.

Crimson Hexagon. 2015. "About Us." http://www.crimson hexagon.com/about/.

Facebook. 2016. "Company Info." http://newsroom.fb.com/company-info/.

Golbeck, Jennifer, Cristina Robles, and Karen Turner. 2011. "Predicting Personality with Social Media." CHI'11 Extended Abstracts on Human Factors in Computing Systems, Vancouver, BC, Canada: 253–62.

IBM. 2015. "IBM Bluemix." https://www.ibm.com/cloud-computing/bluemix/solutions/watson/.

Narayanan, Arvind, and Vitaly Shmatikov. 2009. "De-Anonymizing Social Networks." SP '09 Proceedings of the 2009 30th IEEE Symposium on Security and Privacy, Washington, DC: 173–87.

NodeXL. 2015. "NodeXL." http://nodexl.codeplex.com/.

Overview. 2015. "Overview." https://www.overviewdocs.com/.

Topsy. 2015. "Topsy." http://topsy.com/.

Twitter. 2015. "Company." https://about.twitter.com/company.

Joseph T. Yun is the leader of social media analytics for Technology Services at the University of Illinois at Urbana-Champaign. He is also a PhD student in Informatics at the Illinois Informatics Institute at the University of Illinois and conducts research in the realm of computational advertising.

Brittany R. L. Duff, PhD, is an associate professor of advertising at the University of Illinois at Urbana-Champaign. She is affiliated with the Institute for Communications Research, Illinois Informatics Institute, and the Beckman Institute for Advanced Science.

The Role of Social Media in Crisis Communication: Opportunities and Challenges for Crisis Communication Strategies in the Social Media Era

Jae-Hwa Shin

Since the mid-2000s, social media have played an increasingly important role in shaping the perceptions and responses to crises. According to Duggan and Smith (2013), nearly three-quarters of U.S. adults belonged to at least one social media site. In addition to managing traditional or controlled media, public relations practitioners are today advised to develop a crisis response plan that incorporates social media—not as an afterthought, but as an integral part of crisis management strategies that are unique to the communication channel. According to Coombs (2014), an organization can use social media to quickly report a crisis, which results in less reputational damage than if another source first reports. This diminishes, or at least reconfigures, the gatekeeping role that was once the domain of news organizations. Crises, when they occur, can prove difficult to contain. Like putting out a wildfire with several points of origin, it is often hard to know where to start and when one is finished. On the other hand, as Austin, Liu, and Jin (2012) have contended, a growing number of U.S. adults not only prefer to get information online, but also perceive information gleaned online as more credible than what is available through traditional media channels.

Social media offer a range of specific opportunities and challenges. Among the opportunities, social media have the potential to be collaborative, allowing many voices and viewpoints to find representation, and the possibility of meaningful two-way communication including the opportunity to mobilize and reach a plethora of voices. New media can amplify traditional media or provide a forum for discussion and debate of stories that originate through other media channels. On the other hand, social media often initiate or lead news stories on traditional media. *Columbia Journalism Review* reported that nearly 60 percent of journalists have Twitter accounts, while a study conducted by the University of Indiana School of Journalism found that almost 54 percent were active users. Clearly, even for media professionals, social media have the advantages of timeliness, flexibility, and directness. Timeliness is a key factor. As Cho, Jung, and Park (2013) have shown, news of the 2011 earthquake in Japan began to surface on Twitter 20 minutes before traditional news sources began to report the story. Moreover, the interactive potential of social media, as demonstrated as early as 2007 in the immediate wake of shootings at Virginia Tech, during the Arab Spring and Haitian earthquake, and the 2013 attack on Westgate Mall in Kenya, represents a key advantage in connection to risk communication and fostering public awareness during an emergent crisis (Simon et al. 2014). On a more mundane but nevertheless powerful level, social media present the opportunity for the public to engage directly with organizations or celebrities. Distinctions between content creators, gatekeepers, and audiences, stakeholders, or publics are thus eroded.

Challenges include managing the sheer volume of information. Separating the wheat from the chaff becomes an onerous task and few organizations have the resources to fully scan the social media environment 24/7. Nonprofit organizations in particular historically have failed to recognize the potential for two-way communication embedded in social media (Muralidharan et al. 2011). In contrast to traditional media, the emerging nature of social media makes more apparent the struggle to manage the flow of information amid the noise. According to Cho and Gower, the way a crisis is framed affects how an event is evaluated, as "the public perceives not the objective fact of a crisis event, but the facts constructed by the media or news releases from the party in crisis" (2006, 420). Austin, Liu, and Jin (2012) suggested that it mattered less to many social media users whether or not crisis information was accurate or not. The speed with which a single tweet can travel can incite unanticipated consequences.

The Red Cross learned this lesson in February 2011 when social media director Wendy Harman accidentally posted a tweet about beer that included the phrase "when we drink we do it right" followed by the hashtag "#gettngslizzerd." The tweet went unnoticed for about an hour before it was followed with an explanation issued by the organization: "We've deleted the rogue tweet but rest assured the Red Cross is sober and we've confiscated the keys." The strategy, which mixed corrective action with self-deprecating humor, proved effective and led to a fund-raising opportunity including a partnership with Dogfish Head beer, the subject of the "rogue tweet" ("Case Study" 2011). The same may be said of the way DKNY handled a photographer's claim that the company improperly used one of his images in a display. Claiming it was an accident, the company issued a sincere apology backed up with a donation of $25,000 to a local YMCA.

Applebee's restaurant had less success negotiating social media in 2013 in the wake of the firing of Chelsea Welch, a waitress who posted a photograph on her personal Facebook account of a minister's bill decrying the 18 percent tip added to the bill with "I give God 10% why do you get 18." The company claimed that Welch violated the customer's privacy, a reasonable proposition until it was revealed on social media that the company had itself posted a similar receipt on the corporate Facebook account that clearly identified a client. Applebee's attempts to defend its actions quickly garnered more than 10,000 comments, the majority of which were negative ("Big Op-Ed" 2013). Further complicating the crisis response, the company attempted to delete many of the negative comments and entered into argumentation with customers. Their defensive response violated the public's growing expectation, fostered by social media, for transparency and candor (Wendling, Radisch, and Jacobzone 2013).

Celebrities and public figures often evade crisis situations, distort their responses, and exacerbate the situation in social media environments, often making the crisis more conspicuous and extensive. In the context of revelations about doping, Lance Armstrong concentrated on the crisis communication strategies of attacking the accuser, stonewalling, and bolstering on his official Twitter account, which was inconsistent with a range of strategies such as mortification, conforming, and retrospective regret that he used in his Oprah Winfrey interview. Armstrong failed to exhibit a similar degree of contrition and be consistent in his crisis response strategies between traditional media and social media (Hambrick, Frederick, and Sanderson 2015). He thus missed the opportunity to effectively respond to the crisis and possibly redirect the audience to more positive themes and images.

Organizations can be blindsided by social media attacks. Planned Parenthood proved to be unprepared for the successful attacks mounted on social media by LiveAction. As Wigley and Zhang contended, "Crisis managers should think about social media as a way to prepare for a crisis and develop relationships with stakeholders, by using dialogue, etc." (2011). Social media have become a crucial platform for crisis responses and occurrences as well. Although organizations can monitor or detect a sign or prodrome of crisis, more often they respond to crisis with selected strategies ranging from "simple denial" to "mortification" on social media (Benoit 1995).

A recent illustration of the power of social media to affect attitudes occurred on August 9, 2014, at 12:03 p.m. when Twitter user @TheePharoah posted the now famous message "I JUST SAW SOMEONE DIE OMFG." Within the course of the next few minutes, this and a subsequent photograph of Michael Brown's slain body in Ferguson, Missouri, had been rapidly retweeted nearly 6,000 times. The city of Ferguson failed to respond for more than five hours, heightening the perception that the police had acted improperly. Other blunders, such as lack of sensitivity in communicating with the public, the restricted access to journalists, and the militaristic tactics employed on the ground, led to an escalation of the crisis (DeVries 2015). Considered as an organization facing a crisis, the city of Ferguson would have benefited from advice about the role of social media in a communication strategy offered by Veil, Beuhner, and Palenchar (2011): accentuate open, honest communication from the start, collaborate with the media, and adopt a stance of empathy that suggests partnership with stakeholder publics.

References

Austin, Lucinda, Brooke Fisher Liu, and Yan Jin. 2012. "How Audiences Seek Out Crisis Information: Exploring the Social-Mediated Crisis Communication Model." *Journal of Applied Communication Research* 40 (2): 188–207.

Benoit, William L. 1995. *Accounts, Excuses, and Apologies: A Theory of Image Restoration Strategies*. Albany: State University of New York Press.

"Big Op-Ed: When Private Comments Go Very Public." 2013. *NPR*. Mississippi Public Broadcasting. February 4. http://www.npr.org/2013/02/04/171079146/when-private-actions-go-very-public.

"Case Study: American Red Cross Twitter Faux Pas." 2011. *The Fundraising Journal*. http://www.thefundraisingjournal.com/Archive/1102/redcross.html.

Cho, Seung Ho, and Karla K. Gower. 2006. "Framing Effect on the Public's Response to Crisis: Human Interest Frame and Crisis Type Influencing Responsibility and Blame." *Public Relations Review* 32 (4): 519–32.

Cho, Seung Ho, Kyujin Jung, and Han Woo Park. 2013. "Social Media Use during Japan's 2011 Earthquake: How Twitter Transforms the Locus of Crisis Communication." *Media International Australia, Incorporating Culture & Policy* 149: 28–40.

Coombs, W. Timothy. 2014. "Crisis Management and Communications." Institute for Public Relations. http://www.instituteforpr.org/crisis-management-communications/.

DeVries, Derek. 2015. "The Five PR Crises Most Talked-About on Social Media in 2014." *Lambert, Edwards & Associates blog.* http://lambert-edwards.com/5prcrisesonsocialmedia2014.

Duggan, Maeve, and Aaron Smith. 2013. "Social Media Update 2013." *Pew Research Center.* December 20. http://pewinternet.org/Reports/2013/Social-Media-Update.aspx.

Hambrick, Marion E., Evan L. Frederick, and Jimmy Sanderson. 2015. "From Yellow to Blue: Exploring Lance Armstrong's Image Repair Strategies across Traditional and Social Media." *Communication and Sport* 3 (2): 196–218.

Muralidharan, Sidharth, Leslie Rasmussen, Daniel Patterson, and Jae-Hwa Shin. 2011. "Hope for Haiti: An Analysis of Facebook and Twitter Usage during the Earthquake Relief Efforts." *Public Relations Review* 37 (2): 175–77.

Simon, Tomer, Avishay Goldberg, Limor Aharonson-Daniel, Dmitry Leykin, and Bruria Adini. 2014. "Twitter in the Cross Fire—The Use of Social Media in the Westgate Mall Terror Attack in Kenya." *PLoS One* 9 (8): 412–29.

Veil, Shari R., Tara Beuhner, and Michael J. Palenchar. 2011. "A Work-in-Process Literature Review: Incorporating Social

Media in Risk and Crisis Communication." *Journal of Contingencies and Crisis Management* 19 (2): 110–22.

Wendling, Cécile, Jack Radisch, and Stephanie Jacobzone. 2013. "The Use of Social Media in Risk and Crisis Communication." OECD Working Papers and Public Governance 24. http://www.oecd-ilibrary.org/governance/the-use-of-social-media-in-risk-and-crisis-communication_5k3v01fskp9s-en.

Wigley, Shelley, and Weiwu Zhang. 2011. "A Study of PR Practitioner's Use of Social Media in Crisis Planning." *Public Relations Journal* 5 (3).

Jae-Hwa Shin, PhD, MPH, is a professor of public relations at the University of Southern Mississippi. Her research areas include public relations theory building from the perspective of strategic conflict management including crisis, issue, risk, and reputation management. New media and cultures have been major dimensions in her research. She previously worked as a public relations director for the Federation of Korean Industries. She received her PhD from the School of Journalism at the University of Missouri.

Lessons from the Social Media Revolution?: A Look Back at Social Media's Role in Political Campaigns and Elections

Terri L. Towner

Over the past decade, social media sites have emerged as important hubs of political information and activity. Sites, such as Facebook, YouTube, Twitter, and blogs, have rapidly transformed citizen-to-citizen and citizen-to-government interaction in a manner not seen before. Specifically, citizens can share their political attitudes, gather campaign information, connect with candidates and parties, and become politically mobilized. As a result, scholars from a variety of disciplines have examined how political candidates, parties, and citizens employ social media during campaigns, and, most importantly, how these online sites influence their political attitudes and behaviors. A look back at recent elections suggests that social media transformed political campaigning, but scholarly research implies that it did not revolutionize citizens' political knowledge or participation. This nonrevolution can be attributed to the campaign strategy itself as well as the limitations of existing scholarly research.

Since the 1990s, political candidates have incorporated online technologies into their campaign strategies. By the 2012 presidential election, both Barack Obama and Mitt Romney fully embraced social media platforms to market themselves to voters. In fact, both candidates were locked in a social media war, each employing a variety of online platforms to connect, mobilize, and inform citizens. Candidates used social media to target specific voters, discuss policy issues, trumpet their accomplishments, and attack their opponents (Pew Research Center 2012). Undeniably, social media have changed campaigning, as candidates can communicate with voters without the mainstream media filter and distribute information cheaper and faster. Yet, campaigns fail to employ a distinguishing feature: the social aspect. Campaigns deliver information in a top-down or one-way fashion while neglecting direct interaction and two-way communication with citizens. Considering the latter, social media are best viewed as another mode for campaigns to spread information. As a result, social media's impact on citizens' political knowledge and participation is found to be limited.

Regarding political knowledge, studies suggest that social media's influence in creating an informed citizenry is minimal (Baumgartner and Morris 2010; Dimitrova et al. 2014; Groshek and Dimitrova 2011; Kaufhold, Valenzuela, and Gil de Zúñiga 2010; Pasek, More, and Romer 2009; Towner and Dulio 2011a). Citizens are not employing social media to become more politically knowledgeable. Instead, these platforms are used for entertainment and to connect with friends, family, or people in the community rather than for information-seeking (Anderson and Caumont 2014; Dimitrova et al. 2014).

While it is clear that social media do not enhance political knowledge, research findings on social media's impact on political participation are rather mixed. On one hand, some scholars offer evidence that social media use significantly increases offline political participation, such as voting, signing a written petition, and boycotting (Dimitrova et al. 2014; Gil de Zúñiga, Jung, and Valenzuela 2012; Gil de Zúñiga, Molyneux, and Zheng 2014; Towner 2013; Towner and Dulio 2011a, 2011b; Zhang, Seltzer, and Bichard 2013). On the other hand, other research found no empirical link between social media and offline engagement (Baumgartner and Morris 2010; Groshek and Dimitrova 2011; Towner 2015). Regarding online political participation, research is more promising, indicating that social media use increases forms of digital engagement, such as e-mailing, making an online donation, and following a candidate on a social networking site (Baumgartner and Morris 2010; Gil de Zúñiga, Jung, and Valenzuela 2012; Gil de Zúñiga, Molyneux, and Pei Zheng 2014; Towner 2013; Zhang, Seltzer, and Bichard 2013). In fact, Boulianne's (2015) meta-analysis concludes that social media have only marginal effects on political participation during campaigns, asserting that future research on social media effects must move beyond utilizing college student samples and cross-sectional research.

Due to several reasons, social media's role in campaigning is found to be nonrevolutionary as well as nonimpactful on citizens. First, campaigns transmit information on social media in a one-way fashion with little dialogue or open discussion. Campaigns that employ social media to their full potential, such as utilizing staff to respond to citizens' questions and comments, will likely have more influence on citizens' attitudes and behaviors. Second, the scholarly work on social media effects is limited in research design. For example, research largely focuses on presidential campaigns rather than local- or state-level campaigns. Due to nonpartisan, local elections, "at-large" voting districts, and often competitive gubernatorial races, one could argue that social media have more significant effects on citizen attitudes during state- and local-level campaigning. In addition, scholars examining social media effects during campaigns rely largely on convenience samples of college students, rarely examining national adult samples. Adults, who are increasingly using social media for social and civic reasons, may consume campaign information differently than young people. Thus, the impact of social media could have varying effects on adults' political knowledge and participation. Last, the measurement of political participation requires reconceptualization to include both offline and online forms of engagement (e.g., voting, protesting, e-mailing, "fanning" a candidate) as well as new modes (e.g., adding or deleting an application or "app" about politics) as technology advances. It is possible that current measures of political participation are not capturing all forms of engagement and thus resulting in little to no social media effects. In sum, given that social media use in campaigning is ever-changing, its effects on citizens continue to require examination during future elections.

References

Anderson, Monica, and Andrea Caumont. 2014. "How Social Media Is Reshaping News." *Pew Research Center.* September 24. http://www.pewresearch.org/fact-tank/2014/09/24/how-social-media-is-reshaping-news/.

Baumgartner, Jody, and Jonathan Morris. 2010. "MyFaceTube Politics: Social Networking Websites and Political Engagement of Young Adults." *Social Science Computer Review* 28 (1): 24–44.

Boulianne, Shelley. 2015. "Social Media Use and Participation: A Meta-Analysis of Current Research." *Information, Communication, & Society* 18 (5): 524–38.

Dimitrova, Daniela, Adam Shehata, Jesper Stromback, and Lars Nord. 2014. "The Effects of Digital Media on Political

Knowledge and Participation in Election Campaigns: Evidence from Panel Data." *Communication Research* 41 (1): 95–118.

Gil de Zúñiga, Homero, Nakwon Jung, and Sebastian Valenzuela. 2012. "Social Media Use for News and Individuals' Social Capital, Civic Engagement and Political Participation." *Journal of Computer Mediated Communication* 17 (3): 319–36.

Gil de Zúñiga, Homero, Logan Molyneux, and Pei Zheng. 2014. "Social Media, Political Expression, and Political Participation: Panel Analysis of Lagged and Concurrent Relationships." *Journal of Communication* 64 (4): 612–34.

Groshek, Jacob, and Daniela Dimitrova. 2011. "A Cross-section of Voter Learning, Campaign Interest and Intention to Vote in the 2008 American Election: Did Web 2.0 Matter?" *Studies in Communications* 9 (1): 355–75.

Kaufhold, Kelly, Sebastian Valenzuela, and Homero Gil de Zúñiga. 2010. "Citizen Journalism and Democracy: How User-Generated News Use Relates to Political Knowledge." *Journalism & Mass Communication Quarterly* 87 (3–4): 515–29.

Pasek, Josh, Eian More, and Daniel Romer. 2009. "Realizing the Social Internet? Online Social Networking Meets Offline Social Capital." *Journal of Information, Technology and Politics* 6 (3–4): 197–215.

Pew Research Center. 2012. "How the Presidential Candidates Use the Web and Social Media." August 15. http://www.journalism.org/files/legacy/DIRECT%20ACCESS%20FINAL.pdf.

Towner, Terri. 2013. "All Political Participation Is Socially Networked?: New Media and the 2012 Election." *Social Science Computer Review* 31 (5): 527–41.

Towner, Terri. 2015. "The Influence of Twitter Posts on Candidate Perceptions: The 2014 Michigan Midterms."

In *Media, Message, and Mobilization: Communication and 2014 Mid-Term Elections*, edited by John A. Hendricks and Daniel Schill, 145–66. New York: Palgrave.

Towner, Terri, and David Dulio. 2011a. "The Web 2.0 Election: Voter Learning in the 2008 Presidential Campaign." In *Techno-politics in Presidential Campaigning*, edited by John A. Hendricks and Lynda L. Kaid, 22–43. New York: Routledge.

Towner, Terri, and David Dulio. 2011b. "The Web 2.0 Election: Does the Online Medium Matter?" *The Journal of Political Marketing* 10 (1–2): 165–88.

Zhang, Weiwu, Trent Seltzer, and Shannon Bichard. 2013. "Two Sides of the Coin: Assessing the Influence of Social Network Site Use during the 2012 U.S. Presidential Campaign." *Social Science Computer Review* 31 (5): 542–51.

Terri L. Towner (PhD, Purdue University) is an associate professor of political science at Oakland University in Michigan. Her research focuses on U.S. politics, public opinion, new media coverage of elections, and the politics of race and gender. Her research has appeared in the Journal of Political Marketing *and* Social Science Computer Review.

Saving Face: Applying the Spiral of Silence Theory to Social Media: Self-Censorship in the Midst of Controversial Issues

Juliana Maria (da Silva) Trammel

An image posted on Instagram. Advice on cancer treatment on Facebook. A 140-character political thought on Twitter. Widespread Internet access and the increase of social media sites are transforming the mass communication landscape. Gone are the days that major television networks and companies control the communication pathways and airwaves by using the typical top-down, one-way communication model. Instead, individuals' personal expressions and opinions have become more public than ever. Access to computers, mobile devices, and free social media platforms give everyday people the ability to promote their ideas and ideals. User-generated content has transformed the social media ecosystem, turning into a very complex and transactional virtual community, where communication comes, goes, and intersects like a web. This access has created an oversimplified notion that the Internet has democratized information, but this is not that simple. Instead, social media sites have fostered safer and alternative virtual environments more conducive to the expression of controversial issues, like groups and other less-intrusive platforms, away from the scrutiny of known relationships.

As people are more free to talk and express their thoughts, they have also become more unwilling to share what could be deemed "inappropriate" or opposite to the socially desired answer or perceived public's opinion. This results in a possible social media self-censorship, the process of suppressing one's own opinion, particularly in the midst of controversial issues. This essay uses the Spiral of Silence Theory to explore self-censorship on social media and examines techniques used to relate and "save face" in the midst of controversial issues, including participation in groups or using less invasive social media sites like Twitter.

Although controversial issues such as same-sex marriage, hate speech, racism, or vaccinations often "pop up" on timelines in forms of texts, images, and memes, most people are careful to express controversial issues, even if this means agreeing with it by liking or sharing. A 2014 Pew Research Center study shows that people are less likely to post views if their followers do not share their opinions (Hampton et al. 2014). As with television, social media have a way to crystalize public opinion. It might not show what the majority view is, but it will give people the impression of what it could be, and according to the Spiral of Silence Theory, that impression is enough to keep people with opposing views silent. The Spiral of Silence Theory explains the growth and spread of public opinion, which is an intangible force that "keeps people in line." Coined by Elisabeth Noelle-Neumann, the Spiral of Silence Theory refers to the pressure people feel to conceal their views when they think they are the minority (Noelle-Neumann 1984). It is a communication process in which people who think they hold a minority view do not speak up because of fear of social exclusion and relationship loss.

The Internet expansion in the past 20 years has created an opportunity and platform for freedom of expression. The prevalence of social media sites fostered an assumption that people would be fully free to express themselves, even if they were part of a minority view. The reality is that despite the boom of these social media sites, users are still cautious of what they share, particularly on social media sites with symmetrical relationship ties like Facebook, where the friendship is mutual and, in most cases, personal. Although social media sites and the First Amendment give Internet users the ability to share their personal views, "save face" continues to be a desirable behavior.

While many researchers have questioned the applicability of the Spiral of Silence Theory to online behavior, the fundamental concept of the theory explains that social media users also engage in self-censorship if they fear their opinion is the minority. People's perception of dominant views has a lot to do with their willingness to share personal opinions on social media. Users seek alternative virtual spheres where it is safer to express controversial opinions. One of the advantages of social media, however, is the ability to participate in controversial discourses through alternative pathways, away from the scrutiny of people directly related, where similar views are shared, even if they are the opposite to the perceived majority. These include groups, less-invasive social media sites like Twitter, specific chat rooms and forums, and, in some extreme cases, the creation of aliases and fake profiles.

Facebook, for example, allows members to organize themselves into groups. In 2014, Google indexed 620 million Facebook groups, and a user can join up to 6,000 groups at any given time. In these groups, members are allowed to share updates, photos, and documents and send messages to other group members. There are different types of groups, depending on the desired level of privacy: public, closed, and secret groups.

Public Groups: Anyone can join, be added, or invited to public groups. They are also visible in search results and anyone can see the comments, group members' names, and their posts. Public groups give users a selective audience to share controversial ideas, but these groups are wide open. Closed and secret groups are more likely than the public groups to host members with controversial views.

Closed Groups: In closed groups, anyone can ask to join, see the group description, and view who is in the group, but only members can see what is posted in the group's News Feed. The moderator has to approve a membership request, and depending on the subject and sensibility of the issue, as with the "unpopular" anti-vaccination groups, for example, further steps are taken to avoid the acceptance of "trolls."

Secret Groups: Secret groups are virtually invisible on Facebook. To join, a member must be added or invited by a current member. This provides the ultimate level of privacy to members.

Those who feel they hold the minority opinion on controversial issues may also join less-invasive and impersonal groups like Twitter, which offers a different platform than Facebook. The asymmetrical structure of Twitter gives users the option to follow, without being followed. Conversations are aggregated into hashtags and @mentions, and these interactions often take place among users with little or no personal relationship. The hashtags have also been used as a great tool to diffuse information, regardless of relationship statuses. Hashtags allow topics to be organized and collected as "trends," and due to the lack of personal relationships, ideas are shared with the main purpose of self-expression without the expectation of reciprocation. Of the eleven reasons for using Twitter identified by the American Press Institute, only three were somewhat relational; all the other nine reasons were topic-specific (Rosenstiel et al. 2015). This gives those with minority views a less-invasive platform to express controversial views. There are also other virtual spaces where people are more comfortable to voice their opinions besides the well-known social media sites mentioned, including forums, chat rooms, blogs, and newsgroups.

Social media without a doubt have given an edge to the democratization of information: people are able to speak up more and share their perspectives and points of view. However, the relational nature of human beings, the need for acceptance, and saving face are still valued in human interactions—in some cultures even more than others. Ultimately, social media users, in fear of being in the minority view, seek alternative strategies to voice their opinions. Saving face, overall, continues to be the ultimate human communication goal, even if the opinion is not really the minority view but just perceived to be the minority view.

References

Hampton, Keith, Lee Rainie, Weixu Lu, Maria Dwyer, Inyoung Shin, and Kristen Purcell. 2014. "Social Media and the 'Spiral of Silence.'" *Pew Research Center*. August 26. http://www.pewinternet.org/2014/08/26/social-media-and-the-spiral-of-silence/.

Noelle-Neumann, Elisabeth. 1984. *The Spiral of Silence: Public Opinion—Our Social Skin.* Chicago: University of Chicago.

Rosenstiel, Tom, Jeff Sonderman, Kevin Loker, Maria Ivancin, and Nina Kjarval. 2015. "How People Use Twitter in General." *American Press Institute*. September 1. https://www.americanpressinstitute.org/publications/reports/survey-research/how-people-use-twitter-in-general/.

Juliana Maria (da Silva) Trammel is an associate professor of strategic communication at Savannah State University in Savannah, Georgia. She is a communications researcher and consultant with over 15 years of experience. She earned an MA in public communication from American University and a PhD in communication and culture from Howard University.

Live Tweeting: Fans and Celebrities

Michelle Groover

Social media platforms such as Facebook, Twitter, and Snapchat are used by many people today—including celebrities. Twitter is a microblogging site that allows users to send and receive messages in the form of text, links, photos, or videos up to 140 characters in length. This article will explore the phenomenon of "live tweeting" and take a look at how Twitter is used to tweet during the airing of a popular television program.

In June 2015, Nielsen listed the top 10 television programs in the United States by average audience and average number of tweets during an airing of each program from September 1, 2014, to May 24, 2015 (Nielsen 2015). The report stated the show with the highest average audience tweeting about it was *The Walking Dead*, with a typical audience of more than 4.3 million and averaging 480,000 tweets during the eight months investigated. Also in the top 10 were *Game of Thrones*, *Dancing with the Stars*, and *Pretty Little Liars*.

Many television programs list a hashtag in the lower portion of the screen when it airs. This hashtag provides viewers with a way to join the conversation with others watching the program, which includes other fans and, at times, the stars of the program. Other times, viewers will create a hashtag based around what is happening in the current plot.

The sixth ranked show in the Nielsen list was *Scandal* with an average audience of more than 2.4 million and averaging 282,000 tweets (Nielsen 2015). Not only are fans of the show live tweeting during each episode, but stars of the show are as well. *Scandal* uses a number of hashtags to interact with its audience; however, the primary hashtag is #Scandal.

During *Scandal* episodes, many of the primary cast members will live tweet with the audience. Though all do not participate in live tweeting every week, they try to let their fans know when they are. For example, during the airing of the Thursday night program on April 17, 2015, Kerry Washington [Olivia Pope] tweeted, "On set but will tweet as much as I can! WHADDUP West Coast?! #scandal." Washington is also often asked what clothes her character is wearing and she often answers. When she is not able to tweet, someone handling her publicity will respond. These tweets are noted by the "kw's krew" signature on the tweet. For example, "#PapaPopeisBACK! Watch #Scandal NOW!—kw's krew." In this way, fans know Washington is not participating, but still wants to connect with her fans. Also, some of the actors will tweet photos from the set or where they are watching that evening's show. For example, on December 16, 2014, Scott Foley [Jake] tweeted "#scandal selfie. On location today!," which was accompanied by a photo. Additionally, cast members will tweet about a scene along with viewers. For example, following a scene where Olivia provides advice to Mellie about winning the Senate election, Jeff Perry [Cyrus] tweeted, "Liv reading chapter & verse on how Mellie can win . . . CLASSIC OP! #tgit #scandal." These types of tweets provide the viewers with insights from the stars, news about what is happening on the set, and their thoughts on key storylines. In doing so, viewers feel more invested in what they are watching.

The show's May 2015 season finale used the hashtag #ScandalFinale. While many fan tweets focused on the content of the show, some directed their messages to the stars themselves—with some receiving responses. Prior to the airing of the finale, a fan asked Foley if he could describe the finale in one word, to which Foley responded "Absolutely not!" Other fans asked the stars if they would not only be live tweeting during the East Coast airing, but also the West Coast airing. Tony Goldwyn [Fitz] wrote "Might be a little sleepy but I'll be tweeting." Prior to the East Coast airing, Goldwyn asked on Twitter who would be live tweeting with the cast that evening, which received 57 retweets and 131 favorites. Throughout the finale, the stars originated tweets related to the scenes being aired at the time, with these tweets being retweeted and favorited by the fans. Additionally, the stars tweeted kudos to their fellow castmates. Washington tweeted, "Wow. @KatieQLowes and @guillermodiazyo you ROCKED this scene!!!! #ScandalFinale." Following the airing of the finale on the East Coast, Goldwyn tweeted, "Thanks for another AWESOME season #Gladiators!! See you in September! #Nothing without you #Scandal." In this one statement, Goldwyn let fans know they are the reason the show has become popular.

While many fans will live tweet regardless of whether or not the stars of the show participate, it is interesting how much more lively the conversations and questions are when there is participation from the cast. Even when stars do not live tweet every episode, their participation helps the show succeed, as seen in Goldwyn's response following the show's 2015 season finale.

In conclusion, live tweeting during a television program can bring people closer to their friends, as well as introduce them to other fans of the show. Additionally, fans recognize the possibility their favorite cast member could answer their questions. A show's success is not always found in the number of people watching the program, but in those who are talking about it and what they are talking about.

Reference

Nielsen. 2015. "TV Season in Review: Biggest Moments on Twitter." June 1. http://www.nielsen.com/us/en/insights/news/2015/tv-season-in-review-biggest-moments-on-twitter.html.

Michelle Groover is a senior lecturer in the Communication Arts Department at Georgia Southern University in Statesboro, Georgia, where she teaches public relations courses. She holds a PhD in communication from Regent University. Her research interests include crisis communication, popular culture, public relations, and social media.

Introduction

The tools of social media have helped spread the messages of political, economic, and fund-raising movements to local communities to encourage participation and also to the media and other audiences around the world to raise awareness. Through social media, participants also developed a sense they were part of a greater movement, which likely strengthened their commitment to the cause. This chapter will first highlight the ALS Ice Bucket Challenge, the Arab Spring uprisings, and Occupy Wall Street as important movements that were propelled by social media.

The success of social media platforms has been a direct consequence of the determination, creativity, and business acumen of the entrepreneurs behind the various platforms. This chapter will also profile the founders of today's most popular social media platforms such as Facebook, Twitter, LinkedIn, Snapchat, and Tumblr as well as some of the early social media pioneers of sites such as MySpace and Flickr. This chapter will also highlight key thought leaders, bloggers, authors, marketers, and scholars in the social media industry

---

Massachusetts Governor Charlie Baker participates in the Ice Bucket Challenge to raise money for ALS research during the summer of 2015 at the Statehouse in Boston. Also participating is Pete Frates, former Boston College baseball player and ALS patient, who helped inspire the Ice Bucket Challenge. (AP Photo/Charles Krupa)

as well as those who are making a creative contribution by blogging or posting videos on YouTube.

Movements

ALS Ice Bucket Challenge (2014)

Perhaps no other campaign has ever reached greater success in terms of participation, fund-raising, social media chatter, and attention in popular culture than the ALS Ice Bucket Challenge. This campaign was truly a grassroots effort, fueled by friends of an amyotrophic lateral sclerosis (ALS) victim and spread through social media by millions of participants ranging from average citizens to celebrities. Significant coverage by traditional media and participation by personalities on television and YouTube further accelerated awareness of the campaign and the cause.

The ALS Association (ALSA), which benefited from the campaign, is the only national nonprofit organization that conducts research and provides resources for people living with ALS. The Ice Bucket Challenge was not organized by the organization itself, but has been a tradition in sports that has been used for other causes in the past. Televised ice bucket challenges started with the Golf Channel's program *Morning Drive*, which was followed by *The Today Show*'s Matt Lauer who had been nominated by golfer Greg Norman. The Golf Channel's segment did not mention any donations to charity while *The Today Show* indicated that if the challenge was not taken, the person nominated must donate to a charity. Other ice bucket challenges at the time included motocross racer Jeff Northrop who ran a campaign on Instagram for his nephew's medical needs as well as a women's basketball campaign called #Chillin4Charity that raised money for the Kay Yow Cancer Fund (Levin 2014).

On the same day as *The Today Show*'s ice bucket challenge demonstration, professional golfer Chris Kennedy challenged his cousin, Jeanette Senerchia, and because her husband has ALS, asked for a donation to be made to the ALSA

(ALS Association n.d.). Through the power of social networks, one of Jeannette's friends was connected to Pat Quinn in Yonkers, New York, who was in turn connected to former Boston College baseball player Pete Frates in Boston, both of whom have ALS (ALS Association n.d.). From the northeast of the United States, the campaign spread throughout the country and around the world. Although many different stories exist about the origin of the campaign, Josh Levin of *Slate* offered the following in an article about the invention of the Ice Bucket Challenge: "No matter the answer, it's clear that the year's biggest viral trend isn't about any single person. Rather, it's one of the best examples we've ever seen of the Internet's amazing ability to connect people and spread ideas" (Levin 2014).

The original challenge involved a participant making a choice between donating $100 to the ALSA or creating a video where the participant would dump a bucket of ice water on his or her head. The challenge then quickly transformed into one where the participant would dump the water and still make the donation. Social media played an important role because not only did people create some engaging and entertaining content for their friends to view on Facebook, Twitter, and other platforms, but also the participant used the video to nominate three friends to participate in the challenge, causing participation to spread exponentially. The campaign also peaked in the summer, a time when pouring a bucket of ice water over one's head seemed most appealing. Notable celebrities who were challenged included then-president Barack Obama (who opted to make the donation instead of dumping ice water), Justin Bieber, LeBron James, former president George W. Bush, and Bill Gates.

This campaign was compelling for a number of reasons. In an interview with the *Guardian*, Eb Adeyeri of We Are Social suggested that the campaign indulges certain personality traits that are common to social media users. He noted:

> It encourages a competitive spirit, with each participant trying to make their video more amusing, absurd or

> outrageous than the last. It also plays on the fact people often have narcissistic tendencies on their own social media feeds and enjoy an excuse to post images and videos of themselves. It works perfectly with the guilt factor. Even if you think it's a stupid campaign it's hard to ignore a personal (and very public) nomination from a friend in the name of charity. It also embraces the community spirit of social media; rather than sponsoring someone to climb a mountain or run a marathon, the low barrier to entry means everyone can get involved and feel as though they've done something good with their day. (*The Guardian* 2014)

Other professionals interviewed for the same article suggested that the popularity of the campaign was driven by the appeal of viewing videos featuring friends and family members, the ease of which participants could capture and upload video using smartphones, the simplicity of the supplies involved in the campaign, and the low commitment required to consume the content because the videos are short (*The Guardian* 2014).

The campaign generated more than 17 million videos that were watched by 440 million people a total of 10 billion times (ALS Association n.d.). In terms of financial success, a total of 2.5 million people donated approximately $115 million to the ALSA (Bonifield 2015). The money was divided into five main spending "buckets," including the bulk of it going toward research, then patient and community services, followed by public and professional education, and then a small percentage going toward both fund-raising and external processing fees.

Arab Spring (2010–2011)

The "Arab Spring" was a series of protests, riots, and demonstrations across several Arab countries that began on December 18, 2010, in Tunisia with the self-immolation protest demonstration by Mohamed Bouazizi in the city of Sidi Bouzid (NPR Staff 2011). Some of the first countries to follow with uprisings included Algeria, Jordan, Egypt, and Yemen, which were then followed by many other countries in the Arab world. Many citizens of these countries could no longer tolerate cruel and unfair regimes and demanded the opportunity to live a more dignified life (Goldstein 2014). In Tunisia, Egypt, Yemen, and Libya, the unrest led to leaders being removed from power, and in several other countries, the leaders announced they would not seek a subsequent term. Bahrain, Syria, Iraq, Kuwait, Morocco, and Sudan also experienced civil disobedience and protests, and several other countries throughout the region were also touched by minor protests.

Scholars have debated whether social media were the catalyst of the revolutions or played another role, such as a method for reporting on events. The Arab Spring is even sometimes referred to as a "Twitter Revolution" or "Facebook Revolution." An article in the *Arab Social Media Report* described how the usage of social media in the Arab world exploded after various bans were lifted, allowing citizens "to organize demonstrations (both pro- and anti-government), disseminate information within their networks, and raise awareness of ongoing events locally and globally" and governments "in some cases to engage with citizens and encourage their participation in government processes, while in other cases to block access to websites and monitor and control information on these sites" (Salem and Mourtada 2011, 2).

The impact of social media during the Arab Spring can be explored through the decisions made by various governments, protesters, and the social networking sites themselves. For example, governments of various countries ordered a block or a lifting of the ban on certain social media sites or the Internet itself during the Arab Spring. In Algeria, Facebook and Twitter were partially blocked on January 9, 2011, and in Syria, Facebook returned on February 6, 2011, after having been blocked since late 2007. Egypt blocked the Internet for five days in January 2011, and Libya shut down the Internet in February 2011 for two partial days. Some governments and their supporters started using social media sites to engage with citizens, as was done by the

Egyptian Military Council, or to urge people to stop protests, as pro-government supporters did in Sudan. In some cases, the social networking platforms themselves suspended certain accounts, such as Facebook's shutdown of the Palestinian Intifada page with 350,000 supporters (Salem and Mourtada 2011).

The most significant use of social media, however, was by protesters as many calls for protests made on Facebook developed into actual protests on the specified date. For ten protest calls examined in a research study, all but one in Syria and the initial protest in Tunisia developed into a protest (Salem and Mourtada 2011). In the case of Tunisia, after the initial protest, those that followed were organized on Facebook. The researchers addressed the causality of social media when they noted, "This is not to say that there was a causal relationship, or that the Facebook pages were the defining or only factor in people organizing themselves on these dates, but as the initial platform for these calls, it cannot be denied that they were a factor in mobilizing movements. However, given the small Facebook penetration in most of these countries . . . it can be argued that for many protesters these tools were not central" (Salem and Mourtada 2011, 5). Facebook was likely used by a small, but active group of protesters who then used other means to mobilize a wider set of contacts, possibly through another digital method, mobile phones, or personal interactions.

The same study found that the most popular usage of Facebook for citizens in Egypt and Tunisia during early 2011 was to "raise awareness inside the country on the causes of the movements." For Egypt, the second most popular reason for usage was to "organize actions and manage activists" while the third most popular reason for usage was to "spread information to the world about the movement and related events." In Tunisia, the second and third most popular reasons were the reverse of Egypt. Finally, for both countries, "entertainment and social uses" were the least popular reasons for using Facebook (Salem and Mourtada 2011). Also, the highest percentage of citizens of both countries (88.1 percent for Tunisia and 94.3 percent for Egypt) reported getting news and information during the civil movements from social media sources instead of traditional media, including local, regional, and state-sponsored media (Salem and Mourtada 2011).

Authors Clay Shirky and Malcolm Gladwell considered the role of social media in social activism and revolutions, and their contrasting arguments provided context for the Arab Spring. Prior to events that led to the uprisings, Gladwell had argued in a piece for the *New Yorker* that Twitter and Facebook have been overemphasized by the media as political action tools (Wasik 2011). In *Foreign Affairs*, also prior to the Arab Spring, Shirky claimed that digital media had a crucial role in political incidents, such as the 2009 defeat of the Communist government in Moldova and the 2001 impeachment of the Philippine president (Wasik 2011). He addressed Gladwell's charge that online activism is superficial and argued "the fact that barely committed actors cannot click their way to a better world does not mean that committed actors cannot use social media effectively" (Wasik 2011). At the end of a *Wired* article that addresses the debate between the two scholars, Wasik concluded that "Activists may need 'strong ties' to risk their lives in the streets, but it's clear those ties can stretch across continents, and can consist entirely of bits—right up until the moment when they come together" (Wasik 2011).

Occupy Wall Street (2011)

Occupy Wall Street was a grassroots movement of protests that started in September 2011 against financial inequality and corruption occurring within the financial sector in the United States. The movement's slogan, "We are the 99%," refers to those who are not in the richest 1 percent of the population. The trigger for the movement may have been a July 2011 tweet by anticonsumerism magazine *Adbusters* suggesting a march on Wall Street in September (Preston 2011). The movement, which started in Zuccotti Park in Manhattan, moved outward throughout the United States and around the world.

Social media, particularly Twitter and Facebook, helped the protest spread quickly to others communities throughout the United States. An article in the *Economist* suggested Occupy Wall Street, and not the Arab Spring, was "the world's first genuine social-media uprising" (G.L. 2011). The campaign used a Facebook page that had 170,000 fans as of October 2011, Twitter hashtags #occupywallst and #ows, a website at Occupy Together.org, a Tumblr blog called "We are the 99 Percent," meet-ups in more than 1,300 cities around the world, and a Kickstarter campaign that raised more than $75,000 (G.L. 2011). Counting all Facebook pages for the campaign, a total of 450,000 people had liked the pages as of October 2011 (Kanalley 2011). One month later, another news story reported the movement had 400 Facebook pages with a total of 2.7 million fans (Preston 2011). YouTube housed 1.7 million videos with 73 million combined views tagged with "occupy" in the "News and Politics" category, although it is likely that some of these were not relevant to the movement (Preston 2011). Wikis and Web pages also abounded online including Occupy WallSt.org and HowtoOccupy.org. On Twitter, @occupywall stnyc had more than 94,000 followers in November 2011, and according to Trendrr, an average of 400,000 to 500,000 tweets per day had been shared about the movement since early October with over 2 million tweets on November 15, the day the police broke up the New York City camp (Preston 2011). Live broadcasting using the site Livestream.com and other platforms also helped protesters share the story live, and more than 200 Occupy channels on video-streaming sites evolved over time (Preston 2011).

Researchers who studied this phenomenon using 600,000 tweets during a 36-week period found that communication about Occupy Wall Street had a "highly localized geospatial structure," where many of the tweets were created and consumed by users in the same state (Conover et al. 2013). They found that a high percentage of tweets were related to resource mobilization, which, in the case of Occupy Wall

Street, were tangible resources such as food and tents, increasing the need for communication at the local level. Much of the traffic flowing within New York, California, and Washington, D.C., locations of encampments by protestors, described protest actions, including place and time.

The content shared on social media platforms was particularly helpful to those with a vested interest in tracking the spread, tone, and messages of the campaign. The posts also provided information about possible goals of the campaign and its supporters. For example, the Republican Congressional Committee was monitoring social media to demonstrate to voters how the movement was comprised of people holding extreme views (Goodale 2011). Banks were also particularly interested in the campaign, causing Bank of America, for example, to run a full-page ad in the *Atlanta Journal-Constitution* to share how the bank has helped homeowners in Georgia (Goodale 2011). ListenLogic, one of many companies collecting and analyzing social media communications, found a spike in conversation that mentioned bank transfers prior to November 5, the day consumers were being advised to transfer their bank accounts from large banks and financial institutions to community banks and credit unions (Goodale 2011).

The movement, however, was predicted to be difficult to sustain with social media alone and, according to Harvard Law School professor Yochai Benkler, requires "actual, on-the-ground, face-to-face actions, laying your body down for your principles—with the ability to capture the images and project them to the world" (Preston 2011).

People

Anderson, Tom (1970–)

At the age of 30 with a graduate degree in film studies, struggling musician Tom Anderson saw a flyer that promised $20 to anyone who responded. Needing money for a trip to Singapore, Anderson replied and ended up participating in a focus group for XDrive, an online file storage company that employed Chris DeWolfe as the head of consumer marketing. The moderator was impressed with Anderson, and he was subsequently offered a job as a copywriter with the company. He planned on working at XDrive long enough to pay for his Singapore trip, but instead his relationship with XDrive and several employees led to him becoming the cofounder of one of the most significant early social media networking sites (Angwin 2009).

Anderson's background includes dropping out of San Pasqual High School in Escondido, California, to play in a heavy metal band called Top Hatt. The son of an entrepreneur, Anderson enjoyed computers while growing up. During the time he should have been finishing high school, Anderson was instead writing a technical book called *Using Crosstalk Mk.4* about software that connects computers to other computers or services such as CompuServe (Angwin 2009).

In 1994, Anderson enrolled in the University of California, Berkeley to double major in English and rhetoric. Although he edited a poetry and fiction journal in college, Anderson also stayed involved in technology. He wrote reviews for GameRevolution.com and discussed video games on Usenet newsgroups. When posting on Usenet, Anderson used pseudonyms such as Tom Everett (his middle name) and Melissa Loeffler, the name of a friend (Angwin 2009). After college, Anderson played in the rock band Swank and was poised to move to Tokyo and then later considered moving to Taiwan. He was able to make his dream of moving to Taiwan come true, but returned to the United States to pursue a master's degree in critical film studies at the University of California, Los Angeles. He completed the two-year program in one year and became interested in the pornography industry (Angwin 2009). He operated an Asian porn site called TeamAsian.com, which linked to other content. Click-throughs from the site earned Anderson referral fees.

Anderson's stint at XDrive ended when the company laid off employees and filed for bankruptcy in 2001. DeWolfe, along with Anderson and two other former XDrivers, Josh Berman and Aber Whitcomb, then started a company called ResponseBase, an e-mail marketing company, which later also sold e-books and then became a full-fledged e-commerce business. One of the company's early clients was MySpace.com, which, like XDrive, offered online storage space. When the company failed to pay its online hosting bills, DeWolfe snapped up the domain name.

Launched in 2003, the new MySpace competed with sites like Friendster and Xanga and eventually became the largest online social network in the world. Anderson helped tap into the music community who had become disillusioned with Friendster after being targeted for not adhering to profile regulations and also because of rumors the site would switch to a fee-based model. Musicians found a more welcoming community on MySpace and persuaded their fans to follow them to this new social networking site (boyd 2006).

For all MySpace members, Anderson was automatically assigned to be their first MySpace friend. Throughout his years with MySpace, Anderson used the same profile photo, which is now considered iconic, showing him wearing a white T-shirt positioned in front of a whiteboard covered with writing.

In 2005, Anderson and DeWolfe sold MySpace and the parent company Intermix to Rupert Murdoch's News Corp for $580 million. Anderson served as president of MySpace right after the sale and stayed on with the MySpace team until 2009, later serving in an advisory role (J. T. Miller 2014).

Unlike other social media entrepreneurs, Anderson has not been actively involved in launching or funding other start-ups. He has, however, kept some involvement by serving as an adviser to online gambling site RocketFrog, a role he has held since 2012 (Chang 2014). Anderson has stepped away from running a social media platform, but does use social media for his current passion. At Burning Man 2011, Anderson became interested in photography and worked with a friend, professional photographer Trey Ratcliff, to develop his skills (J. T. Miller 2014).

Anderson now travels the world shooting landscapes and posts to Instagram under the profile name myspacetom.

Anderson said in an interview with ABC News that most people would not have expected him to become a social media pioneer. In the interview, he stated, "If you knew me before MySpace, you'd probably thought I'd have been a scholar teaching philosophy in a university my whole life. If you met me before college, you'd probably have thought I'd be a musician for my entire life . . . I like change" (J. T. Miller 2014).

Armstrong, Heather B. (1975–)

After launching her blog Dooce in 2001, Heather Armstrong grew her readership to the point that she was called "The Queen of the Mommy Bloggers" by the *New York Times* in 2011 (Belkin 2011). She ranks among the first and most prominent bloggers in this now-competitive arena of mommy blogs. Dooce, however, began as a way for Armstrong to rant about coworkers and discuss her disassociation with her Mormon faith and family. The name of her blog came from an AOL Instant Messenger spelling of "doode" for "dude," which Armstrong had misspelled as "dooce" on many occasions (Khazan 2015). When Armstrong started blogging, she was a 25-year-old single woman, and just three years later in 2004, she was married with a young child and able to make blogging her full-time job. Her husband also quit his job to manage the business side of the blog. By 2011, she had 100,000 daily views and was raking in hundreds of thousands of dollars from advertising (Ronan 2015).

Raised in Bartlett, Tennessee, as a Mormon, Armstrong graduated as the valedictorian of her high school class and then studied English at Brigham Young University, graduating in 1997 (Armstrong n.d.). The day she graduated from college marked the day she also left the Mormon Church. Her professional career began as a Web designer in Los Angeles. After launching her blog, Armstrong was fired from her job a year later for talking about coworkers online (Armstrong n.d.).

As a blogger, Armstrong has written much about her life, including a chronicle of moving in with her boyfriend, her subsequent marriage, and their two kids. She has also shared less flattering aspects of her life, including time spent in the hospital suffering from postpartum depression after the birth of their first child. She chose not to, however, write about the separation and eventual divorce from her husband, starting a new relationship, and raising kids as a single mom (Ronan 2015).

Armstrong is not only the author of Dooce, but also a number of books about her life including *It Sucked and Then I Cried: How I had a Baby, a Breakdown, and a Much Needed Margarita* in 2008, *Things I Learned about My Dad in Therapy* in 2009, and *Dear Daughter: The Best of the Dear Leta Letters* in 2012.

Like many bloggers, the daily expectation of posting as well as the desire from readers for personal details took its toll on Armstrong. In April 2015, Armstrong admitted that she had taken up some other projects, including public speaking and brand consulting, which "provided a much needed distraction from . . . a dangerous level of exhaustion and dissatisfaction" (Khazan 2015). Although Dooce is still an active blog, Armstrong is no longer publishing on a daily basis nor is she exclusively posting about being a mom and details about the lives of her children, as they have gotten older. Recent topics include training for a marathon, books, her pets, and home organization.

In addition to the personal strain of maintaining a popular blog, the business model of Dooce and other blogs that relied on banner ads started to implode with the rise of native advertising. Today's click-through rates on banner ads is approximately 0.1 percent, driving down advertising revenues for sites and blogs that sell banner ads (Khazan 2015). Native ads appear on Facebook and Twitter feeds and are a popular form of online advertising used by marketers today because they attract more attention. Also, because of higher views, the revenues generated are greater. Some bloggers have combated the decline of revenue from banner ads by creating sponsored content, which, in Armstrong's case, would involve Armstrong and her family using free products provided by companies and writing promotional blog posts about their experiences. Although sponsored content might work well for travel, food, or fashion bloggers, Armstrong felt her blog was too personal to involve herself and her family (Khazan 2015).

boyd, danah (1977–)

danah boyd (lowercase intentional) is a social media scholar and activist who has focused on how youth incorporate social media into their lives. As Internet scholar Clay Shirky noted about boyd in a *New York Times* interview, "The single most important thing about Danah is that she's the first anthropologist we've got who comes from the tribe she's studying" (Paul 2012).

boyd chooses to present her name in lowercase as a nod to her mother's desire for a visually balanced name (i.e., danah is more balanced than dana) and also as a political statement against the convention of capitalization. As boyd described on her website, "it's my name and i should be able to frame it as i see fit, as my adjective, not someone else's" (boyd n.d.).

boyd's childhood was spent in Lancaster, Pennsylvania, where she was raised by a single mother. She had little contact with her father after her parents divorced when boyd was five years old (Paul 2012). Her high school years were filled with many activities and extra-curriculars including marching band, literary magazine, theater, Model United Nations, volunteering, and athletics. It was boyd's brother who first introduced her to Internet Relay Chat and Usenet, which she started using during her junior year to discuss her teenage issues with strangers she met online. She also created her first website in high school, which still remains online as an Ani DiFranco lyrics page. She graduated as co-valedictorian of Manheim Township High School and then enrolled in college at Brown University where she studied computer science.

boyd's academic credentials include a PhD from the School of Information at the University of California, Berkeley. Her dissertation research was funded through a MacArthur Foundation Initiative on New Media and Learning (boyd n.d.). Her dissertation, titled "Taken Out of Context: American Teen Sociality in Networked Publics," was a two-and-a-half-year-ethnography of how teenagers engage with social media sites and the practices of self-presentation, peer sociality, and negotiating adult society. boyd also has a master's degree from MIT where she studied with the Media Lab's Sociable Media Group.

boyd is currently a principal researcher at Microsoft Research and a research assistant professor at New York University's Interactive Telecommunications Program (boyd n.d.). boyd was also selected as a 2011 Young Global Leader of the World Economic Forum and remains an active member. In 2011, boyd, along with Berkman Center director John Palfrey, was invited to serve as a research fellow for Lady Gaga's Born This Way Foundation (Paul 2012). In an effort to advise the organization, Palfrey and boyd developed a working paper series to summarize existing research and provide useful advice. These papers deal with such topics as youth bullying prevention and anti-bullying legislation. For eight years, boyd also served as a Fellow for Harvard University's Berkman Center for Internet and Society.

boyd is the author of *It's Complicated: The Social Lives of Networked Teens* and a coauthor of *Hanging Out, Messing Around, and Geeking Out: Kids Living and Learning with New Media* and *Participatory Culture in a Networked Era*. In *It's Complicated*, boyd addresses how youth live in a virtual world with conversations conducted through texts, relationship drama playing out on Facebook, and hanging out managed through Skype (Quart 2014). She also explores the concerns of parents over their teenagers becoming "screenagers." Her published papers cover not only youth social media topics such as teen drama, but also privacy, digital backchannels, and social visualization design (boyd n.d.).

In recent years, boyd has explored the implications of "big data," particularly with respect to privacy and publicity, misinterpretation of data, and civil rights (boyd n.d.). Her interests have led her to launch the research institute Data & Society, which focuses "on the social and cultural issues arising from data-centric technological development" (Data & Society n.d.).

Dorsey, Jack (1976–)

Jack Dorsey, cofounder of Twitter, was born into a working-class family in St. Louis, Missouri, to a father who worked in a service department of a mass spectrometer company and a homemaker mother (Max 2013). In his room as a child, Dorsey had a CB radio and a police scanner and later an IBM PC and then a Macintosh. In his youth, he enjoyed participating in Internet Relay Chat and trading code with other programmers. At the age of 14, Dorsey developed a dispatch routing software program, a product still used by taxi companies today (Leonard 2009).

Dorsey attended the University of Missouri at Rolla but left for New York City to work as a programmer for a taxi and courier dispatch service (Max 2013). He enrolled and then dropped out of New York University a semester short of graduating to move to San Francisco to start his own dispatch service using the Internet in 2000. He bounced between cities and other jobs, but returned to San Francisco. At one point, Dorsey decided to get his massage therapy license so that he could start a business doing massage therapy for programmers and, as a programmer himself, also help them through their coding issues (Bercovici 2013b). While working as a programmer for an Alcatraz tour company in 2005, Dorsey noticed Evan Williams in a coffee shop. At the time, Williams was known for selling a company to Google. Dorsey had been pursuing a shoe sales job at Camper, but decided fortuitously to send his résumé to Williams.

Williams was indeed interested and invited Dorsey to join a podcasting platform start-up called Odeo as a programmer. Dorsey had an interest in creating a communication service that updated people without needing access to a computer. Furthermore, he had the idea of sharing "status," or what the user was doing right then.

From a company brainstorming session, the idea for a short message service for internal communication emerged, a project initially called twttr (Carlson 2011). The first message on the site was posted by Dorsey, who tweeted on March 21, 2006, that he was "just setting up my twttr." His Twitter handle, @Jack, was the twelfth created at the company, but only because the first eleven were tests (Max 2013). When a domain name was purchased, the site became Twitter. Debate has swirled about the founding of Twitter, but "Everyone agrees that original inkling for Twitter sprang from Jack Dorsey's mind. Dorsey even has drawings of something that looks like Twitter that he made years before he joined Odeo. And Jack was obviously central to the Twitter team" (Carlson 2011).

Dorsey became the first CEO of Twitter, but created problems by apparently "spending a considerable amount of time going to hot-yoga classes and taking sewing lessons" and not giving enough attention to the fledging company (Bilton 2016). After his ousting just one and a half years into his tenure, Dorsey was replaced by fellow founder Evan Williams, but remained with Twitter as chairman of the board, later becoming executive chairman in 2011 (Indvik 2011). With the encouragement of Dorsey, Twitter acquired Vine in 2014, a social network where users post six-second videos, and Periscope in early 2015, a live-broadcasting service (Malik 2015). In October 2015, Twitter announced that Dorsey would return as CEO with the hope of making significant changes to this important, but struggling, social media platform (Malik 2015). After having Dorsey in place as CEO for a few months, user growth was flat, the stock price was down 60 percent since the previous CEO had been in place, and the company's market valuation had dropped from $40 billion to about $20 billion (Bilton 2016).

Between the years of serving as CEO of Twitter, Dorsey launched Square in 2010, a system that allows any retailer to process credit card payments using a mobile device and a credit card reader (Indvik 2011). In addition to serving as the CEO of Twitter, Dorsey remains the CEO of Square. The Twitter board had asked him to resign as the CEO of Square, but Dorsey refused (Bilton 2016). Dorsey's annual salary at Square is a mere $2.75, a small but significant amount that refers to the percentage that Square charges merchants per credit card swipe. Dorsey also does not receive a consequential salary at Twitter, but his shares in both companies are worth over $1 billion (Rao 2016).

Fake, Caterina (1969–)

Caterina Fake represents an early social media entrepreneur and one of the few women entrepreneurs discussed in this chapter. All the platforms launched by Fake share a common thread—they combine art, technology, and community. Along with her then-husband Stewart Butterfield, Fake founded photo-sharing site Flickr in 2004 through their company Ludicorp. In an interview with *Biz Journals*, Fake explained the perfect timing of Flickr. She said, "When we started, more than 50 percent of houses had broadband. People had phones with cameras. People were familiar with putting pictures online. It was a fast-moving train all at once" (Portillo 2014). Just one year later, the site was acquired by Yahoo for an estimated $35 million, according to experts (Portillo 2014).

Prior to Flickr, Fake and her company Ludicorp had developed the massively multiplayer online game called Game Neverending. The game was available on the Web from 2002 to 2004. The tools they built for Game Neverending then evolved into Flickr. Prior to that, Fake was involved in the Web through her early participation in online discussion board The WELL (The Whole Earth 'Lectronic Link) and she was also a community manager for Netscape communities. She started blogging in 1998 and was a part of a small community of bloggers at the time (Portillo 2014). Other jobs before Ludicorp included working as a temp designing CD-ROM education titles in the IT department at Columbia University, a position with the Web development company Organic, and a stint as an art director at Salon.com (Larson 2014).

After Flickr was sold, Fake spent a few years with Yahoo where she launched Yahoo! Answers and the idea incubator Brickhouse. Fake's next venture was cofounding Hunch, which used collective intelligence to build a taste graph to map people's preferences based on their answers to a range of questions. The tool then offered suggestions, based on a "hunch" that the user would like the recommendation. Like with Flickr, this platform was quickly acquired by a larger company, this time by eBay for a reported $80 million (Portillo 2014).

In recent years, Fake has used her vast wealth to be an angel investor in such companies as Kickstarter and Etsy. Additionally, she served on the Etsy board as chairwoman for five years. In the early days of her involvement with Etsy, she helped the company with day-to-day operations and closing their first round of funding (Bilton 2010).

With $9.5 million in funding, Fake launched Findery in 2014, an app with the slogan "where every place has a story." Through the app, users can share notes and photos on a world map. Some of the platform's strengths are the hidden gems and personal stories that are available to travelers (Portillo 2014). In addition to being the founder, Fake also serves as CEO of the company.

Born in Pittsburgh, Fake's background includes an early interest in writing and art. In college at Smith and then Vassar, she majored in English and then worked as a fine artist in New York City. After moving to San Francisco in 1995, she applied her art skills to a career as a Web designer and programmer. She taught herself HTML and began building websites (Bilton 2010). Fake's many honors include an appearance on the list of *Time* magazine's 100 Most Influential People in the World in 2006 and honorary doctorates from the New School and Rhode Island School of Design.

Hoffman, Reid (1967–)

Reid Hoffman, founder of LinkedIn, is a Stanford graduate with strong ties to the Silicon Valley area since birth. He was born at Stanford Hospital in Palo Alto, raised by two lawyer parents who separated early in their marriage, and attended middle school and then a private high school in Berkeley before transferring to the Putney School, a boarding school in Vermont (Lemann 2015). At the age of nine, Hoffman delved into fantasy role-playing games, particularly Dungeons & Dragons. After learning that the company that published Dungeons & Dragons, Chaosium, had a nearby office, Hoffman joined a group of boys who tested products and later, wrote game reviews for a gaming magazine published by the company (Lemann 2015). After graduating from high school in 1985, Hoffman enrolled in Stanford to study symbolic systems, a major that integrated philosophy, linguistics, psychology, and computer science. He met his future wife, Michelle Yee, during his freshman year, and also became friends with classmate Peter Thiel, who would later play a pivotal role in Hoffman's career. Both Thiel and Hoffman served on the student senate (Lemann 2015).

Post-Stanford, Hoffman earned a master's degree in philosophy at Oxford on a Marshall scholarship to prepare for an academic career. Hoffman then abruptly switched course and returned to Silicon Valley with the idea of starting a software company (Lee 2009). Through a personal connection, Hoffman landed a job at Apple with the intention of learning how to launch a start-up. While at Apple, he worked on the online service eWorld. After learning software development at Apple, he moved on to Fujitsu to develop skills in product management and business operations, focusing on the virtual chat community WorldsAway (Lemann 2015). In 1997, Hoffman launched SocialNet, which focused mostly on online dating, but also helped others connect. The start-up was able to attract funding from venture capitalists, but the business model that involved partnering with newspapers was not sustainable (Lee 2009). Hoffman's departure from SocialNet was followed by an offer from hedge fund owners Peter Thiel and Max Levchin to join them at their start-up, PayPal. While serving as executive vice president of business development at PayPal,

Hoffman gained a greater understanding of "how the world of work was changing" (Lee 2009).

PayPal was sold to eBay in 2002, which gave Hoffman the opportunity and funding to work full-time on his next concept, LinkedIn, a social networking platform for professionals to connect to one another as well as job openings. The platform for LinkedIn was built using a patent for constructing social networks purchased from Six Degrees by Hoffman and Mark Pincus, cofounder of Zynga, for $700,000 (Lemann 2015). Around this time, Hoffman also connected Thiel and Mark Zuckerberg, leading to Thiel's investment in Facebook. Hoffman and Pincus each purchased 0.5 percent of Facebook for $37,500 (Lemann 2015).

Hoffman's initial goal with LinkedIn was to first engage 1 million users and then figure out the business model for the company (Lee 2009). For the first two years, LinkedIn had no revenues (Lemann 2015). By 2005, having reached the first goal, LinkedIn focused on three sources of revenue: job listings, subscriptions for enhanced services, and advertising. By 2008, Facebook's membership was approximately three times that of LinkedIn and fear set in among LinkedIn employees that Facebook might attempt to incorporate a professional networking feature to compete with LinkedIn, but Hoffman remained steadfast that people would want to use different platforms to keep their professional and personal lives separate (Lemann 2015).

Building growth early on was aided by the ability of users to upload their entire e-mail contact list to launch automatic invitations as well as the decision in 2006 to make profiles partially public so that they appear at the top of Google search results (Lemann 2015). LinkedIn also uses a powerful algorithm to make relevant suggestions for connecting.

After realizing that LinkedIn needed further product development in 2006, Hoffman hired a new CEO, Dan Nye, and moved into the product side. Two years later, Deep Nishar from Google was hired as vice president of products to relieve Hoffman of that responsibility and allow him to return as CEO and chair. During the two-year period that Nye had served as CEO, membership grew from 9 million to 35 million and sales increased 900 percent (Lee 2009). In 2011, shortly after surpassing 100 million users, the company went public, making Hoffman a billionaire (Lemann 2015).

Hoffman and Yee married in 2004 and decided not to have children. Although Yee worked as a clinical psychologist, she is pursuing a philanthropic project to focus on and often escapes from Silicon Valley to attend Buddhist retreats (Lemann 2015). Despite his great wealth, Hoffman lives in a four-bedroom home and does not own a private plane, although he did recently splurge on a Tesla (Lemann 2015).

In addition to serving as executive chairman at LinkedIn, Hoffman is also a partner in the venture capital firm Greylock (Lemann 2015). Hoffman is a regular at events such as the annual TED conference, the World Economic Forum, international relations conference Bilderberg, and gatherings organized by Thiel, Google's Eric Schmidt, and technology guru Tim O'Reilly. Hoffman also organizes his own annual conference called The Weekend to be Named Later that includes about 150 power players and their families at a Southern California resort (Lemann 2015). He also travels to China several times a year, which is the fastest growing market for the company (Lemann 2015). Hoffman serves on the boards of Airbnb, Edmodo, Xapo, Wrapp, Mozilla, and Kiva. Previous board positions include shopkick, Zynga, Six Apart, Vendio, and Grassroots. He is also the author of *The Start-up of You*, published in 2012 with Ben Casnocha, and *The Alliance: Managing Talent in the Networked Age*, published in 2014 also with Ben Casnocha and Chris Yeh. Hoffman also enjoys playing the popular board game, Settlers of Catan, and created a version for friends called Startups of Silicon Valley (Lemann 2015).

Hughes, Chris (1983–)

Chris Hughes is not only a social media platform cofounder, but also known for contributing his social and digital media expertise to a successful presidential campaign as the director of online organizing. As described by Ellen McGirt in *Fast Company*, "Hughes has helped create two of the most successful startups in modern history, Facebook and the campaign apparatus that got Barack Obama elected" (McGirt 2009).

Hughes's early life was spent in Hickory, North Carolina, and he was raised as the only son of a paper salesman and a former public school teacher. He applied on his own to boarding schools, and after receiving a generous financial aid package from Phillips Academy, enrolled in the Andover, Massachusetts, school (McGirt 2009). Hughes then attended Harvard on scholarship where he met Mark Zuckerberg. Hughes's early role on the Facebook team was not writing code like Zuckerberg and fellow cofounder Dustin Moskovitz, but instead making suggestions about the functionality of the site as well as opening Facebook to other schools, although Hughes initially argued that each school should have a separate network (McGirt 2009). After spending part of the summer in Palo Alto after his sophomore year, Hughes, unlike the others, returned to Harvard to finish his double major in history and French literature, study abroad for a semester in Paris, and write a thesis on urban space in Algiers (McGirt 2009). He continued, however, working with the Facebook team, and returned to Palo Alto after graduation.

Hughes's work for Facebook bridged his interest in politics when Facebook started offering profile pages to political candidates for midterm elections in 2006, long before fan pages were available to celebrities and brands (McGirt 2009). Although then-senator Barack Obama was not a midterm candidate at that time, he was still interested in having a Facebook page, and it was Hughes who provided the customer service. Soon afterward, Hughes was invited to join the Obama presidential campaign as the third member of the new media team.

For the Obama campaign, Hughes "helped develop the most robust set of Web-based social-networking tools ever used in a political campaign, enabling energized citizens to turn themselves into activists" (McGirt 2009). The digital tool, called MyBarackObama.com or MyBO for short, as well as the main campaign website went live the same day Obama announced his candidacy. Approximately 1,000 groups organized on the first day of the MyBO launch, nearly crashing the site (McGirt 2009).

MyBO provided a way for supporters to organize themselves into groups, plan events, fund-raise, and target possible supporters. Working with contracted and in-house developers, Hughes built a powerful calling and canvassing tool called Neighbor-to-Neighbor. Users could find a list of people who were undecided or leaning toward Obama who could be called or visited. The tool integrated data on these potential Obama voters to match that of the volunteers as much as possible. Neighbor-to-Neighbor is credited with facilitating approximately 8 million volunteer calls (McGirt 2009).

Hughes also led the development of the Vote for Change voter registration site. The site not only registered 1 million people, but also included a strategy to register people in the most advantageous state to the campaign. For example, depending on the rules of the states involved, a college student may be able to register to vote either in the state where he or she attends school or his or her home state. The app decided which state was more important for the Obama campaign and registered the student there (McGirt 2009).

By the end of the campaign, using MyBO.com, volunteers had created more than 2 million profiles, planned 200,000 offline events, formed 35,000 groups, and raised $30 million on 70,000 fund-raising pages (McGirt 2009). After the election, Hughes transformed MyBO.com into Organizing for America, which became a Democratic National Committee project.

In 2012, Hughes purchased a majority stake in the progressive magazine *The New Republic*, but after a major staff exodus in 2014 and a decline in traffic in 2015 of about 40 percent, he sold the magazine in early 2016 (Byers 2016). Hughes had purchased the magazine for an undisclosed sum, which sources have indicated to be about $2.1 million and then invested about $20 million to transform it into a digital media company (Byers 2016). According to *Forbes* in 2016, Hughes is worth $430 million and was listed as number 28 on the list of richest American entrepreneurs under age 40 (Kroll 2016).

Karp, David (1986–)

David Karp, founder of the microblogging platform Tumblr, was once a tech-obsessed teenager who taught himself to code at age 11. Karp's parents noticed he needed more challenge than his prestigious New York City high school, Bronx Science, could offer and began to look at other ways to engage their son. Karp's mother reached out to Fred Seibert, who was running an animation production company, and Seibert offered Karp the opportunity to stop by the office. Eventually, Karp decided to home school, freeing more time to work for Seibert in an attempt to better position himself to gain admission to MIT for computer engineering (Bercovici 2013a). Karp also took Japanese language lessons at the Japan Society and worked with a math tutor to write software for blackjack and poker (Bercovici 2013a).

Instead of applying to MIT, however, Karp continued working as head of product at UrbanBaby, a parenting website. While still working for UrbanBaby, Karp's next venture was taking his coding and limited knowledge of Japanese to Tokyo when he was just 17 years old with an interest in building robots (Halliday 2012). Instead, Karp returned with a desire to become an entrepreneur as well as a handful of contracts and a list of executives to contact (Halliday 2012). After UrbanBaby was acquired by CNET, Karp sold his equity and set up the development company, Davidville, to which he signed Viacom and other major companies as clients (Halliday 2012). One of Karp's projects was tweaking a multiuser blogging platform that he had built for Seibert's company. Through Seibert, Karp met investor Bijan Sabet of Spark Capital who wanted to invest in what would eventually become Tumblr (Bercovici 2013a). The initial offer of venture capital was deemed by Karp to be "too much money with too much pressure" (Bercovici 2013a). When reduced to $750,000 with a $3 million valuation, Karp finally agreed to the investment.

At the age of 21 from the bedroom of his mother's apartment in New York City, Karp launched Tumblr (Halliday 2012). At the time, Tumblr had just one other employee, Marco Arment, who had been recruited through Craigslist. Karp's initial vision for the company was to offer a product that would not require additional investment and would not be later bought out. He saw Tumblr as a way to attract customers for his consultancy business that offered website services. For a few months, Karp was able to keep a foot in both businesses, but then when the user base started doubling every few weeks, Karp realized that he needed to focus exclusively on Tumblr (Halliday 2012). Karp also originally tried to keep the team small, but when the user base surged, the company was not prepared to handle the resulting engineering issues. Offers to move the business to Silicon Valley poured in, but Karp felt that New York was more supportive of start-ups and stayed.

Although Karp was reluctant to base Tumblr's business model on advertising, the company eventually offered promoted posts. After Yahoo purchased Tumblr for $1.1 billion in 2013, Karp remained as CEO. Karp has used his wealth to invest $500,000 in New York start-up Sherpaa Inc., a company that offers an app that connects employees and physicians, and more than $2 million in Superpedestrian Inc., which builds a device that can transform a bicycle into a hybrid electric. Karp has made other investments in start-ups such as Thirty Labs, Elixir, Kitchensurfing, and Picturelife (Crunchbase n.d.). He has stated in interviews that he does not want to use his wealth to be a venture capitalist per se but enjoys supporting the start-ups of friends (Chernova 2014).

Kjellberg, Felix (1983–)

Felix Kjellberg, known online as "PewDiePie," is the world's biggest YouTube star. He built a large following by creating YouTube videos of himself playing video and mobile games.

Instead of merely watching reviews, Kjellberg's audience has the opportunity to view his game-playing experience, hear his opinions, and observe his strange but comedic behavior in this process. As noted in an article in the *Wall Street Journal*, "He contorts, screeches, swears, sings and even 'twerks' to portray his feelings" (Grundberg and Hansegard 2014).

Originally from Gothenburg, Sweden, Kjellberg created the alter ego PewDiePie in 2009. His first video featured the game Minecraft and Kjellberg's commentary in Swedish, followed by several videos with English commentary about first-person shooter games, such as Call of Duty (Hernandez 2014). He continued to upload what is known as "Let's Play" videos, where viewers watch players engage with a video game and learn from the commentary about their strategies. Kjellberg now wields enough power to propel a new game to become a success, and game producers even give shout-outs to PewDiePie hoping he will create a "Let's Play" video based on their games for his channel (Hernandez 2014).

Wanting to focus full time on his YouTube channel, Kjellberg dropped out of Chalmers University of Technology in Sweden where he had been majoring in industrial economics and technology management (Gallagher 2013). He worked at a hot dog stand to support himself while getting started making videos (Regan 2015).

Through his video channel, Kjellberg has created an empire that pulled in revenues of approximately $7.4 million in 2014. He has branched out from his initial video game videos to more comedic sketches. With more than 43 million subscribers, his top 10 most popular videos have more than 30 million views each with his most popular exceeding 72 million. In 2012, he signed a deal with Maker Studios that manages the production of online content, but also takes a percentage of ad sales (Grundberg and Hansegard 2014).

Kjellberg's popularity has attracted criticism from both the public and the press. A Twitter poll reported by Kotaku found that people described PewDiePie with such words as "obnoxious waste of time" and "annoying" (Hernandez 2014). An article in *Variety* magazine attributes Kjellberg's success to his "blathering like a blithering idiot" (Wallenstein 2013). The article continued by saying, "Foul-mouthed PewDiePie jabbers nonsensically to the fans he calls 'bros' primarily about videogames in a voice that reminds you of a young Bobcat Goldthwait between hits of nitrous oxide" (Wallenstein 2013).

Kjellberg ranked third behind two YouTube duos in a survey of 1,500 teens by *Variety* about the influence of 20 well-known personalities, a list that included both YouTubers and traditional celebrities such as actors and singers (Ault 2014). PewDiePie ranked higher than celebrities Jennifer Lawrence, Katy Perry, and Johnny Depp.

His 2014 online earnings generated controversy for the young star when they were released in the Swedish newspaper *Expressen* and the story went viral (Regan 2015). He shared in a video how "It seems like the whole world cares more about how much money I make than I do myself." He further explained that "They [the critics] thought I just sit on my ass all day, and I just yell at the screen over here. Which is true! But there's so much more to it than that" (Regan 2015). Kjellberg also emphasized that he has given a million dollars of his earnings to charity.

Monty, Scott (1970–)

Scott Monty is among the digital pioneers who led social media for a major American corporation in the early years of social media. In Monty's case, it was Ford Motor Company. Ford's CEO Alan Mulally once called Monty "a visionary" (Wernle 2014). He has also been ranked by *Forbes* magazine as one of the top influencers in social media.

For almost six years, Monty served as manager of global digital and multimedia communications for Ford. In this position, he led the company's social media and digital activities including blogger relations, marketing support, customer service, and internal communications (Wernle 2014). He utilized social media to reach new and existing customers, and under his leadership, Ford was the first company to introduce a car on Facebook and the first brand on Google+. For the relaunch of the Ford Fiesta, Monty recruited 100 online bloggers and influencers, gave them each a car to drive for a year, and encouraged them to generate brand content to share through social and digital platforms to build awareness of the car (Wernle 2014). In another campaign for Ford called "Random Acts of Fusion," Monty's team rewarded Internet conversation about the Ford Fusion by surprising users with a car wash, offering critics a test drive, or having comedians create a retweet of their tweets (Fera 2013).

Measuring the impact of social media on the bottom line is a critical task of any social media manager. Monty famously said, "What's the ROI of putting your pants on every day? It's hard to measure but there's negative consequences for not doing it" (Ratcliff 2014). In an interview with Econsultancy, Monty clarified that social media requires different measurement techniques than marketing or other communication functions of an organization (Ratcliff 2014). It is also difficult to isolate and measure social media because they are often tied to advertising and public relations efforts.

Under Monty's leadership, digital and social media at Ford became increasingly important to the company's marketing strategy. Even though traditional methods were still being used by Ford, the percentage of the marketing budget allocated toward digital and social media was 25 percent in 2011 and has been increasing each year since then (Ratcliff 2014).

After leaving Ford, Monty became executive vice president of strategy for SHIFT Communications. He then founded and now serves as CEO for Scott Monty Strategies. In 2016, Monty became the CEO and co-managing partner of Brain+Trust Partners, an executive consultancy firm that focuses on putting humanity into digital communications. As Shel Israel wrote about him in *Forbes*, "Monty has been one of the poster children of making the modern brand—even entrenched, iconic brands like Ford—more conversational, personal and transparent. Along with other social media pioneers who injected this new thinking into other big brands, he believes the real power of this new form of communications lies in listening to the views of customers, prospects, partners and competitors" (Israel 2014).

Monty's educational background includes three degrees from Boston University: a bachelor's degree in classical civilization, a master's degree in medical science, and a master's in business administration with a focus on health care management. After several early positions in communications, marketing, and development in the health care field, Monty entered the agency side as an account director for PJA Advertising & Marketing, which was followed by a stint with the marketing agency Crayon before moving on to Ford. Monty has been blogging since the early 2000s, and his current blog can be found at scottmonty.com. He also distributes the newsletter "The Full Monty" and is executive editor and cohost of "I Hear of Sherlock Everywhere," a website and podcast for Sherlock Holmes fans.

Parker, Sean (1979–)

As one of the youngest people profiled in this chapter to become a technology entrepreneur, Sean Parker cofounded the file-sharing site Napster in 1999 at the age of 19 (Kirkpatrick 2010b). With Shawn Fanning, Parker dramatically changed the music business through Napster, a peer-to-peer music-sharing service. The industry as well as several bands and musicians responded by suing Napster for copyright infringement, which eventually forced the company to close.

Growing up, Parker learned to code on an Atari 800 at a young age by his oceanographer father. Although described as being "painfully cerebral" with an informed opinion on a variety of topics, Parker barely finished high school (Kirkpatrick 2010b). During high school, he honed his hacking skills by tapping into a range of Fortune 500 companies, educational institutions, and military and government websites around the world. He was eventually caught by the FBI and sentenced to perform community service (Kirkpatrick 2010b). During his senior year, he interned as a programmer for Mark Pincus's D.C. start-up FreeLoader and then Internet service provider UUNet, receiving high school credits and an income of $80,000 (Bertoni 2011). After meeting Fanning and learning of his plans to create Napster, Parker decide to forego college to move to San Francisco and work on the project. After the quick ascent and then downfall of Napster because of legal orders that halted users from illegally downloading copyrighted material, Parker was pushed out of the company.

Parker has exhibited a strong sense about the direction of technology and Facebook's Zuckerberg has said that "few people are as smart as he [Parker] is" (Kirkpatrick 2010b). After Napster, Parker cofounded the contact management system Plaxo at the age of 21, but was later fired. After approaching Zuckerberg for a meeting in New York City, the two connected over dinner there. Parker again met up with Zuckerberg in Palo Alto, and he was invited to live in the rented summer home. At age 24, Parker became the founding president of Facebook, a position he held briefly, but that association contributed most significantly to his net worth, estimated to be $2.4 billion in 2016 (Kirkpatrick 2010b).

In 2006, Parker joined Peter Thiel's Founders Fund as a managing partner. He has also been instrumental in bringing digital music service Spotify to the United States. He started the Facebook application Causes with Joe Green, who attended Harvard with Zuckerberg. A recent venture for Parker is Brigade Media, a social media platform for civic and political engagement. In 2016, Parker cofounded The Screening Room, a service that would provide movies to viewers at home the same day they are released in theaters. The pitch involves a $150 set-top box that provides secure, anti-piracy technology and movies that cost $50 to rent (Kosoffmarch 2016).

In 2015, Parker created The Parker Foundation and funded it with $600 million (The Parker Foundation n.d.). The mission of the foundation is to fund life sciences, global health, and civic engagement projects. To date, the foundation has provided $10 million to create an autoimmunity research lab at the University of California, San Francisco (UCSF). Before setting up the foundation, he had funded malaria research at UCSF through a $4.5 million donation and an allergy research center to be named the Sean N. Parker Center for Allergy and Asthma Research at Stanford University with a $24 million donation (The Parker Foundation n.d.).

As a billionaire, Parker has been living lavishly. Parker and his wife Alexandra Lenas were married in 2013 in Big Sur, California, in a $4.5 million ceremony that lasted three days. All guests were provided with Tolkien-inspired costumes by the *Lord of the Rings* costume designer to wear during the ceremony (Kirkpatrick 2010b). He owns a $20 million West Village townhome nicknamed the "Bacchus House" and a $55 million home in Los Angeles called "The Brody House," which was purchased from Ellen DeGeneres (Gross 2011).

Pincus, Mark (1966–)

Originally from Chicago, Mark Pincus, cofounder of social gaming site Zynga, is the son of two professionals, an architect mother and a father who was a partner in a mergers-and-acquisitions firm (Grigoriadis 2011). As a child, he was competitive at a wide range of games including video games, outdoor sports, and board games like Trivial Pursuit and Scrabble (Grigoriadis 2011). Pincus earned an undergraduate business degree from the Wharton School at the University of Pennsylvania and an MBA from Harvard Business School. Between college and graduate school, Pincus worked at Lazard Frères as a member of the bank's first program for postcollege grads and also at Asian Capital Partners (Takahashi 2011). After graduate school, he did not land a job immediately because, as he claimed, "I just didn't have a lot of respect for authority" (Grigoriadis 2011). After deciding that he should change his career path from finance to media, he worked for cable company TCI where he wrote business plans for the Auto Channel and TV Guide Onscreen and also conceptualized the Disaster Channel. Pincus's next position was with a Washington, D.C., venture capital firm, from which he was fired (Grigoriadis 2011).

Prior to founding Zynga, Mark Pincus was a three-time entrepreneur. His first company was FreeLoader, a Web-based push technology service, which he sold for $38 million. Pincus described during a talk at Berkeley that he received a "small share of the total" (Cutler 2009). The sale was one of the first for big Web companies and earned Pincus some recognition in the tech industry (Grigoriadis 2011). After moving to San Francisco, he launched another start-up called Support.com to provide online tech support, which he described as a "service that nobody wanted" (Cutler 2009). When the company went public in 2000, an industry source estimated that Pincus earned $30 million from the deal (Grigoriadis 2011). In 2003, Pincus founded Tribe Networks, which operates the social networking website Tribe.net. Unfortunately for Tribe, some attendees of the annual Burning Man festival held in the Nevada desert eventually gravitated to the site and uploaded photos of themselves naked, offending and driving away users (Grigoriadis 2011).

Despite earning millions from these projects, Pincus described feeling like a failure as an entrepreneur (Grigoriadis 2011). He attended retreats by motivational coach Tony Robbins and started working with a life coach whose clients included other Internet entrepreneurs. Pincus so enjoyed the benefits of working with coaches that he also hired tennis and yoga coaches, as well as a skiing coach during his birthday week. According to Pincus, the coaching paid off because it helped him see gaming in a different way (Grigoriadis 2011). He learned through his coaches that by spending money on a game, a player can compete at a higher level.

Zynga soared to popularity as one of the first companies to allow friends to play games against one another on a social platform, which was Facebook in Zynga's case (Wingfield 2016). The games require a monetary investment to be successful

(Grigoriadis 2011). Eventually, people grew annoyed with the dominance of social gaming content in their feeds, and Facebook made changes that made it more difficult for games and other apps to solicit users. Facebook also insisted that Zynga use Facebook Credits for currency, which would give Facebook a 30 percent share of revenues. This move caused Pincus to threaten to pull Zynga's games from Facebook, but after Pincus and Mark Zuckerberg discussed the situation, they were able to work out a deal. Zynga also missed the opportunity to seamlessly move onto mobile devices, which is where games like Candy Crush and Clash of Clans thrived.

Pincus has been described as a micromanager who has a difficult time delegating or empowering his team (Lynley 2015). Also known for his analytical savvy, Pincus may have helped drive a strong initial public offering for Zynga. His leadership style, however, was criticized by investors. During "greenlight" meetings used to determine the games that would move forward into full development, Pincus was notorious for grilling his team about the monetization strategy of each game and how to engineer the game's virality (Lynley 2015). Insiders claimed this approach hampered creativity within the company. A video of Pincus talking about all the ways the company would exploit users to increase revenues circulated throughout the tech industry and created controversy for the Zynga leader (Grigoriadis 2011).

Before Zynga went public at a $7 billion valuation, Pincus's fortune was estimated to be $2 billion, but his net worth took a dive to around $1 billion upon the company going public in 2011 (Mac 2013a). Throughout the spring of 2012, stock prices rallied and reached a high of $14.69 in March. Then, after Pincus sold 16.5 million shares, which totaled about 16 percent of his stock in the company, investor confidence drove the stock price down and the company never recovered (Mac 2013a). At the time of the sale, other employees were required to hold onto their shares, and Pincus's actions damaged their ability to sell at a favorable price.

Pincus announced in 2013 that he was stepping down from his position as CEO of Zynga and would be replaced by former Xbox executive Don Mattrick. Pincus, however, remained with the company as chief product officer and chairman of the board, two positions he was already holding. At some point, he did step away from day-to-day company operations, but still had an office at Zynga and indicated his support for the future of the company. In an internal memo to employees, he said, "I remain Zynga's largest shareholder and biggest believer" (Lynley 2014).

While Pincus was away from Zynga, he focused on investing. He had previously been an early investor in such successful social media platforms as Facebook and Twitter, and during this period, he is reported to have also invested in Dropbox (Lynley 2014). Sources also claimed that he attempted to be an investor in the app Secret, but was turned down along with other potential investors (Lynley 2014). In 2014, he started a new company that resembled both a start-up and an incubator called Superlabs. With his own funding, he supported work on digital projects that he had been considering since leaving Zynga (Swisher 2014).

In 2015, Zynga announced that Pincus would return to once again serve as CEO, news that caused an 18 percent drop in the company's stock price (Lynley 2015). An initiative of Pincus at the time was to make the company more data-driven and become known for its analytics. Pincus stepped down less than a year later as CEO to become executive chairman and was replaced by board member Frank Gibeau (Wingfield 2016).

On a personal note, Pincus and his wife, Alison, purchased a $16 million home in the prestigious Presidio district of San Francisco in 2012 (Schuker 2012). Alison, also a digital entrepreneur, is the cofounder of One Kings Lane, a flash site for home accessories and furniture.

Rose, Kevin (1977–)

Kevin Rose has been described as having "a way of creating amazing products and then neglecting them" (Lynley 2012).

Along with partners Owen Byrne, Ron Gorodetzky, and Jay Adelson, Rose founded the social news site Digg in 2004 with a $6,000 investment. The concept of the site was that users would share news stories that would become more or less prominent by user votes to "digg up" or "bury" content.

With a self-diagnosed case of attention deficit disorder as well as mild dyslexia, Rose was not a young overachiever like several other prominent social media entrepreneurs (Chafkin 2013). He was raised in a lower middle-class family in Las Vegas by an insurance salesman father and a mother who did nails. He learned some programming in middle school, but overall, he struggled in school with both his studies and girls (Chafkin 2013). His secondary education included computer science night classes at the University of Nevada, Las Vegas, and employment as a technician at a nuclear test site. In 2002, he moved to San Francisco for a production assistant job with the cable network TechTV. He quickly moved on air as the "resident hacker" and then a host (Chafkin 2013).

Rose met Adelson in the late 1990s when Adelson was interviewed by TechTV for a segment about one of his companies (Lynley 2012). Rose was inspired by Adelson's entrepreneurial spirit, and Adelson was interested in video production. It was Rose who first suggested a site that would "democratize the news," and with Adelson's mentoring, Rose built a prototype (Lynley 2012). Adelson then officially joined the team, and Byrne was added to write the code for Digg.

In 2007, after hackers cracked the code for HD-DVD, making it possible to copy and illegally distribute HD-DVDs, a Digg post instructed users how they could do this themselves. After Digg removed the initial post to avoid legal problems, community members continued to repost and also comment on the situation. Rose sided with the community, saying on his blog, "But now, after seeing hundreds of stories and reading thousands of comments, you've made it clear. You'd rather see Digg go down fighting than bow down to a bigger company. We hear you, and effective immediately we won't delete stories or comments containing the code and will deal with whatever the consequences might be" (Marcus 2010).

When TechTV was sold and then folded into another channel, Rose, Adelson, and several others including former TechTV employees cofounded Revision3. A video podcast called Diggnation by Rose and Alex Albrecht launched in 2005 on the site, which further helped to promote the Digg brand by featuring popular stories shared on Digg (Marcus 2010). According to the website, Revision3 provides "all-original weekly and daily episodic community driven programs watched by a super committed, passionate fan base." Rose currently offers a series on the site called "Foundation," where he interviews entrepreneurs. In 2012, Discovery Communications acquired Revision3. Rose also cofounded the microblogging site Pownce in 2007, which was purchased and closed by Six Apart in 2008. His involvement in side projects like Pownce angered the board, who felt that because Digg's designer, Daniel Burka, was working on Pownce, it was a Digg product and that any success of Pownce should benefit Digg shareholders (Lynley 2012). Rose unveiled at the SXSW conference in 2009 another side project, WeFollow, a Twitter directory.

During the early years, offers to purchase Digg included a $200 million offer by Google and a $60 million offer from News Corp (Lynley 2012). In 2006, the Digg board entertained and then turned down the offer from News Corp in a deal that would have earned Rose $36 million at the age of 29 (Lynley 2012). Google's deal was off the table when they looked into Digg's technology and caliber of the technical team and determined it had faults (Lynley 2012). In 2010, after deciding to become more involved in Digg after being distracted by other projects, Rose fired Adelson as CEO. Rose then became CEO of Digg and committed himself full time to the company. His tenure lasted only six months until Matt Williams joined Digg from Amazon as CEO. Rose finally left Digg in early 2011. Digg was sold to Betaworks in 2012 for a mere $500,000 with some additional equity. Some of the company's patents were sold to LinkedIn for $4 million and the engineering team was acquired by a Washington Post Co. subsidiary for $12 million (Lynley 2012).

Since Digg, Rose cofounded the company Milk in 2011, an app workshop company. The company's first product was a review application called Oink (Lynley 2012). Rose and his team clashed when the team wanted to continue working on Oink and launch a second version, but Rose was more interested in pursuing new ideas. With only $1.1 million in funding and a large team, the company could not agree on its direction, and Milk was acquired by Google (Konrad 2015). Rose then joined the Google team and was investing for Google Ventures. In 2015, Rose scaled back his time commitment to Google to focus on North Technologies, a consumer app workshop. The first two projects of North were Tiiny, a photo-sharing app. and then Watchville, a platform for watch collectors. Although neither project gained traction, Rose received $5 million in seed funding from investors, but then closed in 2015 after being in existence for less than a year.

As an angel investor in other social media platforms in their early stages, Rose has been quite successful. His investments include Twitter, Square, Fab, Facebook, Path, and Zynga. Other less familiar companies have also been good investments, including Chomp, which was acquired by Apple for $50 million; OMGPop, acquired by Zynga for $200 million; and Ngmoco, purchased for $400 million by a Japanese gaming company. His return on investment in these companies is estimated to be almost 2,200 percent (Chafkin 2013). As of 2015, Rose moved to New York City to lead Hodinkee, a watch enthusiast website (Green 2016).

Sandberg, Sheryl (1969–)

Perhaps the most important and influential woman in social media is Sheryl Sandberg. Sandberg, who joined Facebook as chief operating officer in 2008, had already become a multimillionaire through her stock options from Google where she was the vice president of global online sales and operations from 2001 to 2008 (Kirkpatrick 2010a). Before Google, she worked as chief of staff to Lawrence Summers when he served as secretary of the Treasury during the Clinton administration. She had met Summers as a student at Harvard majoring in economics when she took his class called Public Sector Economics. Summers later served as her thesis adviser as she explored the relationship between economic inequality and spousal abuse.

From Google, Sandberg brought her experience in working with advertisers to Facebook, which was ambivalent about advertising as a business model, mainly because of Zuckerberg's objections (Kirkpatrick 2010a). Shortly after joining, Sandberg held evening brainstorming sessions to answer the question: "What business are we in?" Options included advertising, selling user data, selling avatars and other virtual goods, or enabling transactions and taking a cut of the fees (Kirkpatrick 2010a). The consensus of the team was that advertising should represent 70 percent or more of the company's revenues. Instead of Google's advertising strategy that fulfills a demand searched for, Facebook's would create demand (Kirkpatrick 2010a). Four years after joining the Facebook, Sandberg became the first woman on the company's board.

In 2013, Sandberg's book *Lean In: Women, Work and the Will to Lead* was published, which started a movement among women as well as backlash toward Sandberg. The book discusses the challenges faced by women, including those as highly accomplished and recruited as Sandberg, in corporate America. In the book, she outlines a plan for effective working relationships between women and men to increase opportunities for women at the top. Some reviews, however, criticized her suggestions as only appropriate for elite professional women who can negotiate the terms of their employment and whose supervisors view them as an asset and will fight to keep them (Gara 2013). Reader backlash contended that institutional factors, such as gender discrimination and income inequality, cannot be overcome by a woman's sheer motivation or persistence for change (Groner 2014).

Born in Washington, D.C., Sandberg moved with her family to North Miami Beach, Florida, at the age of two. She is the daughter of an ophthalmologist father and a mother who gave up her pursuit of a PhD and a position teaching French at a college to raise Sandberg and her two younger siblings. Her parents founded the South Florida Conference on Soviet Jewry, which assisted Soviet Jews immigrating to the United States. Sandberg is a product of the public school system and was always at the top of her class (Auletta 2011). At Harvard, Sandberg cofounded the Women in Economics and Government club to encourage more women to select these majors. She was inducted into Phi Beta Kappa and graduated as the top student in the economics department (Auletta 2011). After graduation, Sandberg worked for about two years as a research assistant to Summers when he was chief economist at the World Bank. She returned to Harvard for an MBA and then took a job with McKinsey & Company.

Sandberg experienced tragedy in her personal life with the sudden death of her husband, Dave Goldberg, in 2015 during a vacation in Mexico (Goel 2015). At the time, the couple had been married more than 10 years and have two children. Like Sandberg, Goldberg was also a technology executive, working for Yahoo and then later as CEO of SurveyMonkey. Thirty days after his passing, Sandberg posted a compelling and heartbreaking post on Facebook about her husband that went viral and received mainstream media attention. Almost a year later, the post had 912,000 likes, 73,000 comments, and 400,000 shares.

According to *Forbes*, Sandberg's net worth in December 2016 was estimated to be $1.27 billion. In 2016, she ranked fourteenth on the *Forbes* list of America's Self-Made Women and seventh on the Power Women list (Forbes 2016b). At the end of 2015, Sandberg donated $31 million of her Facebook stock to the Sheryl Sandberg Philanthropy Fund. The fund provides support for her nonprofit Lean In to benefit working women as well as various education and antipoverty groups (Forbes 2016b).

Silbermann, Ben (1982–)

Ben Silbermann, cofounder of virtual pinboard Pinterest, is an Iowa native who attended a large public high school and excelled at cello and competitive debate. During his junior year, he was invited to participate in the prestigious Research Science Institute, sponsored by MIT and the Department of Defense (Chafkin 2012). Inspired by two ophthalmologist parents, Silbermann was a pre-med major at Yale before changing his career goals his junior year to business. During his first job with the Corporate Executive Board, a consulting company in Washington, D.C., he started reading technology blogs and getting excited about the platforms entrepreneurs were building (Chafkin 2012). He and his girlfriend both quit their corporate jobs and moved to the West Coast. Hired by Google, he worked in customer support and also designed products such as display ads. Without an engineering background, however, he felt his career growth there was stifled and left in 2008 (Chafkin 2012). In an interview with All Things D, Silbermann said, "if Google teaches you anything, it's that small ideas can be big" (Panzarino 2013). After resigning from Google, Silbermann collaborated with college friend Paul Sciarra to design iPhone apps but had little success (Shontell 2012). The team's first project, a shopping app called Tote, generated some seed funding but did not gain popular acceptance. It was useful, however, in demonstrating to Silbermann that although people were not interested in making purchases through the site, they did save photos for later viewing (Chafkin 2012).

An avid collector as a child, especially of bugs, Silbermann recognized there was not a place on the Internet to share collections. After a conversation with Columbia architecture graduate student Evan Sharp about infographics and collecting, Silbermann shared the idea of a digital collection as a method of self-expression (Chafkin 2012). In 2010, Silbermann and Sciarra then started working on this new project, which would become Pinterest. Sharp joined the team to design and code the site, much of which was done while sitting in a Whole Foods on the Upper West Side of Manhattan. In an apartment in Palo Alto, Silbermann and Sciarra collaborated with a single engineer they had added to the team.

Silbermann's strength as an entrepreneur has been credited to his "ability to look beyond the sometimes narrow-minded world of Internet entrepreneurship" (Chafkin 2012). He recognized that, unlike the users of many other social platforms, not everyone wanted to be a creator, but rather a curator of content created by others. He also resisted the popular feature of many other platforms to add an element of gamification to the site, where users compete to be on leaderboards or earn badges.

Pinterest was off to a slow start in the early days. After nine months, the platform had fewer than 10,000 users (Shontell 2012). The slow growth may have been attributed to limited sign-ups in the beginning. The first users were mostly design bloggers personally recruited by Silbermann who were each given a certain number of invitations to hand out to others with good taste.

Understanding the importance of loyal users, Silbermann personally contacted the first 5,000 users and provided many of them his cell phone number to discuss any issue directly with him. He attended blogger meet-ups and sent weekly e-mails to the community, which he had written himself. Despite lack of early success, Silbermann pressed on. He explained why in an interview at SXSW, "The idea of telling everyone we blew it was so embarrassing. I thought, 'Google is never going to take me back—they barely hired me the first time!'" (Shontell 2012).

Silbermann currently serves as the CEO of Pinterest. A 2012 interview revealed Silbermann's work ethic, which includes predawn checking of e-mail, leaving for the office at 7 a.m., and working nonstop until dinner. Silbermann expects the same commitment and work ethic from employees. To build new iPad and Android applications for Pinterest, Silbermann put all employees on "lockdown," which required them to come in early and stay late for several weeks. Employees received commemorative T-shirts emblazoned with the slogan "Summer of Apps." During this period, Silbermann was also on lockdown from all outside contact and did not even respond to business opportunities (Chafkin 2012). The Summer of Apps proved a success, and the iPad app was number one in the App Store within a day (Chafkin 2012).

Silbermann's mother has become a Pinterest celebrity of sorts. Back in 2012, his mother, Jane Wang, had the largest follower count on Pinterest with approximately 3.4 million followers. By 2016, she had dropped to fifth place, but had more than doubled her follower count to almost 7.9 million followers.

Smith, Marc (1965–)

A sociologist by education, Marc Smith studies computer-mediated communication and the organization of online communities. His academic credentials include a PhD in sociology from UCLA, a master's in social theory from Cambridge University, and a bachelor's in international area studies from Drexel University. Smith always had a passion for computers and was interested in interconnections, but not necessarily data or statistics. While growing up, Smith was one of the first owners of a Radio Shack Tandy TRS-80, an early home computer that hit the market in 1977, and he discussed in an interview how he realized that programming was not his niche, but rather that he was someone who could direct coders (De Waal 2010). Smith embraced data visualization as a way for people not versed in math and science to gain insights into the data.

Smith's research focuses on "the ways group dynamics change when they take place in and through social cyberspaces," particularly with visualizing, mapping, and measuring the online groups (Smith n.d.). Smith is the founder and chief social scientist of the Connected Action consulting group, which focuses on applying social science methods and social media network analysis to social media usage. He is also the cofounder of the Social Media Research Foundation (SMRF), a group of social media researchers who work together to create social media tools and host open data. The primary project of the SMRF is NodeXL, an add-on to Excel funded by Microsoft that collects, analyzes, and visualizes social networks. NodeXL's strengths are the simplicity and user-friendliness of the interface, "yet at the heart of the code is an algorithm with deep maths that determines how social structures be given a visual identity. This enables the creation of reliable visualisations of complex data sets" (De Waal 2010).

The visualizations created by NodeXL show each person in the network as a dot, or node, and the connections between people as lines, or edges. The visualization for a Twitter network, for example, will show those who have the most influence on the conversation through retweets and mentions. In an interview with Smith, he explained how professionals and scholars have used NodeXL for a variety of studies, including mapping Alexander the Great's social network, connections between people who author patents together, and the six distinct patterns of network structures in Twitter networks (Rajpurohit n.d.).

Prior to his involvement in Connected Action and SMRF, Smith founded and managed the Community Technologies Group at Microsoft Research. While at Microsoft, he developed "Netscan," which reported on Usenet newsgroups and other threaded conversation sites. He then led development of social media analytics tools at Telligent Systems as the company's chief social scientist (Smith n.d.). Smith's publications include a coedited book with Peter Kollock called *Communities in Cyberspace* as well as a coauthored book with Derek Hansen and Ben Shneiderman titled *Analyzing Social Media Networks with NodeXL: Insights from a Connected World.*

Solis, Brian (1970–)

Brian Solis, a prominent and early thought leader in the area of social media, explores and studies how emerging technologies impact business and society. He is currently principal analyst at Altimeter Group, a company that provides research and strategy consulting on disruptive technology to business leaders. The company also provides free and independent research to the public. In 2015, Altimeter Group was acquired by Prophet, but the team and company name remained unchanged.

At Altimeter, Solis advises companies on how to design digital customer experiences, studies start-up innovation to better understand how to disrupt markets, and helps clients employ digital technology to connect to various publics, such as customers or employees. From 2010 to 2014, Solis ran the Pivot Conference as the executive producer and host. The conference presented the most disruptive trends in business and then helped brand leaders understand how to both appreciate and deal with disruption. Prior to Altimeter, Solis was the principal of FutureWorks, a creative digital and social media agency where he led programs for Fortune 500 companies, celebrities, brands, and technology start-ups (Solis n.d.). In his early twenties, Solis launched *Reality Magazine*, which was a free fashion publication distributed to retail establishments and restaurants (Pitzer 1994). Solis served as publisher and contributing editor of the magazine. At the time, Solis was also working for an advertising agency in Malibu, California, and taking classes at Pierce College, a two-year public institution in Woodland Hills.

Solis is a prolific author of books about digital disruption including *X: The Experience When Business Meets Design*, *What's the Future of Business (WTF)*, *The End of Business as Usual*, and *Engage*. *Engage* is considered the industry reference for companies wanting to use the social Web to engage with consumers (Solis n.d.). He also wrote *Putting the Public in Public Relations*, the first book to explore the role of social media in the practice of public relations. Solis also publishes a prominent blog; contributes to business and trade publications such as *AdAge*, *Forbes*, and *VentureBeat*; and is a frequent keynote speaker at events and conferences around the world. With over 500,000 connections on LinkedIn, Twitter, and Facebook, Solis has been designated a LinkedIn Influencer (Solis n.d.).

In 2008, Solis, along with JESS3, released the Conversation Prism, an evolving graphic that tracks social networks and organizes them by usage and purpose (Solis 2008). The prism puts "You" at the center with spokes that show social media platforms for video, events, music, pictures, livecasting, social networks, and more. The spokes are organized into social sites for adapting, listening, and learning, and then further segmented into platforms for communications, human resources, community, marketing, and sales, among other functions. The most recent version of the Conversation Prism, the fourth edition, was released in 2013.

Solis has received a variety of honors and recognitions including in 2012 being named one of *Billboard Magazine*'s "Billboard's Twitter 140: The Music Industry Characters You Need to Follow" and making Mashable's list of "25 Twitter Accounts That Will Make You Smarter." Solis was also one of eight "Influential Leaders" cited by *CRM Magazine* in 2010 and recognized as one of "Silicon Valley's 40 under 40" in 2008 (Prophet n.d.).

Spiegel, Evan (1990–)

Evan Spiegel, cofounder and CEO of Snap Inc., formerly called Snapchat, is not a coder like several other social media entrepreneurs, but rather a product designer with a visual orientation. In a *Recode* article about Spiegel, his ideas were described as "raw and unorthodox" that "probably wouldn't pass the smell test at larger companies like Facebook or Google" (Wagner 2016). Snap Inc. is also unlike other tech companies in that it is not based in Silicon Valley, but was originally housed in a bungalow on the Venice boardwalk near Los Angeles (Maddaus

2013). The company quickly outgrew that space and leased several properties on nearby Market Street, other properties around Venice, and also space in New York City (Stone 2015).

The son of two Ivy League–educated lawyers whose marriage ended in divorce, Spiegel graduated from the private high school Crossroads in Santa Monica, California. Much has been written about Spiegel's privileged upbringing. In high school, through a proposal written to his father, he demanded his father lease him a BMW 550i because "Cars bring me sheer joy" (Maddaus 2013). After his father refused and other disagreements ensued, he moved in with his mother who leased him the $75,000 car. In high school Spiegel had an internship with Red Bull, which involved organizing promotional parties, some of which were held in his father's home (Maddaus 2013). During his formative years, Spiegel also learned to build a computer from scratch (Maddaus 2013).

After high school, Spiegel pursued a degree in product design at Stanford. He made a number of important connections in college, including Peter Wendell, founder of Sierra Ventures and instructor of graduate courses on entrepreneurship and venture capital. When Wendell invited Spiegel to attend some of this classes, he had an opportunity to sit near guest speakers such as Google CEO Eric Schmidt and YouTube cofounder Chad Hurley, among others. Spiegel also met Scott Cook, the CEO of Intuit, who gave him an opportunity to work on a platform the company would be employing in India (Maddaus 2013). Just a few credits shy of graduating, Spiegel was allowed to walk across the stage at graduation with every intention of finishing his remaining credits, but never did.

Snapchat was born from a conversation about sexting Spiegel had with two Kappa Sigma fraternity brothers, Frank Reginald Brown IV and Bobby Murphy (Entis 2015). Similar to the story of Facebook, Snapchat was launched from a college dorm room, in this case Spiegel's. Brown was later forced out of the Snapchat team, but he contended that the idea to send self-deleting photos through an app was his idea (Maddaus 2013).

Brown sued for a 20 percent stake in the company and a settlement was reached in September 2014 for an undisclosed amount (Entis 2015). Murphy, the coder of the team, stayed on board and now serves as the company's chief operating officer.

Facebook attempted to purchase Snapchat in 2013 for $3 billion, an offer rejected by Spiegel (Entis 2015). The same year, Snapchat received $60 million in funding, giving Spiegel and Murphy $10 million each in the deal (Maddaus 2013). Spiegel's 2016 net worth was estimated to be $2.1 billion, a sum that makes him the youngest billionaire in the world (Entis 2015). He reportedly lives a lavish lifestyle, driving a Ferrari around Los Angeles, traveling around the world, and, in 2015, purchasing Harrison Ford's Brentwood, California, home with supermodel girlfriend Miranda Kerr for $12 million (Gollayan 2016).

Some aspects of Spiegel's personal life have been highly publicized, especially what was revealed in certain e-mail communications. For example, Gawker gained access to e-mails Spiegel sent while at Stanford, including invitations to parties, jokes that certain fraternities have gay members, drug references, and misogynistic suggestions of drunken sex with sorority girls (Biddle 2014). In an e-mail to *Business Insider*, Spiegel attempted to do some damage control, saying "I'm obviously mortified and embarrassed that my idiotic emails during my fraternity days were made public. I have no excuse. I'm sorry I wrote them at the time and I was jerk to have written them. They in no way reflect who I am today or my views towards women" (Entis 2015). A hack of e-mail at Sony Pictures also resulted in exposing e-mails between Sony Entertainment CEO Michael Lynton and Spiegel, who admitted that his board was not aware of critical business issues (Wagner 2016).

Stanton, Brandon (1984–)

Before founding the popular Facebook page and blog "Humans of New York," Brandon Stanton studied at the University of Georgia and earned a degree in history. After graduation, a $3,000 bet he made that Barack Obama would win the presidency in 2008 helped him land a job trading bonds on the Chicago Board of Trade (Stanton n.d.).

After three years of trading and then losing his job, Stanton switched careers from trading bonds to his passion, which was photography. He set out to photograph interesting street scenes in some of America's largest cities, including New Orleans, Pittsburgh, and Philadelphia. From the approximately 1,000 photographs taken each day, he would select 30 to 40 to post on Facebook. He considered selling prints but at the time was just sharing the photos for his Facebook connections to enjoy (Stanton 2013).

In addition to shooting buildings and other objects on the streets, Stanton started photographing people, first as candids, and then as portraits (Stanton 2013). He noticed that the photographs of people were getting the most engagement on Facebook. Upon arriving in New York City in August 2010, Stanton was almost exclusively capturing people and placing the photos in an album on Facebook called "Humans of New York." He then returned to his home of Chicago, packed up, and moved to New York with the intention of taking 10,000 street portraits to plot on an interactive map. After moving the photos from his personal Facebook profile to a "Humans of New York" Facebook page, his follower base grew quickly. Stanton also maintains a blog with his photos and stories. He then added the element of an interview to the photographs, making the content even more compelling and the audience even larger. Stanton explained in an interview with *Crain's* that "having those conversations on the street is a learned skill. It's very much a repetitive process of learning to approach subjects and make them comfortable enough to share intimate details of their lives. I had to practice" (Benson 2015).

In 2013, Stanton's book *Humans of New York* was released after selling 30,000 preordered copies. The book spent 45 weeks on the *New York Times* Best Seller list, hitting number one during that time. In 2015, he released *Humans of New*

York: Stories, which was the number one best seller in travel photography on Amazon and also a number one *New York Times* best seller. He has also released a children's book called *Little Humans*.

During the summer of 2015, Stanton took time away from his New York City subjects to photograph people in Pakistan. His photographs shed light on such serious topics as bonded labor, abusive relationships, and violence, but also expressed common human experiences such as education, recreation, and dating. Within just three days, his followers donated more than $2 million for a campaign to end bonded labor by helping exploited laborers in the brick kiln industry with the legal assistance, education, and rehabilitation needed to escape their situation (Erbentraut 2015). Another success of the campaign was helping a mother in an abusive relationship find housing and medical assistance. A local resident volunteered to connect her with resources. Later that same year, Stanton was in Greece, Hungary, Croatia, and Austria to share the stories of Syrian refugees (LaMantia 2016). Another project in 2015 focused on inmates of five federal prisons in the northeast of the United States. In all, Stanton has traveled to more than 20 countries on five continents to photograph his subjects (LaMantia 2016).

In 2016, Stanton photographed pediatric cancer patients, parents, doctors, nurses, surgeons, and researchers of Memorial Sloan Kettering Cancer Center. This photography campaign comprised of more than 50 Facebook posts raising $3.8 million from more than 100,000 people in 18 days. The campaign was hailed by the administrator of the Department of Pediatrics in an interview with *Crain's* as "life changing" for the hospital by reaching a record-breaking grassroots fund-raising goal in such a short time period (LaMantia 2016). In 2015, Stanton also raised more than $1 million for a Brooklyn middle school called Mott Hall Bridges Academy (Benson 2015). Other campaigns raised funds for the YMCA in Bedford-Stuyvesant and for a family to adopt a child from Ethiopia.

By May 2016, Stanton had more than 17.6 million followers on Facebook and 5.3 million Instagram followers, but he does not monetize the brand beyond the sales of his books and fees for public-speaking events. He has not accepted payment from any source to place content on his blog. Even when he collaborated with the United Nations for a two-month international trip, he paid for the trip himself (Benson 2015). In 2015, *Crain's* honored Stanton as a "40 under 40."

Thiel, Peter (1967–)

Peter Thiel has been a part of many digital success stories, most notably PayPal and Facebook, and he also runs a hedge fund and a venture capital firm. The *New Yorker* said of Thiel, "He might be the most successful technology investor in the world" and that "Few people in Silicon Valley can match Thiel's combination of business prowess and philosophical breadth" (Packer 2011).

Born in Frankfurt, Germany, Thiel moved with his family first to Cleveland, and then his father's engineering job took the family to several other locations including South Africa and Namibia. As of fifth grade, the family had settled in a community in the San Francisco Bay area. While growing up, Thiel demonstrated a strong proficiency for math and was also a nationally ranked chess player. He enjoyed reading *The Lord of the Rings*, and later books by Solzhenitsyn and Rand. It was during this time that he adopted the libertarian perspective that he is known for in the present day. His educational background includes an undergraduate degree as well as a law degree from Stanford. Post-graduation, he worked for a New York law firm and a Wall Street investment bank (Packer 2011).

Thiel rose to prominence in the tech industry as one of the founders of PayPal, along with Reid Hoffman, Max Levchin, and Elon Musk. Levchin had heard Thiel talk at Stanford about currency trading, and during their meeting the next day, they hatched the idea over smoothies of an electronic payment system for e-commerce (Packer 2011). Part of the appeal of

PayPal for Thiel was the potential for transactions to take place outside of government control.

After PayPal went public and then was sold to eBay for $500 million, Thiel received a share totaling $55 million. He then set up the hedge fund Clarium Capital Management, which was mostly funded with his $10 million investment. By 2008, the hedge fund had assets of more than $7 billion, but after the financial collapse, the fund was reduced to $350 million by 2011, with two-thirds of it Thiel's money and representing all of his liquid net worth (Packer 2011).

Thiel's initial involvement with Facebook was as an early investor. He paid $500,000 for a 7 percent stake in the company and a position on the board. As of 2012, he had cashed out almost all his Facebook holdings for a sum just over $1 billion (Pepitone and Cowley 2012). He has since cofounded data-mining company Palantir Technologies with $30 million of his own funding. As of 2016, the company was worth approximately $20 billion. Palantir's software works with government agencies to locate terrorists and other criminals through their information trails.

Thiel has attracted much attention for his political beliefs and unconventional ideas. The online manifesto of his venture capital firm, Founders Fund, which he runs with Sean Parker and others, begins with the statement that sums up Thiel's frustration with forward progress: "We wanted flying cars, instead we got 140 characters" (Gobry 2011). The fund has invested in nanotechnology, space exploration, and robotics. He has also supported the Singularity Institute, an artificial intelligence think tank; the Methuselah Foundation, which works to reverse human aging; and the Seasteading Institute, which wants to build floating city-states on international waters that would not be under the jurisdiction of any country's government.

In 2011, Thiel developed a program for promising young entrepreneurs to provide them fellowships that would allow them to bypass college and start working on launching their own start-ups. Called the Thiel Fellowship, each year the program provides two-year grants for $100,000 to 20 young people under the age of 23. *Forbes* branded the Thiel Fellowship a "failed education experiment" because the program did not produce any revolutionary start-ups and some of the participants, recognizing the importance of a college education, enrolled in college to complete their degrees (Wadhwa 2013). Even Thiel himself has admitted that the entrepreneurs "were not focused on breakthrough technologies that will take civilization to the next level" (Wadhwa 2013).

In May 2016, *Forbes* uncovered that Thiel had been financing several lawsuits against tabloid journalism giant Gawker Media. When Terry Bollea, also known as the wrestler Hulk Hogan, sued Gawker for invasion of privacy for publishing a sex tape of Bollea and a friend's wife, it was Thiel who paid Bollea's lawyers approximately $10 million for their representation. The case resulted in a $140 million jury award for Bollea. An article in *Forbes* explained that, "The $140 million judgment, which isn't covered by insurance, could prove fatal to the company if it's upheld—and could serve as a blueprint for any billionaire who wants to lay siege against a media outlet" (Mac and Drange 2016). Gawker claimed that Thiel is determined to close their operations through litigation. Thiel has stated that he believes his actions toward Gawker to be "one of my greater philanthropic things" to help people targeted by a "singularly terrible bully" (Mac and Drange 2016).

Thiel's antipathy toward Gawker may be traced back to a post on the site on December 19, 2007, that was headlined "Peter Thiel is totally gay, people." Although Thiel has said in interviews that he had been out as a gay man to friends for a few years prior to that, he did not necessarily want this information broadcasted to the general public (Mac and Drange 2016).

Among Thiel's properties as of 2011 are a $7 million mansion in San Francisco and a $27 million oceanfront property in Maui (Packer 2011). *Forbes* ranks Thiel as the seventy-ninth richest person in tech with an estimated net worth of $2.7 billion (Forbes 2016a).

Williams, Evan (1972–)

Evan "Ev" Williams cofounded two of the most important and frequently visited social media platforms: Twitter and Blogger. A *New York Times* profile on leadership changes at Twitter in 2010 called him "famously deliberate and cautious," "ill at ease on the big stage," and "methodical" (C. C. Miller 2010).

Williams hails from Clarks, Nebraska, where he was involved in his high school band, choir, basketball, drama club, and the speech team (Epley 2014). His father, a third-generation farmer, and his mother, a substitute teacher, raised four kids in the community of just 360 residents. After his parents divorced during Williams's senior year of high school, he moved with his mother and sister to Columbus, Nebraska, to complete his schooling at Columbus High School. Williams attended the University of Nebraska–Lincoln, but dropped out before final exams his sophomore year.

After leaving the university, Williams worked for a mentor in Key West, Florida, writing direct mail copy, but returned to Nebraska to focus on other projects, including a historical account of Cornhuskers football on CD-ROM and also selling and setting up Internet domains for local companies (Epley 2014). He also created a video that explained how to use a command line to connect computers in a network, which he sold for a profit (Greene 2007). Williams then started an Internet company, which failed because he hired unqualified people to write software and had a difficult time managing them (Greene 2007). He shut the company down after about a year and set off for California.

In Sebastopol, California, north of San Francisco, Williams worked for O'Reilly and Associates as a marketing coordinator in the software group (Epley 2014). He struck out on his own after just seven months, but did continue working for O'Reilly as a freelance intranet developer. Then, together with Meg Hourihan, whom he met at a networking event and dated briefly, he founded Pyra Labs in 1999. High school friend Paul Bausch joined the start-up shortly after to write code. At the time, Williams was interested in developing software that allowed people to effectively collaborate on projects (Greene 2007).

Pyra Labs launched a tool for publishing "weblogs," which is what blogs were originally called, to help people without coding skills self-publish their own websites. The platform, called Blogger, was later rebuilt by Williams and sold to Google for an undisclosed sum, although he has said it was less than the $50 million reported by gossip blog Valleywag (Greene 2007). Williams's work on Blogger earned him accolades including being named to *MIT Technology Review* magazine's "top 100 innovators under age 35" in 2003 and "Person of the Year" by *PC Magazine* in 2004 (Biography.com n.d.).

Williams invested in a company called Odeo founded by Noah Glass in 2004, and two years later, he bought out their investors' interest in the company, reformed it as Obvious Corporation, and fired Glass (Carlson 2011). However, during that time, the company developed Twitter, which was later spun out as a separate company. In an interview with *MIT Technology Review*, Williams called Twitter a "no-brainer" for "social animals" (Greene 2007). He also explained how "People like other people. So hearing from them, and being able to express yourself to people you care about in a really simple way, is fun, and it can be addictive." After serving as CEO of Twitter for about two years, Williams stepped down but remains on the board and is one of the largest shareholders (Epley 2014).

In 2012, Williams founded and became CEO of Medium, a Web-publishing platform that allows for a more visually attractive presentation of a story. Medium is built on the idea that in the near future people will not be scouring the Web for content posted on blogs or other sites, but rather looking for it on centralized websites (Hof 2015). By posting content on Medium, creators have a higher likelihood of attracting readers.

In a 2013 interview with *Wired*, Williams shared some of his musings about the Internet. "We often think the Internet enables you to do new things, but people just want to do the same things they've always done." He then added, "The Internet is not what I thought it was 20 years ago. It's not a utopian world. It's essentially like a lot of other major technological revolutions that have taken place in the history of the world" (Tate 2013).

When Twitter went public in November 2013, Williams's 12 percent stake in the company was worth more than $1 billion (Mac 2013b). In late 2015, Williams donated 1.8 million shares of Twitter stock to the Sara and Evan Williams Foundation, which sold them for $47 million (Rosoff 2015). The foundation supports causes such as literacy and the environment. Williams currently lives in San Francisco with his wife and two sons.

Zuckerberg, Mark (1984–)

Last on this list is entrepreneur Mark Zuckerberg, who is first on many lists for making the most significant contribution to social media through the launch of Facebook. Zuckerberg, the son of a dentist father and psychiatrist mother, was raised in a modest home in Dobbs Ferry, New York, as the second of four children and the only son (Kirkpatrick 2010a). After two years of public high school, Zuckerberg transferred to the elite boarding school Phillips Exeter Academy. His many awards and honors in various high school subjects such as math, astronomy, physics, and classical languages as well as his participation on the fencing team as captain and most valuable player earned him admission into Harvard (Kirkpatrick 2010a).

Facebook's story begins at Harvard during Zuckerberg's sophomore year while he lived in a suite with roommates Dustin Moskovitz, Chris Hughes, and Billy Olson. During the first week of school in 2003, Zuckerberg developed a program called Course Match that would help students choose courses based on friends who were also registered. Quickly, hundreds of students started using the site (Kirkpatrick 2010a). Zuckerberg's next online project was Facemash, which invited students to compare their peers with the goal of determining "the hottest person on campus" (Kirkpatrick 2010a, 23). Photos for the site were provided from the digital archives of photos taken at freshman orientation used for the "facebooks" produced by each of Harvard residential living houses.

In early 2004, Zuckerberg registered Thefacebook.com with the intention of combining features from Course Match, Facemash, and the social networking site Friendster. Friendster's primary purpose was to connect users for dating, but the site had experienced some technical issues. MySpace also launched prior to Facebook, but had not caught on with Harvard students. Zuckerberg's key idea was to create an online version of the school's printed facebook. After Zuckerberg set up the site with a hosting company, Thefacebook launched on February 4, 2004. Within four days of launching, the site had 650 users, all with a Harvard.edu e-mail address. By the end of the first month, the site had 10,000 users. After four months of successful operation, Zuckerberg was offered $10 million for the company, an offer he quickly declined (Kirkpatrick 2010a).

The summer after Zuckerberg's sophomore year was spent in Palo Alto, California, in the heart of Silicon Valley. At the end of the summer with 200,000 Facebook users and on the precipice of launching at 70 more campuses, Zuckerberg, along with partner Dustin Moskovitz, made the easy decision not to return to Harvard in the fall (Kirkpatrick 2010a).

Through the years, Facebook continued to grow its user base among college students, and then the general public. The company expanded the platform's available languages to accommodate global users. Facebook went public in May 2012 with an initial public offering (IPO) that was fraught with problems. The company raised its IPO price shortly before going public and then technical problems at NASDAQ caused trader confusion (Luckerson 2014). The stock sunk from its initial offering of $38.23 to $18 by August 2012. Since then, however, the stock has continued to climb, reaching $116 in April 2016.

In 2012, Zuckerberg married girlfriend Priscilla Chan, whom he had dated on and off since his sophomore year at Harvard. The wedding was timed to follow Chan's graduation from UCSF's medical school, but it also coincidently took place one day after Facebook's IPO. After the birth of their first child, Maxima Chan Zuckerberg, in late 2015, Zuckerberg announced that he and his wife will eventually give away 99 percent of their Facebook stock, at that time worth about $45 billion (Frankel, Fung, and Layton 2015). According to a letter to their daughter posted on Facebook, the couple stated that their mission is to "advance human potential and promote equality for all children" (Frankel, Fung, and Layton 2015). The money will be directed into the Zuckerberg Chan Initiative, which is not a nonprofit foundation but rather a limited liability company. Previous large contributions given by the company include $120 million to public and charter schools in the San Francisco Bay Area and $100 million to the public school system in Newark, New Jersey, a controversial project that failed to provide sustainable results "because it was a top-down approach that called for wholesale changes in the city's public schools with plans crafted by outsiders, not community members" (Frankel, Fung, and Layton 2015). The couple has also provided $15 million to AltSchool, a corporation founded by a former Google employee that provides personalized instruction through technology, and have plans to open a private, tuition-free school in East Palo Alto for low-income students (Frankel, Fung, and Layton 2015).

References

ALS Association. n.d. "ALS Ice Bucket Challenge—FAQ." *ALS Association.* http://www.alsa.org/about-us/ice-bucket-challenge-faq.html.

Angwin, Julia. 2009. *Stealing MySpace: The Battle to Control the Most Popular Website in America.* New York: Random House Publishing Group.

Armstrong, Heather B. n.d. "About." *Dooce.com.* http://dooce.com/about/.

Auletta, Ken. 2011. "A Woman's Place." *The New Yorker.* July 11–18. http://www.newyorker.com/magazine/2011/07/11/a-womans-place-ken-auletta.

Ault, Susanne. 2014. "Survey: YouTube Stars More Popular Than Mainstream Celebs among U.S. Teens." *Variety.* August 5. http://variety.com/2014/digital/news/survey-youtube-stars-more-popular-than-mainstream-celebs-among-u-s-teens-1201275245/.

Belkin, Lisa. 2011. "Queen of the Mommy Bloggers." *New York Times.* February 23. http://www.nytimes.com/2011/02/27/magazine/27armstrong-t.html.

Benson, Barbara. 2015. "Meet Brandon Stanton, the Man behind Humans of New York." *Crain's.* April 26. http://www.crainsnewyork.com/article/20150426/TECHNOLOGY/150429893/meet-brandon-stanton-the-man-behind-humans-of-new-york.

Bercovici, Jeff. 2013a. "Tumblr: David Karp's $800 Million Art Project." *Forbes*, January 2. http://www.forbes.com/sites/jeffbercovici/2013/01/02/tumblr-david-karps-800-million-art-project/#6eeba4da6969.

Bercovici, Jeff. 2013b. "Twitter's Jack Dorsey: Economist Reader, Accidental Engineer, Would-Be Masseur." *Forbes.* April 24. http://www.forbes.com/sites/jeffbercovici/2013/04/24/twitters-jack-dorsey-economist-reader-accidental-engineer-would-be-masseur/#3933d5a94fa5.

Bertoni, Steven. 2011. "Agent of Disruption." *Forbes.* September 21. http://www.forbes.com/forbes/2011/1010/forbes400-11-networks-sean-parker-napster-facebook-steven-bertoni.html.

Biddle, Sam. 2014. "'Fuck Bitches Get Leid,' the Sleazy Frat Emails of Snapchat's CEO." *Gawker/Valleywag.* May 28. http://valleywag.gawker.com/fuck-bitches-get-leid-the-sleazy-frat-emails-of-snap-1582604137.

Bilton, Nick. 2010. "One on One: Caterina Fake, Flickr and Hunch." *New York Times.* October 6. http://bits.blogs.nytimes.com/2010/10/06/one-on-one-caterina-fake-flickr-and-hunch.

Bilton, Nick. 2016. "Twitter Is Betting Everything on Jack Dorsey: Will It Work?" *Vanity Fair Hive.* Summer. http://www.vanityfair.com/news/2016/06/twitter-is-betting-everything-on-jack-dorsey.

Biography.com. n.d. "Evan Williams Biography." *Biography.com.* http://www.biography.com/people/evan-williams-21402351#founding-twitter.

Bonifield, John. 2015. "One Year Later, Your ALS Ice Bucket Money Goes To . . ." *CNN.* July 15. http://www.cnn.com/2015/07/15/health/one-summer-after-the-als-ice-bucket-challenge/.

boyd, danah. n.d. "danah boyd." *danah.org.* http://www.danah.org/.

boyd, danah. 2006. "Friendster Lost Steam. Is MySpace Just a Fad?" Apophenia Blog. March 21. http://www.danah.org/papers/FriendsterMySpaceEssay.html.

Byers, Dylan. 2016. "The New Republic Is Sold by Facebook Co-Founder Chris Hughes." *CNN Money.* February 26. http://money.cnn.com/2016/02/26/media/new-republic-chris-hughes-win-mccormack/.

Carlson, Nicholas. 2011. "The Real History Of Twitter." *Business Insider.* April 13. http://www.businessinsider.com/how-twitter-was-founded-2011-4#ixzz3hs6oDxwk.

Chafkin, Max. 2012. "Can Ben Silbermann Turn Pinterest into the World's Greatest Shopfront?" *Fast Co. Design.* August 30. http://www.fastcodesign.com/1670681/ben-silbermann-pinterest.

Chafkin, Max. 2013. "Kevin Rose Reigns as the Zen Master of Silicon Valley Chatter." *Fast Company.* January 13.

http://www.fastcompany.com/3004354/kevin-rose-reigns-zen-master-silicon-valley-chatter.

Chang, Lulu. 2014. "What Happened to Tom from MySpace? Oh, Tom Anderson Had the Last Laugh . . ." *Bustle.* April 21. http://www.bustle.com/articles/36429-what-happened-to-tom-from-myspace-oh-tom-anderson-had-the-last-laugh.

Chernova, Yuliya. 2014. "Tumblr's David Karp Giving Back to NY Startups, but Don't Call Him a VC." *The Wall Street Journal.* March 25. http://blogs.wsj.com/venturecapital/2014/03/25/tumblrs-david-karp-giving-back-to-ny-startups-but-dont-call-him-a-vc/.

Conover, Michael D., Clayton Davis, Emilio Ferrara, Karissa McKelvey, Filippo Menczer, and Alessandro Flammini. 2013. "The Geospatial Characteristics of a Social Movement Communication Network." *PLoS ONE.* 8 (3): 1–8. http://journals.plos.org/plosone/article/file?id=10.1371/journal.pone.0055957.

Crunchbase. 2016. "David Karp." https://www.crunchbase.com/person/david-karp#/entity.

Cutler, Kim-Mai. 2009. "Zynga's Mark Pincus: I Got Kicked Out of Some of the Best Companies in America." October 24. http://venturebeat.com/2009/10/24/zyngas-mark-pincus-i-got-kicked-out-of-some-of-the-best-companies-in-america/.

Data & Society. n.d. *Data & Society.* http://www.datasociety.net/.

De Waal, Mandy. 2010. "NodeXL, the Shape of Social Influence to Come." *Daily Maverick.* October 20. http://www.dailymaverick.co.za/article/2010–10–20-nodexl-the-shape-of-social-influence-to-come/#.VxZbQnpFx8k.

Entis, Laura. 2015. "Five Facts about Evan Spiegel, Snapchat's Often Controversial Co-Founder." *Entrepreneur.* July 9. https://www.entrepreneur.com/slideshow/248136.

Epley, Cole. 2014. "Twitter Co-founder Evan Williams' Success Doesn't Surprise Those Who Knew Him Growing up in Nebraska." *Omaha.com.* May 7. http://www.omaha.com/money/twitter-co-founder-evan-williams-success-doesn-t-surprise-those/article_5968322b-2c74-5c7a-97b8-414df1a8e413.html.

Erbentraut, Joseph. 2015. "Humans Of New York Has Helped Raise Over $2 Million to Help End Slave Labor in Pakistan." *Huffington Post.* August 19. http://www.huffingtonpost.com/entry/humans-of-new-york-pakistan-slave-labor_us_55d399a8e4b07addcb446e23.

Fera, Rae Ann. 2013. "Ford Channels Real Tweets into 'Random Acts of Fusion' Campaign." *Fast Company.* April 15. http://www.fastcocreate.com/1682781/ford-channels-real-tweets-into-random-acts-of-fusion-campaign.

Forbes. 2016a. "The Richest People in Tech." *Forbes.* September 9. http://www.forbes.com/profile/peter-thiel/.

Forbes. 2016b. "The World's 100 Most Powerful Women: #7 Sheryl Sandberg." *Forbes.* http://www.forbes.com/profile/sheryl-sandberg/.

Frankel, Todd C., Brian Fung, and Lyndsey Layton. 2015. "Mark Zuckerberg and Priscilla Chan to Give away 99 Percent of Their Facebook Stock, Worth $45 Billion." *The Washington Post.* December 1. https://www.washingtonpost.com/news/the-switch/wp/2015/12/01/mark-zuckerberg-will-give-away-99-percent-of-his-facebook-stock/.

Gallagher, Paul. 2013. "Meet Felix Kjellberg, the New 'King of the Web'." *The Independent.* November 14. http://www.independent.co.uk/life-style/gadgets-and-tech/features/meet-felix-kjellberg-the-new-king-of-the-web-8947100.html.

Gara, Tom. 2013. "Exclusive: First Look at Sheryl Sandberg's New Book." *The Wall Street Journal.* February 5. http://blogs.wsj.com/corporate-intelligence/2013/02/05/sheryl-sandbergs-fight/.

G.L. 2011. "#Occupytheweb." *The Economist.* October 11. http://www.economist.com/blogs/democracyinamerica/2011/10/social-media-and-wall-street-protests.

Gobry, Pascal-Emmanuel. 2011. "Facebook Investor Wants Flying Cars, Not 140 Characters." *Business Insider.* July 30. http://www.businessinsider.com/founders-fund-the-future-2011-7.

Goel, Vindu. 2015. "Sheryl Sandberg's Post on Late Husband Sets Off Meditations on Grief." *New York Times.* June 4. http://bits.blogs.nytimes.com/2015/06/04/sheryl-sandbergs-post-on-late-husband-sets-off-meditations-on-grief.

Goldstein, Eric. 2014. "Before the Arab Spring, The Unseen Thaw." *Human Rights Watch*. January 19. https://www.hrw.org/world-report/2012/country-chapters/global-middle-east/north-africa.

Gollayan, Christian. 2016. "Rich, Famous Millennials Drop $12M on Harrison Ford's Old House." *New York Post.* May 9. http://nypost.com/2016/05/09/rich-famous-millennials-drop-12m-on-harrison-fords-old-house/.

Goodale, Gloria. 2011. "Social Media Drive Occupy Wall Street. Do They Also Divulge Its Secrets?" *Christian Science Monitor.* October 12. http://www.csmonitor.com/USA/Politics/2011/1012/Social-media-drive-Occupy-Wall-Street.-Do-they-also-divulge-its-secrets.

Green, Dennis. 2016. "Why This Tech Icon Turned His Back on Silicon Valley to Run a Wristwatch Blog in New York City." *Business Insider*. July 6. http://www.businessinsider.com/why-kevin-rose-ditched-silicon-valley-for-watches-2016-6.

Greene, Kate. 2007. "What Is He Doing?" *MIT Technology Review.* October 15. https://www.technologyreview.com/s/408856/what-is-he-doing/.

Grigoriadis, Vanessa. 2011. "Ol' Mark Pincus Had a Farm . . ." *Vanity Fair.* June. http://www.vanityfair.com/news/2011/06/mark-pincus-farmville-201106.

Groner, Danny. 2014. "Why the Lean In Backlash Has Returned, One Year Later." *Huffington Post.* May 2. http://www.huffingtonpost.com/danny-groner/lean-in-backlash_b_4886198.html.

Gross, Michael. 2011. "Sean Parker Isn't the First Innovator (or Lothario) to Own the West Village's $20 Million 'Bacchus House'." *New York Magazine.* March 18. http://nymag.com/daily/intelligencer/2011/03/sean_parkers_and_the_20_millio.html.

Grundberg, Sven, and Jens Hansegard. 2014. "YouTube's Biggest Star Wants His Own Network." *The Wall Street Journal.* October 3. http://blogs.wsj.com/digits/2014/10/03/youtubes-biggest-star-wants-his-own-network/.

The Guardian. 2014. "Ice Bucket Challenge: What Are the Lessons for Marketers?" *The Guardian.* August 27. http://www.theguardian.com/media-network/media-network-blog/2014/aug/27/ice-bucket-challenge-lessons-marketing.

Halliday, Josh. 2012. "David Karp, Founder of Tumblr, on Realising His Dream." *The Guardian.* January 29. http://www.theguardian.com/media/2012/jan/29/tumblr-david-karp-interview.

Hernandez, Patricia. 2014. "What People Get Wrong about PewDiePie, YouTube's Biggest Star." *Kotaku.* December 19. http://kotaku.com/what-people-get-wrong-about-pewdiepie-youtubes-biggest-1673109786.

Hof, Robert. 2015. "Medium's Evan Williams to Publishers: Your Website Is Toast." *Forbes.* September 9. http://www.forbes.com/sites/roberthof/2015/09/09/mediums-evan-williams-to-publishers-your-website-is-toast.

Indvik, Lauren. 2011. "Jack Dorsey Officially Returns to Twitter." *Mashable.* March 28. http://mashable.com/2011/03/28/jack-dorsey-returns-to-twitter.

Israel, Shel. 2014. "Scott Monty Leaves Ford: What It Means to Social Media." *Forbes.* May 22. http://www.forbes.com/sites/shelisrael/2014/05/22/will-big-brands-kill-social-media.

Kanalley, Craig. 2011. "Occupy Wall Street: Social Media's Role in Social Change." *Huffington Post.* October 6. http://www.huffingtonpost.com/2011/10/06/occupy-wall-street-social-media_n_999178.html.

Khazan, Olga. 2015. "Can Mommy Bloggers Still Make a Living?" *The Atlantic.* September 4. http://www.theatlantic.com/business/archive/2015/09/mommy-bloggers-money/402535/.

Kirkpatrick, David. 2010a. *The Facebook Effect.* New York: Simon & Schuster Paperbacks.

Kirkpatrick, David. 2010b. "With a Little Help from His Friends." *Vanity Fair.* September 6. http://www.vanityfair.com/culture/2010/10/sean-parker-201010.

Konrad, Alex. 2015. "Digg Cofounder Kevin Rose Grabs $5 Million, Leaves Google Ventures to Build Apps Full-Time at North." *Forbes.* January 4. http://www.forbes.com/sites/alexkonrad/2015/01/14/digg-cofounder-kevin-rose-grabs-5-million-leaves-google-ventures-to-build-apps-full-time.

Kosoffmarch, Maya. 2016. "Sean Parker's New Plan to Shake Up the Movie Industry." *Vanity Fair.* March 10. http://www.vanityfair.com/news/2016/03/sean-parkers-new-plan-to-shake-up-the-movie-industry.

Kroll, Luisa. 2016. "American's Richest Entrepreneurs under 40." *Forbes.* http://www.forbes.com/sites/luisakroll/2016/12/12/americas-richest-entrepreneurs-under-40-2016.

LaMantia, Jonathan. 2016. "Memorial Sloan Kettering Is Blown Away by Response to Humans of New York Campaign." *Crain's.* May 20. http://www.crainsnewyork.com/article/20160520/HEALTH_CARE/160529993/memorial-sloan-kettering-is-blown-away-by-response-to-humans-of-new-yorks-campaign.

Larson, Selena. 2014. "Flickr Co-Founder Caterina Fake: Making Art and Technology Work Together." *Read Write.* October 20. http://readwrite.com/2014/10/20/caterina-fake-flickr-findery-art-technology-builders/.

Lee, Ellen. 2009. "LinkedIn's Startup Story: Connecting the Business World." *CNN Money.* June 2. http://money.cnn.com/2009/06/02/smallbusiness/linkedin_startup_story.smb/.

Lemann, Nicholas. 2015. "The Network Man." *The New Yorker.* October 12. http://www.newyorker.com/magazine/2015/10/12/the-network-man.

Leonard, Tom. 2009. "Profile Twitter Founders: Jack Dorsey, Biz Stone and Evan Williams." *Telegraph.* January 29. http://www.telegraph.co.uk/technology/twitter/4388880/Profile-Twitter-founders-Jack-Dorsey-Biz-Stone-and-Evan-Williams.html.

Levin, Josh. 2014. "Who Invented the Ice Bucket Challenge?" *Slate.* August 22. http://www.slate.com/articles/technology/technology/2014/08/who_invented_the_ice_bucket_challenge_a_slate_investigation.html.

Luckerson, Victor. 2014. "Here's How Facebook Doubled Its IPO Price." *Time.* July 24. http://time.com/3030510/facebook-stock-doubles-ipo-price/.

Lynley, Matthew. 2012. "The Inside Story on Why Kevin Rose Never Had a Big Hit." *Business Insider.* July 17. http://www.businessinsider.com/digg-kevin-rose-untold-history-2012-7.

Lynley, Matthew. 2014. "Mark Pincus's Vanishing Act." *Buzzfeed.* April 23. https://www.buzzfeed.com/mattlynley/mark-pincuss-vanishing-act.

Lynley, Matthew. 2015. "Mark Pincus Is Back—And His Vintage Management Style Might Be, Too." *TechCrunch.* May 6. http://techcrunch.com/2015/05/06/mark-pincus-is-back-and-his-vintage-management-style-might-be-too/.

Mac, Ryan. 2013a. "The Fall of Mark Pincus: From Billionaire to Zynga's Former CEO." *Forbes.* July 1. http://www.forbes.com/sites/ryanmac/2013/07/01/the-fall-of-mark-pincus-from-billionaire-to-zyngas-former-ceo.

Mac, Ryan, 2013b. "Twitter Cofounder Evan Williams a Billionaire After 12% Stake in Company is Revealed." *Forbes*. October 3. http://www.forbes.com/sites/ryanmac/2013/10/03/twitter-cofounder-evan-williams-a-billionaire-after-12-stake-in-company-is-revealed.

Mac, Ryan, and Matt Drange. 2016. "Behind Peter Thiel's Plan to Destroy Gawker." *Forbes*. June 7. http://www.forbes.com/sites/ryanmac/2016/06/07/behind-peter-thiel-plan-to-destroy-gawker.

Maddaus, Gene. 2013. "Snapchat Went from Frat Boy Dream to Tech World Darling. But Will It Last?" *L.A. Weekly*. October 17. http://www.laweekly.com/news/snapchat-went-from-frat-boy-dream-to-tech-world-darling-but-will-it-last-4136959.

Malik, Om. 2015. "Jack in a Box: Can Twitter Be Saved?" *The New Yorker*. October 16. http://www.newyorker.com/business/currency/jack-in-a-box-can-twitter-be-saved.

Marcus, Stephanie. 2010. "A Brief History of Digg." *Mashable*. August 25. http://mashable.com/2010/08/25/history-of-digg.

Max, D.T. 2013. "Two-Hit Wonder." *The New Yorker*. October 21. http://www.newyorker.com/magazine/2013/10/21/two-hit-wonder.

McGirt, Ellen. 2009. "How Chris Hughes Helped Launch Facebook and the Barack Obama Campaign." *Fast Company*. April 1. http://www.businessinsider.com/henry-blodget-how-facebook-co-founder-chris-hughes-got-barack-obama-elected-2009–6.

Miller, Claire Cain. 2010. "Why Twitter's CEO Demoted Himself." *New York Times*. October 30. http://www.nytimes.com/2010/10/31/technology/31ev.html.

Miller, Jared T. 2014. "MySpace Co-Founder Tom Anderson's New Life as a Landscape Photographer." *ABCNews.com*. September 9. http://abcnews.go.com/Photos/myspace-founder-tom-andersons-life-landscape-photographer/story?id=25364138.

NPR Staff. 2011. "The Arab Spring: A Year of Revolution." *NPR*. December 17. http://www.npr.org/2011/12/17/143897126/the-arab-spring-a-year-of-revolution.

Packer, George. 2011. "No Death, No Taxes." *The New Yorker.* November 28. http://www.newyorker.com/magazine/2011/11/28/no-death-no-taxes.

Panzarino, Matthew. 2013. "Pinterest's Ben Silbermann on Turning His Collection Hobby into a Product and Not Making Money." *The Next Web.* May 30. http://thenextweb.com/insider/2013/05/30/pinterests-ben-silbermann-on-turning-his-collection-hobby-into-a-product-and-not-making-money/.

The Parker Foundation. n.d. "About." http://parker.org/about.

Paul, Pamela. 2012. "Cracking Teenagers' Online Codes." *New York Times.* January 20. http://www.nytimes.com/2012/01/22/fashion/danah-boyd-cracking-teenagers-online-codes.html.

Pepitone, Julianne, and Stacy Cowley. 2012. "Facebook's First Big Investor, Peter Thiel, Cashes Out." *CNN.* August 20. http://money.cnn.com/2012/08/20/technology/facebook-peter-thiel/.

Pitzer, Kurt. 1994. "A Publisher's Dream Becomes Issue of Reality." *Los Angeles Times.* February 26. http://articles.latimes.com/1994-02-26/local/me-27500_1_canoga-park.

Portillo, Caroline McMillan. 2014. "Flickr Co-founder Caterina Fake Is Up—and Working—at 3 a.m. Could She Be on to Silicon Valley's Next Big Thing?" *Biz Women.* December 11. http://www.bizjournals.com/bizwomen/news/profiles-strategies/2014/12/flickr-founder-and-serial-entrepreneur-caterina.html.

Preston, Jennifer. 2011. "Protesters Look for Ways to Feed the Web." *New York Times.* November 24. http://www.nytimes.com/2011/11/25/business/media/occupy-movement-focuses-on-staying-current-on-social-networks.html.

Prophet. n.d. "Brian Solis." *Prophet.* https://www.prophet.com/about/leadership/solis.

Quart, Alissa. 2014. "Status Update: 'It's Complicated,' by Danah Boyd." *New York Times.* April 25. http://www.nytimes.com/2014/04/27/books/review/its-complicated-by-danah-boyd.html.

Rajpurohit, Anmol. n.d. "Interview: Marc Smith, Chief Social Scientist, Connected Action, on Why We Need Open Tools for Social Networks." *KDnuggets News.* http://www.kdnuggets.com/2014/07/interview-marc-smith-connected-action-social-networks.html.

Rao, Leena. 2016. "Jack Dorsey's Salary at Square Is Now $2.75." *Fortune.* March 10. http://fortune.com/2016/03/10/jack-dorseys-salary-square/.

Ratcliff, Christopher. 2014. "Q&A: Scott Monty on Ford's Social Media Strategy." *eConsultancy.com.* May 26. https://econsultancy.com/blog/64861-q-a-scott-monty-on-ford-s-social-media-strategy/.

Regan, Helen. 2015. "YouTube's Most Popular Star PewDiePie Hits Back at Criticism over His $7.4 Million Earnings." *Time.* July 8. http://time.com/3950603/felix-kjellberg-pewdiepie-youtube-earnings-criticism/.

Ronan, Alex. 2015. "Heather 'Dooce' Armstrong Talks Life after Mommy-Blogging." *New York Magazine.* May 29. http://nymag.com/thecut/2015/05/dooce-talks-life-after-mommy-blogging.html.

Rosoff, Matt. 2015. "Twitter Co-founder Ev Williams Just Sold $47 Million Worth of Stock." *Business Insider.* December 1. http://www.businessinsider.com/twitter-cofounder-ev-williams-sells-18-million-shares-2015-12.

Salem, Fadi, and Racha Mourtada. 2011. "Civil Movements: The Impact of Facebook and Twitter." *Arab Social Media Report.* May. http://unpan1.un.org/intradoc/groups/public/documents/dsg/unpan050860.pdf.

Schuker, Lauren A. E. 2012. "Private Properties: Zynga's Mark Pincus Buys a San Francisco Home for $16 Million." August 2. http://www.wsj.com/articles/SB1000087239639 0444405804577561700667269124.

Shontell, Alyson. 2012. "Meet Ben Silbermann, The Brilliant Young Co-Founder of Pinterest." *Business Insider.* March 13. http://www.businessinsider.com/pinterest-2012-3.

Smith, Marc. n.d. "Marc Smith." *Connected Action.* http://www.connectedaction.net/marc-smith/.

Solis, Brian. n.d. "About." *BrianSolis.com.* http://www.briansolis.com/about/.

Solis, Brian. 2008. "Introducing the Conversation Prism." *BrianSolis.com.* August 5. http://www.briansolis.com/2008/08/introducing-conversation-prism/.

Stanton, Brandon. n.d. "About." *Humans of New York.* http://www.humansofnewyork.com/photographer.

Stanton, Brandon. 2013. "Humans of New York: Behind the Lens." *Huffington Post.* July 3. http://www.huffingtonpost.com/brandon-stanton/humans-of-new-york-behind_b_3210673.html.

Stone, Madeline. 2015. "Snapchat's Stealthy Real Estate Moves Are Worrying Small Business Owners in Venice." *Business Insider.* April 15. http://www.businessinsider.com/snapchat-taking-over-office-space-in-venice-2015-4.

Swisher, Kara. 2014. "The Pincubator? Former Zynga CEO Mark Pincus Starts a Startup Factory." *Recode.* November 6. http://www.recode.net/2014/11/6/11632640/the-pincubator-former-zynga-ceo-mark-pincus-starts-a-startup-factory.

Takahashi, Dean. 2011. "How Zynga Grew from Gaming Outcast to $9 Billion Social Game Powerhouse." *VentureBeat.* December 12. http://venturebeat.com/2011/12/12/zynga-history/.

Wadhwa, Vivek. 2013. "Billionaire's Failed Education Experiment Proves There's No Shortcut to Success." *Forbes.*

September 11. http://www.forbes.com/sites/singularity/2013/09/11/peter-thiel-promised-flying-cars-instead-we-got-caffeine-spray.

Wagner, Kurt. 2016. "Inside Evan Spiegel's Very Private Snapchat Story." *Recode.* May 9. http://www.recode.net/2016/5/9/11594144/evan-spiegel-snapchat.

Wallenstein, Andrew. 2013. "If PewDiePie Is YouTube's Top Talent, We're All Doomed." *Variety.* September 10. http://variety.com/2013/biz/news/if-pewdiepie-is-youtubes-top-talent-were-all-doomed-1200607196/.

Wasik, Bill. 2011. "Gladwell vs. Shirky: A Year Later, Scoring the Debate Over Social-Media Revolutions." *Wired.* December 27. https://www.wired.com/2011/12/gladwell-vs-shirky/.

Wernle, Bradford. 2014. "Scott Monty, Ford's Social-Media Pioneer, Leaves Company." *Advertising Age*, May 20. http://adage.com/article/cmo-strategy/scott-monty-ford-s-social-media-pioneer-leaves-company/293298/.

Wingfield, Nick. 2016. "Mark Pincus, Founder of Zynga, Is Replaced as CEO Again." *New York Times.* March 1. http://www.nytimes.com/2016/03/02/technology/mark-pincus-will-again-leave-zynga-ceo-job.html.

SATURATION
HIGHLIGHTS
SHADOWS

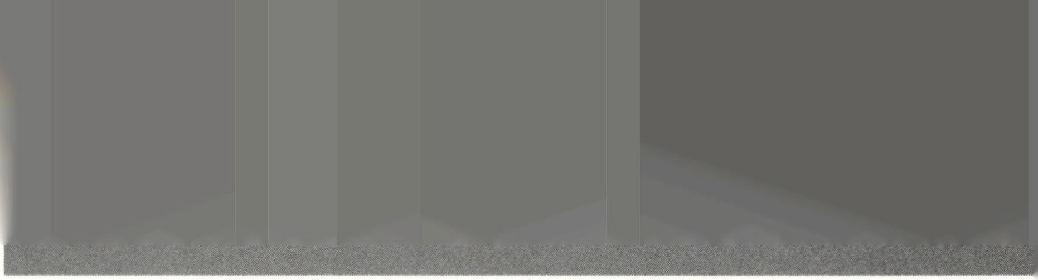

Introduction

Technology is increasingly integrated into the lives of users, impacting a wide range of daily activities including communication, news and information consumption, management of tasks, entertainment, shopping, and work. For many users, the technological devices of mobile phones, tablets, and computers are close at hand throughout the day and interactions with them are common, particularly to access social media sites. The data detailed in this chapter provide evidence for the profound impact of social media on the lives of users.

This chapter presents findings from research studies, which provide valuable insights into Internet, social, and mobile users and usage, including the increasing use of smartphones to access social media sites. Social media addiction is also addressed, and research studies are presented that show the amount of time spent on social media as well as feelings of addiction. This chapter also describes statistics that compare usage of various social media platforms, presents user and usage data about the most popular platforms, addresses the use of social media by marketers, and explores social commerce. Finally, presented at the end of the chapter are documents related to social media privacy

---

Instagram, a social media app that offers full functionality only on a smartphone, was purchased by Facebook for $1 billion in 2012. The content shared includes primarily photos that are enhanced by an Instagram filter. (AP Photo/Mark Lennihan)

legislation for children and in the workplace, testimonies about social media usage in disasters and suppressing stories on Facebook, and a speech related to a popular social media campaign.

Internet, Social Media, and Mobile Usage

This section presents data on Internet, social, and mobile users in both the United States and worldwide and includes trends over time as well as demographic data on social media users. In the United States with a population of almost 323 million as of January 2016, more than 282 million people or 87 percent were active Internet users and 192 million or 59 percent were active social media users. Mobile phone penetration was actually higher than total population at more than 342 million or 106 percent, and 169 million people or 52 percent of the population were active mobile social users (see Table 5.1).

Social media have been embraced by billions of people around the world, and the number of active users continues to rise. As of January 2016, the worldwide snapshot shows that more than 3.4 billion people of the almost 7.4 billion are Internet users, more than 2.3 billion are active social media users, almost 3.8 billion are mobile users, and almost 2 billion people are active mobile social media users (see Table 5.2).

Globally, as shown in Table 5.3, the largest population of social media users are found in East Asia (769 million), followed

Table 5.1 United States Digital and Mobile Usage (January 2016)

	Users	Penetration
Total population	322.9 million	
Internet users	282.1 million	87%
Active social media users	192.0 million	59%
Unique mobile users	342.4 million	106%
Active mobile social media users	169.0 million	52%

Source: Kemp, Simon. 2016. "Digital in 2016." *We Are Social*. January 27. http://wearesocial.com/uk/special-reports/digital-in-2016.

Table 5.2 Worldwide Digital and Mobile Usage (January 2016)

	Users	Penetration
Total population	7.395 billion	
Internet users	3.419 billion	46%
Active social media users	2.307 billion	31%
Unique mobile users	3.790 billion	51%
Active mobile social media users	1.968 billion	27%

Source: Kemp, Simon. 2016. "Digital in 2016." *We Are Social*. January 27. http://wearesocial.com/uk/special-reports/digital-in-2016.

Table 5.3 Social Media Adoption by Worldwide Region (January 2016)

	Active Users in (Millions)	Penetration
East Asia	769	48%
Southeast Asia	234	37%
North America	213	59%
South America	211	50%
Western Europe	201	48%
Eastern Europe	191	45%
South Asia	186	11%
Africa	129	11%
Central America	87	40%
Middle East	63	26%
Oceania	18	45%
Central Asia	4	6%

Source: Kemp, Simon. 2016. "Digital in 2016." *We Are Social*. January 27. http://wearesocial.com/uk/special-reports/digital-in-2016.

by Southeast Asia (234 million), North America (213 million), South America (211 million), and Western Europe (201 million). The highest penetration of social media users can be found in North America (59 percent), followed by South America (50 percent), Western Europe (48 percent), and East Asia (48 percent).

When the Pew Research Center began tracking social media usage in 2005, only 7 percent of American adults used social media (see Figure 5.1). By 2015, almost two-thirds of Americans were users. Growth has slowed in recent years as most mainstream users have already adopted social media.

The Pew Research Center also looked at demographic differences and trends among adult social media users in the United States, which are shown in Table 5.4. In terms of age, at 90 percent, users aged 18–29 are most likely to use social media. Since 2008, women have been more likely than men to be social media users, but the gap is small. In 2015, 68 percent of women and 62 percent of men were users. In 2014, the percentages were closer at 63 percent of women and 60 percent of men. Americans with higher levels of education and higher socioeconomic status have also consistently been more likely to be social media users. Percentages of users with some college or an associate's degree and those with a college degree or more have been close in usage since 2008, but those with a high

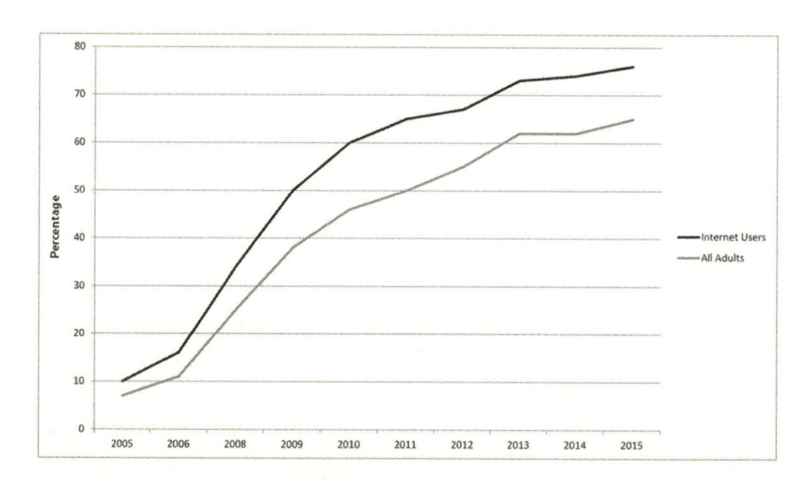

Figure 5.1 Social Media Users among Adult Internet Users and All Adults in the United States as a Percentage of the Population (2005–2015)

Note: Data not collected in 2007.

Source: Perrin, Andrew. 2015. "Social Media Usage: 2005–2015." *Pew Research Center*. October 8. http://www.pewinternet.org/2015/10/08/social-networking-usage-2005-2015/.

Table 5.4 Social Media Users in the United States by Demographics (2015)

Age	Percentage
18–29	90
30–49	77
50–64	51
65+	35
Gender	
Women	68
Men	62
Education	
College grad	76
Some college	70
High school or less	54
Household income	
$75,000+	78
$50,000–$74,999	72
$30,000–$49,999	69
Less than $30,000	56
Race	
White, non-Hispanics	65
Hispanics	65
Black, non-Hispanics	56

Source: Perrin, Andrew. 2015. "Social Media Usage: 2005–2015." *Pew Research Center*. October 8. http://www.pewinternet.org/2015/10/08/social-networking-usage-2005-2015/.

school degree or less have consistently been less likely to use social media. In 2015, for example, 76 percent of Americans with a college degree or more education were social media users, 70 percent of those with some college or an associate's degree were users, and only 54 percent of those with a high school degree or less were users. A similar trend can be observed with income levels, with 78 percent of Americans living in households making $75,000 or more using social media in 2015, 72 percent of those making $50,000 to $74,999, 69 percent of those making $30,000 to $49,999, and only 56 percent of those making less than $30,000. In terms of race, differences in usage are not very pronounced, a trend that has occurred since 2009. By 2015, 65 percent of non-Hispanic Caucasians and Hispanics were users and 56 percent of non-Hispanic African Americans were users, with usage percentages being even closer during the previous five years.

Smartphone Ownership and Social Media Usage on Devices

Because so many people are using smartphones to access social media, smartphone ownership is a key to understanding increased social media usage. This section covers ownership of various digital devices as well as global smartphone penetration, the percentage of users who can access the Web and time spent accessing the Web via a mobile phone, and trends over time for engaging with social media from various devices.

In the United States, as of 2015, 92 percent of the population owned a cellphone, including smartphones. The second most popular device was a desktop or laptop computer at 73 percent, then smartphones at 68 percent, and tablet computers at 45 percent. Other devices included MP3 players at 40 percent, game consoles at 40 percent, e-book readers at 19 percent, and portable gaming devices at 14 percent (see Figure 5.2).

As shown in Table 5.5, trends over time among adults aged 18–29 in the United States show even more dramatic increases for smartphone and tablet ownership from 2010 to 2015. During this time, computer and MP3 player ownership dropped from 88 percent to 78 percent for computers and from 75 percent to 51 percent for MP3 players, suggesting that other devices have replaced computers and MP3 players. On the rise

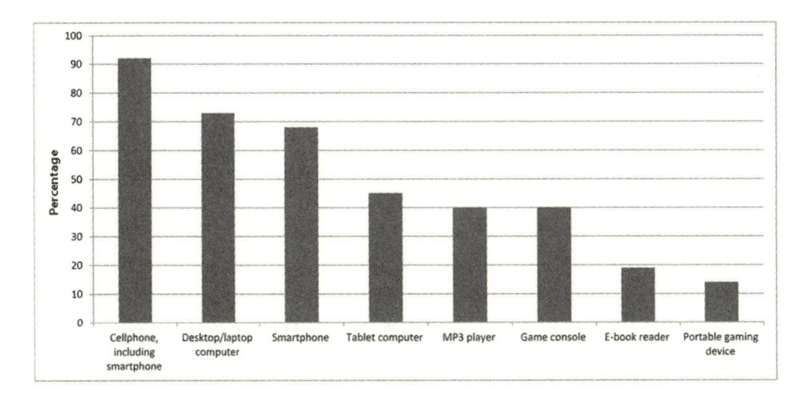

Figure 5.2 Ownership of Devices among U.S. Adults (2015)

Source: Anderson, Monica. 2015. "Technology Device Ownership: 2015." *Pew Research Center*. October 29. http://www.pewinternet.org/2015/10/29/technology-device-ownership-2015/.

Table 5.5 Device Ownership over Time (U.S. Adults Aged 18–29)

	2010	2011	2012	2013	2014	2015
Cellphone	96	95	93	97	98	98
Computer	88	88	89	–	–	78
MP3 player	75	71	–	62	–	51
Game console	62	–	–	71	–	56
Smartphone	–	52	65	79	85	86
Tablet computer	5	13	32	36	48	50
E-book reader	5	8	27	24	28	18

Note: Dashes represent years when the question was not asked.

Source: Anderson, Monica. 2015. "Technology Device Ownership: 2015." *Pew Research Center*. October 29. http://www.pewinternet.org/2015/10/29/technology-device-ownership-2015/.

have been smartphones from 52 percent in 2011 to 86 percent in 2015 and tablet computers from 5 percent in 2010 to 50 percent in 2015.

Data collected in 2015 by the Pew Research Center examined smartphone penetration in various countries as well as ownership among various age groups, education levels, and income. The data showed that a digital divide occurs for likelihood to own a smartphone on the basis of age, education, and income, with younger, more educated, and higher income people more likely to own a smartphone. As shown in Table 5.6, of the top 12 countries in terms of smartphone penetration, South Korea (88 percent), Australia (77 percent), and Israel (74 percent) rank in the top three followed by the United States at 72 percent. Of the countries on this list, Germany, Malaysia, and Turkey all have the largest differences (42 percent) in penetration between users aged 35 and up and those aged 18–34. Education differences are more pronounced

Table 5.6 Top 12 Countries for Smartphone Penetration and Demographic Differences (2015)

	Total Percentage	Age			Education			Income		
		18–34	35+	Diff	Less	More	Diff	Lower	Higher	Diff
South Korea	88	100	83	+17	80	95	+15	79	95	+16
Australia	77	95	70	+25	67	85	+18	62	88	+26
Israel	74	87	67	+20	68	80	+12	63	83	+20
United States	72	92	65	+27	59	81	+22	64	84	+20
Spain	71	91	64	+27	63	85	+22	63	81	+18
United Kingdom	68	91	60	+31	60	80	+20	59	84	+25
Canada	67	94	58	+36	58	73	+15	61	80	+19
Chile	65	86	50	+36	16	74	+58	46	79	+33
Malaysia	65	88	46	+42	26	79	+53	44	75	+31
Germany	60	92	50	+42	48	68	+20	49	68	+19
Italy	60	88	52	+36	56	83	+27	46	74	+28
Turkey	59	81	43	+42	34	86	+52	**	**	**

Source: Poushter, Jacob. 2016. "Smartphone Ownership and Internet Usage Continues to Climb in Emerging Economies." *Pew Research Center*. February 22. http://www.pewglobal.org/2016/02/22/smartphone-ownership-and-internet-usage-continues-to-climb-in-emerging-economies/.

in Chile, Malaysia, and Turkey, where those who are more educated are more likely to be smartphone owners. Similarly, in Chile and Malaysia, the difference between percentage ownership by those with higher incomes and those with lower is the most pronounced.

Asia is also a particularly vibrant region for mobile traffic with 561 million active mobile social accounts. A study by Google described Asia as "mobile-first," referring to the high percentage of Internet users who first went online using a mobile device as well as the high penetration of smartphone usage (Google 2014). Of the top seven countries in terms of percentage of the population that uses a smartphone shown in Table 5.7, five are Asian countries. Singapore, South Korea, Hong Kong, China, and Australia all have higher penetrations than the United States, which is followed by Malaysia. For all Asian countries in the study, computer usage is lower than smartphone usage, but for the United States and Australia, computer usage is higher. Smartphone-only users are highest in Malaysia (35 percent), followed by Singapore (16 percent), Hong Kong (14 percent), South Korea (14 percent), and the United States (11 percent). The implications of such research are that products and services need to be increasingly built with a mobile mindset.

Table 5.7 Worldwide Penetration of Smartphone, Computer, and Smartphone-Only Users (2014)

	Smartphone	Computer	Smartphone-Only
United States	57	72	11
China	70	65	8
Hong Kong	74	61	14
South Korea	80	70	14
Malaysia	51	39	35
Singapore	85	74	16
Australia	66	83	7

Source: Google. 2014. "Asia's Mobile-First World." *Google Asia Pacific Blog*. October 28. https://asia.googleblog.com/2014/10/asias-mobile-first-world.html.

The percentage of adults accessing the Web via a mobile phone has been increasing steadily in recent years. Mobile phones are particularly popular in developing countries that do not have the infrastructure to provide Internet access through a phone network or broadband, but are capable of installing a cell tower. In 2011, only 51 percent of Internet users globally were accessing the Web through a mobile phone, but by 2015, that percentage had reached 75 percent (see Figure 5.3).

The time spent online on mobile phones has also been on the rise in recent years. When looking across age groups, users aged 16–24 report that they spend approximately 3.26 hours per day online on their mobile phones (up from 1.88 hours in 2012) while users aged 55–64 are spending 0.58 hours per day on average (up from 0.37 hours in 2012) (see Figure 5.4).

On average, users in Latin America are spending the most time online on mobile, followed by the Middle East and Africa, Asia Pacific, North America, and finally, Europe (see Figure 5.5).

Between 2008 and 2015, the overall time spent on digital media including mobile devices, desktop and laptop computers, and other connected devices has increased from 2.7 hours

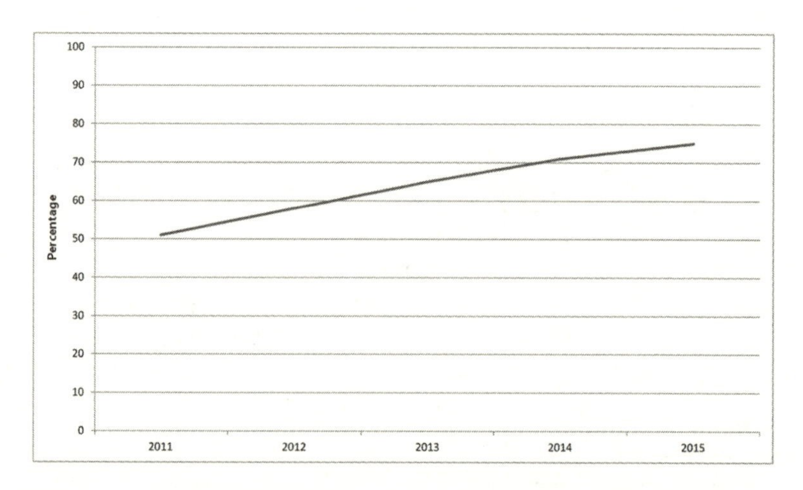

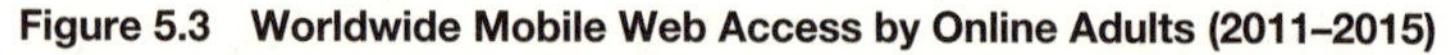

Figure 5.3 Worldwide Mobile Web Access by Online Adults (2011–2015)

Source: GlobalWebIndex. 2016. "GWI Social Summary: Q3 2016." http://insight.globalwebindex.net/hubfs/GWI-Social-Q3–2016-Summary.pdf.

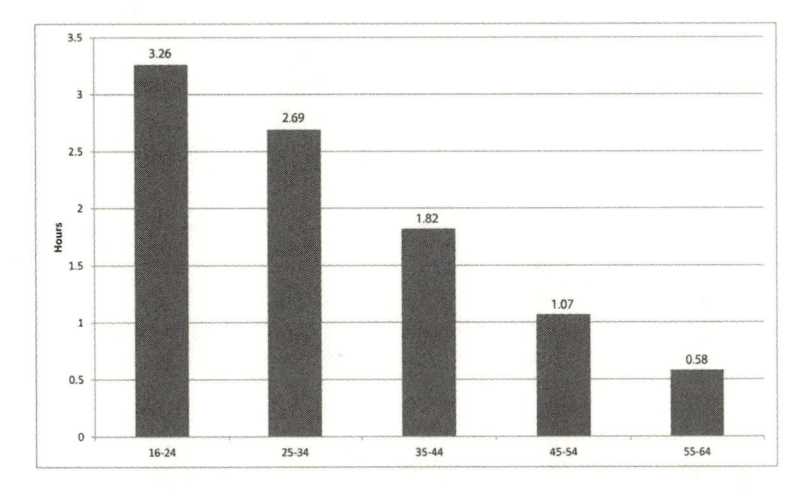

Figure 5.4 Time Spent Online per Day on Mobile Phones, by Age among Global Users (2015)

Source: GlobalWebIndex. 2016. "GWI Social Summary: Q3 2016." http://insight.globalwebindex.net/hubfs/GWI-Social-Q3–2016-Summary.pdf.

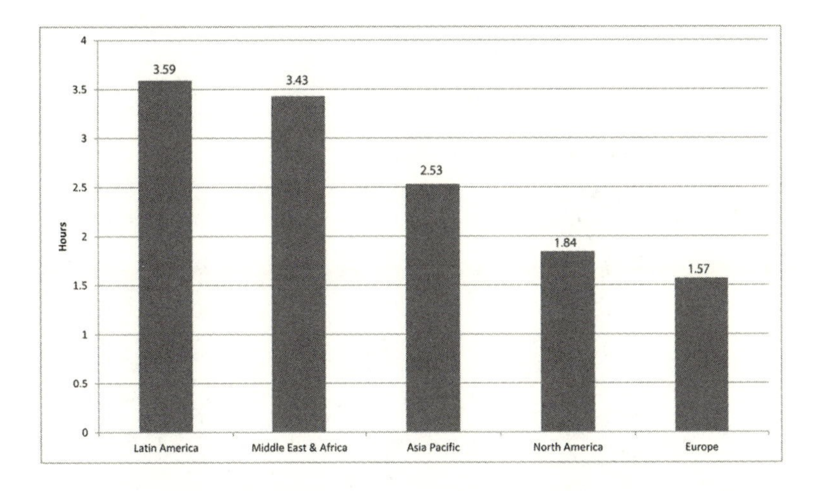

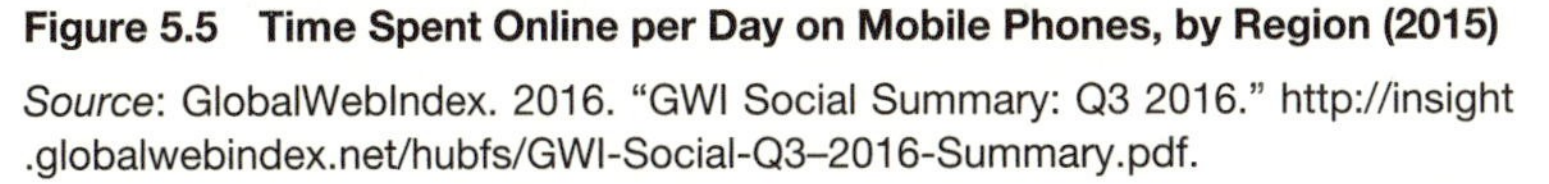

Figure 5.5 Time Spent Online per Day on Mobile Phones, by Region (2015)

Source: GlobalWebIndex. 2016. "GWI Social Summary: Q3 2016." http://insight.globalwebindex.net/hubfs/GWI-Social-Q3–2016-Summary.pdf.

per day to 5.6 hours, as shown in Figure 5.6. Much of this increase is driven by the increased time spent on mobile phones, from just 0.3 hours per day (12 percent of all time spent) to 2.8 hours per day (51 percent of all time spent).

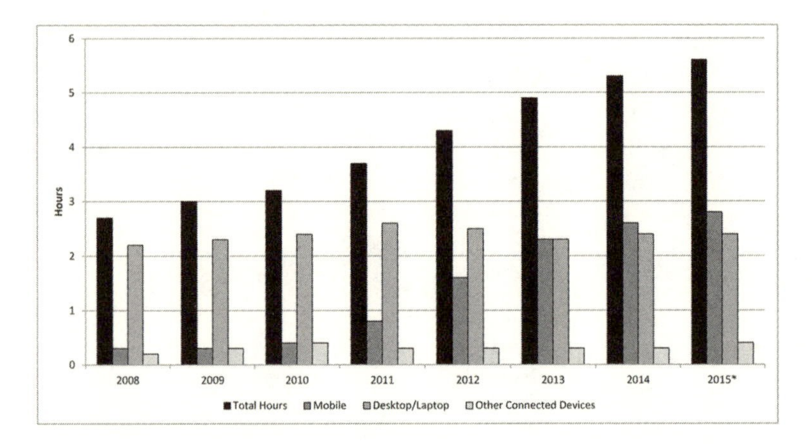

Figure 5.6 Average Time Spent on Digital Media per Day among U.S. Adult Users (2008–2015 YTD)

*Through April 2015.

Source: Meeker, Mary. 2015. "Internet Trends 2015: Code Conference." *KPCB*. May 27. http://www.kpcb.com/file/2015-internet-trends-report.

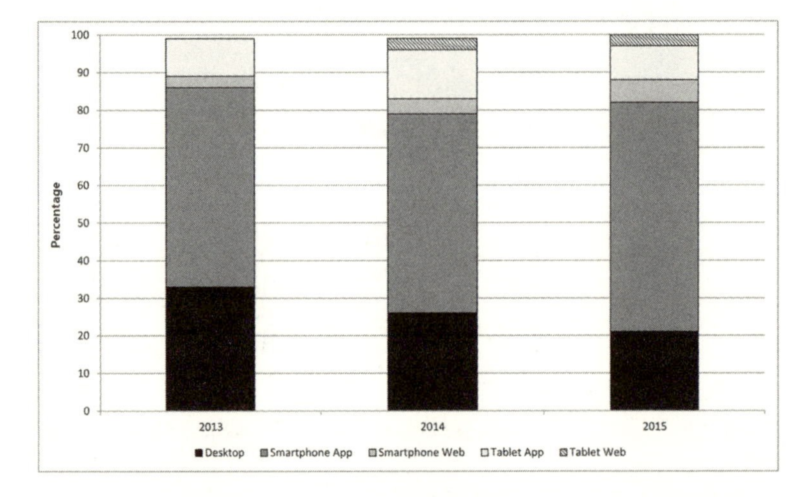

Figure 5.7 Share of Time Spent on Social Media across Platforms (2013–2015)

Source: comScore. 2016. "U.S. Cross-Platform Future in Focus: 2016." March 30. http://www.comscore.com/Insights/Presentations-and-Whitepapers/2016/2016-US-Cross-Platform-Future-in-Focus.

Since 2013, share of time spent accessing social media on smartphones has been increasing from 56 percent in 2013 (through both the app and the Web) to 67 percent in 2015. At the same time, users who access social media from a desktop computer have declined from 33 percent in 2013 to 21 percent in 2015 (see Figure 5.7).

Social Media Addiction

To understand social media addiction, this section starts with a discussion of the global estimates of time per day spent on social media. The section will then cover teen daily usage of screens in general and social media in particular and then feelings of device addiction among both teens and their parents. Finally, this section will cover compulsive phone checking, including the platforms accessed first in the morning.

GlobalWebIndex's quarterly report for the third quarter of 2016 found that approximately one-third of all time spent online is spent on social media sites. As shown in Figure 5.8, this amount has been growing steadily in recent years from 1.36 hours spent per day on social media in 2012 to 1.58 hours spent per day in 2016.

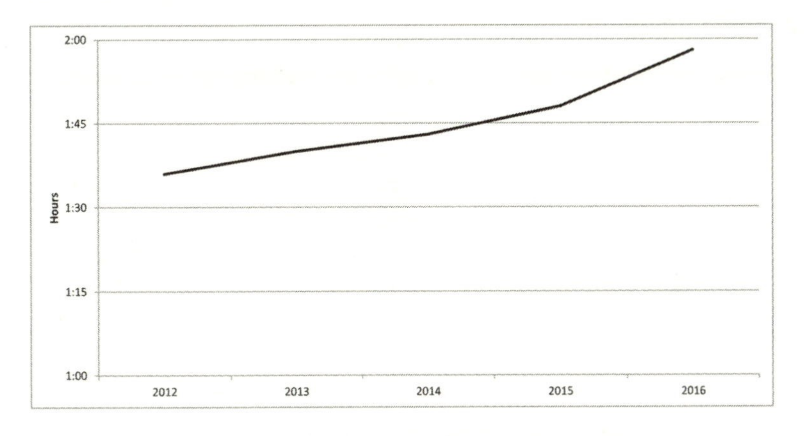

Figure 5.8 Worldwide Daily Average Time Spent on Social Media (2012–2016)

Source: GlobalWebIndex. 2016. "GWI Social Summary: Q3 2016." http://insight.globalwebindex.net/hubfs/GWI-Social-Q3-2016-Summary.pdf.

According to 2014 statistics compiled by GO-Globe, the average social media user in the age range of 15–19 spends three hours a day on social media, while those aged 20–29 spend two hours (GO-Globe 2014). Other studies of teenagers found similar levels of social media usage. A 2015 report by Common Sense Media found that among teen girls who use social media, the average time spent per day is just under 2:30 hours while teen boys who use social media spend slightly more than 1:30 hours (Rideout 2015). Sixty-four percent of teen girls report that they use social media on any given day while 51 percent of teen boys reported the same.

According to the Common Sense Census from 2015, American teenagers spend an average of almost seven hours per day (6:40) using screens for entertainment, including computers, phones, televisions, and video games (see Figure 5.9). Tweens aged 8 to 12 are using screens an average of 4:36 hours per day. Among teens, the highest percentage of users view screens between 4 and 8 hours (31 percent), followed by more than

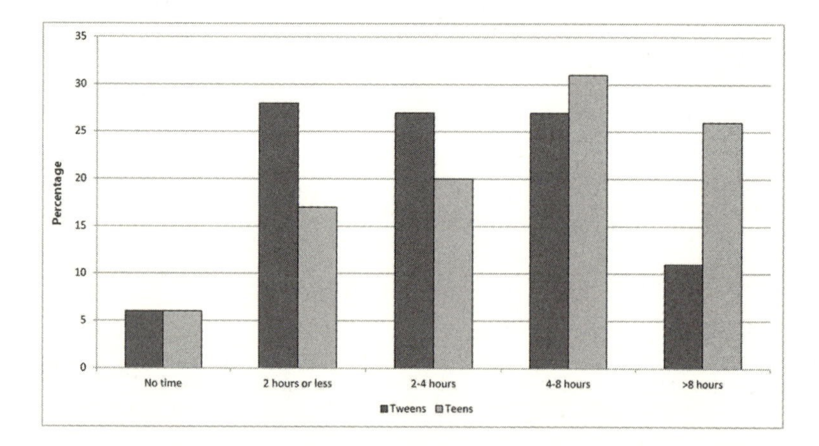

Figure 5.9 Proportion of Teens (13–18 Years Old) and Tweens (8–12 Years Old) Using Screen Media (February–March 2015)

Source: Rideout, Victoria. 2015. "The Common Sense Census: Media Use by Tweens and Teens." *Common Sense*. https://www.commonsensemedia.org/sites/default/files/uploads/research/census_executivesummary.pdf.

8 hours (26 percent) per day. Among tweens, the highest percentages use screens two hours or less (28 percent), 2–4 hours (27 percent), and 4–8 hours (27 percent) per day. Among the teens and tweens who use social media, teens spend approximately more than two hours per day (2:04) on social media and tweens spend 1:43 hours per day using social media (Rideout 2015).

Teenagers are often described as suffering from digital media addiction. In a 2012 Common Sense Media study, 41 percent of the 13- to 17-year-olds surveyed said they would describe themselves as addicted to their cell phones and 20 percent said they were addicted to a social media site (Rideout 2012). A total of 43 percent either strongly or somewhat agreed they wish they could sometimes unplug from social media and 36 percent either strongly or somewhat agreed that they would like to go back to a time prior to Facebook. The report explained that some of the desire to unplug for teens is based on exposure to racist, sexist, or homophobic content on social media sites. Forty-five percent of the teen respondents reported sometimes feeling frustrated when spending time with friends who are distracted by social media, texting, and browsing the Internet (see Table 5.8).

Table 5.8 Teen Desire to Unplug and Other Frustrations (2012)

Among teens aged 13–17 years, the percentage that strongly or somewhat agreed they:

	Percentage
Get frustrated with friends for texting/using social media when hanging out together	45
Wish they could unplug for a while sometimes	43
Sometimes wish they could go back to a time when there was no Facebook	36
Wish their parents spent less time with cell phones and other devices	21

Source: Rideout, Victoria. 2012. "Social Media, Social Life: How Teens View Their Digital Lives." *Common Sense Media*. https://www.commonsensemedia.org/file/socialmediasociallife-final-061812pdf-0/download.

Parents are also frustrated with their teens' use of digital devices with 59 percent of those surveyed for a 2016 Common Sense Media study saying that their teens are addicted to mobile devices and 66 percent of parents reporting that their teens spend too much time with their devices (Felt and Robb 2016). Arguments happen frequently, with 36 percent of parents saying mobile device use causes daily conflict, 43 percent saying less than daily, and 21 percent reporting no conflicts. Surveys of teens also echo what parents are saying. About 50 percent of teens report they are addicted to their mobile devices and 52 percent say they spend too much time on them. Teens are not alone, however, in their addiction. About 28 percent of teens report that their parents are addicted to their mobile devices, and 27 percent of parents say they believe they are addicted (see Table 5.9). About one-half of parents and one-third of teens have tried to cut the amount of time they are spending on mobile devices (Felt and Robb 2016).

Studies have shown that many cell phone users are compulsive phone checkers, with a worldwide average of 150 checks per day, according to the Ford 2014 Trend Report (Ford 2013). Additionally, 80 percent of respondents in the United States surveyed for that report agreed that "Today, the cell phone is a crutch for people's fear of being idle."

Table 5.9 Teen and Parent Addiction to Mobile Devices (May 2016)

	Percentage
Parents who feel teens are addicted to devices	59
Teens who feel addicted to devices	50
Parents who feel addicted to devices	27
Teens who feel parents are addicted to devices	28

Source: Felt, Laurel B., and Michael B. Robb. 2016. "Technology Addiction: Concern, Controversy, and Finding Balance." *Common Sense*. https://www.commonsensemedia.org/sites/default/files/uploads/research/csm_2016_technology_addiction_research_brief_0.pdf.

A 2013 International Data Corporation (IDC) study conducted for Facebook on the topic of smartphones and social media found that 79 percent of people have their phones near them for all but two hours of their waking day, with an average of 32:51 minutes spent using Facebook on the phone over an average of 13.8 Facebook sessions (IDC 2013). GO-Globe reported that approximately 18 percent of users cannot go more than a few hours without checking Facebook (GO-Globe 2014). In a study of parents and teens, Common Sense found that 69 percent of parents and 78 percent of teens check their devices hourly, and 48 percent of parents and 72 percent of teens feel the need to respond immediately to texts, messages, and other notifications (Felt and Robb 2016). More concerning is that 56 percent of parents say they check their devices while driving and 51 percent of teens note that they see their parents checking while driving.

The IDC study also discovered that within 15 minutes of waking up, 79 percent of smartphone owners are checking their phones (IDC 2013). Among those users, approximately 80 percent check their phones before doing anything else. As expected, percentages for people aged 18–24 are even higher with 89 percent of them checking the phone within 15 minutes and 74 percent reaching for the phone immediately upon waking.

As shown in Table 5.10, a study by GfK MRI of U.S. smartphone users found texts and e-mail to be the most popular apps checked first thing in the morning, with millennials and baby boomers most likely to check texts (78 percent and 59 percent, respectively) and Gen Xers most likely to check e-mail first (67 percent) followed closely by texts (66 percent). Two social media sites were included in the top results, including Facebook, which is checked by 48 percent overall, but by the highest percentage of millennials compared to the other age groups (58 percent). Similarly, Instagram, although only checked by 16 percent of all smartphone users surveyed, was checked by 29 percent of millennials, higher than the other two age groups.

Table 5.10 Mobile Apps Smartphone Users Check First in the Morning (November 2015)

	Millennials	Gen Xers	Baby Boomers	Total
Text	78%	66%	59%	67%
E-mail	67%	67%	57%	63%
Facebook	58%	53%	34%	48%
Weather	45%	45%	41%	44%
Calendar	30%	38%	25%	30%
News	19%	22%	21%	21%
Games	21%	22%	13%	19%
Instagram	29%	12%	–	16%

Source: eMarketer. 2016. "Checking Messages Is Part of Almost Everyone's Morning Routine." April 4. http://www.emarketer.com/Article/Checking-Messages-Part-of-Almost-Everyones-Morning-Routine/1013779.

Usage of Various Social Media Platforms

This section begins with a discussion of global usage of social media and messaging platforms in terms of monthly active users, U.S. penetration of various social media platforms, global membership and visitation of social media platforms, and frequency of visitation in the United States. Then, this section will cover changes in millennial usage of social media platforms over time and present a comparison of the two youngest demographic groups in terms of posting or commenting on various social media platforms.

An examination of the social media and messaging platforms with the highest monthly average users (MAU) as shown in Figure 5.10 reveals that Facebook and its products as well as the products of Chinese firm Tencent and other Asian companies dominate. At the beginning of 2016, Facebook continued to lead the social media landscape with 1.59 billion MAU. As the first social network to reach a billion users, Facebook also commands high usage among mobile users at the rate of 1.39 billion average users per month (Facebook n.d.). On a daily basis, Facebook attracts over a billion users.

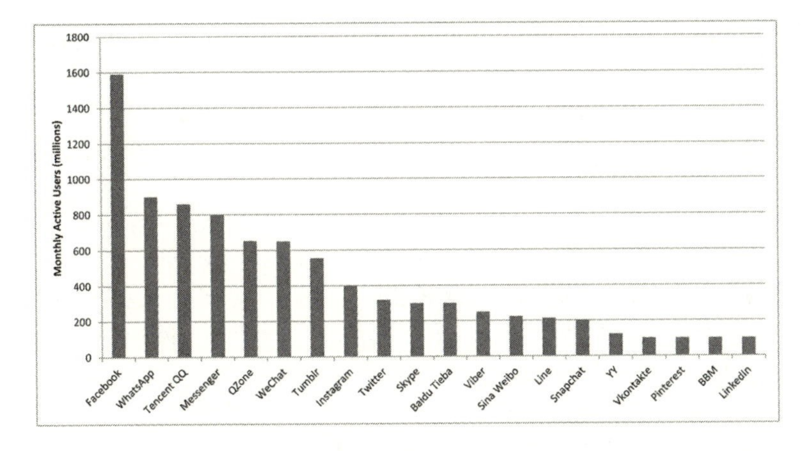

Figure 5.10 Top 20 Social Media Platforms and Messaging Apps with the Most Monthly Active Users (January 2016)

Source: Kemp, Simon. 2016. "Digital in 2016." *We Are Social*. January 27. http://wearesocial.com/uk/special-reports/digital-in-2016.

Facebook-owned WhatsApp receives 900 million MAU. Another messaging app, Tencent QQ, holds third place with 860 million MAU. Owned by Tencent Holdings Limited, most Tencent QQ users live in China and other Asian countries. Facebook's Messenger holds fourth place in usage with 800 million MAU. QZone and WeChat, also owned by the Chinese company Tencent, have 653 and 650 million MAU, respectively. Blogging platform Tumblr has 555 million MAU, and yet another Facebook product, Instagram, has 400 million MAU. Although Twitter has experienced lagging growth recently, it is still solid as the ninth largest among social networks or messaging platforms with 320 million MAU with 80 percent of those users accessing the platform from a mobile phone at least monthly. Other popular platforms include messaging platform Snapchat with 200 million MAU, digital scrapbooking site Pinterest, which reached 100 MAU, and professional networking site LinkedIn also with 100 MAU, but with over 400 million total registered users.

In the United States, the top social networking or messaging platforms in terms of percentage of the adult population who are active users include Facebook (41 percent), Facebook Messenger (26 percent), Twitter (17 percent), Pinterest (15 percent), Instagram (15 percent), and Google+ (12 percent) (see Figure 5.11).

In comparing the top social platforms in terms of membership, visitation (within the past month), and active usage with a global sample of Internet users aged 16–64 (excluding China) during 2015, GlobalWebIndex found that the highest percentage of Internet users are members of Facebook and that the highest percentage have visited YouTube in the past month. Also, for most of the platforms, those who are active users represent approximately half of those who have a profile on the site (see Figure 5.12).

When comparing the frequencies at which U.S. users access social media sites, Facebook continues to dominate with 70 percent of users visiting daily, followed by Instagram, which is visited daily by 59 percent of users, and Twitter, which visited daily by 38 percent of users (see Figure 5.13).

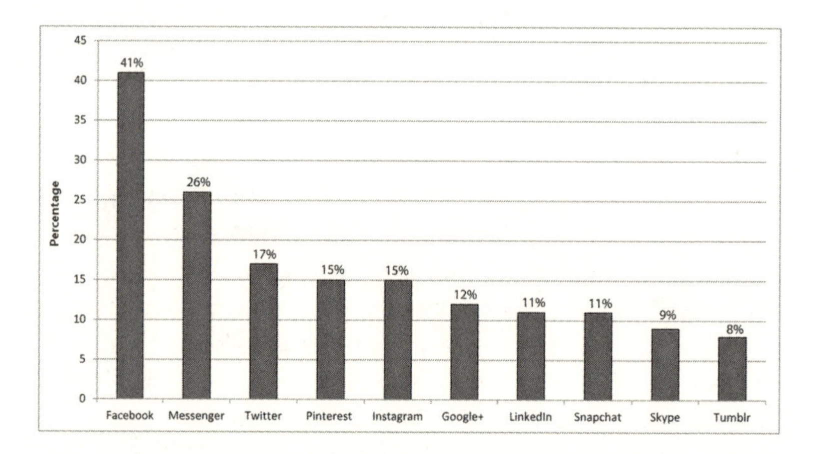

Figure 5.11 Top Active Social Media Platforms in the United States (January 2016)

Source: Kemp, Simon. 2016. "Digital in 2016." *We Are Social*. January 27. http://wearesocial.com/uk/special-reports/digital-in-2016.

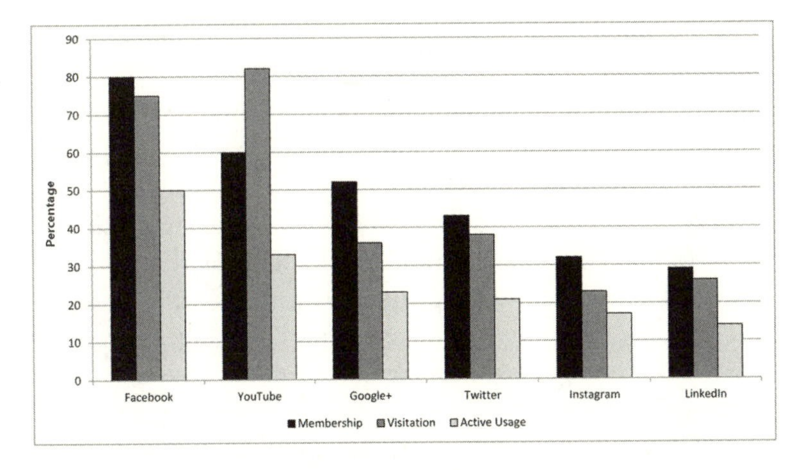

Figure 5.12 Membership, Visitation, and Active Usage of Top Social Media Platforms (2015)

Source: GlobalWebIndex. 2016. "Trends 16: The Numbers That Mattered in 2015, the Trends to Watch in 2016." http://www.globalwebindex.net/hubfs/Reports/Trends_16.pdf.

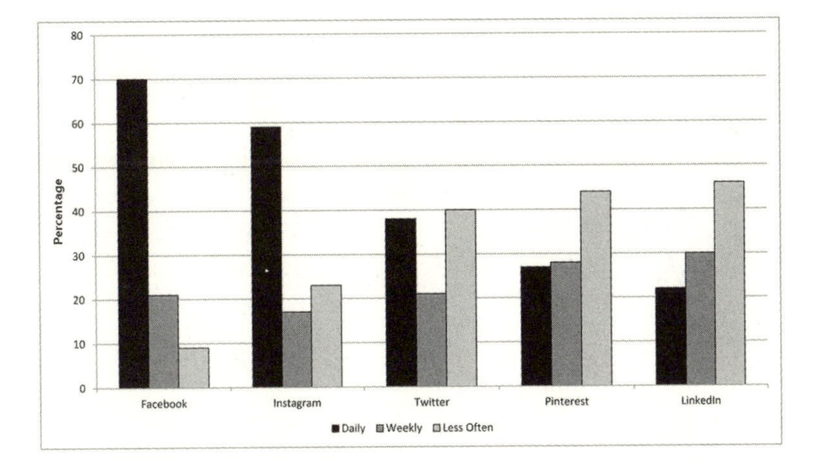

Figure 5.13 Frequency of Usage by U.S. Social Media Platform Users (March–April 2015)

Source: Duggan, Maeve. 2015. "The Demographics of Social Media Users." *Pew Research Center*. April 19. http://www.pewinternet.org/2015/08/19/the-demographics-of-social-media-users/.

As shown in Figure 5.14, an examination of social media penetration over time with teens and millennials aged 13–32 by YPulse has shown slight declines in the usage of Facebook and Twitter among this age group, with growth in the newer social media platforms of Instagram, Snapchat, and Vine. Over the more than two-year time period examined (January 2013–March 2015), the popularity ranking of the platforms remained relatively unchanged with Facebook still the leader and YouTube an increasingly close second. By early 2015, however, Instagram surpassed Twitter as the third most used social media platform.

Comparing teens aged 13–17 to young adults aged 18–32 showed some dramatic differences in social media usage in terms of posting or commenting on the sites daily, particularly for Facebook, where 57 percent of those aged 18–32 post or comment daily and only 28 percent of those aged 13–17 do so (see Figure 5.15). In contrast, Instagram, Snapchat, and YouTube receive daily posts or comments from significantly higher percentages of younger teens than the young adults surveyed.

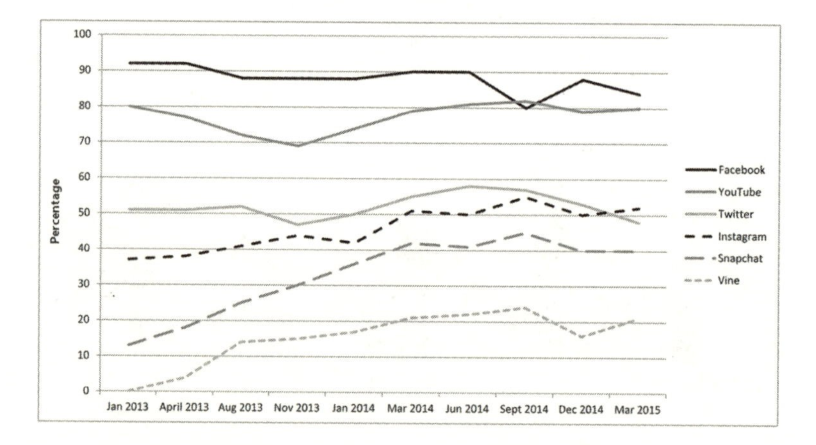

Figure 5.14 Social Media Platform Usage Penetration over Time (Ages 13–32)

Source: YPulse. 2015. "Social Snapshot: The Stats on What Young Consumers Are Using Right Now." May 19. https://www.ypulse.com/post/view/social-snapshot-the-stats-on-what-young-consumers-are-using-right-now.

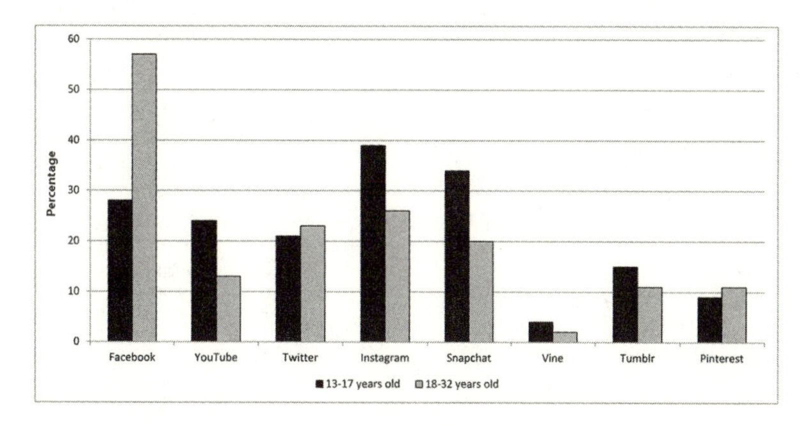

Figure 5.15 Comparison of Daily Posting or Commenting: Teens versus Young Adults (2015)

Source: YPulse. 2015. "Social Snapshot: The Stats on What Young Consumers Are Using Right Now." May 19. https://www.ypulse.com/post/view/social-snapshot-the-stats-on-what-young-consumers-are-using-right-now.

Specific Platform Data

This section describes insights and data related to various specific social media platforms, including Facebook, Twitter, Pinterest, LinkedIn, Instagram, and Snapchat. Video viewing is also discussed.

Facebook

As of June 2016, Facebook had 1.71 billion monthly active users (1.57 billion on mobile) and 1.13 billion daily active users (1.03 billion on mobile). The majority of those users (84.5 percent) live outside the United States and Canada (Facebook n.d.). As of May 2016, the largest number of Facebook users were located in India (more than 195 million), followed by the United States (191.3 million), Brazil (90.11 million), Indonesia (77.58 million), and China (52.87 million) (see Table 5.11).

The dominance of Facebook is further demonstrated in the finding by GlobalWebIndex that 84 percent of online adults in

2015 were members of one of Facebook's platforms, including Facebook, Facebook Messenger, WhatsApp, and Instagram. Not surprisingly, the younger the user, the more likely he or she is to be a member of one of these platforms (see Table 5.12).

Table 5.11 Worldwide Facebook Users (in Millions) (May 2016)

	Users (in Millions)
India	195.2
United States	191.3
Brazil	90.1
Indonesia	77.6
China	52.9
Mexico	46.0
Philippines	39.8
Germany	36.8
United Kingdom	36.5
Turkey	33.1

Source: Statista. 2016 "Leading Countries Based on Number of Facebook Users as of May 2016 (in Millions)." http://www.statista.com/statistics/268136/top-15-countries-based-on-number-of-facebook-users/.

Table 5.12 Global Facebook Product Usage (2015)

	Percentage
Global	84
Female	85
Male	84
16–24	90
25–34	88
35–44	84
45–54	79
55–64	72

Source: GlobalWebIndex. 2016. "Trends 16: The Numbers That Mattered in 2015, the Trends to Watch in 2016." http://www.globalwebindex.net/hubfs/Reports/Trends_16.pdf.

With a penetration rate of 72 percent for Facebook in the United States, a higher percentage of women who use the Internet than men are active Facebook users (77 percent vs. 66 percent) and the highest percentage of users come from the 18- to 29-year-old age group (82 percent) followed by the 30- to 49-year-old age group (79 percent). When comparing racial and ethnic groups, usage penetration is highest among Hispanics (75 percent) (see Table 5.13).

Among Facebook actions, the most prevalent is also the easiest: clicking the "like" button, which is something that 66 percent of active worldwide Facebook users have done. As shown in Figure 5.16, other popular activities include watching a video (51 percent), messaging a friend (50 percent), and commenting on a friend's photo or video (48 percent).

As shown in Figure 5.17, the most popular brands on Facebook during September 2016 (not including Facebook itself) were Coca-Cola with more than 99 million fans, YouTube with

Table 5.13 U.S. Facebook User Penetration (among Internet Users) (March–April 2015)

	Percentage of Internet Users
Total	72
Men	66
Women	77
18–29 years old	82
30–49 years old	79
50–64 years old	64
65+ years old	48
White, non-Hispanics	70
Black, non-Hispanics	67
Hispanics	75

Source: Duggan, Maeve. 2015. "The Demographics of Social Media Users." *Pew Research Center*. April 19. http://www.pewinternet.org/2015/08/19/the-demographics-of-social-media-users/.

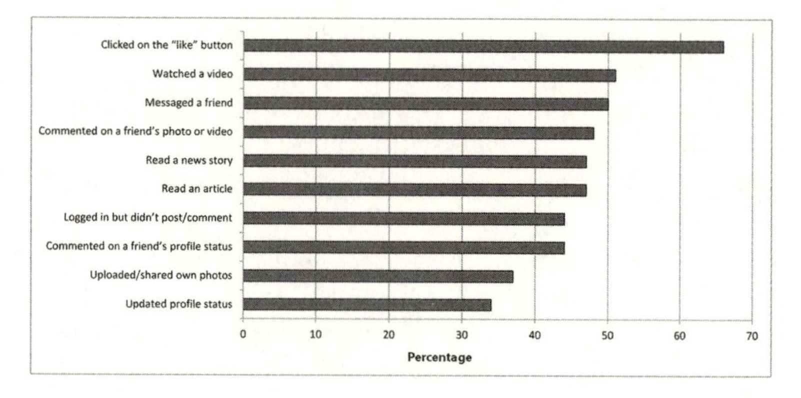

Figure 5.16 Top Facebook Actions Completed by Global Facebook Users within the Past Month (2015)

Source: GlobalWebIndex. 2016. "Trends 16: The Numbers That Mattered in 2015, the Trends to Watch in 2016." http://www.globalwebindex.net/hubfs/Reports/Trends_16.pdf.

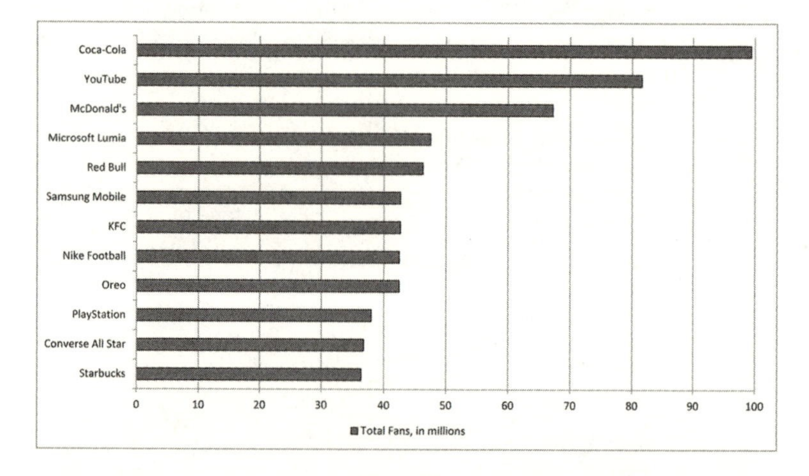

Figure 5.17 Top 12 Brands with the Most Facebook Fans (September 2016)

Source: Fan Page List. 2016. "Top 100 Facebook Fan Pages." http://fanpagelist.com/category/top_users/view/list/sort/fans/page1.

over 81 million fans, McDonald's with more than 67 million, Microsoft Lumia with more than 47 million, Red Bull with more than 46 million, and Samsung Mobile and KFC, both with almost 43 million.

Twitter

Twitter has approximately 313 million monthly active users, as of September 2016, with 82 percent of those users active on mobile (Twitter n.d.). With a penetration rate of 23 percent in the United States, a slightly higher percentage of men who use the Internet than women are active Twitter users (25 percent vs. 21 percent), and the highest percentage of users are from the 18- to 29-year-old age group (32 percent) followed by the 30- to 49-year-old age group (29 percent). Penetration is higher among Hispanics and black, non-Hispanics (both 28 percent) than white, non-Hispanics (20 percent) (see Table 5.14).

As shown in Table 5.15, the top Twitter users in terms of followers as of September 2016 were Katy Perry with more than 92 million followers, Justin Bieber with more than 87 million, Taylor Swift with almost 81 million, Barack Obama with more than 77 million, and Rihanna with more than 65 million.

Table 5.14 U.S. Twitter User Penetration (among Internet Users) (March–April 2015)

	Percentage of Internet Users
Total	23
Men	25
Women	21
18–29 years old	32
30–49 years old	29
50–64 years old	13
65+ years old	6
White, non-Hispanics	20
Black, non-Hispanics	28
Hispanics	28

Source: Duggan, Maeve. 2015. "The Demographics of Social Media Users." *Pew Research Center*. April 19. http://www.pewinternet.org/2015/08/19/the-demographics-of-social-media-users/.

Table 5.15 Twitter Users with the Most Followers (September 2016)

	Followers (in Millions)
Katy Perry	92.5
Justin Bieber	87.5
Taylor Swift	80.8
Barack Obama	77.1
Rihanna	65.2
YouTube	63.9
Lady Gaga	63.1
Ellen DeGeneres	61.9
Twitter	56.6
Justin Timberlake	56.5

Source: Twitter Counter. "Twitter Top 100: Most Followers." http://twittercounter.com/pages/100.

As of March 2016, the top 10 most popular tweets in terms of retweets were dominated by a popular boy band, political statements, and celebrity selfies. The most retweeted tweet at the time was a selfie from the 2014 Academy Awards posted by host Ellen DeGeneres (@TheEllenShow) that also featured Bradley Cooper, Lupita Nyong'o, Jennifer Lawrence, Brad Pitt, Kevin Spacey, Julia Roberts, and others. The tweet that "broke Twitter" was later revealed to be a product placement for Samsung's Galaxy phone (Bulik 2014). In second place, One Direction band member Louis Tomlinson (@Louis_Tomlinson) tweeted about his "love" for bandmate Harry Styles, which has received more than 2 million retweets. Indonesian political analyst Denny Jaguar Ali (@DennyJA_World) posted two tweets with the third and fourth most retweets. One supported presidential candidate Joko Widodo and the other shows a photo of children with T-shirts spelling out the word "love" and calling for an end to discrimination. One Direction member Harry Styles (@Harry_Styles) posted the message "All the love as always" after bandmate Zayn Malik announced he was leaving the band, resulting in the fifth most retweeted tweet. In sixth place, when President Barack Obama was reelected, his staff shared a photo of the president hugging First Lady Michelle Obama with the caption "Four more years." At the time of its posting, this tweet was the most retweeted ever. The seventh most retweeted tweet was posted by One Direction member Niall Horan (@NiallOfficial) about applying to appear on the show *The X Factor*, which catapulted him to fame and the later formation of the band. In eighth place is another tweet by One Direction member Harry Styles quoting a Taylor Swift lyric about "feeling 22." The ninth most popular tweet was posted by former One Direction member Zayn Malik (@zaynmalik) about his love for singer Perrie Edwards. In tenth place, Andrew Malcolm (@AHMalcolm) asked for retweets of a shelter dog photo as part of the #tweetforbowls campaign sponsored by Pedigree. The campaign actually reached its goal of 210,000 dog food bowls three days before Malcolm sent his tweet (Luckerson 2016).

Table 5.16 Top 10 Most Popular Retweeted Tweets (March 2016)

Profile	Retweets
@TheEllenShow	3,341,583
@Louis_Tomlinson	2,100,608
@DennyJA_World (children)	2,089,000
@DennyJA_World (presidential candidate)	998,501
@Harry_Styles ("all the love")	808,091
@BarackObama	785,632
@NiallOfficial	744,612
@Harry_Styles ("feeling 22")	696,114
@zaynmalik	671,085
@AHMalcolm (Pedigree campaign)	652,421

Source: Luckerson, Victor. 2016. "These Are the Most Popular Tweets of All Time." *Time*. March 20. http://time.com/4263227/most-popular-tweets/.

Video

Video viewing is popular with social media users, either through social media platforms like YouTube or Facebook or from apps like Netflix. As of September 2016, YouTube had more than a billion users who watch hundreds of millions of hours on YouTube every day (YouTube n.d.). YouTube also has greater reach among 18- to 34-year-olds and 18- to 49-year-olds than any U.S. cable network. More than half of viewers are coming from mobile phones and the time spent per mobile viewing session averages more than 40 minutes.

Data collected in July 2015 displayed in Table 5.17 reveal that monthly digital video viewers have increased each year since 2012 and are expected to increase through 2017. Similarly, time spent on a daily basis with digital video has increased and is expected to increase during this time period, with most of the viewing growth attributable to viewing on mobile devices. At the same time, traditional television viewers increased between 2012 and 2013, but decreased in both 2014 and 2015 and are expected to continue to drop into 2016 and 2017. In 2015, viewing of digital video on phones surpassed desktop computers.

Almost a quarter of U.S. smartphone users watch television shows or movies on their devices on a daily basis and about

Table 5.17 U.S. Digital Video and Television Viewing (2012–2017)

	2012	2013	2014	2015	2016	2017
Monthly digital video viewers (millions)	171.6	186.2	195.6	204.6	213.6	221.4
Monthly traditional TV viewers (millions)	283.9	286.7	285.1	282.3	278.0	272.5
Daily time spent with digital video (minutes)	50	52	57	64	70	77
—Via mobile devices (minutes)	12	17	25	34	42	51
—Via desktop/nonmobile devices (minutes)	38	35	32	30	28	26

Note: Projected data are provided for 2016 and 2017.

Source: eMarketer. 2016. "Mobile Spearheads Digital Video Advertising's Growth." February 22. http://www.emarketer.com/Article.aspx?R=1013611&ecid=MX1086.

15 percent do so weekly. However, more than two-thirds (36 percent) have never done so and 17 percent have tried once or twice (see Figure 5.18).

As of September 2016, the top 10 most viewed YouTube channels represented the categories of music, movies, entertainment, and toys (see Table 5.18). The top YouTube channel in terms of views is comedic gamer PewDiePie. The top 10 also includes singers Justin Bieber, Rihanna, and Taylor Swift as well as British music label EMI Group Limited (emimusic) and netd müzik featuring videos from the Turkish video-on-demand site. Videos targeted at children also feature prominently on the list including toy advertising channel FunToyzCollector, Russian cartoon and family programming channel Get Movies, and children's educational programming channel LittleBabyBum.

Musical artists have taken over the top spots of the most viewed videos of all time. Leading the pack is PSY's video for "Gangnam Style" at 2.64 billion views, followed by the Wiz Khalifa and Charlie Puth video for "See You Again" at 2.03 billion views (see Figure 5.19).

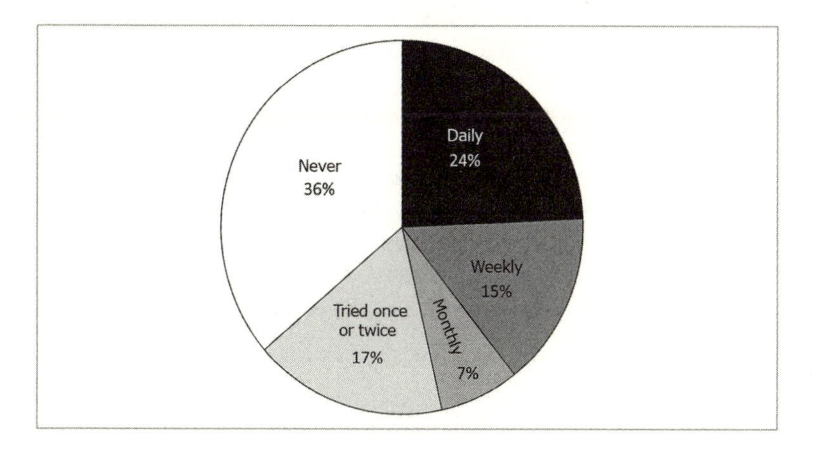

Figure 5.18 Frequency of Television or Movie Viewing on Smartphones by U.S. Consumers (2015)

Source: eMarketer. 2016. "How Often Are U.S. Consumers Watching Video on Their Smartphones." April 7. http://www.emarketer.com/Article/How-Often-US-Consumers-Watching-Video-on-Their-Smartphones/1013802.

Table 5.18 Top 10 Most Viewed YouTube Channels of All Time (September 2016)

Channel	Views (billions)
PewDiePie	13.46
JustinBieberVEVO	12.77
FunToyzCollector	11.77
WWE	11.35
Emimusic	11.32
RihannaVEVO	10.08
Get Movies	9.82
TaylorSwiftVEVO	9.68
LittleBabyBum	9.46
netd müzik	9.36

Source: Social Blade. "Top 100 YouTubers by Most Viewed." http://socialblade.com/youtube/top/100/mostviewed.

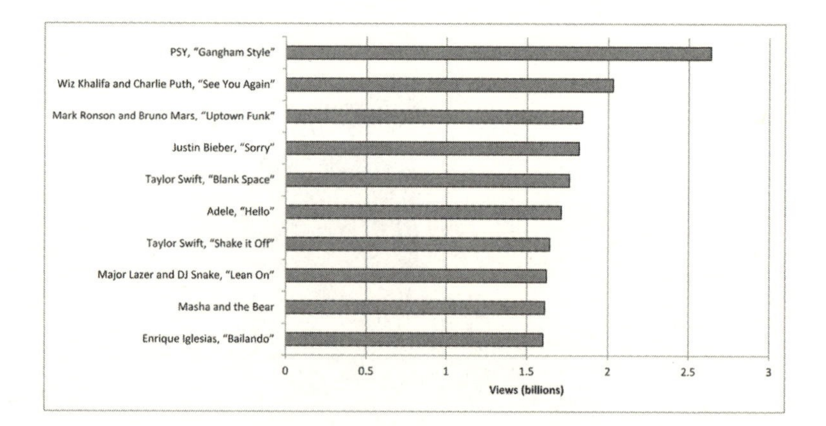

Figure 5.19 Top 10 Most Viewed YouTube Videos of All Time (September 2016)

Source: YouTube. "Most Viewed Videos of All Time." https://www.youtube.com/playlist?list=PLirAqAtl_h2r5g8xGajEwdXd3x1sZh8hC.

Pinterest

A February 2015 eMarketer study estimated that Pinterest would reach 47 million monthly active users in the United States that year and pass 50 million in 2016. Even though Pinterest does not have the activity of platforms like Facebook or Twitter, it attracts users who are interested in making purchases. Females comprise the majority of users, estimated to be almost 83 percent of all Pinterest users in 2016 (see Table 5.19).

A separate study found the penetration rate for Pinterest to be 31 percent of U.S. Internet users as of 2015 (see Table 5.20). A much higher percentage of women Internet users than men are active Pinterest users (44 percent vs. 16 percent) and the highest percentage of users come from the 18- to 29-year-old age group (37 percent) followed closely by the 30- to 49-year-old

Table 5.19 Pinterest Users in the United States by Gender, 2013–2019

Pinterest users (millions)	2013	2014	2015	2016	2017	2018	2019
Female	30.0	35.6	39.2	41.7	43.9	45.8	47.1
Male	4.9	6.6	7.9	9.0	10.0	11.1	12.1
Total	34.9	42.3	47.1	50.7	53.9	56.8	59.3
Pinterest user penetration (percentage of Internet users in each group)							
Female	23.6%	27.4%	29.4%	30.7%	31.8%	32.7%	33.4%
Male	4.1%	5.4%	6.2%	7.0%	7.6%	8.2%	9.0%
Total	14.2%	16.7%	18.1%	19.1%	19.9%	20.7%	21.4%
Pinterest user share (percentage of total)							
Female	86.0%	84.3%	83.3%	82.2%	81.4%	80.5%	79.5%
Male	14.0%	15.7%	16.7%	17.8%	18.6%	19.5%	20.5%

Note: Data from 2015–2019 are projected.

Source: eMarketer. 2015. "Will Pinterest Reach Its Potential in 2015?" February 25. http://www.emarketer.com/Article/Will-Pinterest-Reach-Its-Potential-2015/1012103e.

Table 5.20 U.S. Pinterest User Penetration (among Internet Users) (March–April 2015)

	Percentage of Internet Users
Total	31
Men	16
Women	44
18–29 years old	37
30–49 years old	36
50–64 years old	24
65+ years old	16
White, non-Hispanics	32
Black, non-Hispanics	23
Hispanics	32

Source: Duggan, Maeve. 2015. "The Demographics of Social Media Users." *Pew Research Center*. April 19. http://www.pewinternet.org/2015/08/19/the-demographics-of-social-media-users/.

age group (36 percent). Penetration is higher among white, non-Hispanics and Hispanics (both 32 percent)

Instagram

Instagram, with more than 500 million monthly active users, more than 300 million daily active users, and more than 95 million photos uploaded every day, is a social media platform on the rise (Instagram n.d.)

As shown in Table 5.21, with a penetration rate of 28 percent in the United States, a much higher percentage of women who use the Internet than men are active Instagram users (31 percent vs. 24 percent) and the highest percentage of users are from the 18- to 29-year-old age group (55 percent) followed by the 30- to 49-year-old age group (28 percent). Penetration is higher among Hispanics and black, non-Hispanics (47 percent and 38 percent, respectively).

Table 5.21 U.S. Instagram User Penetration (among Internet Users) (March–April 2015)

	Percentage of Internet Users
Total	28
Men	24
Women	31
18–29 years old	55
30–49 years old	28
50–64 years old	11
65+ years old	4
White, non-Hispanics	21
Black, non-Hispanics	47
Hispanics	38

Source: Duggan, Maeve. 2015. "The Demographics of Social Media Users." *Pew Research Center*. April 19. http://www.pewinternet.org/2015/08/19/the-demographics-of-social-media-users/.

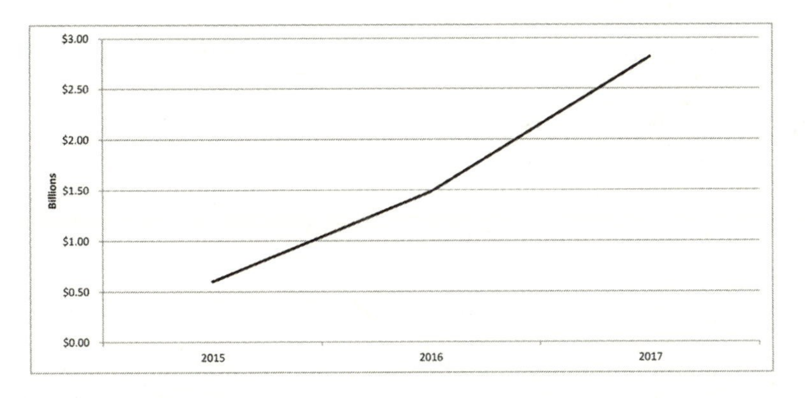

Figure 5.20 Worldwide Instagram Net Mobile Ad Revenues (2015–2017)

Note: Data from 2016–2017 are projected.

Source: eMarketer. 2015. "Instagram Mobile Ad Revenues to Reach $2.81 Billion Worldwide in 2017." July 27. http://www.emarketer.com/Article/Instagram-Mobile-Ad-Revenues-Reach-281-Billion-Worldwide-2017/1012774.

In July 2015, paid mobile advertising on Instagram was expected to be $600 million that year and then explode to $1.48 billion in 2016 and $2.81 billion in 2017, as shown

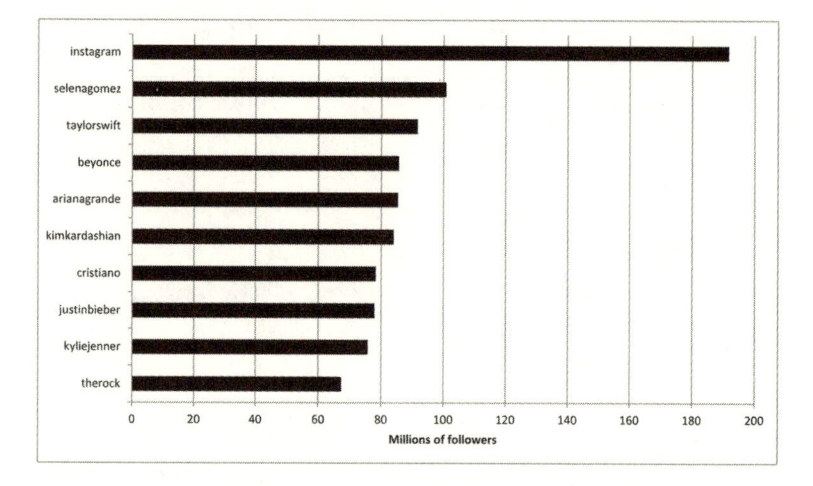

Figure 5.21 Top 10 Instagram Profiles in Terms of Most Followed (October 2016)

Source: Social Blade. 2016. "Top 100 Instagram Profiles, Filtered by Most Followed." https://socialblade.com/instagram/top/100/followers.

in Figure 5.20. An eMarketer report describes how Instagram is expected to surpass both Google and Twitter in 2017 in terms of net U.S. mobile display ad revenues by 2017.

As of October 2016, the most popular Instagram profiles in terms of followers are for Instagram itself, Selena Gomez, Taylor Swift, Beyoncé, and Ariana Grande (see Figure 5.21).

LinkedIn

With a penetration rate of 25 percent in the United States, men and women who are online use LinkedIn in almost identical proportions (26 percent and 25 percent, respectively) and the highest percentage of users are from the 39- to 49-year-old age group (32 percent) followed by the 50- to 64-year-old age group (26 percent). Penetration is highest among white, non-Hispanics (26 percent) (see Table 5.22).

LinkedIn does not command the revenues of other social media platforms, but it was expected to bring in just under

Table 5.22 U.S. LinkedIn User Penetration (among Internet Users) (March–April 2015)

	Percentage of Internet Users
Total	25
Men	26
Women	25
18–29 years old	22
30–49 years old	32
50–64 years old	26
65+ years old	12
White, non-Hispanics	26
Black, non-Hispanics	22
Hispanics	22

Source: Duggan, Maeve. 2015. "The Demographics of Social Media Users." *Pew Research Center*. April 19. http://www.pewinternet.org/2015/08/19/the-demographics-of-social-media-users/.

Table 5.23 LinkedIn Advertising Revenues, United States vs. non–United States (2014–2017)

	2014	2015	2016	2017
United States				
Ad revenues	$450.0	$594.5	$707.0	$819.6
Percentage of worldwide total	60%	64%	63%	62%
Non–United States				
Ad revenues	$296.1	$338.8	$418.0	$506.0
Percentage of worldwide total	40%	36%	37%	38%
Total	$746.1	$933.3	$1,125.0	$1,325.6

Note: Data are estimated for 2016 and 2017.

Source: eMarketer. 2016. "LinkedIn Continues to Grow Ad Revenues." February 4. http://www.emarketer.com/Article/LinkedIn-Continues-Grow-Social-Ad-Revenues/1013551.

$1 billion in 2015, with that number expected to grow in 2016 and 2017. Most of the income comes from U.S. ad revenues, as opposed to non-U.S. revenues.

Snapchat

Penetration of Snapchat is high among the youngest users (70 percent for ages 18–24 and 41 percent for ages 25–34). In just three years, Snapchat has seen significant increases in its usage across all age groups as shown in Table 5.24.

The majority of Snapchat users are millennials born between 1981 and 2000. As of 2016, eMarketer estimates the number of Snapchat millennial users in the United States to be 40.9 million and the percentage of smartphone users in that age group to be 51.3 percent (see Figure 5.22). Growth in Snapchat usage is expected to continue to rise through 2020, but at a slower rate.

At the beginning of 2016, Snapchat users were watching more than 7 billion video clips each day, a number that is approaching Facebook's 8 billion daily video views despite Facebook having 15 times as many users (Frier and Chang 2016). The top actions that Snapchat users are performing, as shown in Figure 5.23, are sending a message (70 percent), sending a photo snap (61 percent), adding a friend (53 percent), sending a video snap (47 percent), and creating or viewing a story (45 percent).

Table 5.24 U.S. Snapchat Penetration by Age (2013–2016)

	April 2013	December 2015	June 2016
18–24	24	64	70
25–34	5	31	41
35+	2	8	14

Source: comScore. 2016. "The 2016 U.S. Mobile App Report." September. https://www.comscore.com/Insights/Presentations-and-Whitepapers/2016/The-2016-US-Mobile-App-Report.

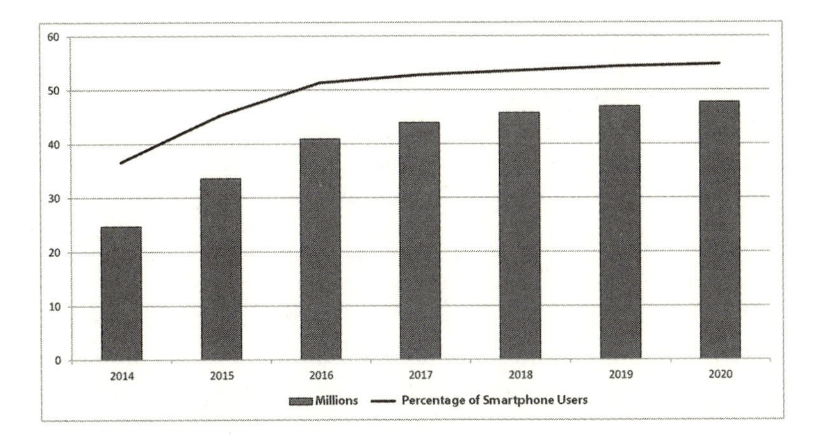

Figure 5.22 U.S. Millennial Snapchat Users and Penetration (2014–2020)

Note: Data for 2016–2020 are projected.

Source: eMarketer. 2016. "U.S. Snapchat Users Will Increase by Double Digits This Year and Next." August 23. https://www.emarketer.com/Article/US-Snapchat-Users-Will-Increase-by-Double-Digit-Percentages-This-Year-Next/1014378.

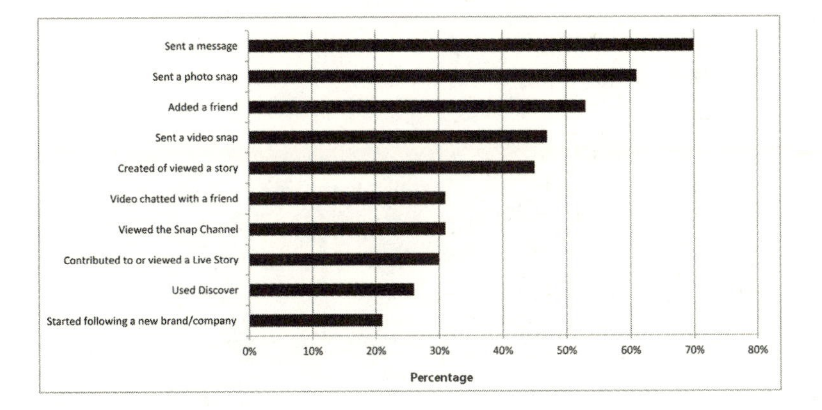

Figure 5.23 Top 10 Snapchat Actions by Snapchat Users in the Past Month (2015)

Source: GlobalWebIndex. 2016. "Trends 16: The Numbers That Mattered in 2015, the Trends to Watch in 2016." http://www.globalwebindex.net/hubfs/Reports/Trends_16.pdf.

Social Media for Marketing

This section presents data on marketers' use of social media platforms as well as the platforms they plan to increase usage of in the future and those perceived to have the best return on investment (ROI). Additionally, this section includes past and projected spending on social media on a global scale and U.S. allocations of digital marketing budgets.

As of May 2015, Facebook, Twitter, and LinkedIn were the top three platforms that worldwide marketers were using to promote their companies, products, or services (see Figure 5.24).

As shown in Figure 5.25, Facebook, Twitter, YouTube, and LinkedIn were all cited as platforms where worldwide marketers would be focusing more attention in the future.

A worldwide study by Social Fresh, Firebrand Group, and Simply Measured of social media marketers found that highest percentage of marketers cited Facebook, Twitter, and Instagram as the three social platforms with the best ROI (see Figure 5.26).

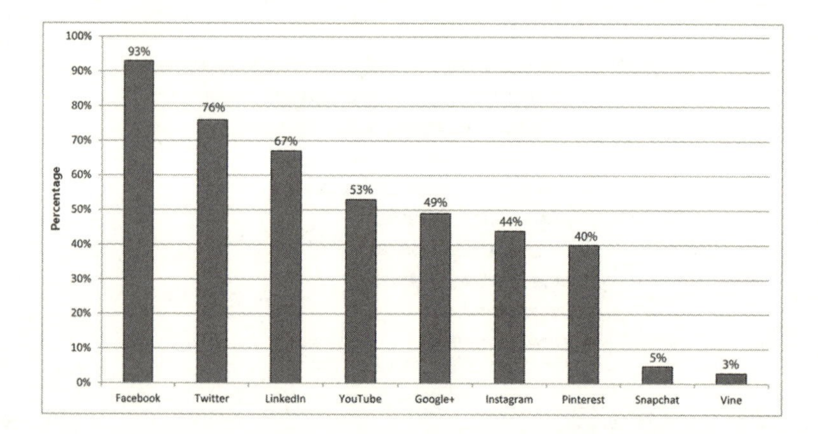

Figure 5.24 Social Media Platforms Used by Worldwide Marketers (May 2016)

Source: Stelzner, Michael A. 2016. "2016 Social Media Marketing Industry Report." *Social Media Examiner*. May 20. https://www.socialmediaexaminer.com/wp-content/uploads/2016/05/SocialMediaMarketingIndustryReport2016.pdf.

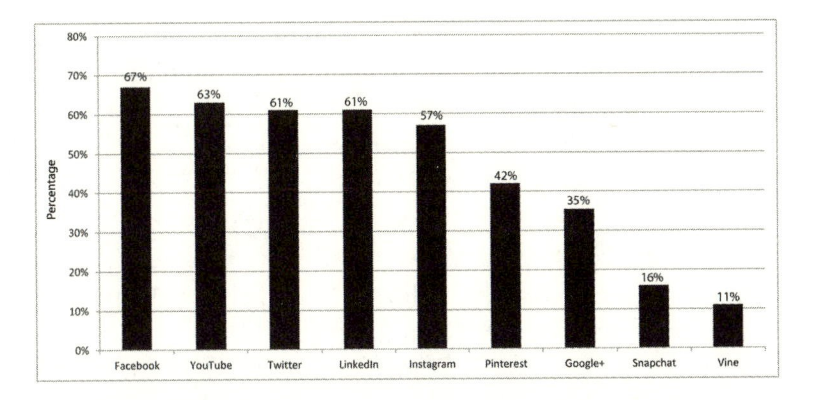

Figure 5.25 Planned Increase in Social Media Usage by Worldwide Marketers (May 2016)

Source: Stelzner, Michael A. 2016. "2016 Social Media Marketing Industry Report." *Social Media Examiner*. May 20. https://www.socialmediaexaminer.com/wp-content/uploads/2016/05/SocialMediaMarketingIndustryReport2016.pdf.

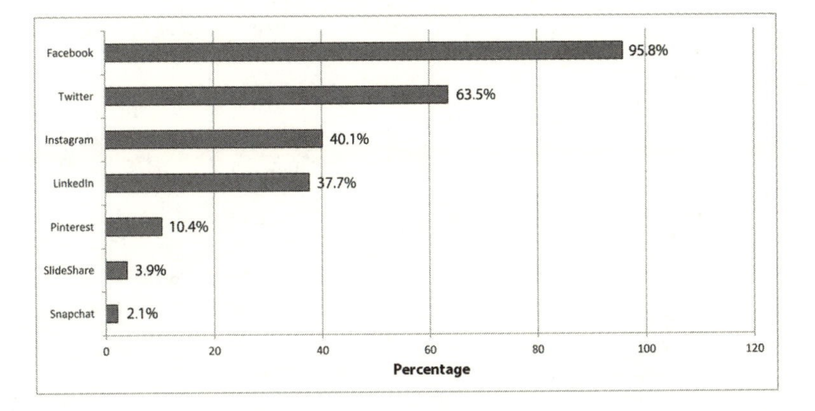

Figure 5.26 Worldwide Social Media Marketers' Perception of Social Platforms with Best ROI (March 2016)

Source: eMarketer. 2016. "For Social Media Marketers, Facebook Produces the Best Results. May 5. http://www.emarketer.com/Article/Social-Media-Marketers-Facebook-Produces-Best-ROI/1013918.

In 2015, eMarketer predicted that global advertising spending on social media would reach almost $24 billion in 2015, a 33.5 percent increase from 2014, and that it would reach almost $36 billion by 2017. Social media ad spending in North America was expected to pass $10 billion for 2015, an increase of 31 percent over 2014. As a percentage of overall digital ad spending, social media advertising was expected to reach almost 14 percent worldwide for 2015 and almost 16 percent in North America (see Table 5.25).

A study by Cowen and Company published in early 2016 by eMarketer found that U.S. marketers allocated more than 22 percent of their digital advertising budgets to social media and almost 20 percent to video advertising. The other digital categories included more than 27 percent for display advertising and more than 25 percent on search advertising (see Figure 5.27).

Table 5.25 Social Network Ad Spending Worldwide and in North America (2013–2017)

	2013	2014	2015	2016	2017
Social network ad spending (billions)					
Worldwide	$11.36	$17.74	$23.68	$29.91	$35.98
North America	$4.94	$7.71	$10.10	$12.67	$15.15
Social network ad spending growth (percentage change)					
Worldwide	51.1%	56.2%	33.5%	26.3%	20.3%
North America	46.3%	55.9%	31.0%	25.5%	19.6%
Social network percentage of digital ad spending					
Worldwide	9.4%	12.2%	13.9%	15.1%	16.0%
North America	10.5%	14.0%	15.9%	17.4%	18.7%

Note: Data for 2015–2017 are projected.

Source: eMarketer. 2015. "Social Network Ad Spending to Hit $23.68 Billion Worldwide in 2015." April 15. http://www.emarketer.com/Article/Social-Network-Ad-Spending-Hit-2368-Billion-Worldwide-2015/1012357.

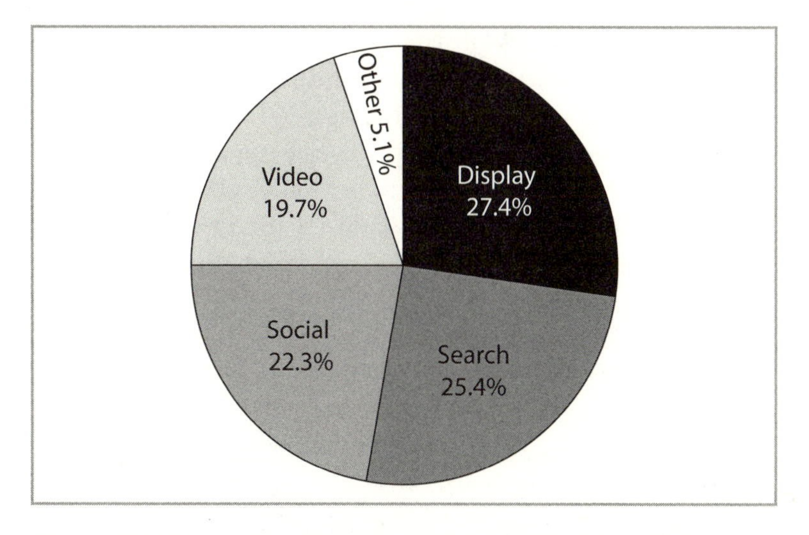

Figure 5.27 Allocation of 2016 Digital Ad Spending by U.S. Ad Buyers

Source: eMarketer. 2016. "How Live Streaming Video Events Can Benefit Retailers." March 25. http://www.emarketer.com/Article/How-Live-Streaming-Video-Events-Benefit-Retailers/1013750.

Impact of Social Media on Online Shopping

For many retailers, online sales contribute significantly to the bottom line. This section provides metrics for online and social commerce, presents adoption rates for social buy buttons, and reports activities that are having the most impact on online shopping behavior. In the United States, online sales for 2015 totaled $335 billion, a number that is expected to increase more than 9 percent annually for the next five years (Lindner 2016). Additionally, 244 million customers browsed or bought online in 2015, which is expected to reach 270 million by 2020. Mobile phones are estimated to have had a $1 trillion impact on online and offline sales in 2015.

Included in online sales are sales through social networks, which is called social commerce. The *Social Media 500* report by Internet Retailer found that, of the 500 leading online retailers, social commerce totaled $3.3 billion in 2014, an increase from $2.6 billion in 2013 (Smith 2015). Traffic to retail websites from social networks had also increased 7 percent during this time frame. Total worldwide social commerce was projected to reach $20 billion in 2014 and $30 billion in 2015 (Statista 2014). The leading social commerce e-retailers in terms of revenue in 2014 included Zappos.com (10.16 percent of traffic from social networks), Fab.com (25 percent), and NoMoreRack.com (35 percent) (Saleh n.d.). The next three leaders included Victoria's Secret (8.5 percent), Nordstrom (8.3 percent), and Nike (8.4 percent). The leaders are all fashion brands, indicating the ability of social media to work effectively for this industry.

Buy buttons on social media sites are helping to drive social commerce. As of August 2015, e-mail and Facebook were the leading platforms for the adoption of buy buttons, used by 27.1 percent and 22.0 percent, respectively, of retailers surveyed (see Figure 5.28). Although buy buttons are available on all other major social media platforms, a small percentage of retailers are using them.

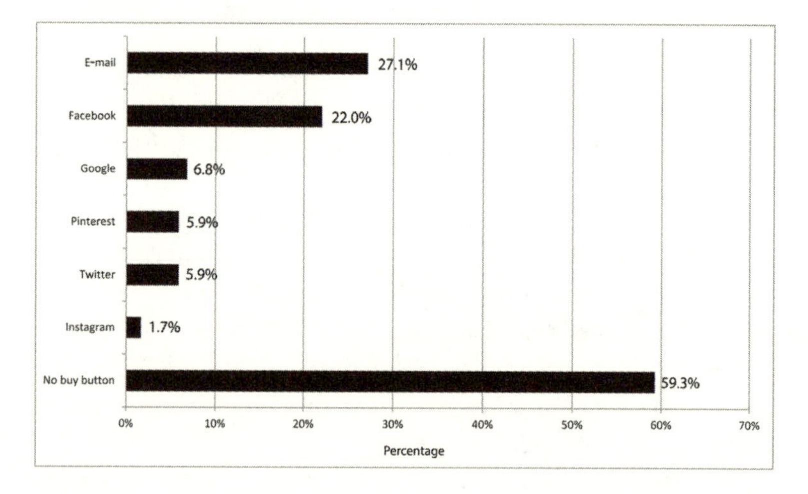

Figure 5.28 Adoption of Buy Buttons among U.S. Digital Retailers (August 2015)

Source: eMarketer. 2016. "How Social Media Influences Shopping Behavior." March 17. http://www.emarketer.com/Article/How-Social-Media-Influences-Shopping-Behavior/1013718.

At this time, however, most worldwide consumers do not believe that a buy button on a social media platform would make them more likely to purchase a product. In a study by GlobalWebIndex, only 10 percent of Internet users said a buy button would make them more likely to purchase, as shown in Figure 5.29. Other findings were that 37 percent follow a favorite brand on social media and 30 percent use social media to research a product.

Digital activities are having an impact on online shopping behavior. A study by PricewaterhouseCoopers of more than 22,000 digital shoppers who had shopped online at least once in the past year found that 45 percent reported that reading reviews on social media sites had an influence on their purchase behavior. Other effective strategies included receiving promotional offers from an online retailer (44 percent), viewing online ads (30 percent), staying on top of trends (25 percent), writing reviews (22 percent), associating with particular brands and retailers online (20 percent), and purchasing directly through social media (16 percent) (see Figure 5.30).

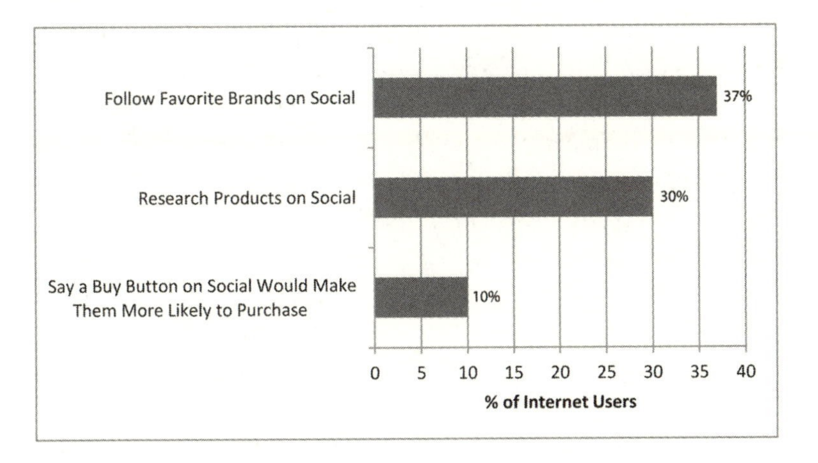

Figure 5.29 Global Social Commerce Prospects (2015)

Source: GlobalWebIndex. 2016. "Trends 16: The Numbers That Mattered in 2015, the Trends to Watch in 2016." http://www.globalwebindex.net/hubfs/Reports/Trends_16.pdf.

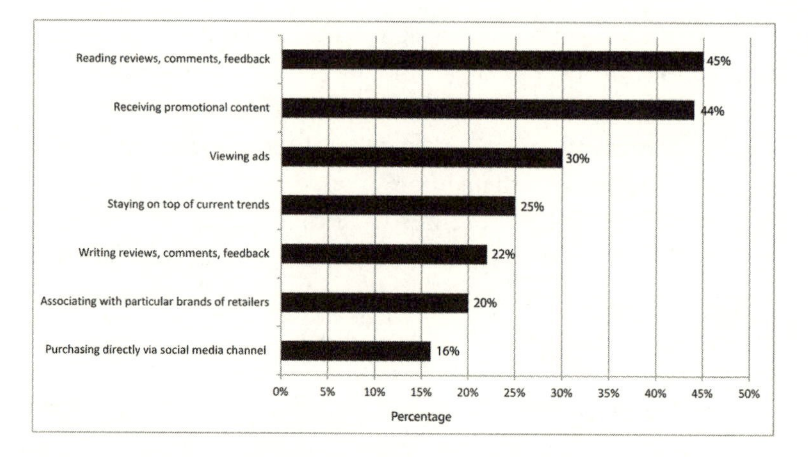

Figure 5.30 Social Media Activities That Influence Worldwide Shopping Behavior (September 2015)

Source: PricewaterhouseCoopers. 2016. "They Say They Want a Revolution: Total Retail 2016." http://www.pwc.ie/media-centre/assets/publications/2016-total-retail-they-say-they-want-a-revolution.pdf.

Documents

Children's Online Privacy Protection Act (1998)

In 1998, Congress passed the Children's Online Privacy Protection Act (COPPA) to require commercial websites to gain parental consent before collecting, using, and/or disclosing information from children under the age of 13. The act gives parents control over the information that is collected about their children online. The act also outlines the contents of a privacy policy, including the responsibility of a website operator to protect the privacy and safety of children on their sites.

(1) In general

It is unlawful for an operator of a website or online service directed to children, or any operator that has actual knowledge that it is collecting personal information from a child, to collect personal information from a child in a manner that violates the regulations prescribed under subsection (b).

. . .

(b) Regulations

(1) Not later than 1 year after October 21, 1998, the Commission shall promulgate under section 553 of title 5 regulations that—

(A) require the operator of any website or online service directed to children that collects personal information from children or the operator of a website or online service that has actual knowledge that it is collecting personal information from a child—

(i) to provide notice on the website of what information is collected from children by the operator, how the operator uses such information, and the operator's disclosure practices for such information; and

(ii) to obtain verifiable parental consent for the collection, use, or disclosure of personal information from children;

(B) require the operator to provide, upon request of a parent under this subparagraph whose child has provided personal information to that website or online service, upon proper identification of that parent, to such parent—

(i) a description of the specific types of personal information collected from the child by that operator;

(ii) the opportunity at any time to refuse to permit the operator's further use or maintenance in retrievable form, or future online collection, of personal information from that child; and

(iii) notwithstanding any other provision of law, a means that is reasonable under the circumstances for the parent to obtain any personal information collected from that child;

(C) prohibit conditioning a child's participation in a game, the offering of a prize, or another activity on the child disclosing more personal information than is reasonably necessary to participate in such activity; and

(D) require the operator of such a website or online service to establish and maintain reasonable procedures to protect the confidentiality, security, and integrity of personal information collected from children.

Source: Children's Online Privacy Protection Act of 1998, 15 U.S.C. 6501–6505.

Barack Obama, "It Gets Better" (2010)

The It Gets Better Project helps lesbian, gay, bisexual and transgender (LGBT) youth deal with bullying and harassment by providing encouraging video messages that describe how the future will be much better for them. In a video posted on the organization's website, President Obama provides a message of hope and support to LGBT victims of bullying in the wake of several tragic suicides.

Like all of you, I was shocked and saddened by the deaths of several young people who were bullied and taunted for being gay, and who ultimately took their own lives. As a parent of two daughters, it breaks my heart. It's something that just shouldn't happen in this country.

We've got to dispel the myth that bullying is just a normal rite of passage—that it's some inevitable part of growing up. It's not. We have an obligation to ensure that our schools are safe for *all* of our kids. And to every young person out there you need to know that if you're in trouble, there are caring adults who can help.

I don't know what it's like to be picked on for being gay. But I do know what it's like to grow up feeling that sometimes you don't belong. It's tough. And for a lot of kids, the sense of being alone or apart—I know can just wear on you. And when you're teased or bullied, it can seem like somehow you brought it on yourself—for being different, or for not fitting in with everybody else.

But what I want to say is this. You are not alone. You didn't do anything wrong. You didn't do anything to deserve being bullied. And there is a whole world waiting for you, filled with possibilities. There are people out there who love you and care about you just the way you are. And so, if you ever feel like because of bullying, because of what people are saying, that you're getting down on yourself, you've got to make sure to reach out to people you trust. Whether it's your parents, teachers, folks that you know care about you just the way you are. You've got to reach out to them, don't feel like you're in this by yourself.

The other thing you need to know is, things will get better. And more than that, with time you're going to see that your differences are a source of pride and a source of strength. You'll look back on the struggles you've faced with compassion and wisdom. And that's not just going to serve you, but it will help you get involved and make this country a better place.

It will mean that you'll be more likely to help fight discrimination—not just against LGBT Americans, but discrimination in all its forms. It means you'll be more likely to understand personally and deeply why it's so important that as adults we set an example in our own lives and that we treat everybody with respect. That we are able to see the world through other people's eyes and stand in their shoes—that we never lose sight of what binds us together.

As a nation we're founded on the belief that all of us are equal and each of us deserves the freedom to pursue our own version of happiness; to make the most of our talents; to speak our minds; to *not* fit in; most of all, to be true to ourselves. That's the freedom that enriches all of us. That's what America is all about. And every day, it gets better.

Source: Remarks of President Barack Obama. Video for the "It Gets Better" Project. Washington, DC: The White

House. Available online at https://www.whitehouse.gov/it-gets-better-transcript.

Social Media in Disasters (2011)

The administrator of the Federal Emergency Management Agency (FEMA), Craig Fugate, testified to the Subcommittee on Disaster Recovery and Intergovernmental Affairs of the Senate Committee on Homeland Security and Governmental Affairs on the topic of using social media for communication purposes in the aftermath of a disaster. Fugate describes how social media can be an effective tool in the toolbox for disaster management and communication.

Senator Pryor. At FEMA, do you all have people in office that are doing your social media focus here? Or is this just part of your overall effort, or do you have to have folks that actually focus on this?

Mr. Fugate. We do have dedicated staff that are working on what we call digital engagement. Initially, when I got to FEMA, the Web page, using things like YouTube to post update videos, and beginning to do partnerships with Facebook where we would do joint Facebook pages per disaster with the State to share information to the public.

When I got there, one of the things that I asked early on was to begin tweeting, which I had done in the State of Florida, so I now tweet "@CraigatFEMA." I actually do my own tweets. So many people keep asking me, Who does your tweets? I am, like, I do not have staff to tweet, I tweet. And I do not tweet about me; I tweet about things that I think are interesting.

A lot of the people that I communicate with are my peers and practitioners. It is actually interesting. Not only is this useful in disasters, but it is helping build a community in the emergency management that traditionally had to go to course or conferences to see and hear across the Nation ideas. There are things that, when you get into the nomenclature of all of these terms, concept of what a hashtag is in Twitter, what it is, it is something that you build into a message that you can link on that can take—-everybody who uses that tag can link everybody else's messages together, so very early emergence in the emergency management community that are asking these very questions about social media applications is a pound sign, social media emergency management (SMEM). That is not led by FEMA, but we have staff that participate.

But this is the conversation taking place with local emergency managers, States, volunteers, researchers, the private sector, and we have never had those kind of—we never saw that interaction outside of conference settings or courses, which was limited.

So we have a centrally directed effort, but it also is underlying some key principles, is give information all the way from high bandwidth to low bandwidth to in-person. We cannot forget there are people who do not use social media. But communicate and provide tools the way people are communicating and using those tools, not limit them to what is just easy for us to administer.

Senator Pryor. All right. You may not have this available, but do you have examples of how social media has actually saved lives?

Mr. Fugate. There are examples. I think you are going to have some people in the next hearing that will talk about this. But some of the examples in Haiti where the wireless infrastructure came back on rather quickly, as people were trapped in debris and rubble and you did not have a centralized government system to receive those calls because of extreme damages to both the government of Haiti and to the United Nations, people were able to get out text messages that were being received by people outside the area. They were able to figure out where those people were, approximately, based upon the towers and went back and worked with the cell providers. And I think you are going to hear stories about how a lot of volunteers and people with a lot of technology experience were able to start mapping and providing data in a way that it allowed the United Nations (U.N.) and other forces from the United States

Agency for International Development (USAID) to get Urban Search and Rescue (US&R) Teams and other resources where needed. And that was just one example in a country that many of us were kind of taken aback on the devastation, but also the resiliency of the Haitians themselves and how much mobile technology had actually been integrated into their country prior to the earthquake.

Senator Pryor. And I think back to Hurricane Katrina, and I think about all those folks in the Superdome and other places, and I guess—was the wireless network up and running at that point? You may not know this, but was it up and running in those early days?

Mr. Fugate. Mr. Chairman, I really do not know, but it is something that—one of the things we have learned in my experience in 2004 and 2005—and I do not know if we have any of the wireless operators that could provide this information. But it has been my observation that the industry learned from those events and how it worked very hard to get in additional resources to both bring back up wireless but also increase capacity. We saw this in the tornadoes where they brought in additional equipment and worked to get cell coverage back up, get wireless back up. And because of that, we have seen—and, again, I kind of look at Haiti as a lesson learned. We actually were assuming until Haiti that wireless communications in areas of devastation would be unreliable and we really would not need to plan for it. Haiti taught me that the industry has learned and is becoming more resilient, and oftentimes it will probably be for many people in the public the first communication that comes back up is going to be the wireless services.

. . .

Mr. Fugate. Mr. Chairman, some of my peers now equate the wireless combined with social media as a revolution in emergency management as powerful as wireless was to original public safety radio systems, except now this is far more reaching in the ability to communicate with the public. And so as we see this, again, I think our role here at FEMA is to keep up with the public and not necessarily fall back into what I call innovation at the speed of government, but really look to the technology industry, and as Senator Brown said, I have had the opportunity to go to Google, I have been to Facebook, I have been to Twitter, and really looking into their insights of how we better utilize the private sector as part of the team and not try to re-create things that they do better than us, but use those tools to better communicate and listen to the public as we deal with disasters.

Senator Pryor. Is it your impression that during a disaster the public will find you using social media? Or do they know where to go?

Mr. Fugate. No, sir. Again, those people that have had disasters do not, and so this is why we work so hard. And I appreciate every time—this is pretty much the drill, is to get people to register with FEMA, get the information out there. So it is always for us important to get people to know where they can get that information. Part of this is working with the States, things like joint Facebook pages. But I think, by and large, most people are not thinking about FEMA, and that is why trying to build systems that are government-specific tend to fail. It is our ability to use the tools they are using and then direct them to things they are used to using. I mean, if you think about it, when we tell people to go to a Web page that is our typical Federal Web page, it is not easy to find the information in a disaster. That is why we built the mobile page so that when you send them there, it is strictly about disaster information that they need, not, the traditional way that we oftentimes put information on a Web page.

Source: Testimony of W. Craig Fugate, Administrator, Federal Emergency Management Agency. "Understanding the Power of Social Media as a Communication Tool in the Aftermath of Disasters." Hearing before the Ad Hoc Subcommittee on

Disaster Recovery and Intergovernmental Affairs, Committee on Homeland Security and Governmental Affairs. U.S. Senate, 112th Congress, First Session, May 5, 2011. Washington, DC: Government Printing Office, 2012. Available online at https://www.govinfo.gov/app/content/pkg/CHRG-112shrg67635/html/CHRG-112shrg67635.htm.

Nebraska Workplace Privacy Act (2016)

The Nebraska Workplace Privacy Act is one of many similar state laws that prevent employers from requiring passwords to personal social media accounts to either gain employment or retain a job. The state legislature passed the act without any opposition votes and governor Pete Ricketts signed the bill on April 19, 2016.

A BILL FOR AN ACT relating to employment; to adopt the Workplace Privacy Act; and to provide severability.

Be it enacted by the people of the State of Nebraska,

. . .

Sec. 3. No employer shall:

(1) Require or request that an employee or applicant provide or disclose any user name or password or any other related account information in order to gain access to the employee's or applicant's personal Internet account by way of an electronic communication device;

(2) Require or request that an employee or applicant log into a personal Internet account by way of an electronic communication device in the presence of the employer in a manner that enables the employer to observe the contents of the employee's or applicant's personal Internet account or provides the employer access to the employee's or applicant's personal Internet account;

(3) Require an employee or applicant to add anyone, including the employer, to the list of contacts associated with the employee's or applicant's personal Internet account or

require or otherwise coerce an employee or applicant to change the settings on the employee's or applicant's personal Internet account which affects the ability of others to view the content of such account; or

(4) Take adverse action against, fail to hire, or otherwise penalize an employee or applicant for failure to provide or disclose any of the information or to take any of the actions specified in subdivisions (1) through (3) of this section.

Sec. 4. An employer shall not require an employee or applicant to waive or limit any protection granted under the Workplace Privacy Act as a condition of continued employment or of applying for or receiving an offer of employment. Any agreement to waive any right or protection under the act is against the public policy of this state and is void and unenforceable.

Sec. 5. An employer shall not retaliate or discriminate against an employee or applicant because the employee or applicant:

(1) Files a complaint under the Workplace Privacy Act; or

(2) Testifies, assists, or participates in an investigation, proceeding, or action concerning a violation of the act.

Sec. 6. An employee shall not download or transfer an employer's private proprietary information or private financial data to a personal Internet account without authorization from the employer. This section shall not apply if the proprietary information or the financial data is otherwise disclosed by the employer to the public pursuant to other provisions of law or practice.

Sec. 7. Nothing in the Workplace Privacy Act limits an employer's right to:

(1) Promulgate and maintain lawful workplace policies governing the use of the employer's electronic equipment, including policies regarding Internet use and personal Internet account use;

(2) Request or require an employee or applicant to disclose access information to the employer to gain access to or operate:

   (a) An electronic communication device supplied by or paid for in whole or in part by the employer; or
   (b) An account or service provided by the employer, obtained by virtue of the employee's employment relationship with the employer, or used for the employer's business purposes;

(3) Restrict or prohibit an employee's access to certain web sites while using an electronic communication device supplied by or paid for in whole or in part by the employer or while using an employer's network or resources, to the extent permissible under applicable laws;
(4) Monitor, review, access, or block electronic data stored on an electronic communication device supplied by or paid for in whole or in part by the employer or stored on an employer's network, to the extent permissible under applicable laws;
(5) Access information about an employee or applicant that is in the public domain or is otherwise obtained in compliance with the Workplace Privacy Act;
(6) Conduct an investigation or require an employee to cooperate in an investigation under any of the following circumstances:

   (a) If the employer has specific information about potentially wrongful activity taking place on the employee's personal Internet account, for the purpose of ensuring compliance with applicable laws, regulatory requirements, or prohibitions against work-related employee misconduct; or
   (b) If the employer has specific information about an unauthorized download or transfer of the employer's

private proprietary information, private financial data, or other confidential information to an employee's personal Internet account;

(7) Take adverse action against an employee for downloading or transferring an employer's private proprietary information or private financial data to a personal Internet account without the employer's authorization;

(8) Comply with requirements to screen employees or applicants before hiring or to monitor or retain employee communications that are established by state or federal law or by a self-regulatory organization as defined in 15 U.S.C. 78c(a)(26), as such section existed on January 1, 2016; or

(9) Comply with a law enforcement investigation conducted by a law enforcement agency.

. . .

Sec. 10. If an employer inadvertently learns the user name, password, or other means of access to an employee's or applicant's personal Internet account through the use of otherwise lawful technology that monitors the employer's computer network or employer-provided electronic communication devices for service quality or security purposes, the employer is not liable for obtaining the information, but the employer shall not use the information to access the employee's or applicant's personal Internet account or share the information with anyone. The employer shall delete such information as soon as practicable.

Source: Nebraska Legislature, LB821, April 20, 2016. Available online at http://www.nebraskalegislature.gov/bills/view_bill.php?DocumentID=28448.

Facebook Suppressing Conservative Views (2016)

In an interview with Gizmodo, a former Facebook contractor described how his team was required by supervisors to suppress certain stories from the trending news module. The suppressed stories tended to have a conservative bent, such as stories about Republican Wisconsin governor Scott Walker or stories from the conservative website Drudge Report. The claims led the Senate to launch an inquiry into the matter. Rep. Lamar Smith (R-Tex.) read a statement about his concerns to the House of Representatives.

Mr. SMITH of Texas. Madam Speaker, recently, it was revealed that the tech giant Facebook may have altered its popular trending news section to suppress conservative views. Facebook's CEO promised to make changes.

Now it has been reported that Facebook removed a viral video that showed how media company NowThis was editing footage of Donald Trump to make him seem insensitive and racist. And last week, a gun range owner in Houston, Texas, said his Facebook page had been blocked after he advertised free concealed handgun classes.

If these allegations are true, Facebook will not be a credible source of information for the American people. Let's hope that Facebook will demonstrate it has no bias against conservatives.

Source: *Congressional Record*, Vol. 162, No. 113, July 13, 2016, H4826.

References

Bulik, Beth Snyder. 2014. "Ellen DeGeneres' Samsung Selfie Ups Social-Marketing Game." *Advertising Age*. March 5. http://adage.com/article/media/ellen-degeneres-samsung-selfie-ups-social-marketing-game/291989/.

Facebook. n.d. *Facebook*. Accessed August 9, 2016. http://newsroom.fb.com/company-info/.

Felt, Laurel B., and Michael B. Robb. 2016. "Technology Addiction: Concern, Controversy, and Finding Balance." *Common Sense*. https://www.commonsensemedia.org/sites/default/files/uploads/research/csm_2016_technology_addiction_research_brief_0.pdf.

Ford. 2013. "Looking Forward with Ford: 2014 Trends." https://media.ford.com/content/dam/fordmedia/North%20 America/US/2013/12/12/Ford_2014_TrendReport.pdf.

Frier, Sarah, and Emily Chang. 2016. "Snapchat's Daily Mobile Video Views Said to Rival Facebook's." *Bloomberg Technology.* January 11. http://www.bloomberg.com/news/articles/2016-01-11/snapchat-s-daily-mobile-video-views-said-to-rival-facebook-s.

GO-Globe. 2014. "Social Media Addiction: Statistics and Trends." *GO-Globe.* December 26. http://www.go-globe.com/blog/social-media-addiction/.

Google. 2014. "Asia's Mobile-First World." *Google Asia Pacific Blog.* October 28. http://googleasiapacific.blogspot.com/2014/10/asias-mobile-first-world.html.

IDC. 2013. "Always Connected: How Smartphone and Social Keep Us Engaged." http://www.nu.nl/files/IDC-Facebook%20Always%20Connected%20(1).pdf.

Instagram. n.d. "Press News." https://www.instagram.com/press.

Lindner, Matt. 2016. "Online Sales Will Reach $523 Billion by 2020 in the U.S." *Internet Retailer.* January 29. https://www.internetretailer.com/2016/01/29/online-sales-will-reach-523-billion-2020-us.

Luckerson, Victor. 2016. "These Are the 10 Most Popular Tweets of All Time." *Time.* March 20. http://time.com/4263227/most-popular-tweets/.

Rideout, Victoria. 2012. "Social Media, Social Life: How Teens View Their Digital Lives." *Common Sense Media.* https://www.commonsensemedia.org/file/socialmedia sociallife-final-061812pdf-0/download.

Rideout, Victoria. 2015. "The Common Sense Census: Media Use by Tweens and Teens." *Common Sense.* https://www.commonsensemedia.org/sites/default/files/uploads/research/census_executivesummary.pdf.

Saleh, Khalid. n.d. "U.S. Social Commerce: Statistics and Trends (Infographic)." *Invespcro.* http://www.invespcro.com/blog/us-social-commerce/.

Smith, Cooper. 2015. "It's Time for Retailers to Start Paying Close Attention to Social Media." *Business Insider.* June 30. http://www.businessinsider.com/social-commerce-2015-report-2015-6.

Statista. 2014. "Worldwide Social Commerce Revenue from 2011 to 2015 (in Billions of US Dollars)." *Statista.* https://www.statista.com/statistics/251391/worldwide-social-commerce-revenue-forecast/.

Twitter. n.d. "Twitter Usage." Accessed September 30, 2016. https://about.twitter.com/company.

YouTube. n.d. "Statistics." Accessed September 30, 2016. https://www.youtube.com/yt/press/statistics.html.

Introduction

This chapter focuses on print and nonprint resources for marketers, business owners, students, teachers, social media users, and anyone interested in learning more about social media. The print section includes books that cover practical uses of social media platforms, explore societal implications of social media, and profile founders of social media platforms and the industry. The nonprint section features e-books, blogs written by digital marketing and social media experts, blogs by companies that offer digital marketing and social media services, online news sites and magazines, videos, and podcasts. Finally, also listed in this chapter are legal, government, and social service resources on issues related to social media, sources of statistics on social media platforms published and updated by the companies themselves, and major research and nonprofit organizations that conduct original research and publish reports on the topic of social media and digital technology.

Logos for Twitter, Instagram, and Facebook are displayed on a window in New York City. Facebook continues to dominate all other social media platforms in terms of usage, but Twitter, Pinterest, and Instagram receive significant traffic from certain demographic groups and for specific purposes. (AP Photo/Mark Lennihan)

Books

Aaker, Jennifer, and Andy Smith. 2010. *The Dragonfly Effect: Quick, Effective, and Powerful Ways to Use Social Media to Drive Social Change.* New York: John Wiley & Sons.

Aaker and Smith describe how to grasp the power of social media to drive change, which is something that anyone can do despite a lack of money or power. This book is modeled on the concept of a dragonfly, a creature that must use all four wings together to fly, and the authors discuss each "wing" of the dragonfly with original case studies of Fortune 500 companies, social media platforms, and start-ups. This book draws heavily on concepts from consumer psychology.

Anderson, Chris. 2008. *The Long Tail: Why the Future of Business Is Selling Less of More.* New York: Hachette Books.

Anderson's book explains how the rise of the digital economy changed the nature of the traditional demand curve. Instead of selling a large volume of highly desired products (aka "hits"), an endlessly long tail of demand exists where smaller quantities of many more niche products can be sold. For example, while a brick-and-mortar bookstore can only stock best-selling books, an online store that is not restricted by space can offer a wider catalog and sell niche products to smaller groups of readers, resulting in increased overall sales.

Angwin, Julia. 2009. *Stealing MySpace: The Battle to Control the Most Popular Website in America.* New York: Random House.

Angwin tells the story of the founding of MySpace by Chris DeWolfe and Tom Anderson and the purchase of the site by News Corp's Rupert Murdoch, who negotiated with the founders to seize MySpace and prevent purchase by Viacom CEO's Sumner Redstone. The book chronicles how the founders fought to regain control of the company after it was taken under News Corp's umbrella.

Barger, Christopher. 2012. *The Social Media Strategist: Build a Successful Program from the Inside Out*. New York: McGraw-Hill Education.

Companies need social media strategists on board to establish and manage their social media programs, and this book explains how to get an organization moving in the right direction. Barger writes from the experience of being social media director at General Motors and blogger-in-chief at IBM.

Baym, Nancy K. 2015. *Personal Connections in the Digital Age* (2nd ed.). Cambridge, MA: Polity.

In this book, Baym focuses on how digital media impacts personal relationships. Topics covered include the role of mediated language and nonverbal behavior in communities and how to maintain existing relationships.

Berger, Jonah. 2013. *Contagious: Why Things Catch On*. New York: Simon & Schuster.

Berger, a Wharton marketing professor, explains in this book how things become popular. He presents six basic principles that drive content, products, stories, policies, and rumors, among other things, to become viral. The book is designed to help people effectively spread their own messages.

Billings, Andrew C., and Marie Hardin. 2016. *Routledge Handbook of Sport and New Media*. London: Routledge.

This edited book covers the integration of social media into the world of sports. Fans use social media to form communities for communication, and information on athletes and teams is widely available on Twitter, fan sites, and blogs. The central thesis is that social and digital media have impacted the way sport is produced, consumed, and interpreted.

Bilton, Nick. 2013. *Hatching Twitter: A True Story of Money, Power, Friendship, and Betrayal*. London: Portfolio.

New York Times columnist and reporter Bilton chronicles the dynamics between and contributions of the founders of Twitter, a story that involves betrayals, power struggles, rises to fame, and great increases in personal wealth.

boyd, danah. 2014. *It's Complicated: The Social Life of Networked Teens.* New Haven, CT: Yale University Press. Available free online at: danah.org/books/ItsComplicated.pdf.

Through extensive fieldwork, boyd explores teen Internet culture through topics such as identity, privacy, safety, danger, and bullying. She contends that although the process is complicated, teens can develop a sense of identity through online interactions.

Brogan, Chris, and Julien Smith. 2010. *Trust Agents: Using the Web to Build Influence, Improve Reputation, and Earn Trust.* Hoboken, NJ: Wiley.

Brogan and Smith's book describes the importance of online influencers who can build trust and relationships with others using social media. The book covers how businesses are using social media tools to create influence networks.

Burns, Kelli S. 2009. *Celeb 2.0: How Social Media Foster Our Fascination with Popular Culture.* Santa Barbara, CA: Praeger.

Burns explores the intersection between social media and popular culture, including how entertainment bloggers changed the nature of celebrity reporting, the use of online communities for discussions of popular television programs, and how movies are promoted using social media.

Christakis, Nicholas A., and James H. Fowler. 2011. *Connected: The Surprising Power of Our Social Networks and How They Shape Our Lives—How Your Friends' Friends' Friends Affect Everything You Feel, Think, and Do.* New York: Back Bay Books.

Christakis and Fowler take a scientific approach to explain how social networks form and influence users in a variety of areas including health, wealth, happiness, beliefs, and tastes.

Cross, Mary. 2011. *Bloggerati, Twitterati: How Blogs and Twitter Are Transforming Popular Culture.* Santa Barbara, CA: Praeger.

Cross explores how social media are changing not only popular culture, but also journalism, language, and perceptions of self.

Falls, Jason, and Erik Deckers. 2011. *No Bullshit Social Media: The All-Business, No-Hype Guide to Social Media Marketing.* New York: Que Publishing.

Instead of competing books that focus on starting conversations and building communities online, Falls and Deckers emphasize using social media to drive sales, research and design products that consumers desire, improve service, and find solid leads. If social media are done right, the authors contend, the results are measurable and can be linked to profits.

Fenton, Nicole, and Kate Kiefer Lee. 2014. *Nicely Said: Writing for the Web with Style and Purpose.* San Francisco: New Riders.

This book explains how to write marketing copy for digital platforms, including finding a voice and appropriate tone and how to build relationships with readers. Real-life examples are included from professionals who write for a living.

Fuchs, Christian. 2013. *Social Media: A Critical Introduction.* Los Angeles: Sage Publications Ltd.

Fuchs explores an understanding of social media with a critical lens to the controversies and benefits. He presents case studies from the leading social media and digital companies and exposes the structures and power dynamics.

Gainous, Jason, and Kevin M. Wagner. 2013. *Tweeting to Power: The Social Media Revolution in American Politics.* Oxford, UK: Oxford University Press.

From a framework of political, communication, and psychological theories, the authors explore how social media influence how voters learn about candidates and engage in elections. Traditional gatekeepers have been replaced by information flowing through social media sites. The authors demonstrate through research how online communities are forums for conversation about politics and how Twitter shapes the information voters use to make decisions.

Garcia Martinez, Antonio. 2016. *Chaos Monkeys: Obscene Fortune and Random Failure in Silicon Valley.* New York: Harper.

Written by a former Twitter adviser, Facebook product manager, and start-up founder, this book compares tech entrepreneurs to chaos monkeys, a test run by engineers to check a system's resiliency and recoverability. These entrepreneurs disrupt and change many aspects of people's lives including transportation, dating, hospitality, and television. Garcia Martinez himself was one of Silicon Valley's most notorious chaos monkeys, thus he writes from experience. He describes not only industry antics, but also trade secrets and power maneuvers.

Gardner, Howard, and Katie Davis. 2014. *The App Generation: How Today's Youth Navigate Identity, Intimacy, and Imagination in a Digital World.* New Haven, CT: Yale University Press.

The authors explore the "app generation" and distinguish between youth who are "app-dependent" and those who are "app-enabled." They explore how identity is formed, intimacy is managed, and imagination is fostered. Some users may lose a sense of identity, fail to develop meaningful relationships, and have their creativity stunted. Others may use digital media to create a strong identity, enhance relationships, and explore creativity.

Godin, Seth. 2008. *Tribes: We Need You to Lead Us*. London: Portfolio.

Tribes are easily formed on social media and need individuals who can provide leadership. In this book, Godin focuses on some inspirational leaders such as wine expert Gary Vaynerchuk who leads a group of wine enthusiasts, Chris Sharma who organizes rock climbers, and Microsoft's Mich Mathews who runs a tribe of marketers.

Golbeck, Jennifer. 2013. *Analyzing the Social Web*. Burlington, MA: Morgan Kaufmann.

Golbeck shows how public data from social media sites can be used to identify similar or influential people in the network, demonstrate the spread of information or ideas through a network, and illustrate the relationships between users of a platform. The book covers network visualization and offers a supporting website with teaching resources.

Golbeck, Jennifer 2015. *Introduction to Social Media Investigation: A Hands-on Approach*. Waltham, MA: Syngress.

In this book, Golbeck provides hands-on instruction and tutorials to use social media sites to gather public data. Crowdsourcing, data mining, and network analysis are also discussed.

Hanson, Jarice. 2016. *The Social Media Revolution: An Economic Encyclopedia of Friending, Following, Texting, and Connecting*. Westport, CT: Greenwood.

Social media have changed all aspects of contemporary society including personal expression, communication, entertainment, and consumer behavior. Furthermore, social media also have an economic impact, serve to equalize power, and create opportunities for social mobility.

Highfield, Tim. 2016. *Social Media and Everyday Politics.* Cambridge, UK: Polity.

Political conversation happens every day on social media platforms. This book considers the range of expressions about politics on social media from selfies, memes, hashtags, and parodies. International examples are discussed including the Arab Spring, Occupy movement, #JeSuisCharlie, and #BlackLivesMatter.

Huba, Jackie. 2013. *Monster Loyalty: How Lady Gaga Turns Followers into Fanatics.* London: Portfolio.

Customer loyalty expert Huba explains how Lady Gaga's command of social media contributed to her musical success. Lady Gaga effectively used social media tools to build a loyal following and community of "Little Monsters." Huba explores seven lessons in loyalty exemplified by Lady Gaga, but also relates the lessons to other businesses.

Humphreys, Ashlee. 2015. *Social Media: Enduring Principles.* Oxford, UK: Oxford University Press.

Each chapter of this book presents a social science theory or concept and relates it to social media. In this foundational and introductory book, Humphreys covers cultural topics like online identity and community and analytical topics like measurement, network analysis, and economics.

Israel, Shel. 2009. *Twitterville: How Businesses Can Thrive in New Global Neighborhoods.* London: Portfolio.

Early social media adopter Israel chronicles the rise of Twitter as well as the diversity of "Twitterville residents." The book focuses on case studies that demonstrate how business and individuals have used Twitter for a range of purposes.

Ito, Mizuko, Heather A. Horst, Judd Antin, Megan Finn, Arthur Law, Annie Manion, Sarai Mitnick, David Schlossberg, and Sarita Yardi. 2013. *Hanging Out, Messing Around, and Geeking Out: Kids Living and Learning with New Media.* Cambridge, MA: MIT Press.

This book explores how youth use digital media for social and recreational purposes. The findings are based on a three-year ethnographic study, and the book features 23 case studies of young people.

Jenkins, Henry, Sam Ford, and Joshua Green. 2013. *Spreadable Media: Creating Value and Meaning in a Networked Culture.* New York: NYU Press.

In this book, media scholar Jenkins along with Ford and Green describe changes in the media environment that have allowed for the creation and distribution of user-generated content. Compelling content is "spreadable," which refers to how it travels through social media. Examples in the book are from the industries of film, music, television, games, comics, advertising, public relations, and transmedia storytelling.

Kawasaki, Guy, and Peg Fitzpatrick. 2014. *The Art of Social Media.* London: Penguin Group.

Kawasaki, the former chief evangelist at Apple, and social media strategist Fitzpatrick offer practical tips and insights to build a compelling presence on a range of social media platforms. The book covers how to optimize a profile, attract followers, and integrate social media and blogging.

Keller, Edward, and Jonathan Berry. 2003. *The Influentials: One American in Ten Tells the Other Nine How to Vote, Where to Eat, and What to Buy.* New York: Free Press.

Although published before the explosion of social media, this book demonstrates the importance of word-of-mouth marketing and the role of influentials, who are generally early adopters with a great deal of power. This book has applications for social media marketing, which relies on networks of influence for ideas and marketing messages to spread.

Kerpen, Dave. 2015. *Likeable Social Media: How to Delight Your Customers, Create an Irresistible Brand, and Be Amazing on Facebook, Twitter, LinkedIn, Instagram, Pinterest, and More.* New York: McGraw-Hill Education.

Kerpen's book explores how social media can help a recommendation travel throughout a network of users. The book offers advice for organizations wanting to use word-of-mouth marketing and online customer engagement to achieve business goals.

Kirkpatrick, David. 2011. *The Facebook Effect: The Inside Story of the Company That Is Connecting the World.* New York: Simon & Schuster.

Through interviews with key Facebook executives, technology reporter Kirkpatrick tells the story of the founding and growth of Facebook. He discusses the successes and mistakes along the way and provides a complete picture of CEO and cofounder Mark Zuckerberg and his relationship with his fellow cofounders and other key people. The book discounts the contribution of the Winklevoss twins, which has been emphasized in other accounts.

Li, Charlene, and Josh Bernoff. 2011. *Groundswell: Winning in a World Transformed by Social Technologies.* Cambridge, MA: Harvard Business Review Press.

Researchers Li and Bernoff provide insights for corporate executives who want to integrate social media into marketing efforts. Addressed in the book are topics such as feedback in public forums, segmenting consumers on the basis of how they will participate in social media, and a four-step process for developing a social media strategy.

Losse, Katherine. 2012. *The Boy Kings: A Journey into the Heart of the Social Network*. New York: Simon & Schuster.

Losse, Facebook's 51st employee, experienced the excitement and promise of the early days of Facebook and then, later, the intensity and commitment that was expected of employees. Employees were encouraged to live within one mile of the office and spend summers at the company pool house. Female employees were expected to wear T-shirts with Zuckerberg's profile photo on his birthday. Losse was eventually promoted to Zuckerberg's ghostwriter and worked closely with this "boy king."

Marwick, Alice E. 2013. *Status Update: Celebrity, Publicity, and Branding in the Social Media Age*. New Haven, CT: Yale University Press.

Scholar Marwick describes how techniques that users employ to build their statuses online, including self-branding and life-streaming, have reinforced traditional distinctions between people in terms of race, class, and gender.

Mezrich, Ben. 2009. *The Accidental Billionaires: The Founding of Facebook, a Tale of Sex, Money, Genius, and Betrayal*. New York: Doubleday.

In telling the story about the launch and rise of Facebook, Mezrich focuses on the relationship between Mark Zuckerberg and cofounder Eduardo Saverin as well as the legal conflict with the Winklevoss twins, fellow Harvard students who sued the company for purportedly stealing the idea of the social media site from them. Mezrich's book is based on interviews with Saverin and public court documents.

Miller, Daniel, Elisabetta Costa, Nell Haynes, Tom McDonald, Razvan Nicolescu, Jolynna Sinanan, Juliano Spyer, Shriram Venkatraman, and Xinyuan Wang. 2016. *How the World Changed Social Media*. London: UCL Press. Available free online at: discovery.ucl.ac.uk/1474805/1/How-the-World-Changed-Social-Media.pdf

Authored by a group of anthropologists who each spent 15 months living in and studying social media in various communities around the world, this book summarizes their findings and explores how social media has both transformed its users and been transformed by users.

Milner, Murray. 2015. *Freaks, Geeks, and Cool Kids: Teenagers in an Era of Consumerism, Standardized Tests, and Social Media* (2nd ed.). London: Routledge.

Sociologist Milner expanded on work done 15 years previously for the first edition of the book. He found a phenomenon among teens where they moved toward the capital of information and status provided by social media. Teens also have new pressures caused by social media and standardized tests.

Musa, Bala A., and Jim Willis. 2014. *From Twitter to Tahrir Square: Ethics in Social and New Media Communication.* Santa Barbara, CA: Praeger.

This two-volume book edited by Musa and Willis addresses how social media have an influence in personal, public, and professional settings with special attention given to the cultural trends and changes that social media are impacting.

Noor Al-Deen, Hana S., and John Allen Hendricks. 2013. *Social Media and Strategic Communications.* London: Palgrave Macmillan.

This edited volume provides scholarly research on how social media impact the practice of advertising and public relations. Topics include how marketers can build relationships on Twitter, Facebook uses at Fortune 500 companies, and legal issues related to social media usage by marketers.

Pariser, Eli. 2012. *The Filter Bubble: How the New Personalized Web Is Changing What We Read and How We Think.* London: Penguin Books.

As users search for information online, make purchases, and communicate likes, they are creating data that form a picture of their interests. A "filter bubble" results when sites only present users with information that they are likely to find valuable or relevant, blocking other information that might challenge users, spur creativity, or create a more democratic exchange of ideas.

Proulx, Mike, and Stacey Shepatin. 2012. *Social TV: How Marketers Can Reach and Engage Audiences by Connecting Television to the Web, Social Media, and Mobile.* Hoboken, NJ: Wiley.

Television and social media can work together to create a more engaging and powerful experience for the viewer. This book is helpful for brands that want to know how to implement an engaging second-screen experience, use social ratings analytics tools to locate audiences, and conduct marketing campaigns via connected televisions.

Qualman, Erik. 2012. *Socialnomics: How Social Media Transforms the Way We Live and Do Business* (2nd ed.). Hoboken, NJ: Wiley.

Qualman's book discusses the role of social media in the daily lives of users and how businesses can use social media to achieve their corporate goals, including increasing sales, cutting costs, and reaching consumers directly. Qualman's insights emerge from interviews with representatives from hundreds of organizations including Fortune 500 companies, universities, small businesses, and nonprofits.

Quesenberry, Keith A. 2015. *Social Media Strategy: Marketing and Advertising in the Consumer Revolution.* Lanham, MD: Rowman & Littlefield.

Marketing professor Quesenberry provides a practical guide to implementing social media for business purposes in this textbook. The book leads readers through the steps of developing a social media plan and how to integrate social media throughout an organization.

Rainie, Lee, and Barry Wellman. 2012. *Networked: The New Operating System*. Cambridge, MA: MIT Press.

Social and digital media have connected users, but at the same time, some users have become lonely and disconnected. Rainie and Wellman focus on the positive outcomes from social media use, including opportunities to learn, solve problems, make decisions, and build relationships. The resulting "networked individualism" calls for new skills to manage networks and utilize connections.

Rheingold, Howard. 2012. *Net Smart: How to Thrive Online*. Cambridge, MA: MIT Press.

Cyberculture expert Rheingold encourages mindful use of digital media so that users are empowered actors rather than passive receivers. He describes the skills that will help users achieve meaningful digital use, including attention, participation, collaboration, critical consumption of information, and network smarts.

Richardson, Glenn W., Jr. 2016. *Social Media and Politics: A New Way to Participate in the Political Process*. Santa Barbara, CA: Praeger.

In this two-volume set edited by Richardson, the ways that social media impact the political process are explored. The books cover hot-button cultural and political issues, shifts in power, and how social media affect political discourse.

Sales, Nancy Jo. 2016. *American Girls: Social Media and the Secret Lives of Teenagers*. New York: Knopf.

Journalist Sales explores the disturbing impact of social media in the development of teenage girls. The research behind this book involves interviews with more than 200 teenage girls throughout the country who explain the new social and sexual norms. Themes include beauty influencers, slut-shaming, and digital exhibitionism.

Sandberg, Sheryl. 2013. *Lean In: Women, Work, and the Will to Lead.* New York: Knopf.

Facebook's chief operating officer Sandberg offers guidance to women who want to achieve greater career success. Advice provided to readers includes how to negotiate, the importance of having a mentor, setting boundaries, and forgoing the idea of "having it all." Sandberg draws upon her personal experiences as a wife, mother, and powerful business leader.

Schaefer, Mark W. 2014. *Social Media Explained: Untangling the World's Most Misunderstood Business Trend.* Mark W. Schaefer.

This book presents simple strategies for social media use and answers questions that business professionals and marketers often ask before launching a social media program. Schaefer not only offers practical advice, but also covers sociological and psychological processes that influence the effectiveness of social media marketing.

Schaefer, Mark W. 2014. *The Tao of Twitter: Changing Your Life and Business 140 Characters at a Time.* New York: McGraw-Hill Education.

Schaefer's book explains Twitter and how to use it for personal and professional reasons. Topics include how to acquire relevant connections, create meaningful content, and gain trust among other users.

Scoble, Robert, and Shel Israel. 2006. *Naked Conversations: How Blogs Are Changing the Way Businesses Talk with Customers.* Hoboken, NJ: John Wiley & Sons.

In this early book on social media, technology experts Scoble and Israel describe how businesses can use blogs to improve communication between companies and customers. The book features more than 50 case studies to illustrate best practices in business blogging.

Scott, David Meerman. 2015. *The New Rules of Marketing and PR* (4th ed.) Hoboken, NJ: Wiley.

Scott's book offers practical action plans for marketers, public relations professionals, and business owners to engage buyers, raise awareness, and increase sales through social media. Featured in the book are case studies from a range of industries and tactics for implementing the latest social media platforms.

Shirky, Clay. 2009. *Here Comes Everybody: The Power of Organizing without Organizations.* London: Penguin Group.

NYU professor Shirky studies social media through a sociological lens to explore the effect digital platforms have on group organization. Previously, group action could only be organized by institutions, but social media tools allow groups to form and coordinate themselves in new ways. Social media also create a phenomenon of mass amateurization as users are able to create and publish content, threatening the traditional news industry.

Solis, Brian. 2011. *Engage! The Complete Guide for Brands and Businesses to Build, Cultivate, and Measure Success in the New Web.* Hoboken, NJ: Wiley.

This book illustrates how to use social media for business applications. The steps of conceptualizing, implementing, managing, and measuring a social media program are covered. Various dimensions, such as psychology, behavior, and influence, of the new social consumer are also explored.

Stafford, Rachel Macy. 2014. *Hands Free Mama: A Guide to Putting Down the Phone, Burning the To-Do List, and Letting Go of Perfection to Grasp What Really Matters!* Grand Rapids, MI: Zondervan.

Stafford, who writes a blog called Hands Free Mama, discusses the addiction some mothers have to technology and how this addiction deprives them of the most important moments of life. This book provides simple strategies to help readers deal with the distractions of technology to enjoy meaningful relationships with loved ones.

Steiner-Adair, Catherine, and Teresa H. Barker. 2014. *The Big Disconnect: Protecting Childhood and Family Relationships in the Digital Age*. New York: Harper Paperbacks.

Through digital technology, children and teens now have access to the world, including adult content and excessive marketing. This book advocates for parents to protect their children from potentially damaging digital technology and also build solid relationships with them, a skill not learned by children who spend a lot of time communicating digitally. At the same time, parents also need to realize their own addictions to technology and create boundaries for its use so that they are not depriving their children of much-needed attention, which will have an emotional cost for the children.

Stone, Biz. 2014. *Things a Little Bird Told Me: Creative Secrets from the Co-Founder of Twitter.* New York: Grand Central Publishing.

Twitter cofounder Stone shares learnings from his early life and career at Google and Twitter. His book is focused on ingenuity and creativity, but he also discusses the role of failure, vulnerability, corporate culture, and ambition.

Tapscott, Don. 2008. *Grown Up Digital: How the Net Generation Is Changing Your World.* New York: McGraw-Hill Education.

This book focuses on the generation of young people (aka "Net Geners") who have grown up around digital technologies. Topics covered include how technology changes the way information is processed, how to engage young employees in the workplace, how educators can teach in ways that meet the needs of today's youth, recommendations for parenting "screenagers," and how young people are using digital technology for activism.

Turkle, Sherry. 2011. *Alone Together: Why We Expect More from Technology and Less from Each Other.* New York: Basic Books.

Based on hundreds of interviews, professor and scholar Turkle explains how communication on social media sites has become a replacement for authentic communication, making users more isolated instead of building closer relationships. The ease at which people can use digital communication and feel like they are experiencing authentic friendships has pushed them closer to technology and further disconnected users from other people in their lives.

Tuten, Tracy L., and Michael R. Solomon. 2014. *Social Media Marketing* (2nd ed.). Los Angeles: Sage Publications Ltd.

Written by two marketing professors, *Social Media Marketing* is the first textbook on social media marketing. The book is organized around four zones of social media—community, publishing, entertainment, and commerce—and explains through practical applications and case studies how to use each zone to achieve strategic goals.

van Dijck, José. 2013. *The Culture of Connectivity: A Critical History of Social Media.* Oxford, UK: Oxford University Press.

This book explores the rise of social media from both a historical and critical analysis framework. Also covered is how the culture of connectivity became an integral part of everyday life. As van Dijck presents various social media platforms throughout this book, she also explains how each functions in the ecosystem of connective media.

Vaynerchuk, Gary. 2013. *Jab, Jab, Jab, Right Hook: How to Tell Your Story in a Noisy Social World.* New York: HarperBusiness.

Vaynerchuk shares advice for beating the competition by connecting with customers. "Jabbing" refers to engaging with customers to build relationships, and then, after trust and interest have been established, the marketer can throw the "right hook" and earn the sale or achieve another result.

Walter, Ekaterina. 2013. *Think Like Zuck: The Five Business Secrets of Facebook's Improbably Brilliant CEO Mark Zuckerberg.* New York: McGraw-Hill Education.

Using Facebook's Mark Zuckerberg as a case study, Walter highlights the five Ps to the company's success: passion, purpose, people, product, and partnerships. In addition to Facebook, successful companies such as Zappos, TOMS, Threadless, Dyson, and others are highlighted.

E-Books

The following free e-books are helpful resources for getting started on social media.

Bolsinger, Kristy, and Moz Staff. n.d. *The Beginner's Guide to Social Media.* moz.com/beginners-guide-to-social-media.

This comprehensive social media resource presents valuable lessons throughout 12 chapters that are supplemented with engaging graphics.

Event Manager Blog. n.d. *Social Media for Events.* books.eventmanagerblog.com/social-media-for-events.

This e-book offers 130 pages of research, tools, advice, and resources for using social media before, during, and after an event.

HubSpot. n.d. *An Introduction to LinkedIn for Business.* offers.hubspot.com/introduction-to-linkedin-for-business.

HubSpot. n.d. *An Introduction to Google+ for Business.* offers.hubspot.com/how-to-use-google-plus-for-business.

HubSpot. n.d. *How to Attract Customers with Twitter and Vine.* offers.hubspot.com/how-to-attract-customers-with-twitter-and-vine.

HubSpot. n.d. *An Introduction to Pinterest for Business.* offers.hubspot.com/how-to-use-pinterest-for-business.

HubSpot. n.d. *A Guide to Facebook Business Page Timelines.* offers.hubspot.com/guide-to-facebook-business-page-timelines.

These free e-books by HubSpot offer step-by-step guidelines for using various social media platforms for business.

Scott, David Meerman. 2008. *The New Rules of Viral Marketing: How Word-of-Mouse Spreads Your Ideas for Free.* davidmeermanscott.com/hubfs/documents/Viral_Marketing.pdf.

Scott contrasts the traditional way of garnering publicity with new ways using social media. This free e-book is filled with examples and case studies to illustrate major points. Other e-books, including his full-length book *World Wide Rave*, are also available for free on his site: davidmeermanscott.com/free-stuff/free-ebooks/.

Solis, Brian. n.d. *Customer Service: The Art of Engagement and Listening through Social Media.* pamorama.net/corepam/wp-content/uploads/2010/02/2233036-Customer-Service-The-Art-of-Listening-and-Engagement-Through-Social-Media.pdf.

Solis addresses in this free e-book how to effectively manage customer service programs with social media tools.

Blogs by Social Media Thought Leaders

Andrea Vahl

AndreaVahl.com/blog

Andrea Vahl, author, speaker, consultant, and former community manager for Social Media Examiner, authors a blog with a heavy dose of Facebook among discussions of other social media platforms, all written to help a small business owner or marketer effectively use social media.

Apophenia

zephoria.org/thoughts

Internet scholar danah boyd explores youth culture, social networking, big data, social software, mobile technologies, privacy, and other "random thoughts" on her Apophenia blog.

Beth's Blog

bethkanter.org

Beth Kanter focuses on social media use by the nonprofit sector and manages one of the longest running and most popular blogs on this topic. Kanter is the coauthor of *The Networked Nonprofit* with Allison Fine, *Measuring the Networked Nonprofit* with Katie Paine, and *The Happy, Healthy Nonprofit* with Aliza Sherman.

Boom! Social

kimgarst.com/blog

Boom Social founder and CEO Kim Garst publishes the Boom! Social blog on her website. Garst's blog is focused on small business owners and empowering them to compete with larger companies by improving their social media skills and knowledge.

Brian Solis

BrianSolis.com

Digital analyst Brian Solis writes about social media, social issues, new communications, and the future of work on the blog hosted on his website.

Chris Brogan

ChrisBrogan.com

Content marketing, social media, and writing expert Chris Brogan covers topics on his blog such as using social media to help business owners achieve success.

{grow}

businessesgrow.com/blog/

Educator, consultant, and author Mark Schaefer publishes a blog called {grow} that provides advice for both professional and personal applications of social media and promises to "stretch your mind, connect you to fascinating people, and provide some fun along the way."

Jeff Bullas

JeffBullas.com

Digital entrepreneur, author, and marketer Jeff Bullas writes a blog on his website, which has the slogan "win at business and life in a digital world." The blog covers entrepreneurship, social media, content marketing, and digital communications.

Katie Paine's Measurement Blog

painepublishing.com/blog

The blog of Katie Paine, the "Measurement Queen," features stories and research related to social media and other metrics. Paine has worked in the field of measurement for three decades, founded two measurement companies, and written several books on measurement including *Measure What Matters* and *Measuring Public Relationships*. Her blog was the first in the blogosphere dedicated solely to communication measurement.

Linked into Business

linkedintobusiness.com/my-blog

Viveka von Rosen was an early adopter of LinkedIn and is the author of *LinkedIn Marketing: An Hour a Day*. Her blog covers many topics related to social media, but posts about LinkedIn dominate. von Rosen also hosts a popular LinkedIn chat on Twitter called #LinkedInChat.

Mari Smith

marismith.com/mari-smith-blog/

"Queen of Facebook" Mari Smith hosts a blog on her website that focuses mostly on Facebook, although she also writes about social media marketing campaigns in general. She covers such topics as how to grow a Facebook following, running a successful Facebook campaign, effectively implementing the features of Facebook, and using Facebook to find clients.

Pam Moore

pammarketingnut.com/blog

The CEO and founder of digital and social media agency Marketing Nutz, Pam Moore, blogs about platforms like Facebook and Instagram, branding, case studies, content marketing, mobile marketing, and key industry events and conferences.

Peg Fitzpatrick

PegFitzpatrick.com/blog/

Social media speaker, trainer, and author Peg Fitzpatrick covers all social media platforms with a business orientation on her blog.

Rebekah Radice

RebekahRadice.com/blog

The blog of content marketer Rebekah Radice offers practical advice to small business owners and other marketers who would like to learn more about using social media.

Scott Monty

ScottMonty.com

Social media strategist and consultant Scott Monty explores how the changes within the tech, marketing, and communications industries can be effectively addressed by business leaders.

A Shel of My Former Self

Holtz.com/blog

Organizational communication expert Shel Holtz, who blogs on his website titled Holtz Communication + Technology, describes his content as "communication at the intersection of business and technology." Holtz is a prolific content creator and curator who shares features from his podcast with Neville Hobson called The Hobson & Holtz Report as well as "Friday Wraps," other topical blog posts, and lots of links to other resources.

Socially Sorted

SociallySorted.com.au/blog

Social media strategist and visual marketer Donna Moritz publishes a blog called Socially Sorted that offers social media advice focused on content strategy and visual social media.

WebInkNow

WebInkNow.com

WebInkNow is the blog of social media marketing strategist and author David Meerman Scott. The blog offers practical tips for using social media.

What's Next Blog

whatsnextblog.com

B. L. Ochman, who writes the What's Next Blog, is a longtime consultant for companies interested in integrating digital and social media into their marketing strategies. The blog cuts a wide swath of content about social media including blogging, video, Twitter, advertising, case studies, and social media marketing.

Corporate Social Media Blogs

Buffer Blog

blog.bufferapp.com

Buffer, a company that offers a social media management tool, publishes a blog with practical advice and case studies on not only social media, but also work culture and development.

Convince & Convert Blog

convinceandconvert.com/blog

Published by digital strategy and media firm Convince & Convert, this blog focuses on content marketing and has been ranked as the world's number one content marketing resource. The company's founder, Jay Baer, is a well-known strategist, speaker, and author who has consulted with more than 700 companies on digital marketing.

HubSpot Blog

blog.hubspot.com

Inbound marketing company HubSpot provides helpful digital and social media resources on its corporate blog. The content is organized into marketing and sales and is targeted at B2B professionals.

Ignite Social Media Blog

ignitesocialmedia.com/blog

Founded by Lisa Braziel and Jim Tobin, Ignite Social Media formed in 2007 to help brands with social media. The company maintains a blog with useful tips and news for social media marketers. One of the regular posts on the blog is "Social You Should Know," a short, weekly update on a specific feature of a social media platform.

Mobile Marketing Watch

mobilemarketingwatch.com

Mobile Marketing Watch is produced by communication software company mobileStorm and covers mobile news, advertising, commerce, and strategy.

RazorSocial Blog

razorsocial.com/blog

RazorSocial, a company that offers technical advice for online marketing, also publishes a blog that focuses on tools and tactics to save time on social media and generate more revenue from social media efforts.

The Simply Measured Blog

simplymeasured.com/blog

Simply Measured is a social media listening and analytics company that produces a blog to help social media professionals get the news they need to make better decisions and improve their results. Some of the categories of content in the blog are social media studies, social media trends, company news, and brand profiles and case studies.

Social Fresh Blog

socialfresh.com

Best known for its annual Social Fresh Conference, Social Fresh also publishes a blog to provide social media best practices to professionals.

360i Blog

blog.360i.com

The 360i Blog, produced by search and digital agency 360i, offers insights into how social and digital media are changing the practice of marketing. The blog puts news stories into context so that they are helpful and actionable for brands wanting to connect with consumers.

TopRank Marketing Blog

toprankblog.com

The digital marketing agency founded by Lee Odden and Susan Misukanis, TopRank Marketing, publishes TopRank Marketing Blog. The blog is geared toward industry professionals and includes content on topics such as blogging and other social media platforms, search engine optimization, and industry news and conferences.

Online News Sites and Magazines

Advertising Age

adage.com/channel/digital/20

Marketing, advertising, and media industry publication *Advertising Age* features social media and technology news in its digital section. *Ad Age* is also available in print.

Adweek's SocialTimes

adweek.com/socialtimes/

Advertising industry trade publication *Adweek* offers a blog network providing information on a variety of specific topics, including social media. The blog dedicated to social media, "SocialTimes," provides breaking reports on social media news and trends. *Adweek* is also available in print.

ClickZ

clickz.com

ClickZ is an online resource for articles on social media, marketing, e-mail, analytics, media, and search. The site, which offers news, information, advice, research, and references, is geared toward helping interactive marketers and others interested in digital and social media stay informed about industry developments.

Digiday

digiday.com

Digiday produces an online news site and events, such as summits and awards galas, and is followed by influencers interested in cutting-edge media and marketing news. The site provides news for brands, agencies, publishers, and platforms.

Econsultancy

econsultancy.com/blog/

This website provides digital media and marketing coverage with a focus on reporting research results. Popular tags on the blog include Facebook, Twitter, and e-mail marketing. Subscribers have access to more comprehensive research reports.

eMarketer

emarketer.com/Articles

eMarketer describes itself as "the first place to look when you need data about digital." Although paid subscriptions are required to have access to most of the company's research reports, many of the findings on topics such as social media, mobile, and video are summarized in free articles.

Entrepreneur

entrepreneur.com/topic/social-media

Entrepreneur, available as a print magazine and an online publication, provides resources that are helpful to business owners. A special section on the website provides resources focused on using social media and digital technology.

Forbes

forbes.com/social-media/

Business magazine *Forbes* is available as a print magazine and an online news site. A special section on technology and social media provides stories related to those industries.

Marketing Land

marketingland.com

Marketing Land covers the digital marketing industry. In addition to daily news stories about industry trends, social media platform news, and new feature announcements, Marketing Land also includes tips, tactics, and strategies for successful integration of digital into marketing plans. The site also offers research and white papers.

Mashable

mashable.com/social-media/

Mashable is a media company that offers a number of online channels for content, including one dedicated to social media. According to its website, the site receives 45 million unique visits, has 28 million social media followers, and gets 7.5 million shares of its content each month. The content on each topic page, including the one for social media, is divided into What's New, What's Rising, and What's Hot.

MediaPost

mediapost.com

MediaPost is a publishing and content company that offers resources to media, marketing, and advertising professionals. Besides conferences and events, MediaPost also publishes Mediapost.com, described as the "largest and most influential media, marketing and advertising site on the net." MediaPost's content is divided into publications that users can read online or have regularly delivered to their e-mail. *Social Media & Marketing Daily*, *Video Daily*, and *Mobile Marketing Daily* are three MediaPost publications that cover the social media industry.

PRWeek

prweek.com/us/technology

Public relations industry magazine *PRWeek* offers stories on digital and social media as they apply to public relations. Many of these stories can be found in the technology news section. Founded in 1998, *PRWeek* is also available as a print publication.

Ragan's PR Daily

prdaily.com/SocialMedia/SocialMedia.aspx

This public relations industry news site has a special section devoted to social media that offers news, advice, tools, and tips for using social media.

Recode

recode.net

Recode offers tech industry news and reviews with a heavy dose of social media insights. Under a special social section, readers can follow breaking news from all the leading social media sites. The site also offers the following podcasts: Recode Media with Peter Kafka, Recode Decode hosted by Kara Swisher, and Too Embarrassed to Ask.

Social Media Examiner

socialmediaexaminer.com

Founded by Michael Stelzner, Social Media Examiner helps businesses use social media to connect with customers, raise awareness of products and services, drive traffic to digital platforms, and increase sales. The site has more than 500,000 e-mail subscribers. Stelzner also hosts a podcast called Social Media Marketing and a video show called Morning Social Media Marketing TALK.

Social Media Explorer

socialmediaexplorer.com

Social Media Explorer provides content on tools and tips for using social media, social media news, features on social media people, and social media cases.

Social Media Marketing Magazine

smmmagazine.com

Social Media Marketing Magazine is an online resource for social media strategies, tactics, and best practices that offers a monthly magazine and blog. The site also provides a list of social media channels organized into the following categories: communication, collaboration, multimedia, reviews, and entertainment.

Social Media Today

socialmediatoday.com

Social Media Today is an online resource, news organization, and community for marketing, social media, and digital professionals who are interested in posts and conversation about social networks, marketing and advertising, technology and data, and social business. The site produces original content and also aggregates content from other sources.

Social Media Week

socialmediaweek.org

Social Media Week is a news platform and annual conference that focuses on how social media and technology are impacting professional and personal lives on a global scale. The site offers a section called Brain Candy that provides useful tips, hacks, insights, and demonstrations to help technology users.

SmartBrief on Social Media

smartbrief.com

Founded by Rick Stamberger, Dan O'Brien, and Tom Wheeler, SmartBrief is a digital media company that delivers industry news to almost 6 million subscribers through the e-mail newsletter. SmartBrief on Social Media is one of the many streams of content provided by the company.

TechCrunch

techcrunch.com

TechCrunch focuses on the tech industry and offers features on start-ups, reviews new Internet products, and reports breaking technology news. Social news is available through a special section in the news channel.

TED Talks, Movies, and Videos

Christakis, Nicholas. *The Hidden Influence of Social Networks.* Filmed February 2010 at TED2010.
ted.com/talks/nicholas_christakis_the_hidden_influence_of_social_networks.

Christakis explains how traits and phenomena such as smoking, ideas, germs, altruism, and emotions can spread through networks of friends and strangers who are connected through social media. He proposes that, by understanding social networks, users can make positive changes in the world.

Golbeck, Jennifer. *The Curly Fry Conundrum: Why Social Media "Likes" Say More than You Might Think.* Filmed October 2013 at TedxMidAtlantic 2013 in Washington, D.C.

ted.com/talks/jennifer_golbeck_the_curly_fry_conundrum_why_social_media_likes_say_more_than_you_might_think.

Computer scientist Golbeck reveals what social media likes and shares say about users and how users should have control over the data they create.

Ohanian, Alexis. *How to Make a Splash in Social Media.* Filmed November 2009 at TEDIndia 2009.
ted.com/talks/alexis_ohanian_how_to_make_a_splash_in_social_media?language=en.

In a quick talk, Reddit cofounder Ohanian describes how a humpback whale named Mister Splashy Pants gained Internet fame.

Pariser, Eli. *Beware Online "Filter Bubbles."* Filmed March 2011 at TED2011.
ted.com/talks/eli_pariser_beware_online_filter_bubbles.

Online organizer Pariser explains how as digital companies learn about user preferences, they deliver content that keeps users in a "filter bubble" of information that does not challenge their assumptions or broaden their perspectives. This phenomenon is detrimental to the political process as citizens are only exposed to information in line with their current views.

Qualman, Erik. *Social Media Revolution 2015 #Socialnomics.* Uploaded January 26, 2015.
youtube.com/watch?v=jottDMuLesU.

Worldwide data about social media, demographics, and social trends from Qualman's book *Socialnomics* are provided in video format. For example, the number of people using Facebook around the world is greater than the population of any given country. Also revealed in the video is that more people in the world own a mobile phone than a toothbrush.

Ronson, Jon. *When Online Shaming Spirals Out of Control.* Filmed June 2015 at TEDGlobal>London.
ted.com/talks/jon_ronson_what_happens_when_online_shaming_spirals_out_of_control.

Ronson discusses how a tweet destroyed a woman's career when people shamed her online.

Shirky, Clay. *How Social Media Can Make History.* Filmed June 2009 at TED@State.
ted.com/talks/clay_shirky_how_cellphones_twitter_facebook_can_make_history.

The news industry no longer has complete control over publishing the news, which changes the nature of political systems. In this talk, Shirky discusses how social media sites allow citizens who live in countries that suppress speech to report on critical news events.

The Social Network. Directed by David Fincher. Columbia Pictures, 2010.

This movie, based on the book *The Accidental Billionaires* by Ben Mezrich, tells the story of the founding of Facebook and the legal battles between Mark Zuckerberg and fellow Harvard students, the Winklevoss twins, who claimed Zuckerberg had stolen the idea of Facebook from them.

Trott, Mena. *Meet the Founder of the Blog Revolution.* Filmed February 2006 at TED2006.
ted.com/talks/mena_trott_tours_her_blog_world.

Mena Trott of Movable Type describes the early days of blogging.

Turkle, Sherry. *Connected, but Alone?* Filmed February 2012 at TED2012.
ted.com/talks/sherry_turkle_alone_together.

Turkle discusses how digital devices are changing the nature of relationships and communication as well as personal lives and sense of self.

Wales, Jimmy. *The Birth of Wikipedia.* Filmed July 2005 at TEDGlobal 2005 in Oxford, UK.
ted.com/talks/jimmy_wales_on_the_birth_of_wikipedia.

Wales describes how volunteers came together armed with tools for creating and collaborating to launch the online encyclopedia Wikipedia.

Williams, Evan. *The Voice of Twitter Users.* Filmed February 2009 at TED2009.
ted.com/talks/evan_williams_on_listening_to_twitter_users.

The cofounder of Twitter shares how the explosion in popularity of the platform can be attributed to some extent to unexpected uses created by the users.

Podcasts

Podcasts are downloadable audio programs that are often formatted like a talk show and released on a regular basis, typically weekly. Consumers can access podcasts through a website (such as the host's website or a site for the show), iTunes, or a podcasting app. iPhone and iPad users can listen to podcasts through the Podcasts app, which either can be downloaded from the App Store or is already downloaded on newer phones or tablets. Many other podcasting apps, such as Overcast, are also available to iOS users in the App Store. Android users can use apps such as Stitcher Radio for Podcasts, Podcast Republic, or Podcast Addict. Through a podcasting app, users can subscribe or listen to podcasts on many different topics. Users can stream podcasts for immediate listening or download podcasts to listen offline. Although there are some paid versions and subscriptions, most podcasting apps and the podcasts themselves are available for free to listeners. All the podcasts presented in the following list offer free content.

The Amy Porterfield podcast, hosted by the coauthor of *Facebook Marketing All-in-One for Dummies*, focuses on action plans for using social media. Topics include Facebook advertising, original online content creation, social media tools, and general tips for growing a business. The occasional guest offers tips on how he or she is using social media.

The #AskGaryVee show, hosted by Gary Vaynerchuk, is based on questions that are submitted by listeners on Twitter related to social media, marketing, and entrepreneurship. The podcast is delivered in both audio and video formats.

Nick Cicero and Nick Robinson host The Creators Class podcast, which features top content creators. The show discusses topics such as branded content, native ads, social influencers, and social media marketing.

Girlboss Radio hosted by Sophia Amoruso, the founder of online retailer Nasty Gal, interviews high-profile women entrepreneurs, some of whom are in the social media and tech industries. Some episodes have featured social media investors, YouTube celebrities, and founders of digital companies.

The Hobson & Holtz Report hosted by Neville Hobson and Shel Holtz provides a weekly commentary on public relations and technology. Hobson and Holtz are longtime podcasters and have recorded more than 800 episodes of the show.

Kim Komando's podcast Komando on Demand addresses how technology impacts the lives of users. Topics covered have included the Dark Web, digital nomads, social media tracking, how devices affect sleep, cyberbullies, and ransomware attacks.

The Marketing Companion Podcast, hosted by Mark Schaefer and Tom Webster, provides marketing insights. Many of the episodes cover social media, such as online influence, the impact of social media on critical thinking, and advertising on podcasts.

Manoush Zomorodi hosts WNYC's Note to Self, which focuses on the relationship between users and technology. The show has run several special projects, including "Bored & Brilliant" to help people control their social media addictions and

"Infomagical" to provide techniques to deal with information overload.

OMFG!, hosted by Deanna Chang and Emily Foster, is a pop culture podcast that features young celebrities, many of whom have risen to fame through popularity on social media platforms or are using social media extensively as a promotional strategy. The premise of the podcast is to help its hosts understand today's youth better, and in the process, they reveal various tactics about social media usage, language, and culture.

Reply All is "a show about the Internet." Hosted by PJ Vogt and Alex Goldman, the podcast covers Internet culture and implications of the Internet through stories about people and their experiences with the Internet.

Scared Sh!tless, hosted by veteran radio personality Tim Hattrick, focuses on the risks of using technology, such as smartphones, the Internet, and social media. Threats to personal security and privacy are addressed, including hacks and cyberattacks.

The #SimplySocial podcast is hosted by Lucy Hitz and Kevin Shively of the social analytics company Simply Measured. The podcast covers brand campaigns and tactics and features interviews with social media marketing professionals.

Social Media Examiner founder and CEO Michael Stelzner hosts Social Media Marketing. Each episode starts with a social media survival tip that can save time and improve effectiveness followed by a guest interview and discussion of a larger social media topic.

Hosted by social media entrepreneur Tyler J. Anderson, Social Media Social Hour addresses specific tactics and resources for social strategies. He interviews marketers and influencers about successful strategies for various social media platforms.

Social Pros Podcast, hosted by Jay Baer and Adam Brown, focuses on social media professionals from some of the most prominent companies in the United States and how they manage and measure their social media programs.

Social Toolkit, hosted by Jason Keath and Jason Yarborough, features an interview with a social media marketing professional with a focus on tools, apps, platforms, and the process of digital marketing.

Research Organizations

The following research organizations produce and publish reports on social media that are available for free. Some of the organizations offer research insights in a blog format, while allowing only paid subscribers access to the complete reports.

BrandWatch

brandwatch.com

BrandWatch, a software company that helps brands gain insights from social data, offers research reports for free downloading with e-mail sign-up on such topics as online conversations about brands, television shows, and luxury fashion. Another report reviews key Twitter campaigns throughout the platform's history. The site also offers a blog, case studies, and guides for social listening. Social Index, an insightful tool offered by the company, ranks brands in various industries on their social performance in five key areas. For example, the top three television networks in terms of their Social Index at the end of the second quarter of 2016 were Discovery, MTV, and the Food Network. The top three MLB teams during the same time period were the Chicago Cubs, Los Angeles Dodgers, and San Francisco Giants.

Cision

cision.com/us/resources

Media monitoring leader Cision produces white papers, e-books, podcasts, infographics, and tip sheets on topics related to social media. Available white papers include the *State of the Media* report, a paper on how social media has become a customer service platform, and an e-book that explores social listening.

comScore

comscore.com/Insights

comScore is a cross-platform measurement company that tracks audiences, brands, and behavior. Reports available cover such topics as global mobile marketing, smartphone app usage, millennial YouTube usage, podcast consumption, Snapchat usage across various age groups, and a comparison of social success across brands.

GlobalWebIndex

globalwebindex.net/blog

GlobalWebIndex conducts the world's largest study of digital consumers for the benefit of marketers and businesses. Although full reports are only available to paid subscribers, the blog of GlobalWebIndex is loaded with research summaries, which are freely available.

KPCB

kpcb.com/internet-trends

Kleiner, Perkins, Caulfield, and Byers is a venture capital firm that publishes an annual Internet Trends report authored by analyst Mary Meeker. The report covers social media trends within the broader scope of the Internet.

Nielsen Social

nielsensocial.com

Nielsen Social focuses on social television measurement, audience engagement, and advertising solutions. The company measures social media activity on Facebook and Twitter related to television viewing. Reports include such topics as the biggest social television moments during a year, Twitter television ratings during a football game, predictions of television show success with Twitter activity, and the elements of a television program that make it social.

Razorfish

razorfish.com

Razorfish, part of the Publicis Groupe, is an interactive agency that provides a range of digital services. The company produces a trends resource called the Outlook Report, which can be found at razorfishoutlook.razorfish.com, and the annual Global Digital Marketing Report.

Selligent

selligent.com/resources

Selligent, a company that offers a marketing engagement platform to manage relationships between customers and Fortune 500 companies, provides a resource site of downloadable white papers, case studies, reports, and e-books.

Spredfast

spredfast.com/social-media-resources

Social media management software company Spredfast offers resources for download when users provide contact information. Resources are divided into case studies, tip sheets, videos, and white papers. Available white papers include the annual Smart Social Report and the Social Media Pocket Guide.

YPulse

ypulse.com/youth-insight

YPulse studies tweens, teens, and young adults to provide valuable data to marketers that help them target this group. This site offers a millennial news feed, a library of resources to all readers who sign up for a free daily newsletter, and additional data and insights to paid subscribers.

Nonprofit Organizations

American Press Institute

americanpressinstitute.org

The American Press Institute, an educational nonprofit organization, serves the news media by helping the industry advance in an era of digital communication. The organization conducts research and provides training for journalists and others in the news industry. Reports and stories on the site provide resources to understand data-gathering from social media sites, how social media users behave like journalists, and engaging audiences on social media, among other topics.

Berkman Klein Center for Internet & Society at Harvard University

cyber.harvard.edu

Established in 1996, the Berkman Klein Center is a research initiative at Harvard that offers scholarly research, builds tools and platforms to address issues, and creates a network across diverse communities. The center focuses on exploring and understanding the Web in terms of development and dynamics as well as the need for legislation. To date, the center has hosted more than 1,000 events, workshops, and conferences; produced more than 700 videos and podcasts; written more than 10 million lines of code; and published more than 250 reports, papers, and books.

Common Sense

commonsense.org

Common Sense is an independent nonprofit organization focused on addressing issues related to technology use by children. The organization offers educational ratings and reviews of movies, games, apps, television shows, websites, books, and music; blogs for parents to better understand the challenges of raising children in the digital age; digital literacy and educational programs for schools and communities; and an advocacy program that works with legislators and business leaders. The organization publishes research reports on the topic of children's use of media and technology and how it impacts their development.

Kinder & Braver World Project: Research Series

cyber.harvard.edu/research/youthandmedia/kinderbraver world

Presented by the Born This Way Foundation and the Berkman Klein Center for Internet & Society at Harvard University with funding from the John D. and Catherine T. MacArthur Foundation, the Kinder & Braver World Project produces a series of short papers edited by danah boyd and John Palfrey on issues related to youth empowerment and action toward creating a better world. The first set of papers edited by the project addressed youth meanness and cruelty, which covers cyberbullying and other forms of digital harassment.

Pew Internet & American Life Project

Pewinternet.org

The Pew Internet & American Life Project offers reports, presentations, and data sets on the topic of Internet use, including social media use. The project is part of the Pew Research Center, which uses opinion polling, demographic research, media analysis, and other social science methods to understand issues, attitudes, and trends impacting the United States and the world. The organization is a nonpartisan nonprofit that does not take positions on policy issues or endorse products, companies, technologies, or certain people. The Pew Research Center is a subsidiary of the Pew Charitable Trusts.

Word of Mouth Marketing Association

womma.org

Word of Mouth Marketing Association (WOMMA), founded in 2004, is the official nonprofit trade association dedicated to word-of-mouth and social media marketing. The website provides free research and white papers in the resources section as well as the WOMMA blog and webinars. Topics covered include the value of word-of-mouth marketing, best practices for disclosure and transparency in social media marketing and native advertising, and social media measurement guidelines. The organization has a strong emphasis on ethical practices through education and training of members.

Legal, Government, and Social Service Resources

.com Disclosures: How to Make Effective Disclosures in Digital Advertising, Federal Trade Commission

ftc.gov/sites/default/files/attachments/press-releases/ftc-staff-revises-online-advertising-disclosure-guidelines/130312dotcomdisclosures.pdf

In 2013, the Federal Trade Commission (FTC) published this document that covers the rules and guidelines advertisers should follow to comply with FTC advertising law. The intent was to explain how to make advertising disclosures clear and conspicuous in an online environment to prevent consumers from being deceived. In addition to a lengthy discussion, examples are provided in the appendix.

Cyberbullying Research Center

cyberbullying.org

Focused specifically on cyberbullying, the Cyberbullying Research Center offers resources, laws, research, and downloadable presentations for groups. This site displays bullying laws on an interactive map of the United States and provides a table to understand the various dimensions of sexting laws in all states.

Guidelines Concerning the Use of Endorsements and Testimonials in Advertising, Federal Trade Commission, 16 CFR Part 255

ftc.gov/sites/default/files/attachments/press-releases/ftc-publishes-final-guides-governing-endorsements-testimonials/091005revisedendorsementguides.pdf

Revised in 2009, this FTC publication explains how and under what circumstances endorsements and testimonials on social media platforms should be disclosed. It covers such topics as product placements, social media contests, and online review sites.

***Internet Safety Resources*, National Criminal Justice Reference Service**

ncjrs.gov/internetsafety/general.html

A variety of publications produced by the Office of Justice Programs on topics such as online safety, Internet privacy, cyberbullying, and cyberstalking are available on the National Criminal Justice Reference Service site.

The National Children's Advocacy Center

nationalcac.org

The National Children's Advocacy Center, which formed to address issues of child abuse, offers a website with a variety of resources to protect the safety and security of online youth. The About section of the website offers resources for kids, teens, parents, and professionals. The section for teens, for example, covers such issues as cyberbullying, sexting, and Internet safety.

***The NLRB and Social Media*, National Labor Relations Board Fact Sheet**

nlrb.gov/news-outreach/fact-sheets/nlrb-and-social-media

This fact sheet explains how the National Labor Relations Board has addressed employee and employer issues related to social media use and policies. Linked from this page are three memos issued by the general counsel and details on two decisions by the board.

***Occupational Outlook Handbook*, Public Relations Specialists, Bureau of Labor Statistics**

bls.gov/ooh/media-and-communication/public-relations-specialists.htm

Public relations is one industry that seeks employees with social media skills. The outlook for a career in public relations is reviewed in this online publication.

***An Overview of State Anti-Bullying Legislation and Other Related Laws*, The Kinder & Braver World Project: Research Series, Dena T. Sacco, Katharine Silbaugh, Felipe Corredor, June Casey and Davis Doherty, February 23, 2012**

cyber.harvard.edu/sites/cyber.harvard.edu/files/State_Anti_bullying_Legislation_Overview_0.pdf

Existing state anti-bullying laws, pending state and federal laws, and other relevant laws as of January 2012 are reviewed in this document. Cyberbullying is addressed within the greater context of bullying.

***Social Media and Employment Law: Summary of Key Cases and Legal Issues*, Heather A. Morgan and Felicia A. Davis, March 2013**

americanbar.org/content/dam/aba/events/labor_law/2013/04/aba_national_symposiumontechnologyinlaboremploymentlaw/10_socialmedia.authcheckdam.pdf

This summary of legal cases covers use of social media in hiring decisions, regulating social media use by employees, employer liability for employee use of social media, unique issues for public employees, and using social media in litigation.

***Social Media Policy*, Society for Human Resource Management**

shrm.org/resourcesandtools/tools-and-samples/policies/pages/socialmediapolicy.aspx

The Society for Human Resources Management, a professional membership association for human resource professionals, provides a sample social media policy that organizations can adapt for their own use.

***Stay Safe Online*, National Cyber Security Alliance**

staysafeonline.org

This website by the National Cyber Security Alliance provides education and awareness of issues related to protecting sensitive information and keeping it secure online. The site is targeted at people who use the Internet at home, work, and school.

StopBullying.gov

StopBullying.gov

StopBullying.gov not only offers resources on the general topic of bullying, but also provides resources that define cyberbullying and describe how to prevent and report it.

Social Media Statistics

The following list provides links to user statistics that are maintained and updated on a regular basis by the respective social media platforms.

Facebook: newsroom.fb.com/company-info/
Instagram: instagram.com/press
LinkedIn: press.linkedin.com/about-linkedin
Twitter: about.twitter.com/company
Wikipedia: stats.wikipedia.org/
YouTube: youtube.com/yt/press/statistics.html

1 Hac

The following chronology first highlights key technological developments that have led to the emergence of social media. The chronology then details the launch, purchase, and sometimes closure of early social media platforms as well as the emergence of modern social media platforms. Finally, the chronology covers noteworthy changes to social media platforms, key milestones and interesting facts about the various platforms, news stories that were shared on social media, notable use of social media by prominent people, and advertising campaigns that utilized social media.

1969 The Advanced Research Projects Agency Network (ARPANET) becomes the first wide area packet switching network using technology that eventually evolved into the modern Internet.

1973 Doug Brown and David R. Wolley of the University of Illinois introduce Talkomatic, a tool for real-time online text communication.

1978 The first use of a home computer to manage a bulletin board system (BBS) is introduced by Ward Christensen and Randy Suess of the Chicago Area Computer Hobbyist

Visitors take photos in front of the Facebook sign outside of the company's headquarters in Menlo Park, California. Silicon Valley, where many social media and tech companies are based, is becoming an unusual tourist destination. (AP Photo/Marcio Jose Sanchez)

Exchange. The idea is conceived during Chicago's Great Blizzard of 1978 and allows the club to share messages through a computer network.

1979 Duke University graduate students Tom Truscott and Jim Ellis develop the Network News Transfer Protocol, which allows for the launch of Usenet newsgroups. Instead of hosting the messages on personal computers as with BBSs, Usenet newsgroups are hosted on a mainframe computer that can manage many users at the same time.

1980 CompuServe develops the CB Simulator, the first dedicated online chat service available to the general public.

1985 Stewart Brand and Larry Brilliant launch the WELL, which stands for Whole Earth 'Lectronic Link. The WELL was originally a dial-up bulletin board system.

AppleLink (which later became America Online) develops an internal chat product available through dial-up modem, and in 1988, it opens AppleLink Personal Edition to all users.

1986 Engineering student Eric Thomas develops LISTSERV software to automate the management of e-mail lists.

1988 Jarrkko "WiZ" Oikarinen launches the first tool and server for Internet Relay Chat (real-time online conversation) at the University of Oulu in Finland. The tool is mostly used for file and link sharing and keeping in touch with others.

1989 America Online (AOL) launches the Instant Messenger chat service.

1992 The first photo, a promotional shot of the band Les Horribles Cernettes, is published on the Internet by Tim Berners-Lee.

1993 Internet service providers such as AOL and CompuServe provide Usenet access to members.

1994 GeoCities launches and allows users to create their own websites and join neighborhoods of themed content areas.

1995 Ward Cunningham launches the first wiki.

Former Boeing executive Randy Conrads releases Classmates, a site that helps users find high school classmates for the purpose of reconnecting or planning reunions.

Craig Newmark launches Craigslist, which started as an e-mail list for San Francisco events.

Match.com introduces the first online dating site.

Jeff Bezos founds Amazon as "Earth's Biggest Bookstore."

eBay, originally called "AuctionWeb," is launched by Pierre Omidyar. The first item for sale is a broken laser pointer.

1996 The Nokia 9000 Communicator, the first cellphone with Internet capabilities, is released.

The 3D animated "Dancing Baby" becomes one of the first viral videos.

1997 MacroView CEO Andrew Weinreich launches Six Degrees, a site often referred to as the first true social network.

Networking site AsianAvenue.com is launched to target Asian users.

John Barger uses the term "weblog" to describe his collection of links on his website.

1999 Dave Winer creates RSS, an acronym for "Really Simple Syndication" or "Rich Site Summary," which allows data to be broken in discrete items that can be syndicated on the Web. RSS feeds make it possible to pull stories from blogs and other sources into a news aggregator, which checks the blog for updates.

Programmer Brad Fitzpatrick launches LiveJournal, a blogging platform that allows users to have a profile page, a friends list, and the ability to follow the blogs of others.

Pitas, founded by Toronto programmer Andrew Smales, releases free blogging software. Smales also launches DiaryLand to build a community among online diarists.

Evan Williams, Paul Bausch, and Meg Hourihan of Pyra Labs release Blogger, which allows users to host a blog on the user's own server.

BlackPlanet, a social networking site targeting for African Americans, is launched.

Yahoo purchases GeoCities for more than $3 billion in stock.

Napster, a peer-to-peer file-sharing platform, is launched by Sean Parker and Shawn Fanning. Music MP3s were commonly shared using the service, which was later deemed to be illegal sharing of copyrighted material.

Korean virtual world Cyworld launches and adds social networking features two years later.

2000 Dial-up Internet access company pioneer AOL announces that the company will merge with media conglomerate Time Warner. Both CEOs would eventually be driven out, and by 2003, AOL Time Warner would revert back to Time Warner.

After three years of stratospheric growth for shares of Internet companies (called the dot-com bubble), share prices fall dramatically and many Internet companies fail. The burst of the dot-com bubble is often referred to as "dot bomb."

Swedish social networking site StajlPlejs is renamed LunarStorm and builds a large following among 12- to 17-year-olds. The site offers friends lists, guestbooks, and diary pages.

2001 Jimmy Wales, Larry Sanger, and others introduce online encyclopedia Wikipedia. In the first year, over 20,000 entries are created.

Six Degrees ceases operations after being sold for $125 million the year before.

Adrian Scott launches Ryze to connect business professionals online, but the platform never achieves a mass following.

2002 Social networking site Friendster is released by Jonathan Abrams and Peter Chin to help users meet friends of friends.

2003 Reid Hoffman and former members of PayPal and SocialNet launch professional networking site LinkedIn.

eUniverse employees Tom Anderson and Chris DeWolfe launch social networking site MySpace.

Google purchases blog platform Blogger.

Linden Lab and founder Philip Rosedale release virtual reality game Second Life.

Social networking site hi5, launched by Ramu Yalamanchi, gains a following in Latin American countries as well as in Mongolia, Tunisia, and Romania.

Apple launches the iTunes Music Store and sells 1 million songs at 99 cents each during its first week.

Blog publishing platform WordPress is released.

Mark Pincus, Paul Martino, and Valerie Syme found Tribe.net, a networking site that gained a following among users in the San Francisco Bay Area.

2004 Mark Zuckerberg and fellow Harvard classmates launch social networking site Facebook, which was initially called thefacebook.com and only available to Harvard students. By the end of the year, Facebook would have 1 million registered users.

Stewart Butterfield and Caterina Fake release image-sharing social media site Flickr.

Social news site Digg is launched by Kevin Rose, Jay Adelson, Owen Byrne, and Ron Gorodetzky.

World of Warcraft, a massively multiplayer online role-playing game, is launched.

R.E.M. offers an exclusive online streaming preview of its album *Around the Sun* on MySpace.

Swedish count Erik Wachtmeister launches elite social network A Small World to cater to an exclusive international crowd. Joining the site is by invitation only or by selection after completing an application.

After losing an opportunity to purchase Friendster, Google launches Orkut, an invitation-only social network. The site never challenges Friendster or MySpace in terms of users.

2005 YouTube is founded by PayPal employees Chad Hurley, Steve Chen, and Jawed Karim. The first video uploaded to the site features Karim and is titled "Me at the Zoo."

News Corp purchases MySpace for $580 million at a time when the social networking site had 22 million members.

Apple iTunes allows for podcasts to be available for download, generating 1 million new subscriptions and increasing listenership for some podcasts to 10 times previous levels in just two days.

Yahoo purchases Flickr for a reported $22–$25 million.

Social news site Reddit is launched by University of Virginia roommates Steve Huffman and Alexis Ohanian.

Husband-and-wife team Michael and Xochi Birch introduce social networking site Bebo, which becomes popular among U.K. users.

Computers connected to the Internet through broadband connections exceed dial-up connections.

2006 Podcasting platform start-up Odeo launches Twitter under the leadership of Evan Williams and employees Biz Stone, Jack Dorsey, and Noah Glass. On March 21, Dorsey posts the first tweet: "just setting up my twttr."

Condé Nast acquires social news site Reddit for an undisclosed price.

Facebook launches the News Feed, allowing users to see a stream of updates from friends.

Facebook opens access of the platform to everyone over age 12 with a valid e-mail address.

Google becomes the exclusive ad sales provider for MySpace in a $900-million, three-year deal.

Teenager Megan Meier commits suicide after a friend's mother creates a fake MySpace profile, presumably for a teen boy, which is used to first attract and then bully Meier.

YouTube is purchased by Google for $1.65 billion in stock.

Tribe.net lays off most employees and Pincus buys the company back through his newly formed corporation. The next year, Cisco Systems buys Tribe.net.

2007 David Karp introduces Tumblr, a short-form blog service.

Facebook introduces a Spanish-language site.

Twitter receives mainstream media attention at the SXSW conference and becomes the breakout social media platform.

Facebook launches the Facebook Platform, which allows open access to the application programming interface so that third-party developers can create applications that work with Facebook.

Mark Pincus founds social gaming company Zynga and launches the first Facebook game, Texas Hold 'Em Poker.

YouTube launches the YouTube Partners Program to share advertising revenues with content creators.

Steve Jobs introduces the iPhone, describing it to a MacWorld audience by saying, "Every once in a while, a revolutionary product comes along and changes everything." The iPhone is priced at $599 for 8G and $499 for 4G.

2008 Twitter is used for the first time in a presidential election campaign.

AOL purchases Bebo for $850 million. The site is sold for less than $10 million just two years later.

Facebook surpasses MySpace in terms of unique worldwide visitors.

Groupon is launched to provide users with a deal of the day.

Apple opens its App Store.

World of Warcraft subscribers total more than 11 million people.

2009 Bystander Janis Krums is the first to tweet a photo of passengers being rescued after the emergency landing of a commercial airliner on the Hudson River, demonstrating the importance of citizen journalists.

Zynga launches its most popular game, FarmVille, followed by Café World later in the year.

Dennis Crowley and Naveen Selvadurai launch geolocation app Foursquare.

Twitter raises $98 million from investors and is valued at $1 billion.

Video viewers enjoy viral videos created by or featuring regular people, including "David after Dentist," Susan Boyle performing on the *X Factor*, "Baby Dancing to Beyonce," and "JK Wedding Entrance Dance."

2010 *The Social Network*, a movie about Facebook based on the 2009 book *The Accidental Billionaires: The Founding of*

Facebook, a Tale of Sex, Money, Genius, and Betrayal by Ben Mezrich, is released.

Photo-sharing app Instagram is released by Kevin Systrom and Mike Krieger.

Cofounders Ben Silbermann, Evan Sharp, and Paul Sciarra launch the first prototype of Pinterest after conceptualizing the idea in late 2009.

Facebook releases the original Web-centric mobile app designed to work on any operating system instead of specifically for iOS or Android. As a result, the app is buggy and slow and has to be redesigned.

Following the success of the Old Spice commercial that ran on television during the Super Bowl, the brand created and posted on YouTube more than 200 personalized video responses within a 48-hour period to questions previously submitted by fans on Twitter and Facebook. The campaign resulted in more than 100 million video views, more than 1 billion media impressions, and significant increases in Twitter followers, Facebook engagement, and website traffic.

2011 News Corp sells MySpace to Specific Media Group and Justin Timberlake for $35 million and rebrands it as Myspace with a lowercase *s*.

Image-messaging app Snapchat is launched by Stanford students Evan Spiegel, Bobby Murphy, and Reggie Brown.

LinkedIn reaches 100 million users and goes public in the biggest initial public offering to date for an online company since Google.

Participants in the "Arab Spring" antigovernment revolutions in the Middle East rely on social media to share information with other participants and the rest of the world. The hashtags #Egypt and #Jan25 spread the word about the revolution in Egypt.

New York congressman Anthony Weiner resigns from his position after a scandal involving an accidental post of a sexually suggestive photo of himself to his nearly 48,000 followers on his Twitter feed.

Facebook settles a second time with the Winklevoss twins in the dispute over who conceived the original idea for Facebook. Cameron and Tyler Winklevoss receive $20 million in cash and partial ownership of Facebook, a deal worth more than $160 million at the time. The first lawsuit, ruled on in 2008, had provided a $65-million settlement.

Google launches its own social networking platform, Google+, to compete with Facebook and Twitter. Google+ allows users to organize friends into Circles for sharing content.

2012 Raising $16 billion, Facebook has the largest Internet initial public offering in history. Since then, Facebook's IPO has only been surpassed by Alibaba Group Holdings, which raised more than $21 billion in 2014.

Facebook releases the Facebook Messenger app, moving the messaging system outside the boundaries of Facebook and into a separate app.

President Obama's reelection tweet hugging Michelle Obama and captioned with "Four more years" becomes the most popular tweet to date. The previous record was held by Justin Bieber.

Dom Hofmann, Rus Yusupov, and Colin Kroll founded Vine, a social media platform based on six-second videos. The same year, Twitter acquires Vine for a reported $30 million and apps are released for iOS and Android the following year.

Facebook purchases Instagram for a $1 billion cash and stock arrangement.

Social news site Digg is acquired by Betaworks, a technology investment and development company, for just $500,000.

Facebook reaches 1 billion monthly active users.

Online video views of Justin Bieber's "Baby" are surpassed by South Korean pop star PSY's video "Gangnam Style."

After being an ad-free platform since its founding, Tumblr changes its business model to include paid advertising in the form of "sponsor products."

Pinterest drops its invitation-only membership process and releases apps for iPad and Android. By the end of the year,

Pinterest is the sixth most popular social network with more than $27 million unique U.S. users.

The Summer Olympic Games in London generates more than 150 million tweets, including spoilers that angered television viewers in the United States.

The Sandy Hook Elementary School shooter is incorrectly identified on social media as the brother of the actual shooter.

2013 Yahoo purchases Tumblr for $1.1 billion.

Photo-sharing app Instagram adds a feature for shooting and sharing 15-second videos.

Twitter is separated from parent company Obvious Corporation and goes public with an IPO price of $26 per share.

When the power goes out expectedly during Super Bowl XLVII for 34 minutes, the Oreo social media team crafts a quick response to post on Twitter. The tweet, featuring an Oreo against a dark background with the caption "You can still dunk in the dark," is retweeted 10,000 times in the first hour.

Snapchat adds the popular Snapchat Stories feature.

2014 Facebook acquires Oculus VR, a company that manufactures virtual reality headsets.

Facebook purchases messaging app WhatsApp for $19 billion.

Social networking site Bebo is reincarnated as a mobile messaging app.

The Ice Bucket Challenge, a fund-raiser that raised more than $115 million for the ALS Association, fills Facebook and Twitter feeds with videos of participants dumping buckets of ice water over their heads.

Foursquare spins off Swarm for location check-ins and finding nearby friends and relaunches the original app as a competitor of Yelp and other review and recommendation apps.

Oscar host Ellen DeGeneres tweets a selfie with celebrities Bradley Cooper, Jennifer Lawrence, Julia Roberts, Meryl Streep, Lupita Nyong'o, Brad Pitt, Angelina Jolie, Kevin Spacey, and others with the caption "If only Bradley's arm was longer. Best photo ever. #oscars." The tweet became the most retweeted to date, displacing President Obama's reelection tweet.

2015 Competing live-streaming services Meerkat and Periscope are launched.

Facebook introduces Facebook Live, allowing users to stream live videos. After testing the feature with a select group of celebrities in late 2015, Facebook rolls out the feature to all users with an iPhone in early 2016.

Facebook and Twitter introduce "buy" buttons, allowing users to make purchases directly from the site.

The earthquake in Nepal inspires more than 770,000 people to donate more than $15.5 million to relief efforts through Facebook.

Two terrorist attacks in Paris result in the extensive use of hashtags #JeSuisCharlie and #PrayforParis on Twitter by users wanting to express support and sympathy for the victims.

Hashtag #BlackLivesMatter trends on Twitter to express dissatisfaction with police brutality and violence toward African Americans.

A photo of a striped dress posted first on Tumblr that spread quickly to Facebook, Twitter, and Instagram had people debating whether the dress was blue and black or white and gold.

Google announces that a Google+ account is no longer a requirement when signing into other Google services.

Twitter purchases live streaming app Periscope for $86 million and integrates Periscope streams into its timeline.

Minnesota dentist Walter James Palmer is identified as the man who paid $54,000 to kill the beloved Cecil the Lion in Zimbabwe. Angry Internet users posted negative reviews on the dentist's Yelp profile and created fake Facebook pages for his practice that served to criticize him for his actions.

President Obama gets a verified Twitter account (@POTUS) that will be handed off to the next president after the inauguration.

Facebook Messenger no longer requires a Facebook membership to use the service.

YouTube announces shopping ads and releases its paid subscription service called YouTube Red.

2016 Twitter acquires the rights to live stream the NFL's *Thursday Night Football.*

Instagram introduces Instagram Stories, a feature that allows users to share a collection of photos and videos from the previous 24-hour period.

Verizon purchases Yahoo for $4.8 billion and gains social media platforms Flickr and Tumblr.

Facebook's WhatsApp messaging app announces that it will start sharing data with Facebook, including usage statistics and phone numbers.

Twitter redesigns its timeline to provide tweets based on an algorithm, rather than showing the most recent at the top.

Instagram increases the maximum video length to 60 seconds from 15 and starts using an algorithm instead of most recent posts to determine the placement of content in the timeline.

Facebook adds emoji reactions to content, providing more options to users than "like." Users can now not only "like" content, but also share such reactions as "love," "haha," "wow," "sad," and "angry."

In the midst of a nasty Twitter exchange, Democratic presidential nominee Hillary Clinton tweets to Republican nominee Donald Trump to "delete your account," a tweet that has received almost 500,000 retweets.

Suffering from a struggling stock price, sluggish ad business, and slowing company growth, LinkedIn sells to Microsoft for $26 billion.

Instagram reaches half a billion users.

Within 20 hours of opening an Instagram account, music artist Kanye West amasses 1 million followers.

Snapchat rebrands as Snap Inc. and introduces Spectacles, a pair of glasses that can record 10 seconds of video at a time with a tap.

Twitter disables the upload function on Vine in preparation for discontinuing the app.

Meerkat shuts down its live-streaming app.

Conversation about the presidential election gets especially heated on social media sites in the months leading up to the election.

After the presidential election, it is revealed that fake news had been widely shared on social media platforms during the campaign. Some of the stories were traced to teenagers in Macedonia seeking advertising revenues from click-throughs to their websites.

This glossary provides a list of key terms related to social media. Specific social media platforms are not defined here, but this list instead includes terms related to social media platform usage and features. Other entries are relevant to the practice of social media marketing. Finally, some entries are popular terms used in social media and digital communication.

algorithm An algorithm is a formula that informs a social media platform, such as Facebook or Twitter, of the content to be displayed in a news feed.

AMA The acronym AMA, which stands for "Ask Me Anything," is a question-and-answer format used on Reddit. During an AMA, guests show up virtually on Reddit and other users pose questions. When President Obama appeared on Reddit for an AMA in 2012, he set the record for the most concurrent visitors in an AMA session with more than 200,000 visitors.

avatar An avatar is a virtual representation of a user. Not necessarily a photo of the user, an avatar is often image that represents the user in some way or cartoon version of the user. Avatar is the Sanskrit word for "incarnation."

blog A combination of the words *Web* and *log*, a blog features posts of text, images, or videos in reverse chronological order. Blog is also used as a verb to mean maintain or add content to a blog.

check-in Platforms like Facebook, Twitter, and Swarm (formerly Foursquare) use check-ins for users to communicate their geographic location to others.

content curation Social media users and the platforms themselves sift through, or curate, Web content to find and post content that will interest followers.

crowdfunding Popular sites like GoFundMe are based on the concept of crowdfunding, where a group of people can direct any amount of funding to a cause or goal promoted by an organization or individual.

crowdsourcing Marketers, other organizations, and individuals can use crowdsourcing to collect content, ideas, or other items from the crowd of people online.

direct message Private conversations on Twitter that can occur when two users are following one another. Often referred to as a DM.

engagement Social media engagement takes many forms depending on the platform, including likes, retweets, shares, comments, and mentions. Engagement occurs when social media users interact in some way with another user, organization, or brand online.

Facebook fans Facebook users who like a Facebook page are called fans, which is the equivalent of a friend on a Facebook profile page.

Facebook page Public figures, businesses, brands, and organizations who set up a profile on Facebook do so using a Facebook page, as opposed to profiles that are used by individual users or Facebook groups that are used for small group communication.

feed A steady stream of information and updates from friends as well as sponsors on a social media site is a feed. Facebook calls its feed the "News Feed," Twitter calls its feed the "Timeline," and Instagram just uses "feed."

filter Social media platforms and a variety of photo apps provide filters that add a photographic effect that can change the look of a photo. Many users first experienced filters on Instagram, where more than 20 filters are available. Snapchat filters can add information such as time, weather, speed, and location.

follower/following On Twitter, a user has "followers," who are other users that follow the user, and "following," who are other users that the user is following.

forum Online bulletin or message boards are also referred to as forums. On a forum, users can start a thread of conversation on a specific topic and other users can reply to that thread.

geofilter Geofilters are Snapchat overlays that communicate the user's geographic location or a branded partner in the nearby area. For example, if the user is at a mall, geofilters from stores in the mall may be available.

geotag Online content can be tagged with geographical coordinates that indicate where the content, often in the form of photos, was created.

ghosting/ghosted Ghosting is ending a romantic relationship by cutting off all contact with the former partner, particularly on social media sites and other digital forms of communication.

GIFs GIF stands for Graphics Interchange Format, a short animation or film clip usually on a loop that can be posted on social media sites. Although often pronounced like "gift" without the *t*, the acronym should actually be pronounced like the peanut butter (Jif).

hashtag A hashtag is a word or phrase that begins with the symbol # and is commonly used on Twitter and other social media sites. Hashtags make content searchable and allow users to follow the posts of others also using the hashtag.

Instagram stalker An Instagram stalker is a user who likes the older photos of another user. Liking an older photo is an indication that the user has looked back through all the posts of the user they are "stalking."

IRL IRL stands for "in real life," which is the offline world of a digital user, not the virtual world of online and social media sites.

Klout score Klout, a service that rates online social influence, provides users with a numerical assessment ranging from a low of 1 to a high of 100. Variables that impact a user's Klout score include the size of social networks and how often other users interact with a user's content.

like The like button originated on Facebook to allow users to indicate their approval or positive reactions to posted content. Many other social media sites now offer a version of like, including the heart button on Twitter.

live streaming Live streaming involves delivering content live over the Internet, often using Facebook Live or an app such as Periscope.

live tweet Posting updates during an event or unfolding situation is called live tweeting.

LOL LOL is an acronym used in digital communication that stands for "Laugh(ing) Out Loud." LOL is commonly misunderstood, particularly by older users who might think it stands for "Lots of Love" or "Lots of Laughs."

meme A meme is a widely shared joke, photo, video, phrase, or concept that can sometimes take various forms as users apply the meme in different contexts. Popular memes include a Dos Equis advertising image of "The Most Interesting Man in the World" and the "Success Kid" image, which features a baby pumping his fist.

microblogging Platforms like Tumblr and Twitter allow users to microblog, or publish small and frequent quantities of content.

newsjacking When a company references a news story or current event as a way to draw attention to or involve itself, this practice is called newsjacking. The reference can be done through the use of a popular hashtag or another reference to the current story. Companies should be wary of newsjacking because when not done properly and respectfully, users perceive that companies are jumping on the bandwagon of a popular story to earn public attention for themselves.

pins Pinterest users store their favorite content by creating Pins and placing them on a visual board called a Pinboard.

podcast A podcast is a digital audio file that can be streamed or downloaded from a website, iTunes, or a podcasting app.

retweet The retweet function on Twitter allows users to forward a tweet viewed in the timeline to the user's followers so that it will also appear in their feeds.

RSS RSS, which stands for Rich Site Summary or Really Simple Syndication, allows Web content to be syndicated. If a user subscribes to a RSS feed through a news reader, he or she can access updated content from blogs, news organizations, and other sites through the reader.

selfie A selfie is a self-portrait that is taken by reversing the camera lens so it faces the user. This form of photography is often shared on Facebook, Twitter, and Instagram.

snap A snap is a photo or video on Snapchat that is available for only a short period of time before it disappears.

Snapchat lenses Lenses allow Snapchat users to add static or animated content to their selfies.

social graph A social graph illustrates all the interconnections between a user and his or her followers.

SoLoMo SoLoMo stands for the combined trends of social media (So), location (Lo), and mobile (Mo). An example of SoLoMo is a mobile app that uses a social media platform to provide location-based information.

tag Tagging allows social media users to link a profile to content shared on social media. It is commonly used to identify people in photos posted on Facebook.

unfollowing/unfriending The act of ending the following of a Twitter user or a friend relationship on Facebook is called unfollowing (on Twitter) or unfriending (on Facebook).

vlog A vlog is a video version of a blog that is commonly shared on YouTube. The user often addresses the viewers directly by talking into the camera.

YOLO YOLO, a common Internet term, stands for You Only Live Once. Users say YOLO to refer to things they probably should not be doing, but that they do anyway because "you only live once." YOLO also refers to grabbing an opportunity or taking a chance.

Aaker, Jennifer, 318
Abrams, Jonathan, 15, 368
Acton, Brian, 33
addiction, 59–67, 267–272, 332–333, 352–353
Adelson, Jay, 21, 218–219, 369
Advertising Age, 343
Adweek's Social Times, 343
Airbnb, 40, 204
Albrecht, Alex, 219
algorithm, 67–71, 158, 159, 379
Ali, Denny Jaguar, 282–283
ALS Ice Bucket Challenge, 25, 183, 184–185, 374
AMA, 379
Amazon, 23, 31, 151, 219, 367
America Online. *See* AOL
American Airlines, 151
American Press Institute, 176, 357
Amoruso, Sophia, 352
Anderson, Chris, 318
Anderson, Tom, 16, 191–194, 368
Anderson, Tyler J., 353
Angwin, Julia, 318
Annual Day of Unplugging, 65
Antin, Judd, 324–325
AOL, 9, 10, 24, 116, 366, 368, 371
  Instant Messenger, 10, 14, 366
  People Connection, 10, 366
Apple, 20, 202, 220
  App Store, 31, 351, 371
  iPhone, 25, 30–31, 66, 199, 371, 375
  iTunes, 20, 22, 26, 351, 369, 383
Applebee's, 163–164
Arab Spring, 121, 162, 183, 186–189, 190, 324, 372

Armstrong, Heather B., 194–196
Armstrong, Lance, 164
ARPANET, 365
AsianAvenue, 14, 367
Assange, Julian, 117
augmented reality, 39, 41
avatar, 16–17, 24–25, 95, 221, 379

Baer, Jay, 341, 353–354
Ban.jo, 40
Barger, Christopher, 319
Barger, John, 367
Barker, Teresa H., 333
Bausch, Paul, 13, 236, 367
Baym, Nancy, 109, 319
Bebo, 24–25, 370, 371, 374
Ben & Jerry's, 151
Benioff, Marc, 150
Berger, Jonah, 319
Berkman Klein Center, 357, 358
Berners-Lee, Tim, 366
Bernoff, Josh, 326
Bernstein, Joe, 38
Berry, Jonathan, 325–326
Beykpour, Kayvon, 38
Beyoncé, 25, 290, 371
Bezos, Jeff, 367
Bieber, Justin, 24, 185, 281, 285, 373
Billings, Andrew C., 319
Bilton, Nick, 319–320
Birch, Michael and Xochi, 24, 370
BlackBerry, 30–31
  BlackBerry World, 31
#BlackLivesMatter, 25, 150, 324, 375
BlackPlanet, 14, 367
blog, 12, 13, 350, 367, 379
blogger, 13, 236–237, 367, 368
Bollea, Terry, 235
Boston Marathon bombing, 77, 113
boyd, danah, 7, 9, 196–198, 320, 337, 358
Brand, Stewart, 366
BrandWatch, 156, 354
Braziel, Lisa, 341
Brilliant, Larry, 366
Brogan, Chris, 320, 337
Brown, Adam, 353–354
Brown, Doug, 10, 365
Brown, Frank Reginald, IV, 38, 229–230
Buffer, 341
Bullas, Jeff, 338
bulletin board system, 8, 9, 10, 365, 366
Burger King, 119
Bush, George W., 117, 185
Butterfield, Stewart, 19–20, 200, 369
Byrne, Owen, 21, 218, 369
bystander effect, 147–148

California Online Privacy Protection Act, 117
Casnocha, Ben, 204

Causes, 213
Chan, Priscilla, 239–240
Chang, Deanna, 353
check-in, 32–33, 119, 379
Chen, Steve, 22, 369
Chick-fil-A, 113, 151
Children's Online Privacy Protection Act, 116–117, 300–302
Chin, Peter, 15, 368
Chipotle, 104
Christakis, Nicholas A., 320–321, 348
Christensen, Ward, 8, 365
Cicero, Nick, 352
Cision, 354–355
Clarium Capital Management, 234
classmates, 366
ClickZ, 343–344
Clinton, Hillary, 75–76, 376
Coca-Cola, 279
Coleman, Daisy, 147
Common Sense, 60, 92, 107, 268–270, 271, 357–358
CompuServe, 9, 192, 366
  CB Simulator, 10, 366
comScore, 355
Conrads, Randy, 366
Conversation Prism, 228
Convince & Convert, 341
Cook, Scott, 39, 229
corporate social advocacy, 152–153
Costa, Elisabetta, 327–328
Craigslist, 367
Crimson Hexagon, 156, 158
Cross, Mary, 321
crowdfunding, xviii, 40, 380
crowdsourcing, 323, 380
Crowley, Dennis, 32, 371
Cunningham, Ward, 14, 366
curated content, 67–71, 379
cyberbullying, 79, 80, 81–83, 358, 359–360, 361, 362
Cyberbullying Research Center, 83, 359–360
Cyworld, 368

data mining, 155–161
Davis, Katie, 322–323
Deckers, Erik, 321
DeGeneres, Ellen, 214, 282, 374
DeWolfe, Chris, 16, 192–193, 318, 368
DiaryLand, 13, 367
Digby, Marié, 74
Digg, 21, 218–220, 369, 373
Digiday, 344
digital detox, 63–65
direct message, 380
DKNY, 163
Dodgeball, 32
Dorsey, Jack, 26, 27, 198–200, 370
dot bomb, 368
Drew, Lori, 82
Duff, Brittany R. L., 155–161
Dyson, 335

eBay, 201, 203, 234, 367
Ebola, 77, 78
echo chamber. *See* filter bubble
Eckler, Petya, 139–145
econsultancy, 344
Electronic Privacy Information Center, 116
Ellis, Jim, 8, 366
Ellison, Nicole, 7, 9, 96, 108
eMarketer, 344
EMI Group Limited, 285
employee privacy, 101–102
Entrepreneur, 344–345
envy, 90–92
Etsy, 201

Fab, 298
Facebook, 4, 16, 17–19, 22, 25, 36, 92–93, 203, 230, 326, 327, 331, 335, 336, 351, 363, 370, 371, 384
  addiction, 60–64
  advertising, 4, 18, 42, 118–119
  algorithm, 67–70, 75
  Arab Spring, 187–189
  body image, 140–143
  buy buttons, 42, 298, 375
  envy, 90–92
  fake news, 74–76
  groups, 175
  hoaxes, 72–74
  Hughes, Chris, 205
  Instagram, 35, 373
  IPO, 17–18, 373
  Live, 5, 34, 38–39, 375, 382
  loneliness, 88–89
  marketing, 294
  Messenger, 18–19, 31, 33, 41, 373, 375
  mobile app, 16, 31, 372
  mood, 86–88, 92–93
  News Feed, 370, 380
  Occupy Wall Street, 190
  Oculus VR, 41, 374
  page, 380
  Parker, Sean, 213
  platform, 370
  presentation, 95, 96–97, 98–99
  privacy, 117, 120–121
  relationships, 106
  Sandberg, Sheryl, 220–221
  social capital, 89–90, 107–108
  suppressing stories, 70–71, 311–312
  Thiel, Peter, 233–234
  time spent, 60, 271
  users, 3, 17, 140, 155, 272–273, 276, 277–280, 373
  WhatsApp, 31, 374, 376
  Winklevoss twins, 19, 373
  workplace, 6, 100–103
  Zuckerberg, Mark, 17, 19, 238–240, 369
  Zynga partnership, 27–29, 215–216, 371
FaceTune, 95

Fake, Caterina, 20, 200–201, 369
Falls, Jason, 321
Fanning, Shawn, 212–213, 367
fear of missing out, xviii, 60–61, 65
Federal Trade Commission, 359, 360
Fenton, Nicole, 321
Ferguson, Missouri, 70, 150–151, 165
Filter bubble, 70–71, 329, 349
Findery, 201
Finn, Megan, 324–325
Fitzpatrick, Brad, 12, 367
Fitzpatrick, Peg, 325, 339
Flickr, 19–21, 159, 200–201, 369, 370, 376
Forbes, 345
Ford, Sam, 325
Ford Motor Company, 210–212
forum, 381
Foster, Emily, 353
Founders Fund, 213, 234
Foursquare, 25, 32–33, 371, 374, 380
Fowler, James H., 320–321
Frates, Pete, *183*, 185
friendster, 6, 15, 16, 193, 239, 368, 369
Fuchs, Christian, 321–322
Fugate, Craig, 304–308
FunToyzCollector, 285
Gaga, Lady, 324
Gainous, Jason, 322
Gap, 151
Garcia Martinez, Antonio, 322
Gardner, Howard, 322–323
Garst, Kim, 337
GeoCities, 11, 366, 367
Get Movies, 285
Gibeau, Frank, 217
Gilkerson, Nathan, 149–155
Girls Who Like Boys Who Like Boys, 42
Gladwell, Malcolm, 189
Glass, Noah, 26–27, 237, 370
GlobalWebIndex, 60, 267, 274, 277–278, 299, 355
Gnip, 156
Godin, Seth, 323
Goffman, Erving, 95
GoFundMe, 40, 380
Golbeck, Jennifer, 323, 348–349
Goldberg, Dave, 222
Goldman, Alex, 353
Gomez, Selena, 290
Google, 13, 20, 22, 33, 36, 74–75, 76, 100, 118, 175, 198, 203, 219, 220, 223, 237, 368, 369, 370, 372
  advertising, 157, 221, 289–290, 370
  algorithm, 74–75
  Cardboard, 41

Circles, 36
Google Play, 31
Google+, 36, 211, 274, 335, 373, 375
Hangouts, 36–37
Photos, 36
Streams, 36–37
Gorodetzky, Ron, 21, 218, 369
Grande, Ariana, 290
Green, Joe, 213
Green, Joshua, 325
Groover, Michelle, 177–180

Halt and Catch Fire, 42
Hanson, Jarice, 323
Hardin, Marie, 319
hashtag, xviii, 24–25, 35, 43, 78, 145, 163, 175–176, 177–178, 324, 381, 383
Hattrick, Tim, 353
Haynes, Nell, 327–328
Hendricks, John Allen, 328
hi5, 368
Highfield, Tim, 324
Highlight, 40
hiring practices, 100–102, 361–362
Hitz, Lucy, 353
Hobson, Neville, 340, 352
Hoffman, Reid, 15, 201–204, 233, 368
Hofmann, Dom, 37, 373
Hogan, Hulk. *See* Bollea, Terry
Holtz, Shel, 340, 352
Horan, Niall, 283
Horst, Heather A., 324–325
Hourihan, Meg, 13, 236, 367
Huba, Jackie, 324
HubSpot, 335–336, 341
Huffman, Steve, 21, 370
Hughes, Chris, 204–207, 238
Humans of New York, 231–233
Humphreys, Ashlee, 324
hunch, 201
Hurley, Chad, 22, 229, 369

IBM Simon, 30
IBM Watson Bluemix, 157
Ice Bucket Challenge. *See* ALS Ice Bucket Challenge
Ignite Social Media, 341
impression management, 64, 95–99
Instagram, 20, 31, 35–36, 60, 70, 78–79, 120, 140, *255*, 271, 273–274, 276, 278, 288–290, 294, 363, 372, 373, 374, 376
Filters, 381
"Instagram effect," 35
Stories, 376
Internet paradox, 88
Internet Relay Chat, 10–11, 196, 198, 366
Internet-use disorder, 62

iPhone. *See* Apple
Israel, Shel, 324, 331–332
It Gets Better, 302–304
Ito, Mizuko, 324–325
iTunes. *See* Apple

Jenkins, Henry, 325
#JeSuisCharlie, 324, 375
job applicant privacy, 101–102
Jobs, Steve, 31, 371

Kafka, Peter, 346
Kalyango, Yusuf, Jr., 139–145
Kanter, Beth, 337
Karim, Jawed, 22, 369
Karp, David, 8, 29–30, 207–208, 370
Kawasaki, Guy, 325
Keath, Jason, 354
Keller, Edward, 325–326
Kerpen, Dave, 326
KFC, 280
Khalifa, Wiz, 285
Kik, 34, 37, 41, 82
Kinder & Braver World Project, 358, 361
Kirkpatrick, David, 19, 326
Kiva, 41, 204
Kjellberg, Felix (PewDiePie), 24, 208–210, 285–286
Klinenberg, Eric, 88
Klout, 382
Know Your IX, 147
Komando, Kim, 352
Koum, Jan, 33
KPCB, 355
Krieger, Mike, 35, 372
Kroll, Colin, 37, 373
Krums, Janis, 371

Law, Arthur, 324–325
Lee, Katie Kiefer, 321
Levchin, Max, 202, 233
Li, Charlene, 326
Linden Lab, 16–17, 368
LinkedIn, 6, 14, 15, 93, 100, 105, 118, 183, 201, 203–204, 220, 273, 290–293, 335, 338, 363, 368, 372, 376
LISTSERV, 9, 366
LittleBabyBum, 285
live streaming, 34, 38–39, 375, 376, 377, 382
live tweeting, 177–179, 382
LiveJournal, 12–13, 367
loneliness, 88–89
lonelygirl15. *See* Rose, Jessica
Losse, Katherine, 327
#LoveWins, 151
LunarStorm, 368
Lyft, 40

Malcolm, Andrew, 283
Malik, Zayn, 283
Manion, Annie, 324–325
Marketing Land, 345
#MarriageEquality, 151
Martino, Paul, 369
Marwick, Alice E., 327

Mashable, 345
Match.com, 14, 15, 367
Mattrick, Don, 217
McDonald, Tom, 327–328
McDonald's, 280
MediaPost, 345–346
Medium, 14, 237
Meeker, Mary, 355
Meerkat, 34, 38, 375, 377
Meier, Megan, 82, 370
meme, xviii, 382
Mezrich, Ben, 19, 327, 351, 372
microblogging, 177, 207, 219, 382
Microsoft, 20, 116, 151, 226, 280, 376
MiGente, 14
Milk, 220
Miller, Daniel, 327–328
Milner, Murray, 328
Misukanis, Susan, 343
Mitnick, Sarai, 324–325
Mobile Marketing Watch, 342
Molina, Marcel, 8, 29–30
Monty, Scott, 210–212, 339–340
Moore, Pam, 339
Moritz, Donna, 340
Moskovitz, Dustin, 205, 238, 239
Moz, 335
Murphy, Bobby, 38, 229–230, 372
Musa, Bala A., 328
Musk, Elon, 233
MySpace, 6, 16, 24, 27–28, 82, 95, 117, 193, 239, 318, 368, 369, 370, 371, 372
  as Myspace, 16, 372

Napster, 212–213, 367–368
National Children's Advocacy Center, 360
National Cyber Security Alliance, 362
National Labor Relations Act, 102, 103, 104
National Labor Relations Board, 102–105, 361
National Security Agency, 117, 156, 158
Nebraska Workplace Privacy Act, 308–311
Nepal earthquake, 375
netd müzik, 285
Network News Transfer Protocol, 8, 366
Neukirchen, Chris, 29
Newmark, Craig, 367
Nextdoor, 39
Nicolescu, Razvan, 327–328
Nielsen Social, 355–356
Nike, 151, 298
The IX Network, 146–147
NodeXL, 158, 226
Nokia 9000 Communicator, 367
NoMoreRack, 298

Noor Al-Deen, Hana S., 328
North Technologies, 220

Obama, Barack, 77, 168, 185, 205–206, 281, 283, 302–304, 373, 374, 375, 379
Obama, Michelle, 76, 283, 373
Obvious Corporation, 27, 237, 374
Occupy Wall Street, 189–191, 324
Ochman B. L., 340
Oculus VR, 41, 374
  Oculus Rift, 17, 41
Odden, Lee, 343
Odeo, 26–27, 198–199, 237, 370
Ohanian, Alexis, 21, 349, 370
Oikarinen, Jarrkko, 10, 366
Oink, 220
Old Spice, 372
Omidyar, Pierre, 367
OneTrip, 31
online shopping, 297–300
online victimization, 79–81
O'Reilly, Tim, 204
Oreo, 68, 151, 374
Orkut, 36, 369

Paine, Katie, 337, 338
Palantir Technologies, 234
Palfrey, John, 197, 358
Palmer, Walter, 112–113, 375
Pariser, Eli, 71, 329, 349
Parker, Sean, 212–214, 234, 367
Parsons, Rehtaeh, 147
Path, 39–40, 220
PayPal, 202–203, 233–234, 368, 369
Pedigree, 283
Perfect365, 95
Periscope, 5, 33–34, 38, 39, 199, 375, 382
Perry, Katy, 210, 281
Persin, Coby, 84
Pew Internet & American Life Project, 63, 97, 118, 358–359
Pew Research Center, 75, 84–85, 119, 140, 153–154, 173, 257–260, 261–263, 358–359
PewDiePie. *See* Kjellberg, Felix
Pincus, Alison, 217
Pincus, Mark, 27, 28, 203, 214–217, 369, 370, 371
Pinterest, 4, 34–35, 42, 78–79, 140, 223–225, 273–274, 287–288, 336, 372, 373–374, 383
Pitas, 13, 367
Planned Parenthood, 164
podcast, 21–22, 26, 351, 369, 370, 383
Pokémon Go, 41

political campaigns, 167–172, 371, 377
impact of fake news, 75–76, 377
Porterfield, Amy, 351–352
Pott, Audrie, 147
Pownce, 219
#PrayforParis, 375
privacy, 116–121
Proulx, Mike, 329
PRWeek, 346
PSY, 285, 373
Puth, Charlie, 285
Pyra Labs, 13, 236–237, 367

Qualman, Erik, 4, 329, 349
Quesenberry, Keith A., 329–330
QZone, 273

#RaceTogether, 150
Radice, Rebekah, 339
Ragan's PR Daily, 346
Rainie, Lee, 330
Razorfish, 356
RazorSocial, 342
Recode, 346
Red Bull, 229, 280
Red Cross, 163
Reddit, 21, 77, 349, 370, 379
R.E.M., 369
retweet, 383
Revision3, 219
Rheingold, Howard, 330
Richardson, Glenn W., Jr., 330
Rihanna, 24, 281
Robinson, Nick, 352
Ronson, Jon, 114, 350
Rose, Jessica, 74
Rose, Kevin, 21, 217–220, 369
Rosedale, Philip, 16, 368
RSS, 12, 367, 383
Rubin, Ben, 38
Ryze, 15, 368

Sacco, Justine, 112
Sales, Nancy Jo, 330–331
Salesforce, 150
Radian6, 156
Samsung, 31, 280, 282
Gear VR, 41
Sandberg, Sheryl, 220–223, 331
Sanger, Larry, 14, 368
Saverin, Eduardo, 327
Scandal, 178–180
Schaefer, Mark, 331, 338, 352
Schlossberg, David, 324–325
Schmidt, Eric, 204, 229
Schultz, Don, 7
Sciarra, Paul, 34, 223–224, 372
Scoble, Robert, 331–332
Scott, Adrian, 15, 368
Scott, David Meerman, 332, 336, 340
Second Life, 16–17, 368

second-screen experience, 43, 329
Secret, 217
self-affirmation theory, 96–97
selfie, xviii, 94, 383
self-presentation, 94–99
self-promotion-envy spiral, 91
Selligent, 356
Selvadurai, Naveen, 32, 371
sexting, 83, 229, 359–360
Sharknado, 43
Sharp, Evan, 34, 223–224, 372
Shepatin, Stacey, 329
Shin, Jae-Hwa, 161–167
Shirky, Clay, 189, 196, 332, 350
Shively, Kevin, 353
Silbermann, Ben, 34, 223–225, 372
Simply Measured, 294, 342, 353
Sinanan, Jolynna, 327–328
Six Apart, 12, 204, 219
Six Degrees, 11, 14, 15, 203, 367, 368
Slashdot, 21
sleep disturbances, 66–67
Smales, Andrew, 13, 367
A Small World, 369
SmartBrief on Social Media, 348
Smith, Adam Mark, 113
Smith, Andy, 318
Smith, Julien, 320
Smith, Marc, 225–226
Smith, Mari, 339
Smosh, 24
Snap Inc. *See* Snapchat
Snapchat, 5, 31, 34, 37, 38, 41, 70, 228–230, 273, 276, 292–293, 372, 376, 383
  geofilters, 381
  Live Stories, 70, 374
  Spectacles, 376
Snowden, Edward, 156
social buy buttons, 4, 42, 297–299, 375
social capital, 89–90, 107–108
social commerce, 4, 42, 297–298
Social Fresh, 294, 342
social graph, 40, 383
Social media ad spending, 296–297
Social Media Examiner, 346–347, 353
Social Media Explorer, 347
Social Media Marketing Magazine, 347
Social Media Research Foundation, 226
Social Media Today, 347
Social Media Week, 347–348
The Social Network, 19, 351, 371–372
SocialNet, 15, 202, 368
Society for Human Resource Management, 100, 103, 362

Solis, Brian, 227–228, 332, 336, 337
SoLoMo, 40, 383
Solomon, Michael R., 334
Specific Media Group, 16, 372
Spiegel, Evan, 38, 228–230, 372
Spiral of Silence Theory, 172–177
Spredfast, 356
Spyer, Juliano, 327–328
Square, 199–200, 220
Stafford, Rachel Macy, 332–333
StajlPlejs. *See* LunarStorm
Stanton, Brandon, 230–233
Starbucks, 150, 151
Steiner-Adair, Catherine, 333
Stelzner, Michael, 346–347, 353
Stephenson, Sam, 29–30
Stone, Biz, 26, 27, 333, 370
Stone, Lindsey, 133
StopBullying.gov, 83, 362
Story Sync, 43
Strikethrough, 12
Styles, Harry, 282–283
Suess, Randy, 8, 365
Super 8, 42
Superlabs, 217
Swarm, 32, 374, 380
Swift, Taylor, 24, 281, 285, 290
Swisher, Kara, 346
Syme, Valerie, 369
Sysomos, 156
Systrom, Kevin, 35, 372

Talkomatic, 10, 365
Tapscott, Don, 333–334
TechCrunch, 348
TechTV, 218–219
Tencent, 272–273
text neck, 65–66
Thiel, Peter, 202, 204, 213, 233–235
Thiel Fellowship, 234–235
Thomas, Eric, 9, 366
Threadless, 335
360i, 342–343
Timberlake, Justin, 16, 372
Tobin, Jim, 341
Tomlinson, Louis, 282
TOMS, 335
TopRank Marketing, 343
Topsy, 157
Towner, Terri L., 167–172
Trammel, Juliana Maria (da Silva), 172–177
Tribe.net, 27, 215, 369, 370
TripAdvisor, 5
trolls, 115–116, 175
Trott, Mena, 350
Trump, Donald, 76, 312, 376
Truscott, Tom, 8, 366
Tumblr, 8, 14, 25, 29–30, 42, 207–208, 273, 370, 373, 374, 376, 382
Turkle, Sherry, 109, 334, 350
Tuten, Tracy L., 334

Twitter, 7, 23, 25–27, 40, 42–43, 119, 145–146, 150–151, 157, 159, 162, 173–176, 190, 282–283, 294, 319–320, 324, 331, 333, 336, 351, 363, 370, 371, 374, 375, 376
algorithm, 69–70, 376
Arab Spring, 187, 189
buy buttons, 42, 375
Dorsey, Jack, 198–200
fake news, 75, 77–78
live tweeting, 177–179, 382
Moments, 69
Periscope, 38, 375
users, 140, 273–274, 276, 281–282
Vine, 37, 373, 376
Williams, Evan, 236–238
workplace, 93, 100

Uber, 40
Urbanspoon, 5
Usenet, 8, 9, 192, 196, 226, 366
uses and gratifications, 86

Vahl, Andrea, 336–337
van Dijck, José, 334
Vaynerchuk, Gary, 323, 334–335, 352
Venkatraman, Shriram, 327–328
Victoria's Secret, 298
Vimeo, 23
Vine, 33, 37, 199, 276, 336, 373, 376
virtual reality, 17, 41, 368, 374
Visa, 151
vlog, 5, 384
Vogt, PJ, 353
von Rosen, Viveka, 338

Wachtmeister, Erik, 369
Wagner, Kevin M., 322
Wales, Jimmy, 14, 350, 368
The Walking Dead, 43, 177
Walter, Ekaterina, 335
Wang, Jane, 225
Wang, Xinyuan, 327–328
Webster, Tom, 352
WeChat, 37, 41–42, 273
Weiner, Anthony, 372
Weinreich, Andrew, 14, 367
Wellman, Barry, 330
Wendell, Peter, 229
Wesch, Michael, 23
West, Kanye, 376
West, Lindy, 115
WhatsApp, 25, 31, 33, 37, 41, 60, 273, 278, 374, 376
Whole Earth 'Lectronic Link, 200, 366
WikiLeaks, 117
Wikipedia, 14, 350, 363, 368
Wikis, 11, 14, 190, 366
Williams, Evan, 13, 26, 27, 198, 199, 236–238, 351, 367, 370

Williams, Matt, 219
Willis, Jim, 328
Winer, Dave, 12, 367
Winkler, Rowena Briones, 145–149
Winklevoss, Cameron and Tyler, 19, 326, 351, 373
Wolley, David R., 10, 365
Word of Mouth Marketing Association, 359
WordPress, 13, 369
World of Warcraft, 369, 371
World without End, 43

Yahoo, 8, 11, 20, 30, 200, 201, 208, 367, 370, 374, 376
Yalamanchi, Ramu, 368
Yarborough, Jason, 354
Yardi, Sarita, 324–325
Yelp, 5, 374
#yesallwomen, 145–146
Youth Internet Safety Survey, 79–80
YouTube, 5, 22–24, 31, 42, 74, 84, 184, 190, 229, 274, 276, 279–280, 284–286, 294, 363, 369, 370, 372, 375, 384
  Partners Program, 23–24, 371
  Red, 375
YPulse, 276, 356–357
Yun, Joseph T., 155–161
Yusupov, Rus, 37, 373

Zappos, 298, 335
Zomorodi, Manoush, 352–353
Zuckerberg, Mark, 17, 19, 72, 203, 205, 213, 216, 221, 238–240, 326, 327, 335, 351, 369
Zynga, 27–29, 204, 214–217, 220, 371
  Café World, 28, 371
  FarmVille, 28, 371
  Mafia Wars, 28
  Texas Hold 'Em Poker, 28, 371

About the Author

Kelli S. Burns, PhD, is an associate professor in the Zimmerman School of Advertising and Mass Communications at the University of South Florida. She is the author of the book *Celeb 2.0: How Social Media Foster Our Fascination with Popular Culture*. Her research has been published in the *Journal of Advertising, Journal of New Communications Research, Newspaper Research Journal*, and the *International Journal of Interactive Marketing and Advertising* and as chapters in several scholarly books. Burns received a doctorate in mass communication from the University of Florida where she was a presidential fellow, a master's degree in mass communication from Middle Tennessee State University, and a bachelor's degree in mathematics from Vanderbilt University. Burns is a frequent public speaker and expert source for news stories on the topic of social media.